GODS OF
ANCIENT
ROME

GODS OF ANCIENT ROME

CONTRACTS WITH THE DIVINE

LYNDA TELFORD

AMBERLEY

First published 2024

Amberley Publishing
The Hill, Stroud
Gloucestershire, GL5 4EP

www.amberley-books.com

British Library Cataloguing in Publication Data.
A catalogue record for this book is available from the British Library.

ISBN 978 1 3981 1164 6 (hardback)
ISBN 978 1 3981 1165 3 (ebook)

1 2 3 4 5 6 7 8 9 10

Typeset in 10.5pt on 13.5pt Sabon.
Typesetting by SJmagic DESIGN SERVICES, India.
Printed in the UK.

Contents

Introduction

For a civilisation such as Rome, the state religion included the pageant of public ceremonies, the pleasure of feast days and the excitement of funeral games, which were the forerunners of the later gladiatorial contests. It gave purpose to the policy of expansion, also providing opportunities for honour in the dedication of new temples to favourite deities, promises to do so often made in the heat of battle, or during other periods of difficulty.

Regular performance, however, gradually becomes mere routine, and begins to lose its relevance, then may wither into 'a lifeless and impersonal formality'.[1] In Rome's case, this stage was followed by the revitalising influence of foreign religious cults, which gave the people a new outlook and refreshed the religious sphere. These imports provided a point of convergence with new excitements, strange and curious ceremonies and even a tantalising whiff of magic. They also, at least initially, brought controversy and opposition, although most of the new ideas eventually achieved acceptance and then popularity. By the reign of the Emperor Domitian, the Egyptian goddess Aset/Isis had become so well accepted by all classes that the Emperor himself became initiated, allowing the imported religion to become orthodox. The requirement for some form of initiation ceremony was not a common feature in Rome's original religion. It served to make individuals feel a part of a group which, while not exactly secret, did set them apart and allowed them access to the inner mysteries not given to outsiders.

Roman religion saw no need for official public commitment. It had no creed to learn, no holy books of instructions for the faithful to follow, no vows to be repeated regularly, and no dogma to rule the lives of followers. Any Roman was free to think what he wished about the state religion, and he could take part in it, or not, as he chose. The only general requirement was that work should be stopped, as a sign of respect, if a procession was about to pass by. This was not merely a courtesy, as the sight of men working in the presence of the priests was considered to be unlucky. Otherwise, the individual had free choice in his personal relationship with his gods.[2]

Even when Gaius Julius Caesar was elected to the office of Pontifex Maximus, thereby becoming the head of Rome's official religion, he was still free to say openly that he believed death to be the end of all things, and that what came after could be no more than a long sleep. Was that opinion shocking to the Romans, or was it a general belief? If the latter, then how could the gods hold such power over human lives? Was it no more than the basic human need for there to be 'something' beyond, some power or scope greater than human experience, particularly something that could be called upon in times of need?

The phrase 'The gods do not die while ever men speak their names' may well be considered true, for the key to continuance is remembrance. They continue to exist while ever devotion lasts, making all gods equally viable as a focus for the attention of their followers. A difference of name or location does not detract from a deity's ability to become that focus, all that is required is for the spiritual connection between deity and individual to be maintained, making all beliefs equally valid, whether the object of veneration is the Christ, the goddess Isis, or even a tree. The Romans were aware of this, and while the state religion continued its annual cycle, there was no brainwashing or persuasion to oblige anyone to follow a prescribed spiritual path.

They were also aware that the more highly educated sections of society tended to be the most agnostic. Cicero was certainly very sceptical, despite being an augur. However, that was less a religious position than an official honour. No particular spirituality was required, not even a basic skill in divination, as models were provided with diagnostic explanations. Cicero was able to say in his *De Natura Deorum* that his countrymen surpassed all others in the performance of their religious duties, despite obvious exceptions, but perhaps most people did not achieve Cicero's level of detachment.[3]

Under Augustus there was something of a religious revival, although this was not a deliberate policy of his reign. He did build temples and provided the means to allow new cults to flourish alongside Rome's recognised deities.

As there was still widespread belief, the multiplicity of gods, both indigenous and imported, gave a wide enough selection to ensure that most people could find what they needed. However, with so many choices, getting the attention of the preferred deity was problematic. Was their usual name actually the one by which they preferred to be known, or would it cause offence to address them incorrectly? If offence were taken, would it result in the god ignoring the request, or could he or she actually become angry and dangerous? This of course had to be avoided and the Romans developed a method of dealing with the problem. A formula was adopted to act as a rider to prayers, needed to cover all eventualities. Therefore, whether the god addressed was happy with their given name or not, they could still be safely addressed by it but with a phrase such as 'or whatever name you wish to be known by' allowing leeway for errors.

It also prevented the deity from wriggling out of the all-important 'contract' between deity and the faithful, for Roman religion was considered to be just that – a contract between parties, where both sides had to provide something. The worshipper gave prayers, devotion, offerings and sacrifices, but the deity was fully expected to reciprocate and help the suppliant, whether that was an individual, or the city of Rome itself. If the deity failed to fulfil their part of the bargain, then the follower was perfectly entitled to consider their contract invalid and was able to take prayers and offerings somewhere else. The idea of a disgruntled worshipper stamping off angrily down the street, clutching his doves or his wine and oil, to offer them to another temple where he hoped to find a more amenable god, is an irresistible one.

It was therefore always understood that a name was powerful, both for gods and for ordinary people. An ugly or silly name could affect a person's whole life, while an old-fashioned one could place a person not only regarding age, but also social class, possibly creating a stigma. A famous name could be a great honour or a terrible burden to be borne, while an infamous name could cause an innocent person to be ostracised.

Jupiter Optimus Maximus was the chief of Rome's gods, and patron of the city. However, Roma could be a goddess in her own right, and Rome was the only city ever to be considered to be a living deity. She was believed to be so powerful that even speaking her secret name could be punishable by death, so great was the risk of it falling into the wrong hands.[4] Servius said 'the Romans wanted to conceal the real identity of the god who looked after Rome, and therefore priestly discipline laid down that the gods of Rome should not be invoked by their proper names, for fear that they should be enticed away.'[5]

In the *Aeneid*, Virgil invokes Jupiter Optimus Maximus with 'or by whatever other style you may wish to be addressed.'[6] There are examples of inscriptions using this form of address. A lead tablet from Arezzo contains a curse being called down upon one Quintus Letinius Lupus and the powers that are being invoked are addressed as 'hot waters, or nymphs, or by whatever other names you wish to be called,' which is similar to the formula used by the Pontifices.

Aulus Gellius tells us that following an earthquake, the Romans held a festival of purification without naming the god to be honoured by it. This was due to fear that invoking the wrong god might cause further offence and make things worse. They addressed their petition merely to 'the responsible deity'.[7]

There was another reason for such care being taken regarding names. If an enemy could discover the secret name of Rome, that could give him power over the city. Similarly, if anyone could entice Rome's protective gods away, then their power might even be used against the city. Names could certainly be delicate and dangerous things.

Protective gods were meant to be available to give help, and an inscription in York, dedicated by Scribonius Demetrius, who accompanied Agricola, the governor of Britain 78-84 AD, was to 'the gods of the governor's residence' who were expected to provide protection to the headquarters building, but also to assist in correct decision making within it.[8]

Each town had its own divine patron, for example Ostia was mainly protected by Vulcan. Praeneste had Fortuna Primigenia, while Falernii had Minerva and Veii was devoted to Juno. Even in Britain the same held true, with Brigantia being the goddess protecting the vast area of the Brigantes, a tribe whose territory covered the larger part of northern England and also parts of the Midlands, the largest territorial area in the country, centred on Isurium Brigantum, now Aldborough, in North Yorkshire.

When dealing with gods, who could be fickle, it was better to leave nothing to chance, so the Pontifices would often invoke all the gods, as a group, after using individual invocations, as it was safer not to risk leaving any of them out.[9] The Romans had also realised that life appeared to work better if they didn't try too hard to search for the hidden meanings of everything, but acted on the assumption that 'all action is associated with, and is the result of, a divine or spiritual agency,' as quoted by Polybius.[10] He also, however, went on to say:

> Those things of which it is impossible to ascertain the causes, may reasonably be attributed to the gods or to fortune, if no cause can be easily discovered. But where it is possible to discover causes, both remote and immediate, of the event in question, then I do not think that we should have recourse to any divine agency to explain them.

That appears to be a call for basic common sense.

Before the familiar anthropormorphic deities evolved, there were entities that controlled springs, rivers or wooded glades. Pliny the Elder observed that 'Trees were the temples of spirits and according to ancient rituals farming communities will, even now, dedicate an outstanding tree to a god. We worship the groves, and their very silences.'[11]

The upheavals at the end of the Republican period left many people adrift and fearful. This also made them more receptive to the call of religion and more susceptible to the assurances offered by it. They were still essentially pragmatic, and this was evident in the way that foreign religions became widely accepted and were absorbed into the Roman pantheon. This was not done to make visitors or foreigners living in Rome feel more comfortable, but the presence of foreign gods, when added to Rome's own, bolstered not only Rome's prestige but also extended Rome's spiritual defence system. Gods residing in Rome became a part of Rome's contract with its deities, whose protection of the city would be required in exchange for worship.[12] Rather than agonising over things or trying to dissect the reasons for religious belief, they simply used them to bolster the Roman state itself and extend that contract with their gods in whose efficacy they believed.

The huge temple of Venus and Rome built close to the Colosseum, the largest ever built in the city, testified to Rome's ability to deify itself, making Roma Eternae a serious focus for attention. For the Romans, religion and politics were closely allied, which was why the Senate, Rome's ruling body, always met in a religious space. The temples were not merely places dedicated for feast days, nor did they have a Sabbath for worshipping on a specific day of the week, or a congregation as we would know it. The gods were ever present, and because of that they were able to oversee and witness the running of the city as a matter of course, while the temples could also be used for other purposes. While Magistrates met in sacred spaces to discuss state business, other areas, apparently public and entirely secular, were also considered to have a close connection to the gods, even if the building concerned was not a 'templum' in the accepted sense.

Likewise, passing laws or holding elections took place on sites which had been chosen by the priests for ritual reasons. The Forum itself could function as a sacred space and in it all kinds of rituals could be performed whether public, political or religious, depending on necessity. This sacred nature of the Forum was a major part of Roman life, in which it was believed that if the Romans honoured the Gods, then they would most likely perform their function of protecting the state.[13]

Many of the deities, such as the ever-popular Fortuna, possessed several different aspects that met varying requirements, making their power more diverse. These deities were the forerunners of the later Christian saints, who would be available to assist in the various aspects of human life. Romans were direct about their gods, knowing what was needed and what they could give in return. They were essentially straightforward in their responses, believing that while the gods were 'fed' they would continue to exist. For this reason, they were given prayers, offerings and animal sacrifices to keep them nourished. While such blood offerings are abhorrent to people in the modern world, they do need to be viewed in the context of their times.

It was believed that to gain the favour of the gods, one must give the very best that was available, or could be afforded. The most perfect doves, the healthiest and strongest bull, or the fastest and most beautiful October horse. What, to us, seems a cruel waste of the life of a creature capable of passing on its strength and beauty to its offspring was for them only just good enough as an offering. After such a gift, the deity could be sure to listen to requests, confidently expressed, and had the power to grant them.

It has always been a belief that the earth was nourished by the blood of sacrifice in this way. The essential 'feeding' of the gods, especially those connected with fertility, by the gift of a handful of grain, a cup of wine, or a full-scale Suovetaurilia, the 'special occasion' sacrifice of a bull, a boar and a ram, all perfect of their kind, would eventually merge with the similar opinions of the priests of the imported gods, and would be carried along with other aspects of Roman culture to the furthest parts of what would eventually become the Roman Empire.

The ban on using any defective creature for sacrifice extended to the priests themselves, and they too had to be without obvious faults. Pliny in his Natural History told the story of Marcus Sergius Silus, who had lost his right hand during the Second Punic War (218-201 BC). Sergius was a great hero, wounded in battle twenty-three times in two campaigns. He still fought and was captured twice and twice escaped. He fought in four battles using only his left hand and had two horses killed under him. He had a right hand constructed of metal, and with this bound to his arm he succeeded in raising the siege of Cremona, saving Placentia, and also captured twelve enemy camps in Gaul. Later, when he was a Praetor, his colleagues tried to ban him from attending sacrifices due to his disability. He then made a famous speech, detailing all his achievements for Rome. Pliny said of him: 'Others conquered men, but he conquered fortune.'[14]

For the Romans, there was always choice. Anyone could be as deeply involved or as distanced from the official religion as they wished. One of Rome's greatest men, Marcus Tullius Cicero, said that he usually took no notice of the religious year, save for using the names of the festivals as dates for his letters, such as 'Floralia' or 'Saturnalia' as we would refer to Easter or Christmas. He cheerfully wrote that the best part of the festivals was getting away from them and retiring to the quiet of one of his country villas and being allowed to read and work in peace.[15] However, most people enjoyed the festivities and at the very least they were an opportunity for merrymaking and taking a day or two off work. Some people could also eat and drink at someone else's expense, as a wealthy patron might provide free food and drink to mark the occasion. It was a time for taking pride in being a part of the greatest city on earth, its security and future prosperity in the hands of its gods.

Throughout Roman history, that link between the religious and secular powers prompted many wealthy people to found temples, not just honouring the gods but also emphasising the social standing of their family, and while they reminded people of the great men who had dedicated them, they also added to Rome's grandeur. However, it was also necessary to maintain these temples, which was not always the case. The poet Horace warned: 'You will continue to pay for the sins of your fathers, Romans, although innocent yourselves, until you restore the crumbling temples and shrines of the gods, and their statues, filthy with black smoke.'[16] So not only were the sons liable for the sins of their fathers, they were also on the hook for their bequests. Merely building temples was insufficient without the commitment to maintain them, to continue the support which formed the basis of Rome's contract with its gods.

1

Faceless Gods

Many people consider that they are familiar with the ancient gods. They are perennial favourites even now, books and films are full of them and they appear to represent a golden age of excitement and adventure. They have the same sins as humans, but more so. Their affairs, quarrels, and battles are shown so often that we feel we know them, just as we imagine what Rome itself must have been like in its heyday.

Rome was always cosmopolitan, and always crowded and busy. Seneca mentioned that at least half of the population were foreigners, and he was not referring to captured slaves.[1] Under the Emperors, the Imperial Guard would enlist Germans, but there had always been Germans in Rome, just as there were always Gauls, Jews, Africans and Egyptians, long before the romance of Antony and Cleopatra; colourfully dressed people, with their wives, families and servants, speaking many languages. These people did not only bring their different skins, costumes and cultures. They brought their gods also – those of the Celts, the Jews, the Orientals and of course the Greeks.

Greece had been the centre of civilisation before Rome became the leader of the known world. Even when Rome was in the ascendant, Greek culture was admired – its architecture, philosophy, art, and theatre – all of which became part of Rome's own cultural life. It was always considered necessary for an ambitious man or one born into authority to have some knowledge of the Greek language. A lack of that refinement would mark out a man as being uneducated. The Greek gods were adopted wholesale. Their names were changed, but their original characteristics were left largely intact, giving Rome a multitude of larger-than-life anthropomorphic figures to commune with.

Behind the huge bearded figure of Jupiter Optimus Maximus (Jupiter Best and Greatest), wielding his thunderbolt, there stood Zeus. Behind Juno, Queen of the Gods, was Hera. Minerva was the Roman version of the Greek Athena, Venus was Aphrodite, and so on. These were imports, sometimes amalgamated with Roman ideas, but still not indigenous. They were just as foreign as Isis, Serapis, Magna Mater and Sabazius would have seemed to be when they first arrived in Rome.

Before Rome thought of itself as a potential world power, before it had even fully settled itself on that rather marshy valley between the hills and decided to stay there, there was another form of religious life. It was a largely agricultural community, consisting of families with small farms, scratching out a living on difficult terrain, fearing droughts and floods, disease for their families and livestock, pests for their crops. They feared also the dark, the storms, and the inevitable approach of death.

These people formed their own ideas about the supernatural world and had gods of their own to invoke and placate, but these gods were quite different from the cheerfully brawling, squabbling, romancing Greek imports. Rome's original gods were faceless and bodiless, entities of pure spirit who bore none of the sins of humans. As such, they were implacable and greatly to be feared. They were not merely gods of material things, such as crops or buildings, as they also inhabited the abstract, such concepts as virtue, truthfulness and good faith.[2] These were the gods who would endure and remain powerful in the minds of the Roman people for centuries, even when Rome itself had changed beyond recognition. Even then, they were feared and respected and the most binding and unbreakable oath was to swear by Sol Indiges, Tellus and the Liber Pater.[3]

They were the Numina, and these original gods would embody the way Rome thought about itself. They were Fides (faith), Virtus (virtue), Virilis (life and potency), Ops (plenty), Spes (hope), and even Mens (the protectress of proper Roman thinking). There were others, affecting and influencing the seasons, plants, harvests, hearth, and all possible aspects of daily life.

What was important about Rome's own religion was that its divine co-operation was as much the responsibility of the domestic group as it was that of the state, and participation on a small scale was equally viable in attracting the favourable attention of the appropriate deities as were the large festivals and ceremonies, and just as important in asking the gods for their help and protection.

Within the state there would always be smaller units, consisting of clubs and tribes, guilds, villages and even regiments, who all had their own divine patrons to whom offerings needed to be made. The performance of these smaller religious duties protected those specific groups as a whole, even as a housewife, in giving her daily handful of grain to the household gods, protected the smaller unit of the family.

If the gods were not appeased, then tragedies could happen. A river could break its banks, drowning people or precious livestock, a tree might fall with killing force, a storm could destroy crops, or even a hillside might collapse, raining down boulders on roads and houses, crushing and destroying.

All these things could have a spirit, and that spirit could be offended and become resentful, therefore it was always safer to offer a short prayer to placate a tree before cutting it, or placate the spirits of animals before they were sacrificed or slaughtered for food. It might be necessary to ask the very earth for mercy before ploughing into it to produce crops. These were the things which kept the world in balance, allowing the different elements to co-exist peacefully. If neglected, these spirits could produce ill health, accidents or other dangers. These elemental forces, both of material and abstract things, were the gods of people at one with the natural world, who were accustomed to the routines of the seasons. However, they were also the gods of people who lived on the edge and were always likely to be faced with some disaster, and such people are helpless in the face of nature and her awesome powers. It is not surprising that they were careful not to offend, not to impose too greatly, and always to ask for assistance from those stronger entities who had the power to protect or destroy them.[4]

Every family clan or 'gens' had its own favourite deity. The family of Fabii had a shrine on the Quirinal Hill dedicated to Quirinus, who represented the concept of Roman citizenship. For them, making an offering at that shrine at the appointed time was vitally important. Rome had finally beaten the city of Veii in 393 BC, after years of trying. The general Marcus Furius Camillus was the man who finally found success after he vowed that, if Veii fell to Rome, he would take their goddess Juno Regina back to Rome. He would build her a magnificent temple there. When Veii fell, the goddess was transported to Rome and installed honourably, along with her flock of sacred geese.[5]

In 390 BC this triumph was followed by tragedy, when the Romans were beaten by the Gauls at the Battle of Allia and the Gauls then marched on Rome itself. Most of the citizens had time to leave, although the Pontifices remained and were duly killed. The rest of the people took refuge on the Capitoline Hill while the Gauls looted the city. General Camillus had been exiled, due to accusations of illegal family enrichment, and Rome was left to suffer the depredations of the Gauls without protection.[6] One young man, Gaius Fabius Dorso, was sheltering on the Capitoline, and he was aware that as the only Fabii member still in the city it fell to him to perform the rites for Quirinus, despite the presence of the enemy. Accompanied only by a slave to help him carry the vessels containing offerings of oil, wine, millet and salt, he decided that he would walk across the city to make the necessary sacrifice on behalf of his family.

It must have been a long walk, and a very frightening one, all the way through the shattered city and out to the Quirinal while surrounded by curious Gauls. Gaius Fabius Dorso kept his head and walked slowly, not allowing fear to show. The scene is easy to imagine, with the young Roman walking steadily and proudly, ignoring the foreigners who must have gathered to marvel at his courage. The tremulous slave followed, possibly obeying rather unwillingly, perhaps looking warily around at the Gauls, fearing sudden attack and violent death. However, they reached their objective, and the duty was performed. Then they had to walk back.

Still watched by the curious enemy, the temptation to speed up and break into a run must have been almost overwhelming, but Fabius and his slave kept their steady pace. Even then it must have been several hours before they were again in sight of safety at the Capitol.[7] Carrying the empty sacrificial vessels, the pair was welcomed back jubilantly, by people who had probably never expected to see them alive again. They were still followed by a whispering crowd of Gauls, but they were not abused. No hands reached out to touch them, and they were helped back behind the barricades. The Gauls had been dumbfounded by the seemingly suicidal bravery of the two young men. The episode was attributed, of course, to Quirinus, having protected the pair in the performance of a religious duty, although their safe return was just as likely to be due to the sheer astonishment of the Gauls at the sight of them, unarmed and unprotected, yet prepared to risk everything in order to attend to their god's requirements.

The Gauls were eventually bought off and left Rome, but their sack of the city led to another tradition, because when Brennus and his men had approached the city the Roman guard dogs had failed to give the alarm. However, the flock of sacred geese belonging to Juno Regina had woken the city with their loud honking and given most of the people time to evacuate.[8] The gratitude of the Romans towards the warning from the geese, and their disgust at the uselessness of the guard dogs, would lead to the celebration of the 'Supplicia Canum' or punishment of the dogs. On this annual occasion, live dogs were suspended from a cross or fork, and sacrificed as a punishment and a reminder of their failure when the Gauls attacked the city. At the same time, geese were decorated with gold and purple and carried through the streets in honour for having saved the people of Rome from even worse losses.[9]

Such was the power of the faceless god Quirinus over the young man Fabius, but there were many others whose influence would be equally long-lasting. For an agricultural society, respect for Tellus is perfectly natural. Tellus was the goddess of the earth, the producer of the warm soil in which seeds could flourish. Her temple would later stand on the Carinae, but even without the building of public shrines Tellus was the deity to whom a prayer was sent each time a plough broke the soil or a handful of seeds was scattered. Upon her the health and prosperity of men and animals depended, for grain was always the most important commodity in Rome, without which famine would threaten. Tellus could avert that, if she chose to do so.

Ops was related to Tellus in that Ops represented plenty. Originally, plenty would mean an abundance of that grain that warded off starvation. Grain that would eventually become an important part of Rome's 'bread and circuses' with its dole of grain to keep the populace from rioting. It would always be a vital element in Rome's prosperity, and a basis for her expansion into the grain-rich regions such as Sicily and eventually Egypt. Rome's demand for such grain would naturally grow with her increasing population.

However, not only grain was represented by the 'plenty' of Ops. There would eventually be a prominent temple on the Capitol Hill, close to that of Jupiter Optimus Maximus, which shows the importance of the deity. Beneath all Roman temples there were basement rooms, and beneath the one dedicated to Ops was an emergency fund of bullion, kept safe for times of need; a reserve to bolster the funds kept beneath the temple of Saturn, which acted as the state treasury.

Spes was another support because Spes was hope. She would eventually possess many temples, and even acquire humanoid form as images and statues were made. She was originally a nature goddess identified with the fruitfulness of orchards and fields, and even with the abundance of offspring. Later she would become connected to prosperity and good fortune in general, and in that guise she was often invoked at birthdays and weddings.[10] Her most ancient temple was in the Forum Holitorium, the vegetable market of Rome, built during the First Punic War (264-241 BC). Spes would later be portrayed as a beautiful maiden, carrying flowers, but her original incarnation was that of sheer hope, that need and desire for the grain to keep growing, that the weather would be kind, and hope of strong and healthy families to ensure future prosperity.[11]

Dis was a deity of the Underworld which was always a concern. Sometimes known as Dis Pater (rich father), he was greatly feared for his power. His riches referred to the other side of the earth, the world below, not death but the mineral wealth that was held in the ground. The prospect of enormous wealth from the earth's minerals often made men forget the awesome powers of nature, if so the other side of Dis might emerge, and a terrible price might be paid for their presumption. He was also associated with Pluto, and sometimes in Hades he would be known as Orcus.

The original Forum in Rome, although a designated meeting space, and one where many famous and important men took the opportunity to speak, was always intended to be a religious space also. Funeral games were originally held there and up to the time of Gaius Julius Caesar, improvements were being made to allow these spectacles to be more exciting and surprising. The dominant feature of the Forum was not its public spaces, or even its very impressive basilicae, but the proliferation of its temples. Among the temples of the later adopted Greco-Roman gods and goddesses, there were always the temples of the Numina, some of whom retained their prime importance throughout Roman history.

Religion and politics were always closely bound together, identical spheres of operation, mutually dependent and connected. That is why the Senate, the main ruling council, always met in a religious space. It often converged in temples within the Forum, such as that of Castor and Pollux (the Dioscuri), although the Senate House itself, the Curia, was also a space with a special relationship with the gods.[12]

It would be very foolish for the Roman people to allow even the oldest of the temples of the gods to decay, as the gods could only protect Rome while they continued to be honoured. As we noted earlier, Horace had lamented the 'statues filthy with black smoke'.[13] The Emperor Augustus in his *Res Gestae Divi Augustae* would certainly claim to have done his duty in this respect by restoring eighty-two of them.[14] He was also keen to represent himself as a model of the four Roman virtues, which were Comitas (humour, courtesy and ease of manner); Clementia (mercy, mildness and kindness); Dignitas (dignity and self worth) and Firmitas (tenacity, strength of mind and determination). He may have aimed at this ideal, although like all men he sometimes fell short, as with his claim of 'finding Rome a city of brick and making of it a city of marble'. The marble was not solid, being merely a facing over the bricks.

The temple of Honos et Virtus was primarily a cult of Roman commanders and was situated close to the Via Appia, which left Rome at the southern end, just beyond the Circus Maximus. This was a sensible place for military men to pay their respects when leaving Rome for a tour of duty in the south.

Closer to the centre of the city, the temple of Concord was at the Capitol end of the Forum, very close to the Comitium where meetings were held outdoors. Concord in this context represented the amiable co-existence of the social classes. Unfortunately, its influence did not always create the harmony wished for, as friction between the Patricians and the Plebeians was a feature of Roman life for centuries.

Women had always played a greater part in Rome's religious life than in its practicalities. However, even in a religious sense the 'concord' was often lacking, and the political conflicts sometimes spilled over into the female religious sphere, as in 295 BC. In that year, a group of Patrician women prevented one other woman, Verginia, from taking her usual part in their rites at the temple of Patrician Chastity (Pudicitia Patricia). Her fault lay in the fact that she had married a Plebeian and had therefore lost status. She responded gallantly by founding her own shrine of Plebeian Chastity (Pudicitia Plebeia).[15]

Public ceremonial went hand in hand with private, in the worship of the Penates. These were spirit gods, beneficial to both the state and the family unit. They were guardian deities, originally gods of the storehouse who became representative of state prosperity and security. They were also present in a domestic setting as the Di Penates, who protected the household, but were mainly concerned with household food supplies. A part of every meal was set aside for them, and sometimes a little food was actually thrown into the hearth fire as a small sacrifice. Fruit and salt were commonly set aside for these protective gods.

Household protection was also entrusted to the Lares (singular Lar), and every home would have a corner dedicated to them, sometimes a grand temple-shaped Lararium showing images of the household gods, with a picture of a snake, which was the genius of the house and the 'begetter' or guardian spirit and a powerful protective household symbol. Poorer homes might only have a shelf on which to leave a small offering for the Lares. The public bar of Asellina's in Pompeii has a magnificent painting on the wall depicting gods and snakes, provided to offer protection for the premises and the customers.

Lares were everywhere in Rome, not only inside buildings, but also in public where they performed their function as guardians (as the Lares Publici) with their temple of the Lares Praestites in a prominent position on the Via Sacra, opposite the Domus Publicus, the official home of the Pontifex Maximus. They could also be the spirits of a location, as at a crossroads or a boundary. These were always considered to be places of potential danger and hotbeds of spiritual activity, due to the Lares congregating there. Because of this, any major crossroads would usually have a small shrine, probably with a fountain. The shrine was for the guardian of the crossroads and was often maintained in conjunction with a nearby wine bar, which might be run by a 'crossroads college' and these small fraternities would hold themselves responsible for the shrine itself, and the bar would be their local meeting place for working men, usually freedmen or slaves, who could congregate there in whatever free time they had. This way, they could feel that along with their social contacts they were also performing a religious duty on behalf of the public good.

At the festival of the Compitales, every free citizen would hang up a woollen doll, and these would be strung across the streets. Every slave was represented by a woollen ball, hung in the same way. The symbolism of this was that every free citizen had a head, counted by the Censors, while slaves had no such head count and did not usually take part in festivals. They did, however, play their part during the Compitalia, making an offering of a fattened pig to their local Lares, under the authority of the Urban Praetor.

The Lares Permarini could protect sailing or anything connected with the sea. Their temple was on the Area Sacra one of the oldest and holiest areas of Rome. Towards the latter period of the Republic, the Lares would tend to take human form, and were often represented as the small figures of two young men, often with a dog. This did not mean that the Romans thought there were only two of them, or even that they had a dog, but it was intended to show their youthfulness and the capable activity of these spirits, who were involved in almost everything. They were certainly present at the festival of the Compitalia (22 December) which was originally an agricultural festival, but later became a general festival.[16]

Reverence for ancestors was a huge part of Roman life, especially for important families such as those who had achieved consular rank or had performed a particular service to the state. For such families the wax ancestor masks, or Imagines, were a feature of their status and devotion to Rome. They were exact copies of the face of the ancestor concerned (always a male) complete with a wig of the correct hair colour. They would be kept in a small temple-shaped box, or cupboard, or were sometimes displayed on shelves in the atrium of the house, and the number of such masks was a great source of pride, showing the length of time the family had been prominent and the amount of effort they had made to support Rome. These imagines were not merely for show, but were used at funerals, where they would be worn by actors who would mimic the walk or known gestures of the person concerned, giving a performance as if the spirit of the man they represented had attended the funeral of his descendant. A large group of these at the funeral of an important man must have been a strange and arresting sight, bringing the spirits of past Romans to life.

The great importance of 'family' was also shown by the ever-present image of the phallus, sometimes known as the Fascinus. This image is the most misunderstood and visitors to ancient sites are often amused (or even shocked) by the number of them they might find. It decorated everything as an image of good luck and fertility and was often thought to point the way to brothels in the minds of early visitors. However, this image of the divine phallus, sometimes left plain and sometimes wearing wings, was on doorframes and lamps, carved onto furniture, painted, modelled and always respected. As the organ of generation, it was responsible for everything and was believed to protect from sorcery, witchcraft, and the evil eye, as well as turning away envy. It was also protective of women in childbirth, along with the babies they bore.

The Fascinus (or Fascinum) was also carried annually in procession and was tended by the Vestals. It was one of the familiar tokens of the safety and security of the state and guarded the city and the people. The related verb 'Fascinare' means to fascinate or enchant. When in procession as 'Father Liber', it could also be associated with Dionysius or Bacchus. Varro said of the ceremonies:

> Certain sights were celebrated which were of such unrestrained wickedness that the shameful parts of the male were openly worshipped in his honour. During the festival of Liber, this obscene member, placed in a little trolley, was exhibited as itself. In this the god Liber was to be propriated in order to gain the growth of seeds and to repel enchantment (fascinatio) from the fields.[17]

Not everyone agreed that the phallus was a disgraceful or in any way obscene symbol. For most people it was a lucky and cheerful one, and it gradually became the very embodiment of a god – it was perhaps even the first god to be worshipped by early people, representing as it does the vital generative force itself, and the source of all life. Its masculine power was located in hearth and home as well as in the wider world. When a Triumph was awarded to a successful general, the Vestals would hang a model of a phallus underneath the general's chariot. This was to protect him from 'invidia', which was jealousy and ill-will.[18]

This connection between the male member and the Vestal Virgins may seem surprising, but their joint role was in protection and security. This continued emphasis on the health and safety of the state reminds us of the importance of Mens in this context, being the goddess of proper Roman thinking. Certainly, in Rome no man (or woman) was an island and it was implicit in 'Romanness' that all would work for the good of the state, whether in a public or a domestic sphere.

The Vestal Virgins may seem to modern eyes to have been merely domestic, attendant as they were on the symbolic hearth fire. However, that would be a mistake. They were absolutely vital to the state, not just to keep the hearth-fire of the goddess burning, whose sacred flame was so important, but their continued virginity was essential to keep the worship of the goddess pure. In this way the small group of women came closer to real power than any other women ever did, until the time of Livia Drusilla.[19]

It was said that the first Vestal Virgins were established by King Romulus himself, when he appointed four young virgins to tend Vesta's sacred flame. King Tarquinius the Elder (r.616-579 BC) increased the number to six, where it was to remain. One of the holy women must always be present to make sure that the flame did not die out. Although led by the senior Vestal, the Virgo Maxima, they were under the direct control of the Pontifex Maximus and originally shared quarters with him and his family at the Domus Publicae in the Forum, close to Vesta's temple. They did, however, have quite separate quarters in which to live and work. Over time, the Domus Publica was expanded and the Pontifex moved elsewhere, giving the new quarters of the Domus Vestae a more familiar feel, situated just behind the temple and having its own gardens. The garden and courtyard were flanked by two-storey colonnades, with columns of green marble below and red and white limestone above. The housing for the six Vestals was most luxurious, with inside and outside spaces and room not only for their work but also for their personal slaves and pets. This accommodation, taking up space in an already crowded city, reflected the immense importance of these half a dozen privileged ladies, who were highly respected and considered personally sacrosanct.

The six Vestals were chosen by the Pontifices (chief priests) from the best of the Roman Patrician families, approximately once every five years. Twenty girls between the ages of six and ten years old were considered, who needed to have both parents still living, and one would be chosen by lot.[20] Once the girl was chosen, she left her family to live in the Domus Vestae, where she would be under the direct guidance of the Virgo Maxima and under the protection and control of the Pontifex Maximus. When she reached adulthood she would even be allowed to make a will, not a privilege generally allowed to women, although in it she could leave nothing to her birth family, neither could she receive anything from them. Nonetheless, the very act of being able to bequeath her cash and belongings as she wished shows the legal independence she had acquired along with her position. If the family of the chosen girl was unable to provide her with her substantial dowry, then the state would provide one for her. By the end of the Republic there were several status-proud but cash-poor families in Rome, so this would help a girl from the correct background to become a Vestal, despite the possible financial losses of her family. The money, which could be as much as two million sesterces, would be invested for her and was intended to provide for her retirement, after thirty years of service.

The Vestal was not necessarily required to retire at the end of that time, although many did. Some even married, not many, despite the attraction of her comfortable financial position. It was not considered particularly lucky for a retired Vestal to marry.

One Vestal, Occia, who had joined the temple in 38 BC, died after fifty-seven years of service. Another, Julia Tarquata, died after completing sixty-four years of service to the goddess.[21]

It was said that a Vestal spent the first ten years of her service in learning, the second ten years in performing her duties, and the third ten in teaching the younger ones. Their highly protected and privileged lifestyle, as part of the only major female priesthood in Rome, reflected their almost sacred status. Prof. Mary Beard described their position as being ambiguous:

> They are paraded as sharing the characteristics of both matrons and virgins ... and they were certainly one of the most ancient of the religious groups, which is why we know more about them, and their lives, than almost any other of Rome's religious communities. [They were] embedded in the religious structure of the earliest Latin communities ... suggesting that they go back to the very earliest history of this whole group.[22]

If one of them became ill, the Pontifex would choose some wealthy household, which must be suitably under the control of a noble and respectable matron, where she could be sent to be nursed in comfort and safety. Apart from tending the sacred flame upon which Rome's good fortune depended, they also took part in several ceremonies which marked Rome's religious year and performed a vital service by storing and keeping safe the wills of Roman male citizen, which were taken (or sent) to them for safekeeping until needed. All these wills had to be recorded until called for at the death of the testator, and this service was provided free. Any citizen was entitled to have his will registered with the Vestals, even the poorest, and all levels of society made use of this facility.[23]

The Vestals played an important part in the 'Sacra Argeorum' in March of each year, when small rush-puppets, resembling human figures, were thrown into the Tiber. They were said to represent the older men who were no longer eligible to vote. It was sometimes described as 'throwing old men off the bridge' which may also have been a reference to the bridge walkway across the Saepta into the voting area. It was not, however, a grim festival, even though the officials behaved solemnly. The watching people wore their best clothes and carried garlands of flowers, which were always an intrinsic part of festivals and celebrations. The present-day Campo dei Fiori continues the Roman love of such floral decorations.

The Vestals also famously took charge of the remains of the sacrificed October Horse. This was the best of the military horses raced at that time of year, when the nearside horse of the winning team was considered to be the best of all – with an anti-clockwise direction on the racetracks this horse needed to be not only the strongest, to balance the turning team, but also the most obedient and responsive to avoid accidents. It is for this reason that this particular horse became the sacrifice, following the tradition of giving only the very best to the gods.

The sexual organs and tail of this horse were removed and burned, and its blood was mixed with the ashes of an unborn calf, killed with its mother and then cremated at the Fordicitia the previous April. This mixture of sacred blood was used at the Parilia, when bonfires were burned to purify the sheepfolds and avert disease from the flocks.[24]

The presence of the Vestals at such ceremonies represents an extreme version of the connection between the religious life of the home and that of the wider community. If anything was to go wrong, then the threat would be to the whole 'salus' or safety of the Roman people, not just that of the city, it would include the whole community, along with its animals and its farms. This is why the continual presence – plus the continued chastity – of those women was vital. Any unchastity in them was not only a domestic offence but a public one, requiring extraordinary measures of expiation.[25]

However, not all of a Vestal's life was spent in religious observance. Although a controlled and virginal life was demanded of them, they were not nuns. They had been removed at an early age from their natural families but were allowed respectable friendships and could leave the Domus Vestae to attend dinner parties at other houses. When they needed to move around the city they often travelled in a litter and would be attended by a Lictor, or bodyguard, in the same way as a civic Magistrate. His presence reinforced the image of the Vestal's importance and to enforce it further the holy lady had the power to annul the sentence of any felon she saw on her journey, and even had the power to stop an execution if she chose.

Vestals were allowed to enjoy the games, and even had front-row seats. They also had the use of a 'carpentum' or carriage if they had to travel far, so that they could do so in comfort. Male relatives were allowed to visit them during the day and their position was often of great value and prestige to their birth family. Livy mentioned their exceptional status as he told the story of a Plebeian man when Rome was facing attack by the Gauls in 390 BC. He made his own wife and children vacate the wagon in which they were escaping to safety, to allow him to offer it to the Vestals to remove them and their sacred objects from the danger. This exaggerated respect was a strong feature of their lives, but if they should break their vows, or even be suspected of breaking them, they were liable to suffer punishment. For an offence such as letting the sacred flame die out, the Vestal responsible could be beaten by the Pontifex Maximus. This man, the high priest of Jupiter Optimus Maximus, was the only man with power over the physical person of a Vestal, who must remain free from the touch of men.

If the virginity on which Rome's safety depended was lost, then the Vestal concerned would be separated from the others, refused permission to sell any of her slaves (who would need to be fully interrogated) and would have to face a trial before the Pontifices. If found guilty, the Vestal would face the death penalty, and the man with whom she had sinned would be beaten to death, but as the Vestal must not be killed by any man, she was sentenced to be buried alive. This would be done in a specially prepared underground chamber furnished only with a bed, a lighted lamp, and a small supply of bread, milk and oil. That was to ensure that no person could be accused of having killed a woman who was entirely in the hands of the goddess.

She would be taken to the chamber under strong guard, in a covered litter, both bound and gagged so that she could neither escape nor cry aloud for help. The people would gather to watch the sad procession, but there was no jeering or attempts to abuse the woman and the occasion was a solemn and silent one. One of these sentences was described by Plutarch:

> People make way without a word and escort the procession in deep disquiet and utter dejection. There is no spectacle in the world more terrifying and in Rome there is no day of comparable horror. When the cortege nears the end of its journey, the attendants undo the bonds and after praying in silence and stretching out his hands to the gods, to explain the necessity of the act, the Pontifex Maximus takes her by the hand, a thick cloak hiding her face, and sets her on the ladder. He and the rest of the Pontifices then turn away while she descends the ladder, then it is pulled up and the entry to the chamber closed and covered with deep earth, and made level with the surrounding ground.[26]

Fortunately, this appalling action was a relatively rare event, and there are fewer than ten occasions in the history of Rome when this punishment is known to have been exacted. However, there was always the possibility that the Vestals could be held responsible for any untoward happening in Rome, such as Rome's unexpected defeat at Cannae, when suspicion of wrongdoing might be directed towards them. It must have been appallingly difficult to prove one's innocence in such a situation, but was that remote possibility an acceptable downside to the life of a Vestal, with its ease and comfort, its respect and reverence? Were they always aware that it just might happen, or was the rarity of the event enough to prevent them worrying about it?

The Roman defeat at Cannae, when Rome came very close to annihilation during the Second Punic War, was fought on 2 August 216 BC near the ancient village of Cannae in Apulia in Southeast Italy. The foe was Carthage and it has been estimated that 20% of Roman men between the ages of eighteen and fifty years lost their lives there. Only 14,000 Roman soldiers escaped with perhaps another 10,000 being captured, all others were killed. The Carthaginians were said to have lost only 6,000 men in the engagement. Livy claimed that the Roman losses were around 55,000 men,[27] while Polybius claimed that the number was nearer to 70,000.[28] Hannibal had not enforced uniformity on his assorted army and expected his men to use their native skills to find success on the battlefield, with men from Africa, Iberia and Cisalpine Gaul all fighting in their own way. Rome, with its trained men and military structure had expected an easy victory, making their utter defeat all the more inexplicable and catastrophic. It was the most terrible and unimaginable blow to Rome's prestige and was quite incomprehensible to its citizens.[29]

The Romans descended into sheer panic, expecting Hannibal and his army to descend upon Rome at any time. Their fear was all the more stultifying because they felt that the gods had turned their faces away from Rome, denying the city the protection it needed, and unless they could restore that divine protection quickly, the whole city could be completely destroyed. To this end, the blame had to be put upon someone, and a punishment carried out to assure the gods that whatever had offended them would not be repeated and they could safely allot Rome their favour again.

As the Vestal's famed virginity was the most important part of their dedication to the goddess, it was decided that the reason the goddess hadn't helped Rome was that the Vestals must be unchaste. An investigation then centred on two young women, Opimia and Floralia, who were accused of having lost their virginity and they were sentenced to die. Floralia suffered the full penalty, as did the men who were accused of being their lovers, but Opimia was terrified of the lingering death ahead of her and managed to commit suicide to avoid it.[30]

Some time later, while the city's mood still verged on hysteria and most families were in mourning, a delegation was sent to the shrine of Apollo at Delphi led by Fabius Pictor (later to become Rome's first prose historian). He was to consult the oracle and find guidance as to how Rome could protect itself from such disasters. In the meantime, the Sibylline Books were also consulted[31] and their priests, the Duoviri Sacris Faciundis, were required to explain their prophecies. These books, along with the auguries having been taken, together with an unfavourable sighting of some passing birds, were recorded and apparently confirmed that the goddess was not satisfied due to one of the Vestals having escaped her punishment by her self-induced death. A further sacrifice was then necessary – and this was considered dreadful, as the sacrifice of humans was not common. However, a Greek man and woman, along with a Gallic man and woman, were subsequently buried alive under the Forum Boarium, the area of the cattle market and one of Rome's oldest areas, which in itself suggests the antiquity of the despised rite.[32]

The victims chosen were probably slaves, in which case their owners would have been reimbursed by the state for the financial loss caused by the destruction of their property. However, it was considered honourable because their lives had been given, in extremity, to placate the goddess and protect Rome.

Two years later, the Vestals were again used as scapegoats when a slave accused three more of them of having lost their chastity. The slave was probably tortured, which action was mandatory when slaves were being questioned. Torture was, however, confined to slaves and Roman citizens were exempt from its use. Its use on slaves was due to the belief that any of them would naturally support whatever his or her master told them to say, unless a far stronger incentive to tell the truth was brought to bear. This was normal procedure, particularly during the Republic. The rule of law, however, still rested on actual evidence, but the theory was that a slave's testimony, if given freely, was so unreliable as to be inadmissible in evidence, therefore the slave would be tortured by instruction of the Magistrates, whether that slave was actually accused of any wrongdoing or not. On that occasion, the Vestals Aemilia, Licinia, and Martia were all found guilty and suffered the extreme penalty.

These accounts of early Rome, with her back to the wall and desperately seeking answers to the apparently inexplicable, shows the immense importance of the Vestals in the hearts and minds of Roman people. It is perfectly feasible that these young women were innocent and that, in one sense, the sacrifice of their lives was seen as a trade-off for the privileges they had enjoyed. Thankfully, the distasteful procedure was rare, and was to become more so.

Even the appearance of wrongdoing could put a Vestal in danger of public censure at the very least. The trial of one Vestal in 420 BC was described by Pliny.[33] A woman named Postumia had aroused suspicion by her apparent general giddiness and her liking for fun and for pretty clothing and jewellery. It must be remembered that the Vestals were taken into the temple very young, when it must have been difficult to deal with the normal longings and dreams of growing up while living a celibate and restricted life. However, for any young woman who had been vowed to Vesta, such natural temptations could be very dangerous.

The girl was taken before the Pontifex Maximus and she must have been terrified, knowing herself to be innocent but that her life could still be forfeit. She was found to be not guilty, but the Pontifex spoke to her very sternly, telling her to stop telling jokes and behaving foolishly, and also that her mode of dress had caused critical comment. He told her that she should in future aim at looking holy, rather than trying to appear smart.

It was probably intended as a salutary lesson for all the Vestals and a reminder than any of them could be in danger at any time, if they forgot the serious nature of their calling. The Urban Prefect Symmachus, attempting to maintain the Roman religion during the rise of Christianity wrote:

> The laws of our ancestors provided for the Vestal Virgins and the ministers of the gods a moderate maintenance and just privileges. This gift was presented, inviolable, until the time of the degenerate money changers who diverted the maintenance of sacred chastity into a fund for the payment of base porters. A public famine ensued, due to this act, and a bad harvest which disappointed all the hopes of the provinces. It was a sacrilege which rendered the year barren for it was necessary that all should lose that which they had denied to religion.

This was reported by Ambrose of Milan as 'The memorial of Symmachus' in the 'Letters of Ambrose' by Tertullian.

The college of the Vestals was finally disbanded and the Sacred Fire extinguished in 394 AD, by the order of the Emperor Theodosius. Zosimus, an advocate at the imperial treasury under the eastern Emperor Anastasius I, recorded how a Christian noblewoman named Serena had taken a silver necklace from around the neck of the statue of Rhea Silvia, and put it around her own neck. An old woman, who was apparently the last of the Vestal Virgins, rebuked Serena for her act, calling down punishments on her for her thieving and her impiety against the old gods. Serena then suffered a series of dreadful dreams and nightmares, which foretold her early death.

The Vestals had a very close relationship with another spirit, that of the water deity Juturna whose pool and small shrine was immediately adjacent to the Domus Vestae. The Vestals had always been required to take their daily water from this natural spring and even later, when the Domus Vestae had been given its own piped water supply, it was still necessary for a token jug of water to be drawn daily from the spring of Juturna. The Juturna waters were widely believed to be health giving and it was a popular place for pilgrims. It was also the site where the shades of Castor and Pollux were seen watering their horses, after the Battle of Lake Regillus in 496 BC.[34]

These twins, who were only half-brothers, were together known as the Dioscuri. They were the sons of Queen Leda of Sparta and their sisters were Helen of Troy and Clytemnestra. They were the gods of sailing and horsemanship and also of athletes and athletic competitions. They were semi-divine as their mother was believed to have slept with her husband, Tyndareus, King of Sparta, on the same night as she was seduced by Jupiter in the form of a swan, after which she conceived a son by each encounter. One of the twins, usually considered to be Pollux, was the son of Jupiter and the other, Castor, was the son of Tyndareus and therefore mortal. Their temple in Rome's Forum was built in 484 BC and at the Battle of Lake Regillus they were said to have transformed themselves into young horsemen again and to have fought on the side of Rome, ensuring success. It was a legendary victory over the Latin League, shortly after the formation of the Republic. The spring of the nymph Juturna, where they were seen after the battle, was spoken of by Plutarch, in his 'Life of Aemilius Paullus' when he said: 'Of this extraordinary and wonderful appearance of the gods there are many monuments in Rome, which the city erected at the place where their apparitions were seen, and the adjacent fountain, which bears the name of these gods, is to this day regarded as being holy.'

The nymph also had a shrine dedicated to her on the Campus Martius by Lutatius Catulus and sacrifices were offered on 11 January, both by the state and private individuals. Arnobius said that Juturna was the wife of the god Janus, and the mother of Fontus the god of Fountains.[35] Frontinus said 'Esteem for springs still continues and is observed with veneration. They are believed to bring healing to the sick, as for example the springs of the Camenae, of Apollo, and of Juturna.'[36]

The front of the shrine in the Forum Romanum itself is a marble well head with an inscription commemorating the first century BC restoration of it by Marcus Barbatus Pollio, a curule aedile responsible for the maintenance of public buildings. The temple of Castor and Pollux, close to it, was restored by Quintus Caecilius Metellus in 117 BC and according to Plutarch was decorated with both statues and paintings.[37]

Nymphs, such as Juturna, would eventually be depicted as young and beautiful women who inhabited streams, trees and groves, although originally they would have been quite without human form. They were not considered to be immortals, although their lives lasted far longer than those of humans. Several elegant Nymphaea, or grottoes, with water supplies, were built to honour them. Artificial grottoes would eventually take the place of natural cave-like ones, and this reverence for the deities of the springs was far-reaching, with a nymphaeum dedicated to a local water spirit named Coventina being built alongside Hadrian's Wall in the northernmost reach of the Empire. Another large and magnificent one was built at Jerash in Jordan in 191 AD and was originally embellished with marble facings and topped with a half-domed roof. Water was piped to cascade through seven carved lion heads into basins. The monumental nymphaeum in Rome, fed by the Aqua Julia and situated near the Via Labicana, had a two-storied façade with arched openings on each side, while its front had a large, curved basin to catch the flow of water. It is attributed to Domitian's double triumph over the Chatti and the Dacians in the 80s AD.[38]

Another goddess, originally faceless but later portrayed and of huge importance, was the Bona Dea, or Good Goddess. The Vestals were involved in the worship of Bona Dea as there was no group of priestesses specifically assigned to the goddess, leaving the Vestals along with the chief ladies of Rome to attend to her ceremonies. Even more than for Vesta, the worship of Bona Dea was entirely in the hands of women. No man could be a part of the cult or be a witness to one of its rituals, even accidentally, although men were fully aware of the goddess's power and of Rome's need of her favour.[39]

This feminine exclusivity naturally provoked some ribaldry among the men, with speculation about what the women got up to during their very secretive meetings. As women during the Republic were not expected to drink wine, as it was believed it could lead to licentiousness, there was a certain excitement around drinking it in the company of other women at the Bona Dea ceremonies. Even then, it was referred to as 'milk' and the vessels holding it were referred to as 'honeypots'. No doubt many men had seen their wives returning home propped up by their slaves and rather worse for wear, and this had prompted further speculation about female drunkenness, with wild theories involving the use of whips and all kinds of erotic carrying on. The secrets were kept, fuelling more imagined behaviour, which became something of a joke.

This did not detract from the importance of the Good Goddess for the safety and prosperity of Rome itself, merely that its exclusively female aspect gave many women an autonomy that they lacked in daily life, however fleeting it may have been. The main festival in the year took place, however, not in any temple, but in the home of a curule Magistrate. The women of the lower classes would continue to worship the goddess in a temple, but the ceremony of putting the goddess to sleep for the winter, which took place in December, was attended by ladies of status; even the Virgo Maxima would be there, and the wives and daughters of the most eminent men in Rome. Not only male pets, male slaves and the statues of men would be removed (or covered if too large to be moved), but also any sprigs of myrtle were taken from the premises, as the plant was believed to have a particularly erotic and sexual symbolism.[40]

At the winter celebration in 62 BC, the ladies were gathering at the Domus Publica, which was at that time the home of Gaius Julius Caesar in his position as Pontifex Maximus. The meeting was not taking place there due to that position, but because he was also Praetor for that year. It was being hosted by his mother, the formidable Aurelia Cotta, despite the presence of Caesar's then wife, Pompeia Sulla. During the early part of the gathering, a slave named Habra drew Aurelia aside to confide her suspicion that one of the musicians present was actually a man![41]

Aurelia was horrified, and the proceedings were immediately stopped and the guests asked to leave. The suspected musician was cornered and Aurelia pulled off the veil to reveal none other than Publius Clodius Pulcher. This young man was the attractive, spoiled son of a wealthy and important family. He and his sisters and his wife Fulvia were fond of making mischief and of scandalising the staider members of their class. Fulvia was the granddaughter of Cornelia, Mother of the Gracchi, and was herself the mother of two children with Clodius. (She would later marry Gaius Scribonius Curio Jnr and then finally Marcus Antonius). Publius Clodius was already infamous for inciting the troops of his brother-in-law Lucullus to mutiny in 68 BC. It has never been explained what prompted the idiotic action of his at the Bona Dea celebration, whether it was sheer curiosity or a desire to cause further embarrassment, but it was typical of his thoughtlessness and desire to always be in the forefront of events.

When the Bona Dea vessels were cleared away, the men were recalled and the situation explained to them. Caesar was furious at the sacrilege and the fact that the entire ritual would have to be repeated. He was also angry at the suggestion that Clodius had entered his house with the intention of seducing Pompeia Sulla. This she tearfully denied and there is no evidence of her having being involved in any intrigue with Clodius, but Caesar divorced her immediately nonetheless, with the famous remark that Caesar's wife had to be above suspicion. Aurelia did not defend her daughter-in-law and may perhaps have been relieved to be rid of an infertile and foolish woman.[42] Aurelia did become a witness against Clodius at the subsequent trial which took place in May of 61 BC. Aurelia was well known to have been devout and eminently respectable and her account was delivered sensibly and backed up by the Virgo Maxima Fabia who was present, half-sister to Cicero's equally formidable wife Tarentia.

The stupidity of Clodius's action cannot be over-emphasised. Despite all the nudges and winks and lewd suggestions about the ceremony, the men were aware that the goddess's ritual had been blasphemed. The trial of the young man was widely demanded and Cicero, under pressure from his wife, became involved and gave evidence against Clodius, thus earning that rather dangerous young man's enmity for years to come. Clodius had claimed that he was not present at the Bona Dea ceremony, and could not have been, as he was at Interamna at the time, which was a good ninety miles away. Cicero's evidence was that Clodius had called to see him at his house in Rome on that same morning, so could not possibly have been at Interamna by nightfall. [43] However, Clodius was acquitted, some suggest by a corrupt jury, while others claimed that the plea of Aurelia Cotta and the Virgo Maxima Fabia was listened to, when they asked that Clodius be freed so that the goddess could deal with him in her own time and in her own way. It was said that the request of these influential women was agreed to by the Pontifices.

Clodius continued to be a nuisance in Rome for several years, but eventually he met a violent end at the hands of Titus Annius Milo in 52 BC, of whom he had made an enemy. They met on the road to Bovillae, both with armed supporters, and a scuffle ensued. Clodius was injured by a lance thrown by one of Milo's men and was then killed. The followers of Bona Dea believed that Clodius had died close to a small wayside shrine dedicated to the Good Goddess, and that she had finally exacted her retribution.[44]

The fact that Bona Dea was a female cult did not prevent the men from appreciating that the goddess was a powerful and important deity. A public slave, named Felix Asinianus, a servant of the Pontifices, had been losing his sight and was very much afraid. After consulting several doctors without any appreciable result, his mistress, the wife of one of the Pontiffs, consulted the goddess on his behalf and had obtained medicines for him to try, possibly through the Vestals, although the story did not stipulate the source.

An inscription records his gratitude and that he had fulfilled his vow for the return of his eyesight:

Felix Asiniacus, public slave of the Pontifices, fulfilled a vow to Bona Dea Agrestis Felicula, by sacrificing a white heifer for his eyesight being restored, after he recovered with the help of his mistress after ten months of taking medicines. He assures the goddess that he is truly grateful for her life saving gift.[45]

The great importance attached to those two goddesses did not rule out the powers of lesser Numen. Roman life was surrounded by deities who must not be offended and even for the devout it must have been impossible to keep up with them all. However, some of them had their rituals performed only by the priests. Even among the more obscure of them, there were many whose influence was sufficient to pose potential problems for the negligent.

The shrine of Jupiter Feretrius on the Capitol Hill was so ancient that it was believed that it had been dedicated by Romulus himself, when King of Rome in the eighth century BC. It was made entirely of tufa blocks without any decorations except for two square columns supporting its small portico. It was windowless and lit only by light from the door. It was very small inside and contained no image of the god, merely an electrum rod two to two-and-a-half feet long, representing the god's power, along with a flint with which the Fetiales sacrificed pigs. It served as a repository for ritual implements and was one of the first temples restored by Augustus due to its dilapidated condition.

Consus, of grain and granaries, was a vital god for a vital commodity in ever-expanding Rome. The festival of the Consualia was also very ancient, as befits an originally purely agricultural society. It was used by Romulus as an excuse to bring together the men of Rome and the surrounding areas for an athletic contest. When the Sabines attended the Roman males, who suffered from a shortage of breeding-age women, took the opportunity to kidnap the Sabine women. This led to much confict between Romans and Sabines over the years, but the stolen women became Roman wives due to having been compromised so they were unable to return to marry men of their own tribe. The altar of Consus was kept hidden during the year and only uncovered for the festival, and Consus would become known as 'the god of secret deliberations' due to the plot against the Sabines. The area where the original athletic contests were held was between the Palatine and Aventine Hills, in a declivity which would later become the site of the Circus Maximus.[46]

Several less well-known deities would need attention at specific times, such as Cardea the goddess of hinges, who was responsible for the smooth running of doors and locks. Forculus was in charge of the door itself, especially double doors, and was a god of security, while Limentinus was of the threshold and the entrance to the home or business. Terminus was in charge of property boundaries, for homes and farms, but in the wider sense for the boundaries of Rome itself and other towns and cities.

These were helpful spirits who could ease daily or even political life. On the other side were ranged spirits such as the Umbrae, who were neither actively bad nor good, they could relay information, or sometimes find things that were lost, but were also capable of haunting in response to some misdeed. The Furies or Furiae were female spirits who carried out the vengeance of the gods on mortals. There were usually three of these (this was borrowed from the Greeks), Tisiphone, Megara, and Alecto, but the Romans added two of their own, Adrasta and the more famous Nemesis. These were all to be respected but also feared.

Even more to be feared were the Lemures, who were spirits of the dead, and there were also the Manes who were the dead belonging to one's own family, regarded as the divine dead, or ancestors, to be revered and celebrated at festivals such as the Feralia, the Parentalia and other times when the Mundus, the vent giving access to the Underworld, was opened. This was situated on the Palatine Hill. At such times, the shades of the dead could be expected to walk in the world again, and families would take gifts of food to share with their illustrious ancestors.

The Lemures were far more fearsome, for these spirits of the dead were malevolent and hostile to humans. They were usually considered to be the potent spirits of those people who had died young, and who therefore resented that life went on for other people while they could no longer enjoy it. They were especially feared in this way if they were the spirits of young children, who could be particularly spiteful and vengeful. They could also represent people whose last wishes had not been adhered to, or those who considered that their families had been neglectful of their duty towards them, particularly in excluding them from family festivals and anniversaries. One ancient scholar described them as 'the wandering and terrifying shades of men who had died before their time', although the name describes 'ghosts' as a whole. The public festivals of the Lemuria were of long standing but there is now no record of which particular sacrifices were made at them.

There is an account from Ovid which describes a ritual carried out by each head of a household privately:

After rising at midnight and washing his hands, he walked barefoot through the house, while spitting nine black beans from his mouth. As he spat each bean he looked away and intoned 'with these I ransom me and mine,' after which the ghosts were expected to creep up and eat the beans. With his back turned, he then washed his hands again and beat a gong loudly. He then intoned nine times 'ancestral ghosts depart' and looked around, when the ghosts would have vanished. It is in any case a regular practice to avert one's eyes when sacrificing or doing any business with the powers of the Underworld.[47]

Antony Kamm notes that 'While a spirit of some kind watched over a person at most times and on most occasions, from conception to death, at the actual point of death there was none. The element of religion in funeral rites was directed towards the purification of the survivors.'[48]

In this, the Romans rather lost out, which might help to explain the later popularity of the eastern gods. The eastern religions assured not only a life after death, but also that someone, such as the jackal-headed god Anubis, would appear to lead the way through to the other side. This was to ensure that no person was left afraid and lost at their death, or was condemned to become a wandering shade. Anubis was in no way a frightening deity, he was a gatekeeper to the life ahead, and his function was to guide the deceased.

There was in Rome a very definite feeling that death would contaminate those people who were in attendance. Attending the dying was one of the times when purification was important, and the idea that a newly dead corpse could make living people unclean was widespread (a practical and effective superstition, as many are). However, various rituals using music, incense, lighted torches and other cleansers could be used to purify both the corpse of the deceased and the area immediately surrounding it. Funeral rituals also had a role to play in showing the wealth and status of the family involved, and the music in particular probably had rather more to do with drawing the attention of the public to the fact that a noble funeral was about to pass, rather than any idea that the music could in itself frighten away any evil spirits or protect the corpse and the family from some unknown contamination. Funeral rites could be very expensive indeed and, far from keeping people at a distance, such an outlay could only be justified if as many people as possible were able to view them, or even join in the procession themselves.[49]

In fact, there could be few more attention-grabbing events than a large, noisy, and expensive funeral, which showed the general population just how much money the family concerned were able to spend on it, and how many important people could be persuaded to attend it. Pliny even recalled a funeral especially arranged to honour a beloved talking pet bird, on which a vast sum had been expended and which 'countless mourners' had attended.[50]

The dead who had been given such attention at their obsequies could hardly come back to haunt their families as malevolent Lemures, or claim that they were being neglected. Even the deceased bird might desist from squawking at his former owners in the night if he'd had such a good send off.

The spirits of dead ancestors, the Di Indigetes, were associated with a particular place and could take an interest in the living family who still inhabited it. They would certainly be around, although invisible, on the dates when spirits generally arose, although their interest in the family would be purely familial and benevolent. The Di Penates concerned themselves with supplies, but not merely on a domestic level. Their sphere of interest concerned Rome itself, and the prosperity of the city. These were gods of general well-being and were concerned with the public good.[51]

One area with an important part to play in Rome's Forum, and often overlooked, is the Regia. This small building, said to have once been the house of the King of Rome, has a very long history. Several buildings have occupied the site, all with similar functions, and there are traces of iron-age huts having been there. At the end of the seventh century BC a brick building was erected on a foundation of blocks of tufa. This was modified and acquired its current ground plan at the end of the sixth century BC after several earlier alterations. It was said to have originally been built for King Numa, the second King of Rome (753-673 BC). Its great antiquity is evident in its orientation, being aligned to the north, out of line with all the later buildings surrounding it.

It was reconstructed yet again in the third century BC and in 36 BC was restored by Gnaeus Domitius Calvinus, who in the same year returned to a Triumph after being the legate of Octavianus while he governed Spain. He rebuilt the Regia as an offering to the state, although by that time it no longer housed any state officials, being considered far too small. It did serve as a useful storage space for the archives of the Pontifex Maximus and by that time its great age was respected.

The Domus Publicae then housed the Pontifex Maximus and his family and the Vestal Virgins (in separate accommodation), and was close to the Regia, as was the temple of Vesta. The Regia still maintained its 'out of sync' orientation and was still a very small building, although it did from time to time have extensions built alongside it. It was essentially a strange triangular property entered from a small courtyard, which had only three interconnected main rooms. The courtyard entrance led into the centre room and the room on the western side held the sacred shields of Mars. The Lastes, or lances, also kept at the Regia. The room also held a small platform which is now believed to have been the base of an altar to Mars.[52]

The eastern room held a sanctuary to the goddess Ops Consiva, who was goddess of the harvest. This area was then so sacred that only the Pontifex Maximus and the Vestals were allowed to enter it. Kept within the Regia were the archives, the civic tablets and the calendars, while official meetings were often held there, as it functioned fully as an inaugurated temple owing to its altars and the presence of the sacred shields and spears of the god Mars.

Cassius Dio suggested that it may have been at the time of the Gnaeus Domitius Calvinus restoration in 36 BC that the outside of the building was decorated with the lists of Consuls and Triumphators, recorded all the way from Romulus to Augustus, which were later found nearby. These are now in the Palazzo dei Conservatori on the Capitol Hill.[53]

One other strange item to be found in the Forum Romanum is the Lacus Curtius. This was once a pool but is now filled in and paved over. The origins of this strange relic from ancient times are disputed, and even the Romans of the Republic were unsure of its original purpose. What is known is that in the Iron Age the Palatine Hill was surrounded on all sides by marshes and small streams. It was said that the area had once been a lake, and the part which would later be known as the Lacus Curtius was the remains of a pool left after the area was drained in the late seventh century BC. This work was attributed to King Tarquinius Priscus and an inscription found close to the site by Giacomo Boni in 1899 near the Lapis Niger[54] supports this. It is now difficult to interpret but appears to contain regulations regarding the execution of profaners along with the ceremony of purification, which usually included a water source. The Lapis Niger itself, a slab of dark marble approximately three metres by four, was in late Republican times believed to cover the tomb of Romulus.

Digging below the water table, Boni found a stela, inscribed in early Latin, which (in part) read 'Whoever violates this sacred space shall be destined for the infernal gods.' Boni also found several burials dated from the ninth to the early sixth century BC on the south side of the temple of Antoninus and Faustina. In 1911-1912 he uncovered the bases of huts of the same dates, below the Flavian Palace on the Palatine. These ancient remains testify to the earliest occupation of the area, and they indicate that it had sacred connections. It was certainly a mysterious place.

One Gaius Curtius Philan, a Consul in approximately 445 BC, was said to have declared the area consecrated ground after it had been struck by lightning. He also gave it his name. However, Livy had a far more intriguing story, involving the opening of a chasm after the area had been drained. It was claimed that there was a demand from the gods in relation to this, and a mysterious 'voice from on high' said that if Rome wished to be saved, the Roman people should throw down into the pit 'whatever constituted their greatest strength'. If they did so, then the Roman nation would live forever.

Various items of value were thrown down into the pit, without eliciting any further response. The people were then beginning to panic, until one Marcus Curtius realised that what Rome valued the most was … youth! He went home, dressed himself in his full armour, mounted his horse, and rode directly to the pit. Once there he urged his horse to jump down into the void, and they both disappeared from sight, with the pit promptly closing over them. It was said to have been named in his honour for his courageous sacrifice on behalf of Rome.[55]

Just as interesting as Livy's romantic and heroic account of the story is the fact that just to the east of the Lacus Curtius, excavations found the skeletal remains of a man, a woman and a child. These unfortunates were all bound together and had apparently been drowned.

Were they some of the 'profaners' referred to in the inscription, or were they some form of sacrifice? The legends surrounding the pool or pit may be recollections of rituals such as those mentioned, making the remains of the lake a place of punishment in earliest times, as well as a place of purification.

It is also interesting to note that this is the place where the Emperor Galba was killed by soldiers on 15 January 69 AD, after he had succeeded the Emperor Nero, when hopes of any improvement in the lot of the people had already faded. Galba did not have the ability to inspire confidence and he was immediately challenged by Otho, after Galba's choice of successor, Lucius Calpurnius Piso, led to Otho's plotting. The Praetorian Guard, stationed in Rome, declared for Otho, causing Galba to panic and attempt to confront the rebels in the Forum. He was cut down there by Otho's men, ending a reign that had only lasted three months; but he had the solace of having died in such a holy space.[56]

The Romans still cherished their traditions, even when the reasons for them had become obscure and faded from popular memory. They were still keen to respect and preserve a holy area, and to do honour to their past, their gods, and the spirit of Rome itself, faithful to the concept of personal sacrifice for the greater good of Rome – as in the self-sacrifice of Marcus Curtius – and this was to carry them forward through many vicissitudes and many changes of government.

2

Female Gods

As chapter one has shown, the lack of autonomy in the lives of Roman women did not prevent female deities from being both important and heavily relied upon for Rome's prosperity and security. Many goddesses, particularly those taken from Greek models and given Roman names, tended to be 'paired off' and considered to be the partners of male gods. Was that yet another need for women to be always under the protection of a male figure? The usual grouping unions were Jupiter with Juno; Neptune with Minerva; Mars with Venus; Apollo with Diana; Vulcan with Vesta; and Mercury with Ceres. These were grouped together by Livy, even though two of those goddesses were considered to be virginal figures, rather than the usual wives or mothers.[1] However, this pairing of the gods was also mentioned by Ennius in the third century BC[2], when the gilded statues of the most important deities had graced the Forum.

The Etruscans had named the most important of the gods the Consentes, because they 'rose and set' thus giving them an astrological significance. However, their twelve most important, considered to be the advisors and councillors of Jupiter, were all male. At the western side of the Forum Romanum is a pillared portico where the images of these gods and goddesses were displayed as the Dii Consentes, or the Portico of Harmonious Gods. It sits at the bottom of the very ancient road which leads up to the Capitol itself and was probably the last functioning shrine in the Forum, having been rebuilt in 367 AD, even though such shrines to the old gods had already been forbidden by law for more than a decade. The paired images were displayed there, ornamented with trophies and victories.

The capitals and the work of the columns are from the beginning of the third century AD, in the time of Septimius Severus, although several marks on the brickwork also bear the date of the reign of Hadrian. It is known that this part of Rome suffered from fire during the reign of the Emperor Commodus, after which Septimius Severus had it repaired. It was suggested – by Robert Burn in 1895 – that these twelve small, recessed rooms may also have served as the offices of the judicial clerks of the Capitoline, although he gives no further details to support this.[3] It is possible that as the Forum became more crowded, available spaces needed to be made more flexible, and an area which had originally been intended for display only needed to be utilised for more practical purposes. Certainly, the bureaucracy of Rome grew unwieldy and there must eventually have been small offices of various departments springing up wherever there was space available.

Over time, the number of gods and goddesses deemed worthy of some kind of worship grew larger, with many more being added to Rome's pantheon of gods, compressing even further the Forum and its immediate area with the increase in temples, but there was still a requirement to continue the worship of the older deities, who could be said to have grown old alongside Rome, and were still respected.

Anna Perenna

One of the most popular of these was the goddess Anna Perenna, who could indeed be referred to as an 'old' goddess, because in the most usual stories about her she is represented as a mature woman, sometimes even as an elderly one. Franz Altheim (1898-1976) suggested that she had originally been an Etruscan mother goddess and one of the enduring legends about her claims that she was a sister of Dido, the founder of Carthaginia, in Virgil's Aeneid. After Dido's death, Anna was obliged to find refuge in Malta, away from her brother Pygmalion, and Bathus the King of Malta gave her sanctuary there. After three years she again had to find refuge elsewhere as her brother prepared for war. She was shipwrecked on the coast of Latium, where she was hosted by Aeneas's settlement at Lavinium. However, Anna's presence provoked jealousy in Lavinia, and she had to move again. She was eventually swept away by the River Numicus and became a nymph, hidden in the perennial stream (annis perennis). Franz Altheim considered that the legend regarding some relationship between Anna and Aeneas was only developed in order to strengthen the Etruscan goddess's ties with Rome.

Another story is that the goddess Anna was requested by Mars to intercede with the virgin goddess Minerva, whom he loved, on his behalf. To teach him a lesson Anna dressed up as Minerva and went, veiled, to Mars's chamber. When he kissed her, she unveiled herself, and laughed at his foolishness. This is one explanation why Minerva's festival of Quinquatrus was celebrated only four days after Anna's own, and was also used as an excuse for the licentiousness which marked Anna Perenna's spring festival, and which actually became a feature of it.

The story of Anna that Ovid preferred, and the one which most closely equates to the Romans' love of her, along with the famous 'carryings-on' which accompanied her festival, dates from the 'secession plebis'. This was in 494 BC when the fledgling city of Roma was ruled by the aristocratic Patricians. However, it was almost divided by the Plebeians, who had grown tired of being enlisted in the military and more tired still of having no voice in the government of the city, despite all that they did to maintain her safety and prosperity. After many disputes, they decided simply to leave Rome and let the Patricians fend for themselves, so they abandoned the city and left the Patricians to struggle on alone. The Plebeians camped on the Mons Sacer or sacred mount about three miles northeast of the city, but the division left both sides unhappy with how the dispute had gone.

The Romans left behind found their situation intolerable, as they were accustomed to being able to rely on the Plebeians. Meanwhile, the angry Plebeians were equally uncomfortable camping out on the mountainside and lacking sufficient supplies. This is where Anna Perenna came in – beginning the Plebeian devotion to her. She daily baked bread and cakes and carried them out in baskets to the hungry Plebeians, helping them to survive. She kept on supplying them with food until the Patricians made them a satisfactory offer, and the Plebeians could return to the city without loss of honour.[4]

There is a strong suggestion of 'loaves and fishes' about this story, although it predates the Christian version by nearly five centuries. Anna Perenna was credited with single-handedly feeding the Plebeians over a considerable period of time, certainly long enough for the Patricians to realise that they would be obliged to make concessions. Her actions resulted in her becoming a goddess, being associated with the restart of the year, a deity of long life and prosperity. Macrobius said that 'private offerings made to Anna Perenna guaranteed that the circle of the year may be completed happily.'[5]

The concession that the Patricians made to the Plebeians was the formation of the Tribunate of the Plebs. This position of the Tribunes was originally intended to protect the common people from being oppressed by the Patrician class. The most important way this could be done was by the right of the Tribunes of the Plebs to veto any move, or proposed law, which was believed to be to the detriment of the ordinary people. It was intended to provide a vital check on the Senate and the Magistrates. However, this estimable intention would eventually prove to be a thorn in the side of progress, as over time the Tribunes (usually ten men) proved themselves to be eminently open to bribes, and because they were not required to give any reason for their veto of any proposed measure, they created not only a check but a block, often preventing changes from being implemented if they had been persuaded that it was not in their interests to do so.

By the fifth century BC, when the Tribunate of the Plebs was certainly in existence, the devotion towards Anna Perenna as a firm supporter of the ordinary people had grown, and her worship had become an important part of the annual cycle. Her festival on the Ides of March (the 15th) dated from a time when Rome's calendar sensibly began in the spring rather than in the middle of winter, and she is connected with life and rebirth. Her name 'Anna' suggests the year itself, while 'Perenna' means lasting many years, and represents the endurance of life itself and of fertility. These are still with us in gardening terms with the description of plants as being 'annual' or 'perennial'.

During excavations in Rome in 1999 (for an underground car park at the corner of the Piazza Eudide and the Via Guidobaldo dal Monte, in Rome's Parioli district), the remains of a rectangular fountain were discovered, between 6 and 10 metres below the present street level. Inscriptions on this bore the name of Anna Perenna, confirming her worship in this area. She is also known to have been worshipped at Buscemi, in Sicily, where in 1899 inscriptions were found linking Anna Perenna to Apollo. In Rome, the importance of her cult also led her to being represented on the Ara Pacis, erected by Augustus to honour the Imperial Family.

The fountain found in Rome's Parioli district dates from at least the fourth century BC and appears to have been in use until the sixth century AD, testifying to her ongoing popularity. At the rear of the fountain was its water tank, which was filled with mud. This mud contained many objects, ranging from a copper pot, many coins, several small oil lamps, to lamellae, which are small, thin lead plates, inscribed with cures and curses. Also among the finds there were small figurines, suggesting their use in specific pleas for intercession to the goddess.[6]

This discovery of almost voodoo-like figures in hermetically sealed containers changes the knowledge we had of the ancient Romans within the sphere of magic and religion. It intimates that the use of spells and curses was far more prevalent than was at first realised, and that the Roman state religion did include not only elements of superstition but an actual belief in magic itself. This dates from long before its connection with the 'imported' cults such as Isis/Serapis and Magna Mater, with their flamboyant priests and exotically exciting rituals.[7]

The festival on the Ides of March took place at a sacred grove by the banks of the Tiber. The celebration itself took the form of a picnic lasting well into the night. It was the time of the first full moon by the old lunar calendar, and the goddess's grove was by the first milestone out of Rome on the Via Flaminia. This was constructed in 220 BC by the Censor Gaius Flaminius and ran from a gate just below the Capitol Hill, in a perfectly straight line, to the Milvian Bridge. Present-day maps of Rome show the Via del Corso, starting at the Piazza Venezia, and going to the Piazza del Popolo where it is once again known as the Via Flaminia, slicing its way across the Campus Martius towards the Milvian Bridge on the Lungotavere Milvio, just as it has done since 220 BC. From there it veers northeast heading for the town of Ariminum (modern Rimini). It was the earliest of all such roads and was a very important route to the fertile agricultural area and onwards towards the Adriatic coast, serving this purpose long before the Empire existed.

A coin dated 82-81 BC was minted by Gaius Annius Luscus, which actually claimed his descent from this goddess. This sort of claim was not unusual, and her appearance on his coin is an example of the trend for prominent Romans to assert claims to mythic or divine ancestors in the first century BC.[8]

Recently published fragments of Decimus Laberius, and further archaeological evidence, place Anna Perenna in a position of importance regarding her worship and associated ritual. This is also confirmed by literary sources and her placement on the Ara Pacis, which was consecrated in 9 BC. This beautiful jewel of a building was originally erected on the northern outskirts of Rome, one mile from the boundary of the Pomerium of the west side of the Via Flaminia, and firmly within the area of worship connected with Anna Perenna. It has been reassembled in its present position, alongside the Mausoleum of Augustus, within a glass and steel pavilion designed by Richard Meier. Anna Perenna also appears on a coin from the period of Lucius Cornelius Sulla, in which she is depicted as a figure in a first-century BC drama, unsurprisingly given Sulla's well-known love of the theatre and theatrical people, for which he was often vilified.[9]

Two further sources refer to Anna Perenna's lasting popularity, one being a description of her worship by Martial, and another a votive inscription in verse recently found in Rome. Her spring festival has been described as 'a mass picnic on the Campus Martius'[10] but its actual significance was much greater than that; the goddess represented far more than merely an excuse for licentious behaviour, although this certainly did play its part in her homage. One of the most well-known aspects of the celebration was the custom of attempting to drink a cup of wine for each year of life the drinker hoped was ahead of him. Ovid gives a description of the general revelry taking place after the Plebeians had pitched their tents in the sacred grove, who even made 'bowers' out of branches:

> The feast has a licentious nature, and has been held in an area not far from the Tiber Banks. During the celebration, abundant wine libations were poured and couples lay down on the grass making love. There were songs, mimes, and other performances, and women were seen dancing with their hair loose, during all of the festival.[11]

He appears to have been as scandalised at the sight of women dancing in public with their hair down as he was at the sight of people copulating on the grass. However, he was totally missing the point. Sexual intercourse has long been an important part of springtime fertility rites and was not merely an unfortunate result of too much wine drinking, which might be expected to have the opposite effect. Romans believed that if women drank alcohol at all they would be unable to control their sexuality, but the drinking, the dancing with loosened hair and the general atmosphere of licence were by no means side issues. On the contrary, they were a vital part of the fertility rites, dating back to the earliest times, and were intended to feed the earth, awaken it from its winter sleep and encourage the new crops to grow as well as livestock to reproduce. These seemingly debauched acts took place in the early spring, and in the sacred grove, which itself was on the road leading to the most fertile agricultural land, in itself significant, as is Anna Perenna's position in the Ara Pacis, which once stood far closer to that sacred grove than it now does.[12]

These origins may well have been ignored or forgotten by the young people enjoying an unusual freedom at the festival, and it is easy to imagine the Patricians turning up their noses at the shameless behaviour of their social inferiors, yet it continued, and remained acceptable in a religious sense even though the origins of the festival became lost in the distant past. Anna Perenna touched on the pride of the ordinary people, along with the fertility of the land. The Flaminia's proximity to the grove was vital, ensuring easy access to the grain-producing lands so important to Rome's continuance and a constant reminder of the goddess's main attribute – that of feeding the people of Rome.

She came to represent not only this nurturing, the essential fertility and the annual rejuvenation of the earth, but the sheer enjoyment of life itself. Her noisy and orgiastic festival was originally performed with these factors at the forefront and was continued with enthusiasm despite the open disapproval of those who forgot the vital requirements of Rome's earliest farming days, as the city became more urban and distanced from its roots.

Many of the city's festivals were very ancient and had gradually lost their derivation from the natural order, even in the minds of those who took part in them. Anna Perenna was an earth mother, a nurturing deity, concerned with food and growth, all of which was marked by the location of her worship. At Buscemi in Sicily her worship was also in another vital grain-producing area. She was not merely an excuse for a drunken picnic and some free love in the woods – pleasant though that may have been – the goddess was concerned with the very basics of life itself.

Angerona

Angerona was very different. Far from being a goddess of the fields and open air, she was a creature of secrets and silence. Statues showed her as a young woman with a finger to her lips, or even with her mouth gagged. She guarded Rome's secret name, a knowledge given to very few and essential for Rome's security. If enemies could discover the secret name, then by evocation they could use it to steal a god away. This 'evocatio' or persuasion of a deity to leave its own location could be achieved by making promises of greater veneration, better temples, greater numbers of worshippers and more sacrifices than the deity enjoyed 'at home'. If the deity could be persuaded away, the protection it gave to its original location would go with it, thereby assisting the people of the new location with its strength, even in battle against its former worshippers.

Angerona's silence also had its place in everyday life. Not only for domestic or personal secrets, but because discretion was always preferred in Rome to cries and lamentations, which were considered to be unlucky. Self-control was admirable and Angerona also controlled that forbearance which caused outsiders to imagine that the Romans, particularly the Patrician class, were distant and unfeeling. She encouraged privacy, concentration, the benefits of meditation and careful consideration, far more than mere silence.[13]

She was also connected to the deep quiet of winter, the patience of waiting for a change back to the brightness of spring and the warmth of the sun, and with this aspect in mind her festival of the Angeronalia (or Divalia) was held on 21 December in the coldest and darkest part of the season. The Pontiffs sacrificed on her behalf at the Curia Acculeis, according to Varro,[14] or at the Sacell Volupiae (the shrine to Voluptas the goddess of pleasure), situated near the Porta Romanula, one of the inner gates at the northern side of the Palatine Hill, where a statue of Angerona has been found.[15]

Georges Demezil (1898-1986) considered her to be a goddess who helped nature to survive to the winter solstice, and that her name derived from Bruma, or Brevissima Dies, the shortest days of the year. He described Angor as being the lack of light and warmth, and Augustiae as designating space and time, in the sense of time itself being too short.

Angerona featured the hidden voice, driving away fears and restrictions, again referring to winter's darkness, although Rome's early calendar did not coincide with the solstice we now know until Caesar changed the calendar to accommodate the extra days more competently in 45 BC. When the Julian calendar was implemented, the beginning of the year was moved from March to the first day of January, that is, to the middle of the winter season.

A further vital use of silence and patience such as Angerona's was found in the sphere of state diplomacy, and there she was the protectress of state sercrets and deliberations. She encouraged careful use of important information. Angerona was, because of her connection with secrecy and the darkest part of the year, also representative of the fertility of spring, in her role as the guardian of the deep sleeps of the winter. She protected the seeds of new growth with the promise of the coming springtime. In this regard she had connections with such deities as Acca Laurentia – a goddess of fertility; Aeternitas – the guardian of eternity; Antevorta – representative of the future; Dea Dia – the goddesss of growth; Decima – the measurer of the thread of life; and Eeria, a water goddess and oracle.

Angerona was also worshipped as Ancaria at Festulae where an altar to her was discovered in the nineteenth century. She was sometimes associated with Feronia, who had a grove and later a temple on the Campus Martius, along with a temple at Terracina where slaves could seek sanctuary, which was a Greek custom rather than a Roman one.

Feronia was also connected to Flora, another deity of spring and growth, celebrating the end of cold and dark weather, so the connection comes full circle. All of these deities could be said to be connected to the resurgence of hope and brightness after the silences and restfulness of the winter season. Therefore Angerona was not only a deity of quiet and peacefulness but one of hope and aspirations for the future. Although a man surrounded by a houseful of women might invoke the silence of Angerona to give him peace, her holy silences were intended to be used for more important and serious purposes.

Bellona

She was a goddess of war, destruction and devastation. Bellona is usually portayed wearing her trademark helmet and holding a shield, the aegis, from which comes our term 'under the aegis' meaning being protected by. She also carried a sword, a spear and drove in a quadriga, a four-horse chariot. Bellona controlled the foreign wars and warfare, in all its policies and its armaments. She was naturally associated with Mars the male god of war and at various times has been described as being his wife or daughter, or even his twin sister. She did act at times as his charioteer.

Her temple was on the Campus Martius, fairly close to the Tiber, and almost level with the Isola Tiburina. It was situated next door to the temple of Apollo Sosianus, devoted to medicine and healing, of which three columns are now standing. Bellona's own temple and its all-important area known as 'foreign territory' have gone. It had been the tradition for the fetial priests to process to the border of Rome's territory and literally hurl a ritual spear over the boundary onto the land of an enemy. This was the first and most symbolic action, showing Rome's intention to wage war.[16] This was particularly the case in Rome's early days, when fighting her Italian neighbours. However, as Rome's boundaries spread until the border between Roman territory and that of its enemy could be hundreds of miles away, or even across the seas, this was no longer feasible. War could not wait for the priests to undertake a long and perhaps dangerous journey, while Rome fretted at delays and the priests might not be able to return at all. A piece of land of one iugera, or approximately half an acre, adjacent to the temple of Bellona, was then set aside and named 'enemy territory', and on this area was a column known as the 'columna bellica' or column of war. It became the tradition for a fetial priest to throw a javelin over that column and into the area designated enemy territory to signify the start of a war. This procedure was then used on all subsequent occasions and the last well-known example was in 179 AD, under the Emperor Marcus Aurelius.

The fetial priests formed a collegium devoted to Jupiter Optimus Maximus as the patron of Good Faith and were responsible for advising the Senate on foreign affairs and international treaties. Theirs was also the responsibility for making a formal declaration of war, and indeed also of peace, and confirming any treaties connected with it.[17]

It has been suggested that these fetiales also took upon themselves the guilt for being responsible for waging wars against any non-aggressive opponents.[18] Despite the fact that Roman law did not allow an aggressive war against a non-aggressive country, merely on the basis of acquiring more territory, it still continued as Rome's own Empire expanded and new land was required – for veterans of Rome's wars, for securing defences, and for the essential grain-lands to feed its expanding population.[19] Therefore, although strictly speaking such warfare was contrary to Rome's peaceable intentions, it was essential to her welfare.

The guilt for such actions was probably assumed by the fetial priests on Rome's behalf, so that the necessary expansion could continue without incurring the censure of the gods against Rome or her people.

The Senate frequently met at the temple of Bellona, particularly when welcoming the ambassadors of other countries. They also received victorious generals there. After the Civil War, when Lucius Cornelius Sulla had finally defeated the Samnites, he met the Senate at Bellona's temple while the remaining Samnite prisoners were killed on the Campus Martius.[20] This was intended less as a show of his personal power than a basic confirmation that a long-drawn out conflict was finally over and that Rome was safe. It must also be remembered, in an effort to be fair to the various Roman generals who appeared occasionally to indulge in a killing spree, that Rome then had no concept of prisoner-of-war confinement, nor did they have anywhere to secure large numbers of enemy prisoners. The idea of permitting hundreds, perhaps thousands, of enemy captives to be set free and allowed to fight again or plot against Rome while it was engaged elsewhere would have been foolish in the extreme. The only way that the ancient world could deal with such a problem was to destroy the foe, to prevent the recurrence of such conflict.

Seneca had a different view of that particular conflict, claiming that the men being killed were Romans and that Sulla took their deaths casually, and had said to the terrified Senators: 'Let us continue our business, a few traitors are being executed on my orders.' The Samnites had, in fact, fought Rome in a long series of wasteful wars, and had beaten Rome overwhelmingly at the Battle of the Caudine Forks during the Civil War of 82 BC. When Sulla finally defeated this very determined enemy at the Battle of the Colline Gate it was very much in Rome's interest to ensure that they were in no position to do further damage and that the long-standing conflict was finally over.[21]

Bellona herself, as Rome's female war-wager, was described as 'loud and active', capable of shouting war cries and driving Mars into battles. She was credited with inspiring violence, both starting and encouraging warfare, and of goading soldiers to make greater efforts to fight and win for Rome.

She had shrines throughout the city, although most of them are now known only from inscriptions and her most important temple on the Campus Martius, which was the scene of such important events, is now barely visible. Bellona had another shrine outside the city at Ostia, the port of Rome, situated on the eastern side of the Campo di Magna Mater, which is made up of a small building with a cella preceded by two columns and three steps. It is made entirely of brick, with the inside including a low podium at the rear, a white marble floor and a marble threshold. Interestingly, it also contains a relief of two pairs of feet, facing in opposite directions, which may have been an offering from a soldier who had gone to war and returned safely. Found on the temple steps was an inscription naming Aulus Livius Proculus and Publius Lucilius Gamala Filius as having rebuilt the shrine on public land.

Bellona's temple in Rome, on the Circus Flaminius, was built in 296 BC by the Consul Appius Claudius. Bellona's festival was celebrated on the third day of June, when the sacrifice of a black ewe, cow or heifer was appropriate, or the offering of female birds. There is some suggestion that in earliest times the sacrifice may even have been that of a human captive. The Dies Sanguinis (Day of Blood) held in Rome on 24 March was referred to as 'Bellona's Day' and her later connection to the imported goddess Cybele changed her rituals to include some masochistic and orgiastic elements. It is difficult to relate these forms of worship to the mindset of the early fetial priests of Republican Rome, yet Virgil claimed that Bellona had a bloodstained image, carried a whip or scourge, and that battles would go well for those who invoked her aid. This tied in with the offering of the returned soldier at her temple in Ostia.[22]

Her name gives us Bellum, or war, and is related to belligerent (warlike or pugnacious), bellicose (aggressive), and to the use of antebellum to describe 'before the war'. In earliest times she was known as Duellona, which was derived from an even more ancient word for 'battle'.[23]

Ceres

She was the goddess of agriculture, particularly associated with grain and cereals. She possessed motherly instincts, controlled fertility, and was said to be the daughter of Saturn and Ops. She was also the mother of Proserpina and Libera. She was the central deity of Rome's Plebeian Triad, along with Liber and Libera, otherwise known as the Aventine Triad, due to her temple being on the Aventine Hill. Liber was known as 'the free one' or Liber Pater as the free father, whose festival was the Liberalia on 17 March. Libera was a goddess of wine and wine making.

Ceres had a seven-day festival in April, the Cerealis, which included the popular Ludi Cerealis games. She was also honoured at the May 'Lustratio' of the fields, at the Ambarvalia festival of the harvest, and during the Roman marriage and funeral rites.[24]

Vitruvius, in his 'On Architecture', described her temple as being 'near to the Circus Maximus, with widely spaced supporting columns, wooden architraves instead of stone ones, clumsy, heavy low-roofed and wide ... with pediments showing statues of clay or brass, gilded in the Tuscan fashion.'

Archaic cults of Ceres are well-documented in Rome's neighbours, the Latins, Oscans, and Sabellions. Archaic fertilisation inscriptions dated from 600 BC ask Ceres to provide 'far' or spelt flour, the dietary staple. Her name was synonymous with grain and the bread it provided. Ceres is also widely credited with the discovery and introduction of wheat, with the yoking of oxen and with ploughing of the land, sowing seeds and protection of the growing plants. It was said that she taught these skills to men, for before her intervention men had lived on acorns and wandered aimlessly, knowing nothing of farming. They had had no settlements to live in or laws to live by. In January of each year she was offered spelt flour and a pregnant sow was sacrificed to her, along with the earth goddess Tellus, at the moveable feast of Feriae Sementivae, which was held before the annual grain sowing.

Regarding the apparently wasteful sacrifice of pregnant animals, Cato the Elder remarked that offering pregnant victims to the gods, particularly fertility deities, was intended to fertilise the earth and multiply the seeds, and worked more successfully than when offering the deity a barren sacrifice.[25] Cato also described the offer of a Parca Praecidanea sacrifice (before the sowing), and before harvest the goddess was offered a grain sample known as the Praemetium – again, the sacrificial animal was usually a sow. Ovid said of Ceres, 'She is content with little, provided that her offerings are "casta" or pure.'[26]

The priest responsible for the rituals of Ceres was the Flamen Ceriales, who would invoke Ceres (and probably also Tellus) along with twelve specialised minor gods, known as the 'Indigitamenta' when asking for divine help and protection at each stage of the growing cycle of the grain, and this would begin before the Feriae Sementivae.

The Indigitamenta or assistant gods to be invoked were Vervactor, or 'he who ploughs'; Reparator, 'he who prepares the earth'; Imporcitor, 'he who ploughs a wide furrow' (also called the maker of pigs); Insitor, 'who plants the seeds'; Obarator, 'who traces the first ploughing'; Occator, 'he who harrows'; Serritor, 'he who digs'; Subruncinator, 'he who weeds'; Messor, 'he who reaps'; Convector, 'he who carries the grain'; Conditor, 'he who stores the grain'; and Promitor, 'he who distributes the grain'.

In bridal processions a boy carried a torch ahead of the bride, and the wood for these torches was usually taken from the Spina Alba or mayblossom tree, which was also a very powerful fertility symbol. Adult males at weddings waited at the house of the groom and there they made a sacrifice to Tellus, on behalf of the bride, the victim usually a sow.

From the Republican era, Ceres was more associated with Proserpina to reinforce the connection with the Roman ideal of correct feminine virtues. The promotion of this part of Ceres worship coincided with an increasing birth-rate among Plebeian commoners along with a corresponding reduction among Patrician families. This created concern among Patricians who felt themselves under threat from the Plebeian rise. Women therefore needed to prove their fertility yet also be loyal in the best Roman tradition, to ease the growing sense of insecurity.

By the late Republic, Ceres was being described as 'Genetrix' or ancestress, sometimes also known as Alba meaning nourishing, as she was believed to have nourished and increased the Plebeians. By Imperial times, Ceres became an Imperial deity and a part of the joint cult with Ops Augusta, who was the mother of Ceres in Imperial guise and a bountiful ancestress in her own right. Several of her ancient Italic precursors are closely associated with human fertility and motherhood. The Pelignan goddess Angitia Cerealis has also been identified with Angerona and thereby associates her with childbirth. Ceres was seen as the protector of Plebeian laws and rights, particularly those of the Tribunes of the Plebs. Her temple on the Aventine served as a cult centre for Plebeians, as a legal archive, and as a treasury, possibly also possessing a law court. This area is considered to be contemporary with the Lex Sacrata, which established the office and persons of Plebeian Aediles and Tribunes as the representatives of the Plebeian people in Rome. These officials held a secure and powerful position, being immune to threats or arrests and holding the power of veto. Anyone who violated the freedom of a Tribune faced losing his property or even his life, being forfeit to Ceres.[27]

The Lex Hortensia of 287 BC extended the Plebeian laws to the city and to all its citizens. The official decrees of the Senate (Senatus Consulta) were kept in the temple of Ceres, under the guardianship of the goddess and her Aediles. Livy approved: 'The Consuls could no longer seek advantages by arbitrarily tampering with the laws of Rome.'[28]

The temple on the Aventine may also have been used as a sanctuary, where people threatened with arrest by Patrician Magistrates could be under the protection of the goddess. The poet Virgil called her 'law-bearing Ceres'. The temple, cult and games of Ceres were, at least in part, funded by the fines paid by those who offended the laws regarding her protection. The grain-lands were so vital to Rome's survival that the Plebeian Aediles were empowered to impose fines on anyone who allowed flocks or herds to stray onto or trample them. Such fines were issued in the name of Ceres and the people of Rome.

Ancient laws of the original Twelve Tables also forbade anyone 'charming by magic that the crops of a neighbour should move onto his own fields.' This begs the question of how it could possibly be proved, and whether an inefficient farmer could blame his own lack of decent crops on the 'bewitching' of some neighbour whose own grain was more abundant.[29]

The possibility of some innocent person being severely punished due to the malice of a neighbour concerns the modern mind, however in its own time it was considered an acceptable risk. In the same way as the accusation of witchcraft is considered ridiculous; although most accused were found not guilty, this did not deny the reality of witchcraft.

Likewise, the death penalty could be invoked in the event of deliberate removal of field boundaries, and any youth found guilty of this offence was liable to be whipped, as well as being fined double the amount of any damage caused. These field boundaries were merely marker stones, and it might be possible to move one inadvertently when ploughing, but the consequences could be serious if the accidental nature was not acknowledged by others.

Cicero refers to the killing of Tiberius Gracchus in his 'In Verrum' (Against Verres), of 70 BC. He was then prosecuting Verres, the ex-Governor of Sicily, for extortion.[30] It must be remembered that Cicero hated Verres, and his eloquence at that time was not entirely concerned with the matter in hand. The murder of Tiberius Gracchus in 133 BC had not been directly concerned with the movement of boundaries, although this was one of the points raised at the time. It was, rather more seriously, concerned with the distribution of Latifundia, or state land and large farms used to grow profitable crops. Although some suspected that Gracchus had ambitions to rule, he was in fact protected by the Lex Sacrata and his person should have been inviolable, resulting in his death being punishable. The case against Verres concerned, in part, his exploitation of the grain farmers in Sicily, and these people were under the protection of Ceres at the place of her 'earthly home', plus the fact that Verres had stolen from many temples, including a statue of Ceres herself.

The boundaries of Ceres also included those between the living and the dead. She could function as a gatekeeper when the Mundus was opened, to allow the occupants of the Underworld access to the land of the living. This took place on 24 August (between the rites of Consualia and Opiconsivia), on 5 October (following the Leiunium Cereris), and on 8 November during the Plebeian Games. She prevented spirits from wandering or becoming Lemures, or vengeful shades.[31] One lady named Lassia, possibly of the old Lassii family from Pompeii, was a priestess of the goddess Ceres and her tombstone remains outside Pompeii. Her family were workers in wine and one of their boats was wrecked off Cannes with wine jars aboard, stamped with the family name in Oscan script, dated to the first century BC. It shows that the cult of Ceres did not choose its priestesses only from Patrician families, as the Lassii, though prosperous, were in trade. In Republican times that would have been an unsuitable background for a priestess of Vesta.

The Cerealia itself was held in mid- to late April, organised by the Plebeian Aediles to include circus games or 'Ludi Circenses', which opened with a horse race in the Circus Maximus facing the Aventine and the temple of Ceres. The festival included religious theatrical events during mid-April, while the turning point at the far end of the Circus Maximus was sacred to Consus, the god of the storage of grain.

The Mundus Cerealis, or underground pit, was opened to release the shades when the time for offerings to them should be made. It was also believed that Romulus had dug the pit as part of the foundations of his new city of Rome. Fowler noted that again pigs were a favourite offering, along with seed corn, probably 'far', from the new harvest.[32] Plutarch, however, compared the Mundus pit to similar pits dug by Etruscan colonists to contain soil from their parent city, which was then used to dedicate the first fruits of the harvest.[33]

Fowler also speculated that the Mundus was Rome's first grain storage pit or 'penus' which later took on symbolic significance. The large number of festivals concerning the goddess, and the dates of opening the Mundus, show the immense importance of Ceres to Rome. Her priests made sure that the fields were blessed for the grain to grow, and the Arval Brethren led a rural version of the rites. The Plebeian Aediles also held a minor priestly function at the Aventine temple, responsible for its financial affairs, including the collection of fines. They organised the Ludi Cerealis and possibly also the Cerealia itself, as well as caring for the grain supplies and the Plebeian grain doles, which were part of a government subsidy to give free, or cheaper, grain to the poor citizens of Rome, and was used by around 200,000 people.

Juvenal called it 'bread and circuses' as a way of keeping the people quiet, which in some ways is a fair assessment.[34] Grain riots were not uncommon and the poorer citizens were quick to pick a fight if ignored. The doles of grain and the regular festivals provided not only a basic food supply but also an opportunity to release public tensions in pleasurable shows. It is interesting to note that when public interest in minor festivals waned, the games still drew huge crowds, who may have forgotten the original religious elements.

The most important sources of wheat were Egypt, Libya, Tunisia, Algeria, Morocco and of course Sicily. Many hundreds of ships transported the grain, and there was an extensive distribution system within Rome. In the early Republic (509-287 BC) the government had sporadically distributed grain to the people, but after 123 BC regular donations began with the grain law proposed by Gaius Graccus when all male citizens over fourteen years of age could buy, at below market price, five modii (33kg or around 73lbs) of grain per month. In 62-58 BC the number of people eligible for doles was expanded, and grain became free to its recipients. The number of people receiving free or subsidised grain then rose to an estimated 320,000 before being reduced by Gaius Julius Caesar back to 150,000 and then set at a basic 200,000 by the Emperor Augustus, which number remained stable almost until the end of the Empire.[35]

In the third century AD, bread replaced the actual grain, and Septimius Severus began to provide olive oil to residents of Rome, while Aurelian also ordered the distribution of wine and pork. The grain dole during the early Empire is believed to have accounted for 15% to 33% of the total grain imported and consumed within Rome. Ceres, with her Plebeian connections and her all-important grain should certainly have been pleased.

Diana

The goddess of hunting in later times also became a deity of the moon and of chastity. Cypress trees were sacred to this daughter of Jupiter and his mistress Latona, and she was the twin sister of the god Apollo. She was revered as a goddess of woods, children and the wild creatures, as well as domestic animals. She probably originated as an indigenous goddess of the woodlands, but later absorbed identification with Selene (Luna) and also with Hecate, who was an infernal deity, which led to the 'Triformis' used in Latin literature. This Triad consisted of Diana the huntress, Egeria the water nymph who served her, and the woodland god Virbius.

Her most famous place of worship was the Grove of Diana Nemorensis (Diana of the Wood) on the shore of Lake Nemi near Rome. This was a shrine common to the cities of the Latin League and associated with Diana there was Egeria, the spirit of a nearby stream, and the hero Virbius who was said to have been the first priest of Diana's cult in the area. A particularly strange custom for this priesthood was that the incumbent priest must always have been a runaway slave who had personally killed the previous priest. It must have been an uncomfortable position to hold, knowing that one day another runaway slave would appear to challenge the holder of the priesthood, just as he had challenged his predecessor.

Rome's most important temple of Diana was also perhaps the earliest in the city, on the Aventine. There she was referred to as Diana Aventina. There was a large precinct there and a temple building, the whole complex being known as the Dianium. The rules governing the precinct and its rites were inscribed in detail on a bronze stele, the Lex Arae Dianae, and the temple itself was known to still be standing in the fourth century AD. Diana was considered to be another protector of the lower classes, particularly slaves, given the original status of her chief priests. Her festival in Rome on the 13th (the Ides) of August was a holiday for all slaves. Many votive offerings have been found at her sanctuaries and women whose prayers had been answered visited the grove in processions from Rome on her festival day. They carried torches and wore garlands of flowers. The celebration was always so popular that the later Christians could not stop it, so finally had to adopt it as their own festival of the Assumption of the Virgin Mary.

Diana was identified with the Greek goddess Artemis – there is a beautiful wall painting of her, holding a bow, which came from Stabiae.[36] The worship of this goddess probably began in Crete in pre-Hellenic times. However, the virginal sister of Apollo is very different from the many-breasted Artemis of Ephesus, whose cult usually included the wild and lascivious dances of nymphs of the wells and springs, as she was originally a deity connected with trees.

Diana is usually pictured holding a bow, accompanied by a hunting dog or a stag. However, the cults could vary considerably, especially in the Artemis versions, which included the devotion in Attica to Artemis as a bull goddess, who was honoured by a few drops of blood drawn by a sword from the neck of a living man.[37] According to Homer and later poets, even Artemis was originally virginal despite the orgiastic nature of some of her followers. She also showed wrath towards humans, drawn from wild nature's suspicions of, and hostility towards, human beings. Until the milder and gentler aspects of this goddess prevailed, around the fourth century BC, she was not wildly popular and only after that date did the great sculptural schools begin to portray the more beneficent form of Diana.

She is presently revered in modern Pagan religions such as Roman Neo-Paganism, known as Stregheria, and also in Wicca.[38] She was always lauded for her purity and it is said that once, when she was hunting in a sacred forest where no humans had ever been, she and her attendant nymphs bathed in a nearby stream. Later, while they rested, a hunter named Actaeon, who was lost, saw the naked Diana. To prevent him from telling others what he had seen, Actaeon was turned into a stag, then set upon and killed by his own hounds.

In a related story, Ovid tells of her sacred chastity. Diana's follower Callisto was out hunting and was seen by Jupiter, Diana's father. He felt lust for the girl and turned himself into an image of Diana in order to get closer to her, greeting her with a kiss. He then embraced Callisto, revealed his true self, and raped her. She was deeply ashamed and the next time Callisto saw Diana she feared it could be Jupiter in disguise again. Ovid pointed out that 'if Diana had not been a maiden, she would have known of Callisto's guilt by a thousand signs,' for Callisto was pregnant by Jupiter. The pregnancy was revealed soon enough, and Diana sent Callisto away from the river, saying 'Be off from here, do not defile these sacred waters!' Callisto was obliged to leave, despite her innocence, and later Jupiter's wife Juno turned her into a bear.[39]

Diana is the only Pagan goddess to be mentioned in the Christian Bible, and as a result she became associated with many of the folk beliefs involving supernatural figures which the early church wished to demonise. In Acts 19 (24-41) she is referred to as an incarnation of the warlike and lustful Astoreth, a connection forced onto Diana by early Christian writers. On the contrary, Diana had always been revered as a virgin goddess and an upholder of stern morality. Astoreth was quite the opposite, known for rampant sexuality and immorality, the antithesis of all Diana stood for.

The temple of Diana at Ephesus had been the early centre of worship and she was referred to as 'the idol whom all Asia and the world worships.' There was a very lucrative trade for silversmiths there, making small replicas of her for sale, but this trade was totally destroyed as a result of Paul's ministry, and not only did the silversmiths' trade receive a death blow, but a great deal of ancient art and many books of divination, which would have become great treasures for later generations, were burned in Christian purges. Paul was only saved from a savage mauling by the irate silversmiths due to the intervention of the town clerk of Ephesus, who proved to be by far the more tolerant and sensible of the two men.

Interestingly, despite Diana's virginity, she was often prayed to by women who needed to conceive, and also by those already pregnant, in order to ask for an easy birth. Her reputation for protecting such women earned her a place of great honour. She was considered to be intelligent and is reputed to have directed the movements of the moon and was a goddess of light. Her worship on 13 August was a festival of torches, especially at Lake Nemi, where the torchlight joined the moonlight on the surface of the lake and was then referred to as 'Diana's mirror'. In this regard she was known as Diana Nemorensis or Diana Nemoralis. [40]

Flora

The goddess of flowers and the springtime, of fertility and vegetation, Flora never assumed a high position among Roman deities, although she did have an important function and was one of the oldest of the Roman gods. Her temple stood near the Circus Maximus and her festival, the Floralia, began in 240 BC being held on 27 April during the Republic, and following advice given in the Sibylline Books, was held on 28 April when the calendar later changed. The Ludi Florae lasted for six days under the Empire and included gladiator contests, theatrical performances (according to some sources these included naked dancing), and various other events stretching in total from the 28th until the 3rd of May.[41]

Flora had her own Flamen, or priest, the Flamen Florialis, who was one of the Flamines Minores. Her temple was inaugurated in 238 BC and during her festival it was customary for everyone to wear wreaths of flowers, while the women also tended to wear brighter colours, which were usually avoided by the respectable matrons.

Five days of farces and mimes were performed that centred on the phallic symbol, ever-present in Roman fertility culture, and included a good deal of nudity.[42] These events were followed by a further day of the release of goats and hares for hunting. Flora also had a festival of roses in her honour on 23 May.

Fortuna

She could easily be said to be the most important goddess of ancient Rome. She was certainly the most wide-ranging, being present in all everyday life, whether public or private, all depended on her goodwill. Fortuna controlled luck, chance, fate, increase, prosperity and fertility. She controlled the good fortune of the state and the lives of millions of people across the Empire, for her worship continued from the earliest times as an agricultural goddess responsible for the fields, right up to Medieval times, when images of Fortuna were familiar with her 'Rota Fortuna', or wheel of fortune, by which she could affect the lives even of kings and popes. There is evidence that she was worshipped as far north as Castlecary in Scotland, on the Antonine Wall; there is a statue of her in the Hunterian Museum in Glasgow that was found at Castlecary.

Her name possibly derived from Vortumna, who revolved the seasons of the year. There was also a minor goddess named Felicitas, but this benign creature did not and could not usurp any part of Fortuna's enormous power, because Felicitas was concerned only with happiness, like another minor deity named Hilaria, whose feast day on 25 March was one when any man believed he could do as he pleased. These two deities represented only pleasure, however brief it might be. Fortuna's influence touched everything, and her power was absolute. She was greatly revered – and also greatly feared – due to her capricious nature. Her presence could be delightful and comforting or it could be terrifying in its calamity, for Fortuna could just as easily bring bad luck as good. She was sometimes shown blindfolded or veiled, due to the sheer randomness of her dispensing and it was, and still is in Italy, said that 'La dea della Fortuna e cieca' or that 'the goddess of luck is blind' and this blinded image of her is still alive in many aspects of Italian culture, where the dichotomy of 'fortuna/sfortuna' or good luck/bad luck is still familiar, with sfortuna in this instance meaning actual mischance or misfortune, rather than merely an absence of good luck.

As the eldest child of Jupiter, Fortuna could be as bountiful as her father, and was also tied to Virtus, or strength of character, an essential requirement for public officials, but the lack of which often brought ill-fortune to Rome. Sallust said '…truly when in the place of work, idleness in the place of the spirit of measure and equity, caprice and pride invade, fortune is changed just as with morality.'[43]

The Wheel of Fortune was first mentioned by Cicero, who said of her: 'It is difficult for one who has enjoyed uninterrupted good fortune, to have a due reverence for virtue.' This could mean that those favoured by her could expect to do as they wished – but also that, due to her capricious nature, opportunities should always be grasped immediately they presented themselves, lest they slip through one's fingers.

Ovid said of her: 'Only he who is the favourite of Fortuna is loved,' doubtless by being surrounded by admirers in the hope that one's good fortune would rub off on them, while Petronius pragmatically warned that 'While Fortune lasts, you will see your friend's face,' implying that fair-weather friends would disappear along with Fortuna's goodwill.

Plautus commented that 'This goddess Fortuna single-handedly frustrates the plans of a hundred learned men,' successfully expressing her darker side and her influence over state business, while Ovid's description is typical of the Roman representation of the goddess, as in a letter from exile he called her 'the goddess who admits, by her unsteady wheel, her own fickleness. She always has the apex beneath her swaying foot.'[44]

An oracle at her immense temple at Praeneste (present-day Palestrina, east of Rome), used the art of divination, where a boy would pick out oak rods to indicate the future for a supplicant. Dedications to Fortuna have been found showing her many aspects, for example Fortuna Dubia (doubtful fortune) and Fortuna Brevis (fickle or wayward fortune), or Fortuna Mala (bad fortune), in efforts to turn her kinder aspects back towards her worshippers.

An amulet was found in the House of Menander in Pompeii which linked Fortuna to Isis, sharing not only the Isis worship as Isis/Fortuna but also as Fortuna Augusta, the good fortune of the Emperor's family. She could also be linked to the god Bonus Eventus, who is represented as her counterpart, as both appear on intaglios and engraved gems all over the Roman world, including Pompeii.[45]

Fortuna could also be connected to an even earlier Egyptian god, Shai, who was also a deity of fortune and was believed to be 'born' with each person and control their fate throughout their life. He could also be positive or negative, bring good luck or dispense misfortune. He was linked to Renenutet, a goddess of good fortune who gave each child its true name, as with Angerona and her knowledge of Rome's most secret name, which was not only personal but could be powerful. Fortuna was a deity of many different aspects, and her incarnations as Brevis, Mala and Dubia have already been mentioned, but there were others:

Fortuna Virilis, the character of potency of men. Worshipped during Veneralia on the first day of April, in honour of Venus Verticordia (the changer of hearts), and Fortuna Virilis, this involved ritual bathing and the adornment of a cult statue of Venus. There was a temple to Fortuna Virilis in Rome.

Fortuna Annonaria served farmers and crop growers.

Fortuna Belli concerned herself with battles and other warlike aspects, while Fortuna Atrox was the goddess of terrible and horrible fate.

Fortuna Redux was the homebringer, who allowed travellers safe journeys, and the worship of this aspect is first known by the dedication of the Senate made in gratitude for the homecoming of the Emperor Augustus in 19 BC. The temple on the Campus Martius was built by Domitian to celebrate his own triumphs in Germany and altars to her have been found in military bath houses on Hadrian's Wall.

Fortuna Balnearis was also often found in military bath-houses, along with Fortuna Salutaris (health and well being), reflecting the personal preoccupations of the troops in those outposts of Empire, and their desire to return safely home. Two dedications to this aspect of Fortuna were found in Spain.

Fortuna Equestris was the patron of the Eques, or knights. Her temple was vowed by Quintus Fulvius Flaccus in 180 BC during his Spanish campaign. It was on the Campus Flaminius and was dedicated on the Ides of August 173 BC, with the festival of Fortuna Equestris also being on the 13th.

Fortuna Respicians was a provider, with a temple on the Esquiline Hill and a shrine on the Palatine Hill.

Fortuna Mullebris was concerned with the affairs of women in general, and her temple was about four miles outside Rome, on the Via Latina.

Fortuna Victrix was for victory in battles, while Fortuna Conservatrix could preserve life.

Fortuna Obsequiens was goddess of indulgence, and of an indulgent future. There was a shrine to her near the Vicus Fortunae Obsequens on the Caelian Hill.

Fortuna Privata and Fortuna Publica were for private devotions and public good fortune. Privata had a temple on the Palatine, while the temple on the Quirinal was in an area which became known as the 'Three Fortunes' – one of these aspects was for Privata, one was for Primigenia, and the third was dedicated to Fortuna Publica Citerior, which is believed to have meant 'nearer the city.'

An altar dedicated to Fortuna Populi Romani (the luck of the Roman people), is known from Chesterholme Fort on Hadrian's Wall. Fortuna Romana was the luck of Rome itself, and in Constantinople the Emperor Constantine built a temple to Fortuna in which he set up a statue of Fortuna Romana.

There were even more, Fortuna Faitrix who represented the fate of life; Fortuna Virgo for virgins; Fortuna Barbarta for adolescents who were becoming adult; and Fors Fortuna who was connected with astrology and the surrounding world.

One of the most important aspects of the goddess was Fortuna Primigenia, this was for the protection of first-born children and her temple in Rome occupied a prime position on top of the Capitol Hill, close to that of Jupiter Optimus Maximus. The goddess's name is also thought to refer to her first cult at Praeneste, meaning that she was the original Fortuna. Her festival was on 13 November, and she also had a temple on the Quirinal Hill in Rome.

Fortuna Huiusce Diei is fortune of the present day. She had a temple dedicated to her in the Area Sacra, which is one of Rome's most ancient temple complexes. Her lovely circular temple there was dedicated in 101 BC by Quintus Lutatius Catulus after he vowed it at the Battle of Vercellae. The Area Sacra stands on the Campus Martius, and the ruins are now several yards below present road level. The theatre complex of Gnaeus Pompeius Magnus with its vast Forum of a hundred columns almost touched the ancient Area Sacra at one end and was topped by a temple to Venus Victrix. The Area Sacra excavation in 1926 revealed not only the remains of four early Republican temples, but also fragments of a colossal statue of Fortuna Huiusce Diei. These are now in the Museum of Centrale Montemartini. There is no present evidence that another temple to her, in this aspect, ever existed and the vow of Lutatius Catulus at Vercellae (proving to be the final battle between Rome and the Cimbri people) was believed to have turned the tide in Rome's favour. This event is documented by Plutarch in his 'Life of Gaius Marius,' as Marius then held Imperium as Consul and commander during that battle [46]

Cicero described the delightful temple (which then had eighteen 11-metre-high Traventine columns, with tufa Corinthian capitals, above a 2.5 metre podium) as a 'splendid monument, that one visits to refine and enrich the beholder.'[47] Cicero also said that Fortuna Huiusce Diei '... should be cultivated because she empowers each day.' The sculptor of the immense statue of the goddess is believed to have been the famous Greek, Skopas Minor, who was then living in Rome. It is spectacular in that, as well as head, arms and feet of Parian marble, it once possessed a bronze body with a full robe and cloak. The existing pieces of the head, neck and right arm and one sandaled foot give some idea of the original height of the full statue, hypothesised as having been around eight metres tall, in a standing position, placed in the centre of the temple. It would have been usual for her to have been holding a cornucopia and wearing a diadem. Presumably, the bronze body was melted down after the fourth century AD, when Christianity took over Rome.[48]

The nature and importance of the Area Sacra finds is obvious and further excavation may be able to reveal more information about this goddess. The other temples there, whose ruins are also visible, are believed to be temple a, Juturna, built in the third century BC possibly by Gaius Lutatius Catulus after his victory against the Carthaginians in 241 BC. The temple of Fortuna Huiusce Diei is the only circular one and is usually referred to as temple b. Temple c is probably that of Feronia, an ancient fertility deity and is likely to be the oldest of the group, possibly dating to the fourth century BC. The largest of the four is temple d, possibly dedicated to the Lares Permarini, the protectors of sailors, dating to the second century BC. Only a small part of this one has been excavated as it still runs under the present road, the Via Florida. This was vowed by the Praetor Lucius Aemilius Regillus while he was engaged in a naval battle against Antiochus the Great in 190 BC. The temple was later dedicated by Marcus Aemilius Lepidus, the Censor, on 22 December 179 BC.[49]

A temple to virgins and pubescent girls in Fortuna's name once stood on the Forum Holitorium (the vegetable market), and various others were built extensively around the Empire. However, none of the many temples could compare, either in size or in importance, to the temple of Fortuna Primigenia at Praeneste. This had been founded by Publius Sempronius Tuditanus in 204 BC. Parents would take their first-born children to gain the goddess's blessing and improve their chances of a successful life. Rome never had anything to equal this amazing structure, the remains of which still stand, now with a medieval palace on the top. It was formed of a spectacular series of terraces, in a huge pyramidal style, with a theatre on the top level similar in design to the later Theatre of Pompeius Magnus in Rome, also with an oracular shrine. Those consulting the oracle would be asked to choose at random from a collection of inscribed oak tablets, and then they had to interpret the reply themselves.

During the war between Marius and Sulla, and later when Lucius Cornelius Sulla was opposed by Marius Junior and his followers, Praeneste suffered damage. When Sulla was victorious he undertook to restore Praeneste, which became a veteran's colony in 82/81 BC. Sulla had a great devotion to Fortuna, and although he had previously carried an image of Apollo, he turned to Fortuna believing that she had given him success in battle. The full restoration of the temple to its original magnificence was done out of his respect for Fortuna Primigenia.[50]

Juno

Juno was Queen of the Gods of Rome, the wife of Jupiter Optimus Maximus, and another goddess holding power in several different aspects. As the mother of Mars, Vulcan, Bellona and Juventus, she concerned herself with women and childbirth, but as the daughter of Saturn she also had warlike associations and was often depicted carrying a spear and wearing a goatskin cloak and a diadem.[51] She was a part of the Capitoline Triad, along with Jupiter and Minerva, and could function as a councillor of state and protectress of the Roman people and empire.

Her large temple of Juno Moneta (giver of timely warnings) was situated on the Arx, which was the mound alongside Capitol Hill, now occupied by the church of Santa Maria in Aracoeli. This connection with warnings was due to the invasion of the Gauls into Rome in 390 BC during which the guard dogs had slept, but the warning of impending danger was given by Juno's sacred flock of geese. Livy tells us that the temple had been vowed by Lucius Furius Camillus during the war against the Aurunci and was actually dedicated in 348 BC, having been built on land where the house of Marcus Manlius Capitolinus had once been.

The goddess Juno was taken to Rome in 396 BC after originally being the patron deity of Veii. During conflict with that town, the Romans wished to have her assistance and the great statue of the goddess was asked if she would prefer to live in Rome, where she would have a bigger and better temple, and more worshippers and sacrifices. The goddess is reputed to have replied 'Yes, take me now,' so she and her protective influence went to assist Rome, amid great rejoicing, and the people of Veii were defeated. The temple was close to where the first Roman coins were minted, and it probably began the tradition of storing coins and bullion in the basement rooms attached to the temples. In addition, the Libri Lintei, or records of the annually elected Consuls which dated from 444-428 BC were also stored there.

Tradition suggests that there may have been an earlier temple on this site, as archaic terracotta artefacts were found there in medieval times, and the remains of squared-off walls and stones are preserved there which go back to both archaic and mid-Republican phases of temple building. Remains of a building made from blocks of cappellaccio, the local volcanic tufa of which Rome's hills are formed, can still be seen in the garden in front of the Sixtus VI entrance to the Palazzo Senatorio, which space faces the Forum. It was from there that Augurs observed the flight patterns of birds in order to interpret the will of the gods.

Juno had a presence in many towns, being revered as Sespeis Mater Regina at Lanuvium, Tibur, Falerlii and Veii, and also as Juno Regina at Tibur and Falerlii. She was known as Juno Lucina at Tusculum and Narbo, and had a temple in Rome under that name on the Clivus Suburanus leading to the Via Labicana. There she also had a registry and was responsible for the recording of Roman citizen births.

As Juno Regina, or ruler, her temple was in the Circus Flaminius close to that of Jupiter Stator, the stayer of soldiers in retreat. Closer to the Forum Holitorium stood the Sospita temple where Juno, as saviour, was close to the temples of Pietas, Janus and Spes. Also as Sospita, Juno was the patron deity of Lanuvium, a Latin town just south of Rome, and her aid was equally invoked by Rome to pacify the often rebellious Latins.

The temple to Juno Sospita, vowed by the Consul Gaius Cornelius Cathegus in 197 BC, had by 90 BC become derelict due to prostitution in its precinct, and an incident where a pregnant bitch had delivered her puppies beneath a statue of the goddess. Juno Sospita was probably an offshoot of the Greek Mother of Pessinus, Juno of the snakes from Lanuvium, and considered a saviour of women. At the time of the Italian War, Metella Belearica, the wife of Appius Claudius Pulcher, dreamed that the goddess appeared to her and complained about the state of her temple. She told Belearica that it was by then so filthy that she could no longer live in it. Belearica went with her husband to the Consul Lucius Caesar and asked him for his help to clean it to pacify the goddess. They cleaned it together and made the temple pristine, so that the goddess could take up residence there again. Two months later, Caecilia Metella Belearica died in childbirth, and the child she gave birth to survived her, being Publius Claudius Pulcher of Bona Dea infamy.

Ovid in his 'Fasti' had certainly described the temple as being 'dilapidated to the extent of being no longer discernible because of the injuries of time.' However, that may have been an exaggeration, as parts of that temple are still visible today. Gaius Julius Caesar had ordered its complete restoration and it is possible that Ovid was referring to an even older temple on the site, which he confirmed had been 'near the temple of the Phrygian Mother goddess (Cybele) on the Palatine'. Outside of Latium, in Campania, Juno was known as Populona (she who increases, either people or understanding). At Samnium she was known as Regina Populona and at Pisarum as Regina Matrona.

She was associated with Fluvium or Februalis and with the essential rites of purification which were undertaken in February of each year, to provide a good start to the New Year. Ovid[52] said that the name derived from these Februae or expiations, which were lustrations designed to remove possible spiritual contamination. Rituals were performed to cleanse the influences from the previous year. On the first day of the month a black ox would be sacrificed to Helernus, a minor Underworld deity related to the cult of Carna, a nymph who may have been another image of Juno Sospita, and as Juno Lucina the goddess was also celebrated on 15 January at the festival of the Lupercalia.

The Lupercalia was connected to the Caprotina festival, where free and slave women could celebrate together, with mock battles, some obscene language, and the sacrifice of a male goat. It took place at the site of an ancient wild fig tree and this fruit was considered to have a strong sexual element due to its fertilising power, but also to the shape of its fruits and the white viscous juice of the tree itself. The Lupercalia was also a fertility rite, derived from the stealing away of the Sabine women, in order to increase the population of the young city of Rome. However, it would appear that many of the stolen women then had trouble conceiving the all-important children, leaving the future of Rome still under threat.

Ovid described the fertility rite:

Beneath the Esquiline Hill there was a grove, uncut for many years, named after mighty Juno, and when the wives and husbands went there they went down on bended knees in supplication. Suddenly the tops of the trees shook, and through the grove the goddess spoke wondrous words … 'Let the sacred he-goat enter the Italian matrons,' so the Augur slaughtered a male goat and cut its hide into strips, with which he struck the girls, who then became pregnant.[53]

This rite was to become an important part of the month's rituals, intended to promote health and particularly fertility. It can be traced back to the sixth century BC and the ritual began with the sacrifice of one or more male goats, and one dog.

These rites were performed by the Luperci, young and active men, who were then smeared with the blood of the animals on their foreheads, which blood was then wiped off by a piece of wool dipped in milk. The Luperci then had to laugh aloud. Further strips of the goatskins were named Februa, and they wrapped some of these around their bodies, but remained almost naked as they ran around the streets, striking any woman of child-bearing age with the strips of hide they carried. The women welcomed and offered themselves for these light whippings, after which they hoped that they would become pregnant.

It was said that, over time, the nudity aspect of the Lupercalia became less of a feature, at least less 'authorised'. However, a youthful Marcus Antonius caused a scandal in 44 BC due to his display of his genitals, when young women present pretended to swoon over him, much to his delight. It was during that year's feast that he offered a diadem to Gaius Julius Caesar, intimating kingship, which Caesar spurned seeing that the crowd was not pleased. He would eventually become Dictator in Perpetuity instead, knowing that the title of king would be unwise.

The sexually charged atmosphere of the Lupercalia, accompanied by drinking, feasting, and random sex, would eventually be replaced in the Christian calendar by the mild St. Valentine, whose own feast day happened to coincide. Two festivals so opposite can hardly be imagined, however, the Lupercalia was always enormously popular despite (or perhaps because of) its reputation for immorality. The Emperor Augustus certainly disapproved of it and ruled that no adolescents should be allowed to take part due to the dubious carryings-on, but despite all the official disapproval the festival survived intact until 494 AD, when Pope Gelasius I abolished it and replaced the February purification rites with the festival of the Purification of the Virgin Mary.

The name Lucina, often used for Juno, is revealing in that it reflects the two aspects of her function, being the cyclical renewal of time, in the waxing and waning of the moon, as well as referring to her involvement in births. Juno in this aspect is credited with 'bringing light to the new-born' in the form of the vigour of the life forces. The temple of Juno Lucina was built in 375 BC in the grove sacred to the goddess and stood on the Cispius, near to the shrine of the Argei. Inscriptions for Juno Lucina were found at the nearby church of San Pressede, on the Via di Sante Pressede near the church of Santa Maria Maggiore. It appears that there was another shrine, built before the fourth-century BC temple, where Servius Tullius had ordered gifts to be placed in the treasury of the temple on behalf of the city's new-born children.

The Kalends (or first day of each month) were Juno's and in Laurentium she was known as Juno of the Kalends. In Rome on that day the Pontifex would invoke her when he announced the date of the Nonae or Nones, which were the fifth or seventh day of the month. This was done from the Curia Calabra, a templum used for the ritual observation of the new moon. Its exact location is now unclear, but it was probably a roofless enclosure in front of an Auguraculum to the southwest of the Capitoline Hill.[54] On that day, a white sow was sacrificed to Juno in the Regia.

The festival of the Matrinalia was also celebrated at Juno Lucina's temple on the first day of March, which was the anniversary of the temple's dedication. The Matrinalia was a form of Mother's Day, when small gifts and flowers were usually offered to mothers and also to the goddess and were even given by lovers to their mistresses on that date.

The aspect of Juno Martialis shown on coins issued by the Emperor Trebonius Gallus (251-253 AD) showed her seated on a throne inside a domed temple, but here Martialis more likely refers to her connection with the month of March, rather than any warlike association, and she had a festival on 7 March, the Nones of that month. This was identifiable with Juno Perusina, a cult of Perusia (modern Perugia), which was imported into Rome by the Emperor Augustus in 40 BC, but which never attained any great popularity.

Juno could therefore be a contradiction of heavenly and worldly functions, and due to her connection with the Kalends all new beginnings were under her influence. She was primarily a goddess of youth, liveliness and strength, and promoted the births of children for women, while also giving protection to the state's soldiers in her aspect of Juno Iuvenes. These youthful characteristics probably imply youth in the sense of a bride, and the Romans recognised an individual 'iuno' as being the spirit of protection for a woman, in the same way as a 'genius' protected a man.

In Rome, throughout both the Republic and the Empire, there were times when some public calamity created general fear. This would cause the priests to call for a propritiatory offering to be made. They had 'discovered' that in such cases the deity who most required such propritiation was Juno. A call would be made for a 'thrice-nine' of unmarried girls (27 virgins) or sometimes married women (matronae) of the same number, to be clad in long gowns with sandals on their feet, who would sing the goddess a particular song, while beating time with their feet. Balsdon, in his *Roman Women*, described the song as 'barbarously uncouth' but tantalisingly gives no further details. This performance took place in 207 BC and was required again seven years later. After the great fire of Rome in 64 AD a group of married women were again required to perform it, and these choirs of women were believed to have had a calming effect.

Minerva

She was originally derived from the Etruscan goddess Menrua, and was associated with the Greek Athena. Minerva was the goddess of wisdom, medicine, poetry, the arts, handicrafts, trade and the strategy of war – although unlike Bellona she was only concerned with defensive conflict, and was sometimes shown with a drawn sword pointing downwards, to offer respect to all those who had fallen in battle. She was believed to be tall, with an athletic build, often wearing armour and carrying a spear. She was one of the virgin goddesses who had vowed never to marry and was a member of the Capitoline Triad along with Juno and Jupiter, with whom she was a favourite.[55]

She was prominently worshipped on the Capitol, but also had a temple dedicated to Minerva Medica where the church of Santa Maria Sopra Minerva now stands, just behind the Pantheon, which was dedicated in around 50 BC by Gnaeus Pompeius Magnus.

Her festival was celebrated from 19 to 23 March, during the Quinquatria, the fifth day after the Ides of March. This was an important time for artists and craftsmen and according to Ovid it lasted five days, although the first day was considered to be the birthday of the goddess, so that no blood could be shed on that day. The following days were full of 'games of drawn swords', however, held in celebration of Minerva's military connections.

Suetonius tells us that the Emperor Domitian celebrated the Quinquatria by appointing a college of priests to stage plays and animal hunts, as well as organising poetry and oratory competitions, and there was also a smaller version, known as the Minisculae Qinquartria which was held on the Ides of June (the 13th) by flute players, as Minerva was also believed to have invented the instrument. This apparent contradiction between the violence and bloodshed of the games, sacrifices and animal hunts against the sweet music of flutes may be explained by the fact that such music was always played at sacrifices, and flute players were a necessary part of the rituals of Roman festivals. There were also players of hand drums, tambourines, and (for the legions) trumpets, cornets, horns (buccinae) and the cornu, most of which were used to provide directions and issue orders to the troops. Rome was never a quiet place, and at gladiator games they even had a water-powered pipe organ, adding to the general clamour.

The Aventine sanctuary of Minerva was an important centre for the arts for much of the Republican era and Livy in his 'History of Rome' said that an annual ceremony of 'marking the year' by driving a nail into the temple wall took place at the temple there. Minerva was also believed to have invented numbers, so this act would be performed by the Praetor Maximus.[56] At the side of the temple of Jupiter was a sacred space dedicated to Minerva, and here that ritual of the 'clavus annalis' was long established. That literally means 'year nail'. Livy said that it had long predated the common use of written letters, and by the late Republic the origins of the by-then rusty nails were presumably forgotten. There was the phrase 'clavum fingere' meaning 'to fix the nail' which may have had a connection to the sealing or fixing of fate. The fixing of such nails was also believed to be connected to the occasional appointment of a Dictator, usually in extreme circumstances, for a limited period of six months, and this was named by Livy as the 'Dictator clavi figendi causa', or the reason for fixing the nail. A Dictator could be nominated for a national emergency, and if he were to hold military command against a specific enemy it would be referred to as 'Rei gerundi causa', or for the matters to be dealt with. For the holding of a Comitia, or an election, if the Consuls were unable to do so, it would be known as 'Comitorium habendorum causa' and the actual 'clavi figendi clausa' when the nail was driven into the wall of the temple of Jupiter Optimus Maximus was an important religious ritual, believed to be a protection against pestilence.

Various other reasons for the driving of nails into the temple wall could include that of establishing a religious holiday in response to a portent, holding the Ludi Romani or Roman games, which were religious in nature, and in one unusual but vital case it was used to meet an order to fill the ranks of the Senate after the appalling losses at the Battle of Cannae. Records show that a Dictator was appointed in 363, 331 and 263 BC. In 363 BC, Rome suffered from a plague that had lasted three years, but when the newly appointed Dictator drove his nail into the temple wall, the pestilence began to abate.

A further ceremony was begun by the Emperor Augustus in 1 AD when he revived the old tradition to allow a Censor to place a nail in order to mark his retirement from his term of office.

One of Minerva's temples was outside the Pomerium, then the boundary of Rome's religious centre, which was marked by white stones known as 'cippi', although this boundary was extended by Lucius Cornelius Sulla in 80 BC. Several of the white marker stones dating from the reign of the Emperor Claudius are still in situ, marking the extensions made by him in 49 AD, during which he was the first to include the Aventine within the Pomerium boundary, including Minerva's temple there.

The Pomerium was not actually a walled area and did not even cover all of Rome's hills. In early times while the Palatine was within the Pomerium, even the important Capitoline Hill was not, although these anomalies were later corrected.

The sacred area had been intended to only contain the centre of Rome, including the Forum and its immediate environs, but that left many areas, including the Area Sacra on the Campus Martius, outside the official boundary. This allowed the Campus Martius to be used as a 'waiting area' or camping ground for generals and their troops.

This area, originally a sheep pasture, was public property and was used as a place of assembly, as well as a temporary camp for troops. It was the place where the Comitia met, where votes were cast, and where foreign ambassadors were given audience when they could not enter the city proper. Imported foreign religious cults also tended to erect their temples in the area.[57] Minerva's temple on the Aventine was close to, but not aligned with, the nearby temple of Diana. It was mentioned during the Second Punic War (218-201 BC) and became a well known centre for writers and actors.

A cow was sacrificed to Minerva on 13 October 58 BC, along with other sacrifices, in order to celebrate the coming to power of the Emperor Nero. He would have been familiar with the area and with the acting fraternity that gathered there, as he was a great theatre lover who believed strongly in his own thespian talents.

On 3 January 81 AD, two cows were sacrificed as part of the New Year vow to secure the well-being of the Emperor Titus, and of Domitian Caesar, Julia Augusta and their children. A similar New Year vow records that a cow was sacrificed on 3 January 87 AD in honour of Minerva, attesting to her continued popularity.

Pietas

She was a deity of respect and duty, to the gods, to the state, and also to one's parents. She was often shown in human form, as a young woman who was accompanied by a stork, which symbolised filial duty. During the Empire she often appeared on coins, representing the moral virtues of the reigning emperor, whether or not he had any. In the city she had a temple at the Circus Flaminius, on the Campus Martius, and another on the Forum Holitorium (the vegetable market) between the Forum Boarium (the cattle market) and the Circus Flaminius. The small temples to Janus, Spes and Juno Sospita were in the same area.

The festival of Pietas was on the first day of December and her worship connected families in insisting on the moral responsibility of maintaining good relationships within the family group, with friends, institutions, and with one's fellow citizens in general. It had a far wider meaning that today's word 'piety' as it signified more than religious observance. The veneration of a deity alone would come under the word 'cultus', which would mean the correct observance of one's religious obligations, intended to preserve peace and harmony with the gods. Pietas was a more abstract concept, more wide-ranging and designed to produce and maintain favourable accord with not only close family and friends but also with those other Roman citizens with whom one was likely to come into contact – thus preserving the 'mos maiorum', which meant ancestral custom and was defined by time-honoured principles, good behavioural models and social practices ensuring harmonious dealings in private and in public life.

Sibyls

The Sibyls were prophetesses rather than deities, although the Cumae Sibyl was famous and highly respected. Their importance was in their ability to prophecy by way of their supernatural connections with the gods themselves, and also with natural forces, which made them very useful as an adjunct to actual religious worship. This was not merely a private act of consultation, as a person might in modern times visit an astrologer, as the consultation of an Oracle was just as often done on behalf of the state, in times of need.

The Cumae Sibyl was believed to have written the Sibylline Books and had apparently arrived from the mysterious East and settled in a cave. The Books were written in Greek, originally on palm leaves, and were offered to King Tarquinius Superbus, the last king of Rome. According to Roman traditions, there had been nine books of oracles for which the old woman demanded an exorbitant price. The king refused the offer, upon which the Sibyl burned three of the books then offered the king the remaining six, at the same price. He again refused, so she burned three more, and repeated her offer, demanding the full original price for what was then only a third of the Books. Tarquinius, probably by then not only suspicious but close to panic, consulted with his Augurs, who deplored the loss of the other six books which were then in ashes, with their vital secrets lost forever. They urged their king to buy the final three at whatever price the old crone demanded, which the king did.

This story is mentioned in Varro (quoted in Lactantius 'Institutiones Diviae' as Varro's original works are now lost to us). It was also told by Aulus Gellius in his 'Noctis Atticae' (Attic Nights), associated of course with residence in Attica, rather than a room under the eaves.

The Senate kept close control over the all-important Books, which were entrusted to the care of two Patricians. By 367 BC this committee of protection had increased to ten men, consisting of five Patricians and five Plebeians, known as the 'Decemviri Sacris Faciundis'. By the time of the Dictator Lucius Cornelius Sulla, this number had probably increased to fifteen custodians, known as the 'Quindecimviri Sacris Faciundis' who were usually ex-Consuls or ex-Praetors. These men held this important office for life and were exempted from all other public duties. This level of responsibility was not only to keep the Books safe and secret, but to be at the state's command whenever they needed to be consulted. They would not expect to discover exact predictions but would be given clues to the actions necessary to avert calamities and prevent 'prodigies' such as earthquakes, plagues, comets, and other things up to and including 'showers of stones'. It makes one wonder what possible advice could be given to avoid showers of stones, except perhaps a pragmatic instruction to build a roof, although perhaps it was intended more to suggest defence against attacks.

This gives rise to an assumption in the modern and perhaps more literal mind that there was an element of farce in these consultations, but they were taken absolutely seriously. The advice was given in the form of verse, which then required interpretation, on what would prevent further problems of a similar nature. The fact that the Oracle needed to be interpreted could presumably lead to opportunities for abuse and gave a particular importance to the group of men whose concern this was.

As a further duty, these men also had to supervise the worship of Apollo, of Magna Mater, and of Ceres, and the Books motivated the construction of a further eight temples in Rome, possibly on contracts which benefited the favourites or relatives of the Custodians. Having been written in Greek, they also influenced the Roman acceptance of Greek cult practices and religious ideas. The Custodians were obliged to employ two Greek interpreters to assist in deciphering the Oracles, but when the temple of Jupiter on the Capitol burned down in 83 BC, the Books burned with it, as they had been stored there. The Senate sent envoys in all directions, in 76 BC, to collect any similar oracular sayings, which were eventually put into the restored temple along with the writings of other Sibyls which were found in private hands, quickly taken over by the state.

The Quindecimviri then had the task of sorting them all out, retaining only those which 'appeared to them to be the truth' according to Tacitus in his 'Annals'. This seems to have been a task comparable to sorting out the Gospels, when few were retained and everything considered unacceptable became 'Apocryphal' and was subsequently discarded as being untrue.

Augustus, as Pontifex Maximus, in 12 BC transferred them to the temple of Apollo Palatinus, where they remained until 405 AD with the last known consultation of the Books taking place in 363 AD. Some supposedly genuine Sibylline verses are still available, continuing a long history from the time of the kings of Rome over 2,500 years ago.

Tellus

She was an earth goddess, a female representation of productive power and the vegetation of nature. She was sometimes known as Tellus Mater and was associated with other agricultural deities. Her festival was on

13 December, and she was also worshipped at the Sementivae in January and at the Fordicitia in April, when a cake of spelt (hulled wheat, cultivated since around 5,000 BC) was given as an offering.

A pregnant sow was sacrificed at the Sementivae and a temple vowed by Publius Sempronius Sophus and dedicated in 268 BC was on the Carinae, perhaps on the site of an earlier shrine. The Senate met there on the day after the assassination of Gaius Julius Caesar at the Curia in the Forum of Pompeius Magnus in 44 BC. She is shown surrounded by the fruits of the earth on the Ara Pacis in Rome.

Venus

This is another goddess of fertility, but representing the more sexual aspects, love and beauty and the attraction between men and women, rather than concentrating solely on the production of children. She could also represent prosperity and victory and some Roman families claimed lineal descent from her, like the family of Gaius Julius Caesar, supposedly through her son Aeneas who fled Troy for Italy and became the ancestor to Romulus and Remus, the founders of Rome. This in turn led to the arrogant belief of Caesar that his lineage bested everyone else's, and that if there ever was a king in Rome, then he should be it.

Venus was thought to have been born by rising fully formed from the foam of the sea, produced from the severed genitals of Caelus-Uranus.[58] As such, she embodied all the power of sexuality and was often portrayed nude. At her festival on the first day of April, it was customary to ask her advice on matters of love and marriage. The planet which bears her name was known since prehistoric times, but she was also considered to be an original creation of the Roman pantheon, a native goddess combined with Aphrodite.

She represented all the female charms, along with the seduction appropriate to the divine, in direct contrast to the usual contractual relationships between the Romans and their gods. As such, she was of a very fluid and feminine nature, in contrast to her supposed counterparts, Mars and Vulcan, who were fiery. She absorbed and cooled the male essence, was essentially benign, and served in several different functions.

She gave both sexual and military success, promoted good fortune, and (as Venus Obsequens) could turn vice into virtue. Brides would offer her a gift before their wedding (although probably not their childhood toys, which were usually given to the household Lares). In dice games the best throw was known as 'the Venus', so her followers no doubt hoped to be lucky in life *and* love.

She was associated with the rose and the myrtle, and myrtle 'crowns' or wreaths were often worn at her festivals. Although a victorious general wore a wreath of laurel at his Triumph, a man awarded an Ovation wore myrtle. The earliest temple to Venus was known to have been built in 290 BC and the Emperor Hadrian built one in Rome in 135 AD. Her official day was Friday, known as the Dies Veneris. As Venus Acidalia at the Fountain of Acidalia, her daughters, the Graces, were said to bathe. Servius also connected the name to the arrow, in the form of the dart of love.

As Venus Caelestis or the heavenly Venus, a name used for her from the second century AD, she was the first known Roman recipient of the Taurobolium, which was a form of bull sacrifice originally associated with the Great Mother, Magna Mater, a Syrian goddess. This was performed at the shrine at Pozzuoli (modern Puteoli) on 5 October 134 AD. After 159 AD, all private Taurobolia refer to the Magna Mater. The earliest inscriptions from Asia Minor from the second century suggest a bull chase, in which the victim is overcome and then sacrificed. The testicles were removed and Rutter suggested that this substituted for the earlier self-castration of Cybele's devotees, which practice was unacceptable to the Romans.[59] The rite of the Taurobolium was performed for the welfare of the Empire or the community, for purification or for regeneration. It usually involved the followers being covered in the blood of the sacrificial victim and its good effects were believed to last for twenty years. The vows of an initiate would also last that long, and the practice was not limited by sex or class. It did, however, become the hallmark of the Pagan nobility and the place of the ritual was latterly known to be near to the present day St Peter's, where excavations have uncovered several altars and Taurobolia inscriptions. Sometimes a ram would be substituted for a bull, in which case the ceremony was known as a Criobolium.

Venus Calva was a purifier. The Etruscan goddess Cloacina had an ancient shrine above the outfall of the Cloaca Maxima, Rome's main sewer, although in earlier times the mighty Cloaca Maxima had been a stream, running placidly through the marshy area which would later become the Forum Romanum. Pliny identified this shrine with Rome's earliest history, when Romulus led the Romans to meet the Samnites led by Titus Tatius. The intention of the meeting was to make peace with the Samnites, after the rape of the Sabine women, and myrtle branches were carried to the meeting as a sign of peaceful intentions. Titus Tatius was responsible for the introduction of lawful marriage and Venus Cloacina protected and purified the sexual intercourse between married couples.

Venus Erucina was derived from a Punic Idol captured from Sicily and worshipped by elite women on Capitol Hill. Later, a temple outside the Colline Gate preserved some of the features of the Sicilian cult, but it was then considered more appropriate for common women and prostitutes.

It was usual for sex workers to donate a little of their earnings regularly to Venus Erucina in order to ensure her protection.

During the Second Punic War, Rome suffered defeat at Lake Trasimene and the Sibylline Oracle declared that if Venus Erucina could be persuaded to change her allegiance from Carthage to Rome (she was at that time the patron of Carthage's Sicilian allies), then Carthage would lose power and could be destroyed. Rome laid siege to Eryx where the goddess then was, and offered her a better temple to tempt her back to Rome. They took her statue and in Rome she became Venus Genetrix, or the Ancestress, with a festival in her honour on 26 September. Gaius Julius Caesar dedicated his own temple to Venus Genetrix in his Forum in 46 BC.

This Capitoline Cult appears to have been reserved for people of status, the Patricians. A more Plebeian version of this deity was established at the Colline Gate in 181 BC, which was then a Plebeian area of the city, and this new version was also dedicated to Venus Erucina.

Venus Verticordia was the changer of hearts, and had a shrine dedicated to her in 114 BC, which had links to the ancient Venus/Fortuna combined cult. Venus Verticordia was intended to change the hearts of women from feelings of lust and loose behaviour into those of chastity. The shrine to this aspect of the goddess was dedicated personally by the most chaste of the women in Rome, who had been chosen from over a hundred candidates, at the suggestion of the Sibylline Books. Under this title, Venus was worshipped by respectable married women, although the real purpose of the cult was to control the sexuality of women in general – always a preoccupation of Roman men – and according to Ovid to 'correct any wanton ways and make them chaste'.[60]

Venus Victrix was quite different from the charming and sensual image of the usual Venus cults. She was of a warlike aspect and gave victories in battle to both Lucius Cornelius Sulla and Gnaeus Pompeius Magnus in the first century BC. Pompeius dedicated his temple, on the top of his great theatre complex on the Campus Martius, to Venus Victrix in 55 BC and celebrated his Triumph in 54 BC by issuing coins showing her crowned with laurels.[61]

When Sulla captured Pompeii from the Samnites in 89 BC he resettled the town with Roman army veterans, creating a colony with the name of 'Colonia Veneria Cornelia Pompeiianorum' in honour of Venus and his illustrious family.[62]

Later, during the earthquake at Pompeii in 62 AD the temple of Venus was completely destroyed and was not rebuilt in the intervening years before the eruption of Vesuvius in 79 AD destroyed the entire town, so there are now few traces of what was once a large and impressive building.

Venus Obsequens was considered an indulgent deity, and her first known temple was vowed by Quintus Fabius Gurges while in battle against the Samnites. It was actually finished and dedicated in 295 BC near to the Aventine and was said to have been funded by the fines paid by Roman women when they were punished for sexual misbehaviour.[63]

Venus Libitina functioned as the recorder of Roman citizen deaths and that connection put her temple outside of the city walls, as all connected with death had to be. The undertakers, the 'Libitinarii', had their business premises beyond the walls and it was common to give a coin to Libitina's temple when a death in the family took place. This temple is said to have been beyond the Agger, which was the double rampart protecting Rome on its most vulnerable side, along the Campus Esquilinus. There were also the lime pits in that area, which were for the disposal of the bodies of the unfortunates. The Agger was part of the Servian Walls, built by Servius Tullius in the early fourth century BC.[64]

As a goddess usually devoted to life and pleasure, it may seem odd that Venus should also be connected to death. However, the interconnection between life and death showed the natural cycle and that death was nothing to fear. Libitina had originally represented freedom and the passions, but mortality gradually predominated. On the Esquiline, all things necessary for the respectful treatment of the dead could be hired, not merely the services of the undertakers but also mimes, actors, the essential flute players and other musicians and professional mourners. All were available at different prices, making it a very busy and prosperous area.

Venus and Rome was by far the largest temple in Rome, begun in 121 AD and dedicated to Venus Felix (good luck) and Roma Aeterna (eternal Rome). It was built between the Forum Romanum and the Colosseum by the Emperor Hadrian. It was finally inaugurated in 135 AD and was completed by Antoninus Pius in 141 AD. It was built on a huge site which once held part of the Domus Transitoria built by Nero, parts of which still exist beneath the temple area. This enormous palace was built as part of Nero's Domus Aurea, or Golden House, an architectural paean to extravagance. The temple which replaced it is built over the portico entrance to Nero's immense palace and includes a domed rotunda, several multicoloured pavings and marble-lined pools. The original burned down in the Great Fire of Rome in 64 AD and Nero commenced to rebuild in an even grander style. Suetonius claimed that his palace, when completed, covered the entire area between the Palatine and Esquiline Hills.[65]

Hadrian's temple to Venus and Rome was also palatial, being built on a great podium of Travertine 145 metres long and 100 metres wide. The building on it was 110 metres long and 58 metres wide, with ten huge white marble columns at each end and twenty more on each side. The temple roof was over thirty metres high.[66] The two cellae dedicated to the goddesses were arranged back-to-back, with Roma facing west towards the Forum, while Venus Felix faced east towards the Colosseum. Within the cella of Venus was an altar where newly weds made offerings. The arched and coffered ceilings of the two cellae displayed seated statues of the goddesses. Hadrian's architect, Apollodorus, was reputed to have criticised the enormous scale of the cellae and the statues inside it, saying that if the statues could stand up they would bang their heads on the ceilings. Hadrian was unimpressed by the architect's criticism and Apollodorus was said to have been executed shortly afterwards.[67]

Unfortunately, with the passing of years, the enormous building would become a target for people wishing to reuse its materials. It had survived largely intact until 630 AD, when Pope Honorius removed the gilt bronze tiles from its roof, which allowed the temple to decay rapidly. In 850 AD, Pope Leo IV ordered the church of Santa Maria Nova to be built on the ruins of the temple of Venus and Rome, and vast quantities of marble were then dispersed to be used on various building projects around the city. From the fourteenth to the sixteenth centuries the site was used as a quarry. Fortunately, the church has now gone and present-day visitors can receive some impression of the magnificence of the largest temple in Rome, erected for the glory of Roma herself.

Venus Felix also represented Rome's military achievements and Sulla adopted the name 'Felix' out of respect for her. Plutarch translated this from 'Epaphroditus' meaning the favourite or beloved of Aphrodite.[68] Venus would again be concerned with aspects of love, and Vitruvius thought that temples to her should be built in accordance with the rules of the Etruscan Haruspices and 'near the gates', where her influence was less likely to 'contaminate matrons and youths with lust'. He suggested light and airy spaces 'appropriate to Venus's character and disposition' and that her two divine consorts Mars and Vulcan should be kept outside the city, so that 'no armed forays disturb the peace of the citizens, that this divinity be ready to protect them from enemies and the perils of war.'[69]

3

Male Gods, Joint Festivals, Divine Locations

Aesculapius

Also known as Asclepius, Aesculapius was a god of healing of Greek origin, son of Apollo and a mortal princess named Coronis. He represented the healing aspect of medical arts and had a group of daughters who were also connected to healing. First was Hygieia the goddess of cleanliness, then Iaso who was connected to recuperation from illness. Aceso was in charge of the healing process itself, while Aegle was the goddess of good health, and finally came Panacea who was goddess of the universal remedy.

Aesculapius carried a snake-entwined staff, although unlike the caduceus it only bore one snake. He was originally named Hepius but received the well-known name after he had cured the ruler of Epidaurus, Ascles, of an eye ailment. Aesculapius became a proficient healer and was not only able to evade death himself but could haul others back from the dividing line between this world and the next.

The cult of Aesculapius was readily absorbed into Roman belief, which also looked to the gods for the preservation of health. Some of Rome's physicians were sceptical about the healing sanctuaries, which became a feature of the worship, but many accepted them as being useful. The cult of Aesculepius spanned approximately a thousand years, and he was usually represented as a bearded middle-aged man, powerful in body, with a cloak over his left shoulder. He either carried, or leaned on, that distinctive staff, with its entwined snake. His daughter Hygieia was also shown with a staff, and her own cult ran alongside his. The snake was considered beneficial and quite without the sinister connotations given to it by Christians. For the ancients, all snakes were a symbol of rebirth, rejuvenation, and the restoration of good health. They were certainly not evil and were appropriate for a healer god.[1]

The followers of Aesculapius performed rituals such as bathing and offered a sacrifice, after which the afflicted were sent to a dormitory to rest. It was through this 'temple sleep' that the cure was decided. Treatment given after priestly interpretation could include drugs, specific diets, or exercise regimes.[2]

Votive offerings of plaster or terracotta-shaped body parts could be bought, which indicated the diseased areas. These were often arms, feet, legs, eyes and ears, breasts or genitals, and even occasionally representing a uterus. These would be left at the temple, or details could be inscribed on votive columns describing the cures received by grateful patients.

By far the most votive models were of legs and feet. Models of heads and chests had flattened bases, so they could stand upright, but most were perforated so that they could be hung on walls, and female parts were coloured white and male parts coloured red. These anatomical votives give intriguing evidence of the Roman reaction to disease and its hoped-for cures. There was a healing sanctuary dedicated to Aesculepius at Ponte di Nona in the Republican era.[3]

Studies of over 8,000 votive models from Ponte di Nona have led to the conclusion that the area specialised in foot and hand complaints. The shrine was established in the late fourth or early third century BC and appeared to serve a rural area primarily, and some of the hand and foot votives are detailed enough to show the stresses that farm labourers were subjected to – they show fallen arches, ingrowing toenails, torn ligaments, arthritic joints (these were very common), and deformities such as club foot.

There was another healing sanctuary at Campetti, in the city of Veii, and this had a large proportion of votive models depicting male and female sexual organs, with ailments such as testicular tumours. There were breasts and wombs, although some of these were possibly offered in gratitude for a successful birth. Some models attempted to reproduce images of organs with cystitis, urethritis, and gonococcal disease. The presence of these does not necessarily suggest that any cure was received.[4]

Hot and cold mineral springs were increasingly popular in Roman Republican Italy, showing a medical predilection for hydropathic treatments. These places were also known as 'safe havens' from plagues and epidemics such as typhus or malaria. As Rome was originally a marshy area, malaria was a regular problem in the summer months.

The god Aesculepius was usually shown with a small, hooded figure beside him. This was Telephorus, and he was the god of convalescence.

Convalescence was considered a very important part of the healing process, and patients were often sent to the country to recuperate. Pliny the Younger, who was very fond of his wife and attentive to her needs, sent her to Campania to recover from such an illness in order to regain her strength. He also rested often at his country villa to secure his own health and to relax in pleasant surroundings in order to ease his mind. For poorer people who did not own villas, the public baths would have to do. Problems affected everyone and few diseases were entirely curable whatever one's financial or social status. Cleanliness was sensibly viewed as a preventative.

Apollo

He also had connections with healing, and was the chief god mentioned in the Hippocratic Oath – 'I swear by Apollo, physician, and by all the gods and goddesses, making them witnesses that I will fulfil, according to my ability and judgement, this Oath and covenant.'[5]

First introduced into Rome as a healer, Apollo would eventually become a god of oracles and prophecies, along with hunting, music and poetry. The famous Sibyl from Cumae was a priestess of Apollo and wielded great power. The Emperor Augustus regarded Apollo as a favourite deity and built a temple dedicated to him next to his own house on the Palatine. In the city, games in honour of Apollo took place in July, with a festival on 23 September. He was one of only three gods to whom a bull could be sacrificed.

The oldest temple to him in Rome was vowed in 433 BC due to a plague in the city. It was dedicated in 431 BC by the Consul Gaius Julius. Because the cult of Apollo was then still considered a foreign one, it was placed outside the Pomerium on the Campus Martius, between the Circus Flaminius and the Forum Holitorium. It stood next to the temple of Bellona, goddess of war. This juxtaposition of warlike and healing elements is a very common one. In the pantheon of Egyptian gods it is represented by Sekhmet, who is goddess of war and healing, and a Nemesis-like figure to be reckoned with.

In 1940, three of the columns of Apollo's temple were re-erected and its podium is now beneath the cloisters of Santa Maria in Campitelli. It remained the only temple to Apollo in Rome until Augustus built his own on the Palatine in 28 BC. The Apollo temple on the Campus Martius was restored by Gaius Sosius in 32 BC and had previously been known as Apollo Medicus, but it became known as Apollo Sosianus after its restoration. Sosius, a Consul in 32 BC, is said to have furnished the interior with many beautiful works of art. Augustus's later temple was known as Apollo Palatinus and was described as an 'aedes', a 'templum' and a 'delubrum', which was a grander temple within which the aedes or temple building stood. It could also refer to a courtyard in which an altar was sited.[6]

Apollo's healing sites were particularly important, as sanctuaries in his name were dedicated to him all over Italy. As well as healing, there was an element of prophecy, which involved the ritual of incubation. This entailed lying down on the ground, or even beneath the ground in an underground chamber, and was intended to encourage a prophetic dream or perhaps, by falling into a state of semi-consciousness, one might experience a vision.

Around the ancient city of Baiae, where the villas of the wealthy once flourished facing the Bay of Naples, are many deep caves and underground galleries, where this practice quite likely was followed. The mysterious 'Oracle of the Dead' complex, sinking almost 500 feet into the earth, is situated only a mile or so from the Grotto of the Sibyl, with connections to Cumae, where the Sibylline Books were said to have originated. Livy reported that in 209 BC Hannibal had made a sacrifice at the Oracle of the Dead. These tunnels and corridors, cut from the rock, are evocative even now. The lovely city of Baiae itself, once a playground for wealthy Romans, has largely been lost due to the volcanic activity in the area, whereby the sea level has been raised. Underwater exploration has since revealed villas, statues and mosaics under the water, and it is frequently visited by divers.

There were many different aspects of Apollo. He was often linked with Celtic gods such as Atepomarus the Horseman. At healing shrines in Gaul, Apollo had figures of horses dedicated to him. Being also a sun god, he was believed to be closely associated with horses via the Celtic cult of the sun. Apollo Belenus was a Celtic sun and healing god, popular in Gaul and northern Italy, while Grannus was another, known throughout Europe. He was associated with medical springs and an inscription to him was found at Musselburgh in Scotland. The Celtic god Moritasgus was named at a healing shrine in Alesia, in France, and the complex there included healing baths and a polygonal temple, along with a pool where the sick could bathe. Numerous votive body parts were found at the site, along with surgical instruments.

Apollo Vindonnus was the link between the sun god and healing at Essarois in France. Vindonnus means 'clear light' and there appear to have been many eye problems treated there. Many bronze plaques were found there depicting eyes, other body parts were shown as ordinary votive models. Some offerings show the image of a hand holding out fruit, or a cake. Other connections with Celtic gods were Apollo

Virotutis, with Virotutis probably meaning 'benefactor of humanity' and with Cunomaglus, known from a shrine found at Nettleton Shrub in Wiltshire, which may also have been a place of healing. Diana and Silvanus were worshipped there, which suggests a cult of hunting, as hunting and healing could also be linked.[7]

Apollo was always shown as a god of youth and male beauty, the ideal of health, although he was also credited with being the father of numerous children, including Aesculepius. As well as being a healer, he was a god of Oracles, particularly at Delphi, and he could also help to ward off evil. As the Delphic Apollo he protected seafarers, foreigners, fugitives and refugees of all kinds.

He was concerned with the health and education of children and presided over their development into adults. The long hair which boys usually wore while young was cut at their coming of age, and then dedicated to Apollo. There were many temples to him in Greece and a large one at Pompeii, built in 120 BC but with possible origins as far back as the sixth century BC. It was reconstructed after Pompeii's earthquake in 63 AD.

There was also a temple to Apollo at Melite (modern Mdina in Malta) where remains of a second-century AD building were found in the eighteenth century.

In Rome, the Ludi Apollinares were games held annually in his honour, established after the inspection of a collection of prophecies known as the Carmina Marciana. These dictated that the Romans should use Greek ritual and the Sibylline Books confirmed it during the Second Punic War. As in other times, the establishment of these games distracted the Romans, on this occasion from Hannibal's invasion of northern Italy.[8]

These games were held in the Circus Maximus with stage performances as well as equestrian games. The future Ludi Apollinares received less funding from the state due to being shorter – a vow had initially been made in 212 BC to hold them only once – and having only one day of horse racing. Lucius Varus, then the Praetor Urbanus, renewed the vow in 210 BC and celebrated the games that year, but he turned them into an annual festival by law in 208 BC when he was Curule Aedile. A plague in 208 BC may have swayed the decision by the Senate to make them a permanent feature, due to Apollo's connection to healing, and they were then celebrated on 13 July. Over time they gradually grew to last eight or nine days. Livy claimed that it was due to Caius Calpurnius Piso that the games were made permanent in 211 BC:

> The games of Apollo had been exhibited the previous year, and when the question of their repetition the next year was moved by the Praetor Calpurnius, the Senate passed a decree that they should be observed for

all time... Such is the origin of the Apollonarian Games, which were instituted for the cause of victory, and not, as is generally thought, in the interests of public health.[9]

For the generally horse-racing-mad Romans, the distinction was probably irrelevant, so long as the games were indeed held.

Bonus Eventus

Although not now widely remembered, he was the god representing the 'good outcome' of things. Originally an agricultural deity, he eventually became popular as a god of general success. He had a temple on the Capitol and another one on the Campus Martius and was usually depicted holding a cup in his right hand and a bunch of wheat ears in his left. The late Republican scholar Varro[10] lists Bonus Eventus as one of the twelve gods influencing agricultural matters, and pairs him with Lympha the goddess who oversaw the provision of the essential water for the crops.

His temple on the Campus Martius is mentioned by Ammianus Marcellinus (330-391 AD) a Roman soldier and historian, in connection with the building of a portico there by the Urban Prefect Claudius in 374 AD. Five Corinthian capitals of 'extraordinary size' uncovered in the 19th century, may have originally belonged to this portico.

These porticos, or colonnades, were usually long galleries bordering a street, attached to the adjacent buildings. They provided shelter from sun and wind and could be decorated with statuary. A porticus took its name from its builder, or some structure of which it formed a part. The Campus Martius was well-suited to their addition, offering sufficient space for the erection of long walkways, and there are records of twelve of them being in Regio IX by the second century AD. It was then possible to walk from the Forum of Trajan to the Pons Aelius under shelter.[11] The Pons Aelius is the present-day Sant'Angelo Bridge, leading to what is now known as the Castel Sant'Angelo, but was originally the Mausoleum of Hadrian. The original bridge has been dated to 134 AD. There are inscriptions in the provinces referring to Bonus Eventus and a shrine was dedicated to him at Sirminium in Pannonia.[12] This was erected on behalf of members of the city council.

In Britain, a mosaic floor at Woodchester Villa near Stroud in Gloucestershire has an inscription reminding passers-by to 'worship Bonus Eventus duly' and he was frequently depicted on carved or engraved jewels, which were very popular at the time and also feature as part of the jeweller's hoard found at Snettisham in Norfolk in 1985. Along with coins, this hoard had some ceramics but was mainly a collection of silver rings, bracelets, and chain necklaces. The completed rings and 117 engraved carnelian stones have intaglio engravings for good luck, and include the deities Fortuna, Bonus Eventus and Ceres.[13] The epithet of Bonus, or good, is shared by other deities, such as Bona Fortuna for luck, Bona Mens for good thinking, Bona Spes for valid hopes, as well as the women's goddess Bona Dea, the good goddess.

Coins showing Bonus Eventus were issued in 69 AD, the year of the four Emperors (Galba, Otho, Vitellius and Vespasian), which was a time of great turmoil in Rome after the death of Nero. The suicide of Nero left a vacuum filled by civil war and Galba reigned only for only just over three months (October 68 AD to January 69 AD), to be killed and replaced by Otho, whose own luck ran out equally quickly, as his reign lasted from January to April 69 AD. He was threatened by the march of Vitellius's legions from Germany to Rome, and after his three months of rather shaky authority he committed suicide. It was said that he had done that to 'spare Rome from further mayhem', but more likely to spare himself from an even more unpleasant ending.

Vitellius had serious opposition from the start of his reign, particularly from Vespasian, who was a low-born career soldier who had risen through the ranks. Vitellius was proclaimed emperor in April of 69 AD and was assassinated by December of that year, leaving Vespasian to attempt to do better, being proclaimed emperor on the first day of July 69 AD and managing to reign for ten years, despite his low birth and that of his wife and his mistress. It is obvious why, during a time of such upheaval and uncertainty, the assistance of Bonus Eventus was considered necessary, and why his 'good outcome' was earnestly requested.

Vespasian's act of tearing down Nero's Golden House and the building of the Flavian Ampitheatre in its garden area, later to be known as the Colosseum, was not only done as a monument to the old traditions which he embraced, in attempting to present himself as a ruler in the mould of Augustus, or even the end of the Jewish Revolt after the capture of Masada in 74 AD, but was more a reminder that the Roman people required to be placated and considered. Failing in this objective the new emperor might only too easily find himself following in the footsteps of his three unfortunate predecessors, rather than being the embodiment of the 'good outcome' that Romans had asked for.

Castor

He was the brother of Pollux and one of the Dioscuri, who were originally Greek, then known as Castor and Polydeuces, but they were worshipped in Rome from earliest times. The name 'the Dioscuri' comes from the Greek, 'Dioskouroi' meaning the sons of Zeus. They were also known as the Twins, although they were allegedly born of two fathers.[14] Their mother Leda, Queen of Sparta, was wife of King Tyndareus, but was seduced by Zeus in the guise of a swan. The King of Sparta was said to be the father of Castor, who was therefore a mortal, but Zeus's fathering of Pollux made his son a demigod.

This form of double birth is now known as 'heteropaternal superfecundation' and is less rare than formerly following the development of artificial insemination techniques. It is unlikely that a modern mother could claim that she had been impregnated by a swan, although in Greek mythology this trickery happened not only to Leda of Sparta, but also to Alcmene who also laid with Zeus, in her case because he disguised himself as her husband, Amphitryon. Again, the result was two sons, Iphicles by Amphitryon and Heracles by Zeus. The Dioscuri were patrons of sailors and also known as superb horsemen. They were associated with helping mankind and were extremely popular, with the common Roman oaths 'mecastor' (or ecastor) and 'edepol' being derived from their names.

There was a temple to them in Rome in the Forum, known as the Aedes Castoris or Templum Castoris, which according to tradition was vowed by the Dictator Postumius during the Battle of Lake Regillus. The temple was actually dedicated by the son of Postumius in 484BC. It was after that battle that the twins were seen watering their horses at the shrine of Juturna next to the temple of Vesta.

In 117 BC the temple rebuilding by Lucius Caecilius Metellus was begun and the floor level was raised by three metres. In 74 BC, Gaius Verres was in charge of restoring the temple, but was accused of corruption by Cicero.[15] The temple was known to be one of the finest in the Forum Romanum during Republican times and from as early as 160 BC was used for political meetings, including those of the Senate. It was also used as a safe deposit for not only the Imperial treasury but for private individuals.

In the civil wars Gnaeus Pompeius Magnus rose to prominence while serving Sulla, and he celebrated three Triumphs. In March of 81 BC, when Pompeius had returned from an African campaign to enjoy the pleasure of his first Triumph, he was only twenty-five years old. He intended to make the day memorable and instead of having his Triumphal chariot pulled by four horses, as was usual, he replaced them with four elephants.

The Dictator Lucius Cornelius Sulla was waiting with other officials on the steps of Castor's temple for Pompeius's procession to pass by, but there was a long delay. On making an enquiry, Sulla was told that Pompeius's four elephants were too large to get through the Porta

Triumphalis, the gate by which all Triumphators must enter the Via Sacra. The elephants had to eventually be changed for four horses to allow the procession to proceed in the normal way. Sulla was reported to have been greatly amused by the young man's pretensions.[16]

The two large statues of the Dioscuri were once used as gatekeepers during the reign of the Emperor Caligula, when he incorporated the temple into his palace on the Palatine Hill, turning it into a monumental form of vestibule. It was later restored to its original function under the Emperor Claudius and was still standing in the fourth century AD.

The statues of the Twins, with their horses, now stand on the stepped ramp leading to the Piazza di Campidoglio, the original Capitol Hill. These ancient statues were unearthed from the site of their temple in 1561 and were erected in the Campidoglio in 1583. There was also a temple to Castor and Pollux in the Circus Flaminius, which had been built around 100 BC. On the third century AD marble plan of Rome known as the 'Forma Urbis Romae' it was shown as a hexastyle temple, approached by steps, with a circular feature in front which was probably an altar.[17]

Consus

This was the deity who protected the all-important grain and was represented as a grain seed. He was a 'chathonic' or underground god, whose altar was located at the first 'meta' of the Circus Maximus. Sources say that it was actually under the ground, but it may have been covered by earth which was swept away during the two festivals dedicated to him, which were the Consualia on 21 August and 15 December. There was also a sacrifice performed there on 7 July when the Flamen Quirinalis and the Vestal Virgins officiated at the rites.[18]

The festival of Opiconsivia (or Opalia) followed close behind those of Consus, being held on 25 August and 19 December. These dates represent both the reaping of the harvest and the seeding of the new crops.

Consus was also a god of secrets, as his name was interpreted in relation to 'consilium', which meant a council or assembly. Tertullian said that one of the metae at the Circus Maximus held an inscription reading 'Consus consilio, Mars duello, Lares coillo potentes' – the meditation of Consus, the fighting of Mars and the power of the Lares.[19] The metae were the three turning posts at either end of the spina in the centre of the Circus Maximus. They were situated on plinths and crowned by egg-shaped finials. The Romans loved horse races and the racing of horses, or sometimes mules, was an important part of this festival.

In Rome, Consus was also connected to Vulcan, as Vulcan's own festival was close in date, on 23 August. Vulcan was the god of fire, metalwork and volcanoes: Pompeii and Herculaneum were apparently destroyed at around the time of his festival in 79 AD. However, expert opinions now vary as to the actual dating of the eruption, after examinations of foodstuffs left in the town suggested that it probably took place in October. Even more telling, an inscription has since been found which dates the tragedy to mid-October of 79 AD. Pliny the Younger left an account in letter to Tacitus, a Roman Senator and historian, in which he states clearly that 'on 24 August, about one in the afternoon, my mother desired him (her brother Pliny the Elder who was to die at Stabiae during the eruption) to observe a cloud' as the eruption began. However, a charcoal scribble discovered in the new area of excavations is dated to 'sixteen days before the Kalends of November' which would make the date 17 October. As this inscription was in fragile charcoal which could not last over the years when exposed to the weather, it is highly probable that it can indeed be dated to October of 79 AD, suggesting that the eruption date was actually two months after the one usually quoted.[20]

As Pliny wrote his account of the eruption some twenty years after the event, it has been suggested that his original dates were slightly different to the copies we now have. The new possibilities are a fascinating discovery. The Italian Culture Minister Alberto Bonisoli proudly claimed that 'The new excavations demonstrate the exceptional skill of our country' in his statement on the matter in October 2018.

A temple to Consus was either vowed or actually dedicated by Lucius Papirius Cursor, probably in 272 BC when he won a victory in Southern Gaul and he was depicted on the temple walls wearing his Triumphal robes. The building was on the Aventine and was probably one of those restored by the Emperor Augustus some time after 7 BC. It has been suggested that it was close to the shrine to Vortumnus.[21]

The Dii Consentes

These were the twelve most recognised deities, whose gilded statues were displayed in the Forum Romanum. On the slope of the Capitoline Hill, close to the temple of Saturn, stands the Portico of the Dii Consentes, the remains of which were first discovered in 1834. During subsequent restorations in 1858 some of the columns were re-erected. Behind the portico of marble columns were open rooms, built of brick, and at a level below the portico the remains of a line of small shops have been found. The portico was probably built in the first century AD, in the Flavian period, possibly following the fire of 80 AD that destroyed so many of the buildings on the Capitol. It was restored in 367 AD by the Prefect of the City, Vettius Agorius Pretextatus, as an inscription on one of the architraves explains. He was a staunch supporter of the 'old' gods, in a city which was becoming ever more under Christian influence, so it would seem that the portico was the last of the Pagan monuments to be erected in the heart of the city.

Varro mentioned that there were twelve gilded statues, containing six of the chief gods along with six goddesses in the Forum, and the inscription of 367 AD confirms that this is the monument that he described.[22] The twelve deities represented were Jupiter and Juno; Neptune and Minerva; Apollo and Diana; Mars and Venus; Vulcan and Vesta and Mercury and Ceres. The remains of this monument, but without its statues, are still in the Forum.

Dii Conservatores

These were deities who had at some time or another responded to a worshipper's plea for assistance, and had provided help. The term was a collective one to describe any and all of these 'saviour' deities.

An altar dedicated to the Dii Conservatores, now in the British Museum, is believed to have been a thanks offering for the safe return to Rome of the Imperial family of the Emperor Septimius Severus, after they had been in Britain. It was dedicated by one Antonius, who was a 'libertas', or freed slave. He held the position of Secretary of the Petitions to Septimius Severus (r.193-211 AD) and part of his duty was arranging for such dedicatory monuments or for vows. The emperor is mentioned, along with his wife the Empress Julia Domna, and their two sons Caracalla and Geta.

The name of Geta was later erased after he had been murdered, and the wife of Caracalla, Fulvia Plautilla, also had her name removed, after she had been executed following her implication in plots against her husband. In January 205 AD, Gaius Fulvius Plautianus the father of Plautilla, was executed for treachery and all the family properties were confiscated. Plautilla and her brother were exiled to Sicily, then to Lipari. They were treated very harshly and eventually strangled, probably on Caracalla's orders, after the death of Septimius Severus in February 211 AD. Plautilla would then have been in her mid-twenties and is reputed to have had a daughter (un-named) with Caracalla. She had been forcibly married to him in 202 AD and the marriage had proved to be very unhappy.

The translation of the inscription reads 'To Fortuna, protectress of the emperors, Antonius freedman and imperial secretary for petitions, dedicates this as a gift from a vow made for the wellbeing and (safe) return of our Emperors Severus Pius and Antoninus Pius (Caracalla), and

Prince Geta (erased), and the Empress Julia (Julia Domna) mother of the emperors (erased) … and Empress Plautilla. [23]

Di Manes

These were the collective spirits of the dead, having become immortal through death. They were worshipped at the Feralia, the Parentalia and the Lemuria. They were later identified with family dead and originally graves were often dedicated to the dead collectively, although during the Empire it became usual to name individuals. The Manes were considered to be powerful spirits who required regular propitiation.

Di Parentes

They were the spirits specifically of the ancestors, parents and other deceased close relatives. They were worshipped at the festival of the Parentalia, when several days were devoted to the private commemoration of the ancestors, followed by a final day of public ceremony. During this festival all respect was shown, with marriages being forbidden and all temples closed. The Parentalia began on 13 February and culminated on the 21st, with the Feralia on 22 February. The Carista was also on the 22nd, a day of renewing family ties, and was celebrated well into Christian times, eventually becoming the feast of St Peter until the twelfth century.

Di Penates

These were household gods, usually known simply as Penates, and were the gods of the store cupboard supplies. A portion of every family meal was set aside for them, and on the Kalends, Nones and Ides of each month they were especially honoured with offerings of garlands. Any notable family event involved making an offering and a prayer to the Penates.

Dis

He was a god of the dead and ruled over the Underworld. He was also known as Dis Pater (father of riches) as Dis was a contraction of Dives, meaning rich. He was equated with Hades (also known as Plouton, from which the Latin name Pluto derives, and which also means rich). It may suggest the richness of the fertile lands and their mineral wealth and possibly Dis was originally a deity of the land. As Dis Pater he is sometimes associated with the Sabine god Soranus, and in his work 'De

Bello Gallica' (the Gallic War), Julius Caesar mentioned that the Gauls believed themselves to be descendants of Dis Pater.

Dius Fidius

A god to swear oaths by, his name derived from divine and faith, he had a festival on the fifth day of June. He was linked with the deity Semo Sanctus and there was a temple to Semo Sanctus Dius Fidius on the Quirinal Hill.

Hercules

He was the personification of manly strength, of victory, and even of commercial enterprise. He had a reputation for gluttony so there was no restriction on what kind of sacrifice could be offered to him. Essentially, he would accept anything. He tended to be depicted as a strong and mature man, usually wearing very little in order to display his muscular body, but generally with a lion skin over his head and carrying a club.[24]

There are several busts of the Emperor Commodus in this guise, as he fancied himself as an image of the god. Unfortunately, as well as being muscular and attractive in the Herculean mould, Commodus was also a homicidal sociopath who enjoyed gladiatorial games so much he often took part in them. His opponents could expect to be killed, even during practice bouts, and it was sometimes said that he would use real weapons while his opponents were given wooden ones. The appearance of Commodus in the arena meant the deaths of many helpless animals, along with the defeat of his human opponents, usually by being executed after they had already submitted to him.

He was also fond of devaluing the currency and playing the heroic ruler, yet leaving the actual tedious administration of Rome to others. His sister Lucilla began to plot his downfall with two of her lovers, but bodyguards rescued him in time. The male plotters were sentenced to death, while Lucilla and her daughter were exiled to Capri for a year, before Commodus finally ordered their execution. The common people, not knowing him personally, continued to find him attractive and to favour him, especially during his impressive impersonations of Hercules, but even to them he could be casually cruel and unjust. He always emphasised his godlike status as one who could fight both men and beasts, and as Hercules he could claim to be a son of Jupiter. His megalomaniacal tendencies grew worse after a fire in 191 that damaged the city extensively, and he declared himself to be not only Hercules but also the new Romulus. As such, he ritually re-founded Rome, naming the city 'Colonia Lucia Annia Commodiana' and then changed the months of the year to his newly chosen names of Lucius, Aelius, Aurelius, Commodus, Augustus, Herculeus, Romanus, Exsuperatorius, Amazonius, Invictus, Felix and Pius, positioning himself as the fountain head of all Roman life.

In November of 192 AD, he held the Plebeian Games, killing animals and fighting gladiators who again were only armed with wooden swords. A conspiracy was formed to supplant him and his food was poisoned, but he vomited up the poisoned food, so that it was then necessary to send his wrestling partner Narcissus to strangle him while he was bathing. The statues of him were demolished and he was buried in the Mausoleum of Hadrian.[25]

The god Hercules would have been unimpressed with such a posturing imitator, who had actually achieved nothing and from whom the decline of the Roman Empire is usually measured. Hercules the deity was a strong and productive force, the epitome of masculine power and was popular from the very earliest times, when the Ara Maxima (ara refers to an altar) on the Campus Martius, dedicated to Hercules, was the place for business deals to be agreed on and firm oaths to be made. The Ara Maxima (greatest altar) was the oldest and therefore the most important to Roman sensibilities. Its full name was the Ara Maxima Hercules Invicti, or the altar of unconquered Hercules. It stood on the Forum Boarium, probably between the later temple of Hercules Victor and the Circus Maximus. The title of 'Maxima' refers to its importance rather than its size. It was the earliest known cult centre in Rome, officially adopted by the state in 312 BC. The merchants who used it were accustomed to giving a tithe of their profits to Hercules.

His other temples were numerous, and some of them were round, like that of Vesta, to represent the round huts of the ancestors. The Porta Collina had a temple there, as did the left bank of the Tiber near to the Pons Aelius. As Hercules Magnus Custus (Hercules the custodian) there was also a temple on the Circus Flaminius. Another – which was either built or restored by Gnaeus Pompeius Magnus – was known as the Hercules Pompeianus and its remains may well be the those found under a part of the church of Santa Maria in Cosmedin. This was destroyed by Pope Hadrian I in the late eighth century when the church was enlarged.[26]

There was a temple to Hercules of the Muses in the Circus Flaminius close to the Porticus of Octavia, which was built by Augustus in honour of his sister. This temple to Hercules had been built by Marcus Fulvius Nobilior in 189 BC with statues of the Muses and one of Hercules playing a lyre inside it, along with a small bronze shrine (an aedicula) which dated from the time of Numa Pompilius. As with many of the Hercules temples, this is understood to have been circular in design.

Hercules Invictus (unconquered) or Hercules Victor (victorious) was always popular in Rome, and he was associated with Celtic deities of strength and manly prowess. These included Ilunuss who was worshipped in France, and Saegon who is known from an inscription from Silchester, near Reading, where city walls and the remains of an amphitheatre attest to Rome's presence.

Hercules Magusanus was very popular as a Celtic god and is known from eleven dedications found in north-eastern Gaul. The temple of Hercules Victor, in the Forum Boarium is still extant, another circular building. It stands close to its rectangular counterpart, the temple of Portunus.

Honos Et Virtus

The Honos et Virtus temple was originally founded to Honos alone by Quintus Maximus in 234 BC. This was restored and re-dedicated by Marcus Claudius Marcellus in 208 BC when it was renamed in honour of the twin virtues of Honour and Virtue. However, the Pontiffs opposed the double renaming, saying that the two gods could not share the same space, so a new cella was added to accommodate Virtus, thereby making the temple a double one. This was finally dedicated in 205 BC by the son of Claudius Marcellus and stood beside the Porta Capena and was known to have contained many works of art. It may have finally been destroyed in Nero's fire in Rome but was last mentioned in the fourth century AD.[27]

Janus

He was the god of doors and doorways, of beginnings and endings, of looking back at the past as well as ahead to the future and was one of the oldest Roman gods, with dealings in many aspects of Roman life. Legends say that he ruled alongside a king named Camesus, and that Janus built a city on the hill which came to be known as the Janiculum. He presided over peace and plenty and was deified when he died. While Janus had reigned on the Janiculum, Saturn had reigned in Saturnia, which was a village on the Capitoline Hill.

As the god of beginnings, he was always the first god to be named in any lists of prayers and also the first to receive a portion of any sacrifice. The first day of January was naturally dedicated to him, but he also had a festival on 17 August.

His capacity for looking both ways made him a contemplative god, one who remembered past events and learned from them, as well as being able to turn aside from them to look ahead to future opportunities. He was always young, and was new in the New Year, but equally old and wise in the old one. A coin from the reign of the Emperor Commodus (180-193) showed the emperor as Janus Bifrons, with the old year, as four seasons, behind him, while the New Year, depicted as a child holding a cornucopia, stood ahead of him.

The most important shrine to Janus was that of Janus Geminus, which stood between the Forum Romanum and the Julian Forum. It was a permanently inaugurated bridge (ianus), carrying the Via Sacra over the Cloaca Maxima, the main drain, to the Comitium or assembly area. It may have been a double bridge, as it was referred to as Ianus Geminus (twin) and when the doors at one end of the building had to be closed for religious reasons, the other half could still function as a bridge for access. It was believed to be from the time of King Numa Pompilius and it represented peace and war. When Rome was at war, the doors were kept open, and if at peace they were kept closed. In 179 BC the Cloaca was diverted and the bridge was removed to make way for the building of a basilica. It was not rebuilt in the same manner, but as a long rectangular structure with doors at each end, and it is shown as such on the coins of the Emperor Nero.

Domitian eventually moved this to the Forum of Nerva (the Forum Transitorium), where it was replaced with a Janus image with four faces, and the old site covered over, with the Curia being built on the area. A new temple was later built in front of the Curia, being a small shrine made entirely of bronze, and was probably completed before 193 AD.[28]

Jupiter Optimus Maximus, or Jupiter Capitolinus

The tradition of Jupiter Optimus Maximus (Jupiter best and greatest), is that his temple was begun by the last king Tarquinius, finished by the end of his reign, and was actually dedicated by the very first college of Magistrates of the new Republic. It crossed the boundary between monarchy and republic and although the king had intended the temple to be an expression of his own power, it passed smoothly into the new Republican mindset, actually becoming central to the religious side of the Republic, and a focus for all that the new Rome stood for.[29]

What had been intended as royal ceremonial changed easily enough into Republican ceremonial, and even though the new order was to be almost paranoid about any possibility of one man, or one family, ever again taking control of Rome, the priests of what was to become the state religion were elected for life to positions of great responsibility. Nevertheless, their authority was diffused and no man could expect to have the overriding authority that the kings may have had, even over religious matters. This may have been bad news for the god Jupiter, in his brand-new temple overlooking the heart of Rome, but somehow Jupiter avoided being cast out along with the old regime, and instead became a symbol of the power of Rome itself. He was regarded as the chief of the gods, like his Greek counterpart Zeus, and sometimes was also identified with Egypt's chief god, Amon or Amun-Ra.

Jupiter was originally a sky god, controlling the weather, particularly rain and lightning. In fact, any building struck by lightning was then considered to be sacred to him. His new temple on the Capitol was built on a site which was already well occupied by other deities. They apparently agreed to be moved elsewhere, except for Terminus, the god of boundaries and their stones and markers. His own stone was in the area needed for Jupiter, but although the god refused to move this was considered to be a good sign, indicating the permanence of the cult of Jupiter, and also that of the new Rome. The shrine of Terminus was eventually incorporated within the new temple to Jupiter, and the shrine of Juventas would eventually join it. Juventas or Juventa was a goddess who protected youths, or men of military age. When a young man first put on his adult toga it was customary for an offering to be made to the goddess in the small shrine dedicated to her, which stood within the cella of Minerva inside Jupiter's temple. Juventas had her own temple also, near to the Circus Maximus, and a festival of 19 December may have also been dedicated to her. Even later, it was claimed that Mars had also refused to move and so room had also to be found for him within Jupiter's temple.

Jupiter already had his wife Juno Regina in residence with him, and his daughter Minerva. These three deities formed the Capitoline Triad, a powerful amalgamation of familial gods. There were festivals in honour of Jupiter on 15 March, 15 May and 15 October and he was worshipped at the festival of Vinalia Priora on 23 April. The Capitoline Games took place on 15 October and the Ludi Plebeii or Plebeian Games were held from the 4th to the 17th of November, while the Ludi Romani and its accompanying festival was held on 13 September.

Jupiter Optimus Maximus was Rome's supreme god, but he did have plenty of human failings, certainly with regard to his eye for ladies other than his wife. Juno Regina had need of her famous patience with him, as he shape-changed into a bull, or a swan, or another woman's husband in order to have his way with the ladies concerned. Thus he fathered many children, including Mercury, Proserpine, and Minerva, along with Bellona, Juventas, Hercules and Vulcan.

He was, like other Roman gods, associated with several Celtic gods, with Beissirissa from southern France, with Brixianus from northern Italy, Cernenus from Gaul, Digus from Spain; and with Dolichenus, a local god associated with Baal, worshipped in Turkey. His temple of Jupiter Freretrius was traditionally believed to have been established by Romulus and was said to be Rome's oldest temple. It served as a repository for spoils and booty from foreign wars, and the ritual implements used by the Fetiales. There was no cult statue within it, merely the sceptre. It was restored by Augustus as one of his first duties, but unfortunately no trace of it has been found.

As Jupiter Fulgur, he hurled thunderbolts in the daytime, whereas if he hurled them at night he was called Jupiter Summanus. A temple to Fulgur was on the Campus Martius with a festival in his honour on 7 October. As Jupiter Heliopolitanus he was equated with the Syrian god Hadad, and there was a cult for him in Athens. A temple to him in this aspect was on the Janiculum Hill but was destroyed by a fire around 341.

Jupiter Latiaris was worshipped on the Alban Mount, a volcanic peak about 13 miles southeast of Rome. Latiaris had the Feriae Latinae festival on 27 March in his role of god of the Latin League. There was a temple at the Alban Mount from the sixth century BC but no trace of this now exists. However, the Via Triumphalis, which once led to this temple, has been identified.[30]

Jupiter Stator was an important aspect of the chief god, known to be the 'stayer of soldiers in retreat' and his temple was on the Circus Flaminius before the early second century BC. Foundations of another temple to him were found on the Via Sacra in the Forum Romanum, at the foot of the Palatine Hill, when a medieval tower was being demolished in 1829. On 8 November 63 BC the Senate had met there for the only recorded time, when Cicero delivered his first oration against Catilina.[31]

Jupiter Stator's ability to stop any flight of Rome's troops from the battlefield was vital. One of his temples was said to have been vowed by Romulus during the battle between the Romans and the Sabines. That temple, however, was apparently never built, although a similar vow was made by the Consul Marcus Atilius Regulus during the battle with the Samnites. On that occasion the Roman troops rallied and stood their ground, which resulted in the building of the temple on the Via Sacra as a mark of gratitude.

Jupiter was often pictured holding a thunderbolt, and as Jupiter Tonans (the thunderer) he was greatly feared. His anger could strike at anyone, as was shown when the Emperor Augustus was very nearly struck by lightning in 26 BC. Augustus had responded by vowing a temple to Jupiter Tonans on Capitol Hill. This aspect of the god had a festival on the first day of September.

In the first century, Vitruvius had observed in his 'De Architectura' that propriety required all temples to Jupiter Tonans to be open to the sky, so it may be presumed that the temple dedicated after the narrow escape from a lightning strike enjoyed by a relieved Augustus while on campaign in Cantabria was built on this plan. It allowed Jupiter's sky to be visible to the priests and the worshippers and possibly for them to be visible to the god.[32]

Lares

Otherwise known as an Aedicular, the Lararium was a small private shrine within a house, premises, or even a public bar, which could take the form of a miniature house, a freestanding shrine, a cupboard or shelf, or even a picture painted on the wall. These held images – or a painted picture – of the Lares, the household gods. There was often a snake present, as in the picture mentioned earlier painted on the wall of Asellina's bar in Pompeii, and this creature represented fertility and prosperity. Other images could include the toga-clad figure of the family genius, or ancestor figure, and often two Lares were shown as young men. They would often be in dancing or running mode, often accompanied by a dog.[33]

In Pompeii the House of the Vetii had two Lararia, one being out of public view and probably used for private household rites. Another was in full view of any visitors, with statuettes of patron divinities. The guardian spirits who inhabited the family Lararium, whether it was a finely made temple-like shrine or merely a shelf holding a pottery statue, were central to Roman domestic life. They were witnesses to all important family occasions and represented the religious hub of the home. Small offerings would be made to them and, although their protection was restricted to the domestic sphere, they were necessary for family life. When a young man began to wear his first toga, or when a young girl was about to be married, they were remembered, joining the family in these rites of passage.

They were particularly worshipped on the Kalends, Nones and Ides of each month, and the Paterfamilias was responsible for ensuring that proper respect was paid to them, although it was usually the wife who actually made the small daily offerings to them.[34]

Lares Compitales were the guardian spirits who presided over the crossroads. Each district in Rome had a central point, where roads met. These areas were considered relatively dangerous and were guarded by Lares from two adjoining areas, to ensure peaceable relations and a smooth flow of foot and vehicular traffic. They had their own festival, the Compitalia, and the Emperor Augustus decreed that at this festival (held between 17 December and 5 January, a period that would be announced and confirmed by the City Praetor), should show two statues of the Lares and one of the Genius of Augustus at each shrine, thereby making a semi-private celebration into a fully state one, with a public aspect.

Even at a small 'open' crossroads in a remote rural area, a small shrine would be erected, open on all sides to allow passage for the Lares from each direction. A sacrifice and some feasting would follow. When Augustus transformed the worship of the Lares within Rome, the worship and its sacrifice had to be performed by a priest, rather than a private individual, as it was believed to be the concern of all the people and was done on their behalf.

Lares Permarini were the protectors of sailors and all people who worked on the sea, such as traders, fishermen and all who had to sail. Their temple was on the Area Sacra, on the Campus Martius.

Lares Viales were the guardians of roads and had altars dedicated to them at intervals along all the main thoroughfares outside Rome.

Lares Prestites were the public Lares and guarded the Roman State itself. There was possibly an altar in Rome in the area of the Colline Gate, with a festival devoted to them which took place on the first day of May.

Lectisternium

This comes from the Latin 'lectis sternere' meaning 'to spread a couch' and it involved preparing a feast to honour certain gods, being a propitiatory ceremony when their assistance had been needed. The images of the gods required would be carried out into the open street, where a banquet had been prepared for them to enjoy. Then the images of the gods, or sometimes just wax masks, would be arranged on couches before the feast, as if they were actually present and about to eat.

Livy describes what he called the first of such ceremonies, which took place in 399 BC after a pestilence in Rome had caused the Sibylline Books to be consulted. He told of the three pairs of couches for three pairs of gods, some paired with their goddesses. Apollo with Latona, Hercules with Diana, and Mercury and Neptune on the occasion he wrote about. The feast is said to have lasted for seven or eight days and was also celebrated by private individuals who kept open house, allowing others to enter and feast within. Quarrels were forgotten, debtors and prisoners were released, and all was done in an effort to 'banish sorrow'.[35]

In 217 BC, after the terrible defeat of Rome at Lake Trasimene, a three-day ceremony of Lectisternium was held, during which twelve gods were feasted. Jupiter, Juno, Neptune, Minerva, Mars, Venus, Apollo, Diana, Vulcan, Vesta, Mercury and Ceres were all honoured.

Such ceremonies continued into the Imperial era, although in later times the couches for reclining were replaced by chairs for sitting upright, in the case of goddesses. In Republican times it had been the custom for only men to recline, while women sat respectably upright on chairs. It was considered unseemly for women to loll on couches alongside men. Livy had reported on one ceremony where the image of Jupiter had reclined on a couch, but the other members of the Capitoline Triad, Juno and Minerva, had been placed on upright chairs, one on each side of him.

A Sellisternium was a similar festival, but for goddesses only, with only chairs for sitting upright and no couches.

At times, even the members of the Triad varied, and when the foreign religions arrived, particularly from Egypt, Jupiter could be seen sharing a Lectisternium not with his own wife and daughter, but with Isis and Serapis.[36] Such a ceremony was not merely used as an invocation, however, but after an event was settled it could be used as a thank offering to the relevant gods who had assisted with it.

The Lesser Quinquatrus

This was the festival of the Guild of the Flute-Players. (The Major Quinquatrus was for Minerva and was held on the 5th day after the Ides of March. It was named for the fifth day itself, not for the fact that it lasted for five days, although it actually did). The festival of the flute players (tibicines) was very different to Minerva's festival. Flute players were very important in religious ceremonies and they played not only to attract the attention of the gods but to drown out any unwelcome noises from the sacrificial victims. Each animal was supposed, ideally, to go willingly to its death, and to achieve this they were usually drugged, having a soporific added to their food prior to the event. However, drugging creatures of various sizes and weights is a very hit and miss matter, and the sacrifices quite often did not go according to plan. There were many images showing docile creatures standing placidly by, while the toga'd priests and spectators prepared themselves, but these only show the ideal. If an animal was unwilling to be offered to the god and made a fuss, or if it was in any way imperfect, then the priests were likely to refuse to use it. If the creature went so far as to actually kick over the altar, and run off, then it would cause a very embarrassing situation. This was not unknown, and there were even manuals prepared to give advice on the correct procedure to adopt in such cases.

Usually, the man on whose behalf the sacrifice was being performed would have to take the animal back to its vendor and try to get his money back. The argument between vendor and purchaser can easily be imagined, with the vendor unwilling to take back an animal which the priests had rejected – and which he might then be unable to resell – and the purchaser, hot and humiliated, attempting to get the matter completed so that he could make another appointment with the priests and musicians to go through the whole procedure again. However, in reality it was unlikely to end even there, for while the sacrifice would have to be performed again, properly, with a more suitable or placid victim, the musicians such as the flute-players would expect to be paid for both appearances, whether completed correctly or not.

These musicians had their festival of the Lesser Quinquatrus between 13 and 15 June, and they certainly had a good time. So much so, that after the feasting was done, they were in the habit of roaming the streets (by which time they were very drunk), wearing long robes, masks and making an appalling noise. This festival was so notorious for its rowdy behaviour that respectable people stayed inside and locked their doors while the gangs of inebriated musicians were out of control and roaming the streets, night after night, for the duration of their festival.[37]

Liber or Liber Pater

Liber the Father was an ancient fertility god with a temple on the Aventine. He shared his temple with Ceres and his female equivalent Libera, while during a famine in 496 BC the Sibylline Books instructed that the worship of Demeter, Iacchus and Kore should be identified with Ceres, Liber and Libera. The festival of the Liberalia was on 17 March. It was usually celebrated with feasts, sacrifices, vulgar songs and the hanging of masks on trees. There may originally have also been games, but by the time of Ovid these were no longer held.[38]

Mars

The god of war was associated with the wolf, the woodpecker and the month of March. He was one of only three gods to whom a bull could be sacrificed, the others being Neptune and Apollo. The woodpecker was a link to the agricultural roots of this god, and he was also well known as a guardian of fields and boundaries.

Mars had an altar (the Ara Martis) on the Campus Martius, the open area in Republican times, which was also named for him as a war god. Armies camped, trained, and waited there for the Senate's permission to re-enter Rome after a campaign.

Also associated with Mars was the Regia, the small consecrated templum in the Forum Romanum. This contained a shrine to Opiconsivia and was where the sacred shields were kept, along with the sacred sword of Mars, although it was not known which of the sacred shields was the one Mars had sent down from the sky. In early times a blacksmith named Marmurius had been told to make eleven identical ones, to prevent anyone identifying the sacred one. Also stored at the Regia were the sacred lances, which were said to vibrate if danger threatened Rome. The Regia was the official headquarters of the Pontifex Maximus during the Republic, and only he and the Vestals were allowed inside, except for the Salii, priests of a minor priesthood who were divided into two colleges, each of twelve men, who were responsible for the safety of the shields and lances.

On the first day of March, Vesta's sacred fire was relit and homes were decorated with laurel, which was sacred to Mars. On the 14th, horseracing, the Roman passion, took place, while on the 23rd the sacred trumpets were purified and the Quinquatrus festival, a favourite with the people, was performed. The Salii priests, carrying the sacred shields and banging them with sticks, danced around the streets, also performing ritual songs. These dances and songs could be performed in October, but at the Quinquatrus the merriment lasted for days, while a double team of the Salii (whose parents both had to be of noble family and still alive), performed in the streets. Every so often they would stop their dance to chant, and each night they would be feasted in a different house. They were known in other areas, notably in Tibur (Tivoli) where they were attached also to Hercules.[39]

A combined sacrifice of a bull, a boar and a ram was known as the Suovetaurilia, and this was usually made to Mars, who had a number of festivals celebrated in his honour. Also for Mars's sake, the Armilustrum was on 19 October, and was a festival of purification of the weapons used in war. This took place in the square named the Armilustrium on the Aventine Hill. It was probably one of the occasions when the Salii performed, before the weapons were put away to await the next campaigning season.

The festival of Equirria was held on 27 February and was another spectacle of horse-racing. It was said to have been established by Romulus and was held on the Campus Martius or – if that flat area happened to be flooded – on the Caelian Hill, at a place named the Campus Martialis. A similar festival was on 14 March, which may have been another celebration of Mars, although such meetings tended to be held on odd-numbered days, which were considered more auspicious.

The Feriae were literally days of feasting, when wealthy people would pay for a meal for the poorer citizens to enjoy. The Flamen Martialis was the sole Flamen who served Mars, and he sacrificed the October Horse after the racing held on the fifteenth day of that month. Like other Flamens, the Flamen Martialis had to be a Patrician, born of parents married in the old formal (and almost unbreakable) rites of Conferreatio, and he was chosen by the Pontifex Maximus to serve for life. He was only obliged to resign if a major ritual fault was committed.[40]

Women known as Salii Virgines were hired as priestesses to act for a short time each year, accompanying the Pontifex Maximus at an annual sacrifice, which probably took place in the Sacrarium Martis. These women were probably not free-born, and they assisted with the sacrifice dressed in the costumes of the male Salii, which would have been considered improper for free-born or higher status women.

As with many other gods, Mars had several different aspects, some of which connected him to Celtic deities, such as Alator, Albiorix, Barrex, Camulos, Cocidius, Latobius, Lenumius and others. As Mars Gravidus, he was connected with the Palatini, which was one of the Salii priestly groups, who were particularly devoted to him in that aspect. Mars Gravidus was also highly respected by the legions, and the courage said to be given to each man by Mars in this form made each individual a part of the Roman army machine. It helped them to work together against all odds and it lent them determination to ignore dangers and to fight in such a way that they were, as far as possible, invincible. It was that discipline, strict and sometimes unforgiving, which made the Roman legionary far superior to the soldiers of any other power, and Mars Gravidus epitomised that level of training. In the era of Augustus, troops were not allowed to marry, making their entirely dependent on their unit, which in effect became their family. Mars Gravidus became known as 'the Marching God', an important part of any soldier's life, one which promoted endurance.

As Mars Invictus (the unconquered) the deity had a festival on 14 May and had a temple dedicated to him in Rome. The main temple to Mars was on the northeastern side of the Via Appia, outside the Porta Capena. This district came to be known as Ad Martis, between the first and second milestones. The temple contained a statue of Mars and possibly also images of wolves, and was vowed during the invasion of the Gauls, being dedicated on the first day of June, probably in 388 BC. The Roman army commonly assembled there before leaving on campaign.

Another temple in honour of Mars was in the Circus Flaminius and was built by Decimus Junius Brutus Callaicus after his Triumph in 133 BC. It contained a colossal statue of the god and a naked statue of Venus, both by the renowned sculptor Skopas Minor. Julius Caesar had also intended to build an enormous temple to Mars on the site of the lake he used for mock sea battles, but the plan was abandoned and the site was eventually used for the Pantheon.[41]

As Mars Silvanus, the deity was connected to the Roman god Silvanus, who protected woods and uncultivated land, hunting and also boundaries. His cult is well known from over eleven hundred inscriptions dating from 39 BC to 339 AD. He was a deity of private rather than public devotions, and as such had no state festival or holy day and although shrines to him were numerous throughout the Empire, they tended to be small and simple. He was associated with many minor deities of woods and wild spaces, as far from Rome as Hadrian's Wall, where he was possibly a god of hunting. He was usually depicted with the fruits of the fields and often also with a dog.

Mars Ultor or Mars the Avenger had a temple built in his honour by the Emperor Augustus when his new Forum was built, the forum forming the temple's precinct. Over 120 yards long and 57 yards wide, (110m by 52m), it had been vowed at the Battle of Philippi when Augustus was still Octavianus. He intended it to commemorate the deaths of Brutus and Cassius, and the final avenging of the assassination of Julius Caesar, who was the adopted father of Octavianus. It was dedicated in 2 BC and the standards that had been recovered from the Parthians in 20 BC were kept there.

There had possibly been an earlier temple to Mars Ultor on the Capitol Hill, but the temple built by Augustus was intended to be a showpiece. It stood on a high podium, dominating the Forum of Augustus and inside it were housed statues of Mars, Venus, and the deified Caesar, along with Caesar's own sword. The temple and its forum precinct were used for the enrolment of military training, and as a place from where Governors left for the provinces, as well as being a repository for triumphal insignia. The state would meet there when considering the awarding of Triumphs or when receiving reports of military successes.[42]

Mercury

In Latin Mercurius, he was another of the children of Jupiter. He was a messenger of the gods and was associated with trade, particularly anything concerned with grain, where he represented both abundance and commercial success. In Rome he had a temple on the Aventine and was depicted with a winged hat and sandals. He carried a caduceus and was sometimes also shown with a cockerel, as the herald of the new day. He is reputed to have invented the lyre, made from a tortoiseshell. Mercury did not have a Flamen of his own, which indicates that he was not one of Rome's earliest gods, but he did have a festival in his honour on 15 May. Julius Caesar had written that Mercury was the most popular god in Britain and Gaul, where he was regarded as the inventor of the arts.

His temple on the Aventine overlooked the Circus Maximus and was outside the Pomerium. It was traditionally believed to have been dedicated on the Ides of May in 495 BC by the Primi Pili Centurion Marcus Laetorius. It became the meeting place of the guild of traders and merchants, although no trace of it has been found. From coin evidence, Marcus Aurelius rebuilt the temple, probably in circular style, and it is the only temple dedicated to Mercury known to have been in Rome. The sestertius of Marcus Aurelius dated 172-173 AD shows the inscription 'Imperator for the sixth time, Consul for the third time, the religion of the Emperor is commemorated by order of the Senate.'

It shows what appears to be a round temple with tributes to Mercury on the roof, and apparently refers to the god Mercury having gone to the assistance of Marcus Aurelius during a military campaign.[43]

Neptune

The god of water, primarily of the seas, was by 399 BC identified with the Greek god Poseidon, and also with Consus, due to Poseidon's association with horses. A temple on the Circus Flaminius was dedicated to him and a festival known as the Neptunalia was held on 23 July, with another celebration for him on the first day of December. He was the brother of Jupiter and also of Pluto, god of the underworld, and was often shown carrying a trident.

The festival of the Neptunalia took place at the height of summer, when water could be scarce, making it a propritiatory ceremony. In earlier times it was the god Portunus who oversaw ports and who was thanked for naval victories, but by the first century BC Neptune had supplanted him. Sextus Pompeius (the son of Gnaeus Pompeius Magnus) called himself 'a son of Neptune'. Neptune was also considered the legendary progenitor god of a Latin people, the Faliscans, who referred to themselves as Neptune's Proles.

In recorded times, the Neptunalia festivals were performed outside, in branched huts, in a wood between the Tiber and the Via Salaria, and there people drank wine and spring water to escape the fierce heat. It was a time for unrestrained merrymaking, when men and women could mix freely, without the usual social constraints.[44]

Neptune's temple on the Circus Flaminius was shown on a coin struck by Gnaeus Domitius Ahenobarbus in 40 BC, probably due to some restoration carried out by him. It contained a famous marine group sculpted by Skopas Minor.

The Basilica Neptunae built on the Campus Martius was dedicated by Marcus Agrippa in honour of the naval victory of Actium and probably replaced an earlier building on the same side. The Battle of Actium, between Rome led by Octavianus and Egypt led by Cleopatra and Marcus Antonius, took place in 31 BC off the coast of Greece. Marcus Agrippa very skilfully dominated the sea lanes, and although details of the battle are sketchy, one piece of evidence does testify that a full-scale engagement did take place. There are some later reports that the battle was largely engineered by Octavianus and that several ships were later scuttled to make the engagement seem to be more dramatic than it actually had been, but there is no direct evidence of this.

Shortly after his Triumph, Octavianus founded the settlement of Nicopolis (Victory City) on a peninsula on the Ionian Sea. It was decorated with the prows of the ships taken in battle, indicating that Antonius's losses had indeed been heavy. It appeared that he had tried to break through the ships of his opponents, and as he did so Cleopatra's squadron turned about and fled. Antonius followed her, first in his flagship, then later in a faster vessel. The remainder of his fleet retreated to the bay and later surrendered to Rome.[45]

Oceanus

The Greek god of the ocean, the 'great river surrounding the earth', was also worshipped by the Romans. His consort was his sister Tethys, a goddess of the sea. The Bocca della Verita, or mouth of truth, into which modern-day visitors to Rome like to place their hands to determine whether or not they are truthful, and which used to be a drain cover in Rome, is believed to show the face of Oceanus.

Pax

Peace was represented by the temple of peace, built by Vespasian and dedicated in 75 AD. It was considered to be very beautiful, was surrounded by lawns and housed the monumental marble map of Rome, known as the Forma Urbis Romae, which was created on the orders of the later Emperor Septimius Severus between 203 and 211 AD, which was apparently based on the city's property records. It hung on an interior wall of the temple of peace and had been carved into 150 Proconnesiun marble slabs. It was considered detailed enough to show the floor plans of nearly every temple, bath and insula in central Rome. The map was destroyed during medieval times and the wall upon which it once hung is still visible, now a part of the church of Ss. Cosmo and Damiano and is open to the elements. About 10% of the fragments of the map have been recovered from the area and are now housed in the Vatican Museum. (See Chapter 3, note 17.)

Still in existence is Augustus's own Altar of Peace, the Ara Pacis. This has been restored and is now housed in the pavilion built for it, alongside the Mausoleum of Augustus on the Campus Martius. The decoration on it is an allegory of peace, which Augustus gave Rome after the upheavals of the end of the Republican era. The Ara Pacis had been vowed in 13 BC and shows the imperial family and various processions. It would have been originally painted in bright colours, but is now pristine white marble, which glows in the light from the surrounding windows.

Priapus

He was a god of fertility, whose statues were a common feature of the countryside. Although a god, he was often regarded with amusement and is often shown with a huge phallus, sometimes so heavy that he is obliged to have it held up. The general use of phallic symbols as protective charms, particularly against the evil eye, was widespread and Priapus was sometimes worshipped as a part of the rites of Dionysus.

Quirinus

He was the most Latin of the Roman gods, possibly originating as a Sabine war deity; there was once a Sabine settlement on the Quirinal Hill before Rome was founded. The temple of Quirinus was believed to have been founded by Romulus, who appeared to Julius Proculus in the mid-sixth century BC to tell him to build a temple on the site.

However, the earliest record is of its dedication by Lucius Papirius Cursor in 293 BC when it is quite likely to have replaced an even earlier building. It was one of the temples rebuilt by Augustus and re-dedicated in June 16 BC. It was one of Rome's largest temples, and in 45 BC a statue of Julius Caesar was placed inside it, by order of the Senate. It stood in the garden of what is now the Palazzo Quirinale until at least the fourth century AD.

An inscription at the north end of the Eumachia Building in Pompeii reads:

Romulus Martis (f)ilius urbem Roman (condi) dit et regnant annos duodequadraginta isque primus dux duce hostium Acrone Rege caeninensium interfecto spolia opi(ma) Iovi Feretrio consecra(vit) receptusque in deo(rum) numerum quirinu(s) appellatu(s) est.

Romulus, son of Mars, founded the city of Rome and reigned for thirty-eight years and was the first general to dedicate the enemy spoils to Jupiter Feretrius having slain the enemy's general King Acro of the Caeninenses, and having been received among the company of the gods, was called Quirinus.[46]

This appears to claim that Quirinus and Romulus was the same person. Quirinus was the divine concept of an idea, the embodiment of Roman citizenship itself and the god of the assembly of Roman men. His priest, the Flamen Quirinalis, was one of the three major Flaminates, and his festival was the Quirinalia. In certain circumstances the senior Flamines (Dialis, Martialis and Quirinalis) could claim to have precedence even over the Pontifex Maximus, and there were certainly disputes between them on several occasions.[47]

The festival of the Quirinalia was held on 17 February and the name came to refer to Roman citizen males in general, so long as they remained civilians. In front of his temple grew two myrtle trees, representing the Patricians and the Plebeians. There may also have been a shrine at the Porta Quirinalis, although the deity's popularity began to decline with the arrival of the imported foreign gods, leaving his Flamen to perform the rituals on his behalf.[48]

Saturn

Known mainly as a god of seed sowing, he had a festival at the winter solstice, the Saturnalia. He was believed to have taught humans to cultivate the ground and grow crops. His temple was at the foot of the Capitoline Hill and was built in the early Republican period, possibly in 501 or 497 BC by the Consuls. It was rebuilt by Lucius Manius Plancus in 42 BC.

From Republican times it housed the state treasury in the basement rooms beneath the building, and also contained the state archives. There was a much older altar outside the temple, which was traditionally believed to have been founded during the Trojan War, or possibly even built by Hercules. Whatever its real age, its antiquity was shown by the fact that the rites were performed by a priest with his head uncovered, in the Greek style, and not with a fold of his toga pulled over to cover his head, in the Roman way.[49]

The festival of the Saturnalia lasted from three to seven days and began with a great sacrifice at the temple. This was followed by a public feast which was open to everyone. All businesses were closed and a general holiday was held, when people were allowed to play gambling games in public. Everyone wore less formal clothing, and the slaves and servants were allowed to exchange places with their masters and be served by them for the duration of the festival. It can easily be imagined, however, that any sensible servant would make his time of authority over his masters a very mild one, or else he would have to suffer resentment, or even punishment, later, if he should forget himself and his real position.

The Saturnalia was taken over by the Christians and turned into the feast of Christ's birth, and they even used the change of social positions by appointing a Lord of Misrule in large households during medieval times. For a short while this person could order others around and make them do stupid things for the amusement of others. There were even 'boy bishops' appointed temporarily, and the usual societal norms were turned upside down, making the winter solstice the time for revelry and parties and for the eating of the animals that could not be over-wintered on the farms. It had been, since earliest times, the darkest and coldest and most frightening time of the year, so the feasting, noise and generally rowdy behaviour was intended originally to scare away the demons of the dark times, and bring back the light, the spring, and renewed life.

Sol

The sun god was a very ancient deity and essential to the growth of all new life. His worship became increasingly important from the first century BC and his temple in Rome, on the southwestern side of the Circus Maximus, was probably built then. There was a festival on 28 August and there are many inscriptions referring to Sol and to his consort Luna, although outside of Rome the worship was less frequently performed. Sol Indiges (native sun) had a festival on 9 August and may have been worshipped also during the Agonalia on 11 December.

Sol Invictus was the unconquered sun, and a Syrian variant which spread across the Empire, particularly during the second century AD. He was associated with Mithraism rather than the original concept of Sol, the ancient Roman deity.

The sun god as Deus Sol Invictus was established as the supreme deity by the Emperor Aurelian in the late third century and in 274 AD Aurelian built a temple to him in Rome, establishing a college of Senators as 'Pontifices dei Solis'. Under Aurelian the imperial power became more closely connected to the god of the sun. Some coins from the period have the words 'Sol Dominus Imperi Romani' on them, meaning Sol Lord of the Roman Empire. Some coins from the time of Constantine also show 'Soli Invicto Comiti', claiming Sol as the 'ally' of the emperor.

When referred to as Indiges, this probably is intended to indicate he is Rome's own sun god, not an import. He was represented from earliest times by the image of a young man crowned with solar rays. What is certain is that the festival of Sol Invictus on 25 December was not suppressed by the rise of the Christian cult as is sometimes imagined. Instead, it was eventually absorbed by the Christian religious calendar and from the fourth century AD was 'made out to be'[50] a celebration of the birth of Christ, which had in fact originally been celebrated on 6 January. It was the usual super-imposition of one cult belief over another, in order to suppress, or better, erase.

Invictus was victory incarnate, after rising every morning to banish the darkness of the night. He also represented battle victories and became a deity favoured by soldiers and was known as the patron of the legions – however, it must be remembered that Invictus was quite different and separate from Sol in the aspect of Sol Indiges.

It was claimed that the Emperor Constantine imposed Christianity on Rome after he had had a 'vision', but the reality is that the state religion at that time remained the worship of the Sun, and Constantine always performed the rituals as its Chief Priest. His reign was actually described as that of a 'sun-emperorship' and Sol Invictus appeared everywhere throughout the reign, including on the Imperial banners and the coinage. Constantine was not baptised into the Christian cult until 337 AD, when he was on his deathbed, so was then probably unable to protest at any changes made in his name. Likewise, he cannot be credited with the Chi Ro monogram, which was found incised on a tomb at Pompeii, dating from two-and-a-half centuries earlier.[51]

A temple to Sol Invictus had been built by the Emperor Aurelian in 273 AD after his victories in the east, and it was known as the Templum Solis Aureliani. A large structure, recorded by Palladio, which stood to the east of the Via del Corso and west of the San Silvestro church, may well have been the remaining part of this temple [52]

Terminus

He was the god of boundaries and marker stones, whose own boundary found itself inside the temple of Jupiter Optimus Maximus on the Capitol Hill, because the god refused to move to make way for the new building. As we have seen, this was regarded as a fortunate sign rather than one of mere stubbornness and was believed to represent the determination of the Roman people to stay where they were and a general sign of permanence.

When a boundary was set up, it was celebrated by a religious ceremony when a sacrifice was made. The blood of the sacrificial victim and other offerings from the sacrificial fire were placed in the bottom of the hole where the boundary stone would stand, and the marker was then placed on top. Each boundary stone was considered to have its own individual spirit deity, and these Termini were worshipped together at the Terminalia. This rite was held on 23 February, and rituals were performed at boundaries when all the stones were decorated with garlands. It was also celebrated at the boundary stone at the temple of Jupiter Optimus Maximus.

The shrine within Jupiter's temple had an opening above it, because Terminus should always be left uncovered to allow him to see the Heavens, as stones outdoors would, and as Terminus would have been, had Jupiter's temple not been built around him.[53]

The Underworld

The resting place of the dead was also the dwelling house of some of the deities associated with death. Souls went there, rather to a Heaven or a Hell, but those who for some reason were not admitted would have to wander as Shades forever. Virgil described the world of the dead as a 'Limbo' between heaven and hell, but most Romans dismissed his ideas. Some believed that the dead lived in the sky and the old Greek idea of being ferried across the River Styx by Charon was frequently shown on Roman coins.

Ideas were to change with the importation of eastern religious beliefs, notably those of Aset/Isis, who promised reincarnation. She – unsurprisingly – became very popular indeed. It was a reassuring belief compared with the 'long sleep' that had been propounded by Julius Caesar.

Vediovis

Also known as Vedius, Veiovis, or Vendius, he was closely associated with Jupiter. However, he was Jupiter's direct opposite, being vengeful and harmful, rather than having Jupiter's fatherly and rather sensual aspect. There was a temple to Vediovis behind the Tabularium in Rome, and his sacrificial animal was a female goat, which was killed on behalf of the dead. His festivals on 1 January, 7 March and 21 May were not much celebrated outside of Rome itself.

A temple to him on Tibur Island (the Isola Tiburina), was vowed in 200 BC by the Praetor Lucius Furius Purpurio during the Battle of Cremona against the Gauls. Lucius Furius also vowed another temple when he was Consul in 198 BC, which was dedicated by Quintus Marcius Ralla in 192 BC. That one was built on the Capitol Hill and was described as being 'between the two groves', that is between the twin peaks of the Capitol and the Arx. This was restored in 78 BC after the Tabularium was built. The remains of this temple were discovered in 1939 at the southeastern corner of the Tabularium, and it was found that the foundations were oriented differently from the later rebuilding works. A cult statue was found there, of colossal size, which appeared to be a first-century BC copy of a fifth-century Greek original.

Vortumnus

Vortumnus or Vertumnus was originally an Etruscan deity who was worshipped at Volsinii, which was captured by the Romans in 264 BC. The god was regarded as having 'gone over' to Rome by the process of 'evocatio', persuading a god to defect from its original home and worshippers by promises of a greater temple, better sacrifices and a larger group of worshippers. If the deity concerned agreed to be transferred to Rome, then it meant that his or her protection was removed from the original city and also transferred to Rome.

Vortumnus had a temple on the Aventine and offerings were also made to him at his statue in the Vicus Tuscus at the entrance to the Forum Romanum. His festival was on 13 August and he was regarded as being a god of changes, and so he came to preside over the changes of the seasons. He was also consequently regarded as a god of fruiting trees and of fertility.

Vulcan

The god of fires, blacksmiths, metals and all metalwork, and of volcanoes was sometimes referred to as 'Mulciber', or the smelter of metals. He had an important cult in Ostia, where he was the patron of the town, and had festivals on 23 May (the Tubilustrium) and on 23 August (the Vulcanalia). In Rome, the temple of Vulcan was attributed to Romulus and was situated on the Campus Martius. His priest was the Flamen Vulcanalis and the usual sacrifice to him on the festival of the Vulcanalia was said to be small live fish, which were thrown into the ashes of the bonfires lit in his honour. This rather unusual practice was said to be due to the fact that the fishes of the sea did not fear the fire god.

He was said to have fathered the fire-breathing monster Cacus, and also his sister Caca. In Roman legend, Caca betrayed his brother Cacus to Hercules by showing him where Cacus had hidden stolen oxen. In return, she was given a shrine containing a perpetual flame at which the Vestal Virgins worshipped. Cacus was supposedly killed after his sister betrayed him to the Etruscans, but others claim he was merely a seer who had once lived on the Palatine Hill.[54]

4

Foreign Gods

As discussed above, the bringing of foreign gods into Rome was not an act of altruism, aimed at making visitors or foreign residents feel more at home. Rome's whole aim in conquering foreign territories was to expand Rome's sphere of influence and extend Rome's power. The inclusion of foreign people into Rome's way of life was a part of this, a way of showing outsiders the huge benefits to be enjoyed by their association with Rome. The question 'What has Rome ever done for us?' was the base for a good joke, but when the huge strides forward Rome had made in a comparatively short space of time are considered, it would seem that the spread of Roman civilisation did a great deal. Rome's buildings, its open Fora, its many fountains, statues, and beautiful temples were intended to awe, and no doubt they did, but her other advances were equally important.

There was the subtle spread of the Latin language, throughout a world accustomed to speaking Greek. There were trading links, taking prosperity to other areas because of Rome's insatiable need for grain, wine, oil and luxury items from the east. There were were ideas and expectations that were essentially Roman, introducing a new way of life.

What Rome needed it tended to take, in some senses it had no reverse gear, yet Rome also preferred to find a way of obtaining what was needed with some semblance of legality, along with balance, and hopefully acceptance, even a little gratitude from those involved. Of course, if any barbarian people resisted too strongly, they could always be flattened, conquered, and made to accept what they had refused to take willingly, perhaps on the assumption that they would eventually benefit from Rome's civilising influence in the process, but if not...

The first steps outward, into the wider world, were for two reasons only, security and sustenance. The most important was naturally security. Nobody can feel secure with a potential enemy living next door, therefore the enemy has to be made into a friend, or better still, one takes over next door so that it becomes a part of one's own property. That not only eliminates any potential threat but ensures growth.

An ever-expanding Rome needed more food. Trading with others is all very well, but deals might fail, old friends can become enemies again, and there is always the problem of increasing costs, once the people at the other side of the deal realise that they have you over a barrel and can charge what they like. This situation can only be solved by cutting out the other side altogether, and ensuring that all that was necessary, the grain-lands, the cattle ranges, the wool pastures, the vineyards and the ports, became a part of Rome. The original owners become workers on the farmland they once owned, and more amenable to persuasion, or at least are in no position to argue.

That leaves the gods, and they are always to be placated, to be honoured and to be feared. If a foreign area is taken over, how are they likely to react to their loss of influence? Even the gods of barbarians may have great powers and resent what happens, so they must also become a part of Rome. This was sometimes done by the process of 'evocatio' mentioned earlier which was effectively the transference of such gods to Rome itself, from territory fallen under Roman control. Then the power of the gods must be harnessed for Rome's benefit.

Bringing in new gods did not mean that the Romans were dissatisfied with their own gods, quite the reverse, for just as Rome's citizens gave Rome her military stength, so did the increasing numbers of deities, both domestic and foreign, give Rome another kind of strength; as they increased her 'armoury' of spiritual protection, the safer she would become.[1]

It was believed that a town could be more easily conquered if its patron deity had already defected to Rome, thus leaving its people without heavenly protection. Evocatio was very useful in this situation, as with taking Juno to Rome, leaving her town of Veii bereft and easily beaten. Many of Rome's gods were easily 'twinned' with gods from Gaul, Syria, or from Egypt because they performed similar functions. In this double aspect, the original deity would gain additional power, and the new deity would give its people a new focus: as their gods had a place in Roman society, so did they.

In some cases, where a new deity was being introduced, the Augurs would conduct a rite called 'exauguration', intended to prevent jealousy and resentment from the original deity. It even, on occasion, would require the deconsecration of a temple and its replacement with a new shrine, but the original deity would have to be placated and assured that they would still have respect and would be given an equal or better shrine in a new position.[2]

Isis

The most important of the foreign acquisitions was the Egyptian religion, which brought into Rome the mother goddess Aset, or Isis as she was called in Greece. Her name derives from the throne, which was her symbol, and her name was usually pronounced Ee-set or Ee-sa, because the last 't' in the name was a feminine suffix which was dropped in the later stages of the Egyptian language. She was by far the most powerful figure in Egypt's pantheon and would eventually assume the virtues of practically every other important goddess. She was also a powerful magician, having learned the secret name of Ra from the god himself.

Wife and sister of Osiris, sister of Nepthys and Set, she was the mother of the Horus child, the son of god, called Harpocrates outside of Egypt. Her cult started at Abydos near the Delta in the North (in Lower Egypt), but she became universally worshipped. She was associated with motherhood, with nurturing and was kindly towards her followers. She was adored for her supreme loyalty towards her husband and child, and for all her protective qualities.

Osiris was killed by his jealous brother Set and his body parts scattered. Aset/Isis searched for those parts and brought Osiris back to life just long enough to conceive their son, Horus. Thus, Isis was the beginning of the resurrection myths later copied by the Christians, just as they also appropriated her titles of Queen of Heaven and Virgin Mother for their own lady, Mary.

Isis wears the symbol of the throne on her head, or else is shown with the cow's horns of Hathor. She often carries a sistrum, or rattle, which was used as an intrument during rituals, or she is occasionally seen with a vessel containing Nile water, which was used for purification in her worship.

The belief reached Rome early in the first century BC and was at first considered to be a 'mystery' religion. It required initiation, which was unusual in Roman worship, and this gave it a secretive aspect, which was at first considered suspicious. However, the new ideas quickly spread beyond the walls of her temples, and were understood to involve a particular devotion, a set of moral rules to live by, and a level of purity to strive for. In exchange for this commitment, resurrection after death in the form of reincarnation, giving a life, or indeed many lives, and an idea of interconnected identities and future continuance was offered. This was one of the main attractions which made the worship popular, initially among women and the downtrodden and also with slaves, who might be expected to wish for something better than their present life. It suggested that the apparently natural order could be overturned, and that if one lived a 'good' life then one could benefit next time round. For this reason, the cult was frowned upon as disputing the 'mos maiorum', basically for giving low-born people ideas above their station.[3]

Isis worship faced many early difficulties due to these factors, but also because of its shaven and celibate priests who appeared very different to Rome's ideals of masculinity, whose priests married and produced families. They had always preferred the robust, muscular, 'normal' type of soldierly male. Augustus, in particular, had his own issues with it, mainly due to his earlier problems with Cleopatra and Marc Antony, and he preferred to consider it incontinent, although in actual fact the Isis priests preached sexual self-control and moderation. The belief went through phases of being suppressed, with its priests being executed and its temples destroyed. There are in existence some temple statues and images of priests found in the Tiber, which very likely ended up ther during one of these periods of suppression.

The popularity of the religion grew nevertheless, as it offered new hope to all levels of people, even though its acceptance meant that it drew revenues away from the more traditional gods. After the earthquake in Pompeii in 63 AD, the Isis temple was one of the first to be restored and re-opened to its worshippers, while the temple of Venus on the other side of the Forum was not rebuilt at all and was finally destroyed, as everything was, in the eruption of 79 AD.[4]

Caligula legitimised the religion, finally assuring its safety. The emperor already had an Egyptian chamberlain and both Hadrian and Marcus Aurelius were friendly towards the cult. Hadrian ordered a new gate for the temple complex at Philae during his reign.[5]

Isis worship was not confined to one gender, or one social class. The Romans, always quick to incorporate the deities of others into their own pantheon where possible, began to equate Osiris with Serapis, leading to the building of a huge temple complex for Isis/Serapis on the Campus Martius (close to where the pantheon now stands). The first Ptolemy, a far-sighted and sensible man, had the idea of bonding the city of Alexandria more firmly to Egypt by having a high priest of Ptah, named Manetho, construct what amounted to a hybrid religion. This part-Greek and part-Egyptian hybrid was to gain the confidence and sympathies of the prople. The result was the Zeus-Osiris-Apis combination that became Serapis, and the Artemis-Isis combination, which helped to make the Aset/Isis goddess more acceptable to the Hellenistic and Roman worshippers. In Rome itself, Serapis was often shown as a muscular male figure, with a full size bull's head.

Caracalla would eventually dedicate a temple to Serapis on the Quirinal Hill, within the sacred boundary of the city, with the Greek connection emphasised rather than the Egyptian, to permit easier assimilation for the Romans. The priesthood in Rome, in particular in the nearby port of Ostia, was Greek in nature, which helped to co-mingle the different aspects, particularly the problem of animal worship, which many Romans initially found disagreeable.

The elephant, now in front of the church of Santa Maria sopra Minerva (St Mary above Minerva, as the remains of the Minerva temple were below), carries on his back one of the Egyptian obelisks from the adjacent Isis temple complex, and the fountain in the Piazza della Rotunda outside the Pantheon holds another. The Vatican Museum has an Egyptian Department which has a great many statues of the Egyptian deities, including Sekhmet, Thoth, Bastet and of course of Isis and Horus, along with a delightful pink granite crocodile, representing Sobek, which once was in the channel of water than ran through the Isis/Serapis complex, to represent the Nile. There are also some grey granite columns from the temple, showing carved priests of Isis performing the rituals. The complex was once known as Isis Campensis, due to its position on the Campus Martius.

The Iseum, like all Egyptian temples, was not open to the street like Roman ones but was enclosed and with an inner sanctuary. Temples to Isis usually also had a small building within the precinct wall which held Nile water, to be used during rituals.

On 5 March, Isis had a festival when she sailed the seas looking for the body parts of her husband Osiris. One 28 October, 'Passion Plays' were performed, telling the story of his resurrection and the eventual birth of the holy child, Horus. The similarity between these and later Christian beliefs is obvious.[6]

There were several Isis temples or shrines in Rome, sometimes combined with Serapis the Apis bull. His appearance gradually changed into a more masculine figure, along with several other of the Egyptian gods, who took on a strangely Romanised appearance, for example Anubis, who took on a distinctly Roman look, wearing a toga yet still sporting the head of a jackal. Several Isis temples were dedicated around 200 BC on the Sicilian coast. The first temple to Isis in Pompeii was probably built in around 100 BC. There was an Isis cult in Rome by the 30s or 40s BC, although it was kept rather private, but Isis-themed names had already begun to emerge, such as Isidora, showing its spread and influence.

The Isis Metellinum, which is still partly visible, is on the Via Labicana, where the Piazza Iside still carries the name. The remains are made of brick, and recent studies identify this structure with the temple to Isis, which was probably founded by Quintus Caecilius Metellus Pius, Consul with Lucius Cornelius Sulla in 80 BC. The building was a substantial one, with arcades and fountains on a series of terraces connected by ramps and stairways. It must have been similar in design to the temple of Fortuna Primigenia at Praeneste, but on a smaller scale. (Interestingly, the Fortuna temple at Praeneste was also associated with Isis.)

It was a tripartite structure, enhanced with granite columns and a swimming pool a little way upstream. Numerous Egyptian sculptures were found in the surrounding area, which are now in the Capitoline and Centrale Montemartini Museums. In 1653, some paintings with stuccoes and Egyptian figures were excavated and in 1886-1887 a head of Serapis and other gods were found there. In 1889, an inscribed stone was unearthed which commemorated a gift made by a freedman and imperial procurator named Mucianus, referring to Isis as 'Lydia and educator' the actual words used were 'Isidi Lydiae educatrici valvas cum Anubi'.[7] This Iseum gave its name to the area of Regio III in Rome, which became known as 'Isis et Serapis'.[8]

The Isis Capitolinum was very likely the first to be built in Rome, in order to worship Isis, Serapis, Anubis and Harpocrates (Horus). This branch of Isis worship probably originated on the Island of Delos, in Greece. However, this caused some problems, as Delos was known as a slave-trading centre, and Isis and Serapis were both firmly associated with the freeing of slaves. Indeed, slaves could be liberated by being 'sold' by their owners to the goddess, becoming owned only by the deity, therefore technically and legally free.

The Capitoline Isis was subjected to pressures in 58 BC and in 48 BC – particularly in 48 when a swarm of bees settled at the nearby sanctuary of Hercules during a sacrifice to Isis. It was considered to be 'nefas' and the temple was destroyed in retribution, although this did not stop the worship of the goddess in Rome. Five years later, during the Second Triumvirate (43-32 BC of Octavianus, Marcus Aemilius Lepidus and Marc Antony) a new temple was built to Isis/Serapis and this may well have been the complex of the Iseum Campense. Queen Cleopatra, who had been staying outside Rome until just after Caesar's death, may have influenced the rebuilding. This Iseum/Serapeum on the Campus Martius was exempted from the various bans put on other Isis shrines, as it was just outside the Pomerium. Isis worship was banned within the city in 28 BC and again in 21 BC, but the worhip continued without interruption on the Campus Martius. In the second century AD Appuleius notes that

'Isis in Rome is worshipped with supreme devotion and, due to the place where her temple has risen up, she is called Isis Campensis.'[9]

Its position corresponds to the latest sinkhole, which opened up in the Piazza della Rotunda in the summer of 2020, with the canal trench found beneath the present road level. This is where the pink granite crocodile in the Vatican Museum probably once stood guard. It shows that the Iseum/Serapeum was actually just behind the Pantheon, and not beneath it. The Via Santa Catrina di Siena is directly over the double temple site, side by side with the processional way.

Isis Curiana, probably built by Quintus Curius, was mentioned by Cicero, and the Isis Patricia may have stood on the Vicus Patricius in Regio V. The Isis Pelagia, a shrine for her as the protectress of sailors, is known only from an inscription of 'Aeditus ab Iseum Pelagiam.'[10]

Isis Invicta's worship received imperial sanction, flourishing during the reigns of Caligula and Vespasian. Caligula may also have been responsible for rebuilding the Campus Martius complex. The Iseum burned down during the fires of 80 AD but was restored by Domitian and enhanced by some of his successors. Many shrines were opened and one Roman graffito reads: 'Una quai es omnia dea Isis' or 'Being one, thou art all, goddess Isis,' meaning she was so popular that all other gods were considered to be aspects of her. The Iseum Metellinum on the Labicana is now the only temple with any remains above ground, and the property is a part of the convent of the Sisters of Good and Perpetual Help, between the Piazza Iside and the Via Pasquale Villari.

The house of the Emperor Tetricus (270-283 AD) stood on the Caelian Hill and was said to be facing the Iseum Metellinum. There were then two 'groves' just inside the Porta Querquetulana. Their position may well have been the reason why the large complex of the Iseum Mettelinum was built nearby, in or close to an area already considered to be sacred. The Iseum Metellinum can be associated with the Isis and Serapis on the Via Labicana, and an imperial inscription addressed to 'Isis Regina' was found nearby.[11]

Filippo Coarelli argued that the foundation there was a Republican one, as the Caecilii Metelli died out during the Imperial period. He suggested that it was founded by Quintus Caecilius Metellus Pius between 72 and 64 BC, and he placed its position on the Caelian Hill. Quintus Caecilius Metellus Pius was a firm supporter of Sulla and was made Pontifex Maximus in 81 BC.[12]

The fullest description of the ceremony of initiation was described by Appuleius in his story 'The Golden Ass', which is also known as 'Metamorphosis'. His character Lucius fell asleep on a beach at Cenchreae in Greece, and Isis appeared to him. She told him that she alone decided who was to be initiated after she calls each person to her service. He described the initiation ceremony as if he knew it personally, and he did describe her as 'Mother of the stars, the parent of the seasons, the mistress of all the world', so he sounds like a worshipper.

Before initiation 'Lucius' had to be purified, by waiting for ten days during which time he must abstain from meat and wine. When he finally attended the temple, the priest read out the procedure from a book. Looking around the initiate saw that 'the walls of the temple were covered with all sorts of animals.' He was bathed by a priest who asked the gods to forgive his sins. The confession of the sins and the repentence for committing them placed great emphasis on chastity, which other sources confirm was an important feature of this religion. He was then sprinkled with water, and on the evening of the final day he received a variety of gifts before dressing in a clean white robe and entering the deepest part of the temple. Plutarch confirms in his 'On Isis and Osiris' that the vast majority of Egyptian temples had secret chambers and corridors: 'in another portion, the temples have secret vesting rooms in the darkness underground, like cells or chapels.'

The temple of Dendera has ten of these rooms, some single small cells, with corridors and long galleries on three levels. The temple of Horus at Edfu likewise had two chambers underground, accessed from the wall of the main chapel into a tunnel within the walls. Archaeologists often claim that these were for storage, but Plutarch, who was an initiate of Delphi, confirms that they were used for initiations and men and women were shown the mysteries there, so that they could teach others, and these included the priestesses of Isis. The proceedings were to be kept secret from those who were unitiated, but Lucius reveals that he 'travelled to the boundaries of death and, having trodden the threshold of Proserpina, I moved through all the elements and returned in the middle of the night. I saw the sun, flashing with a bright light, and I came face to face with the gods below and the gods above, and paid reverence to them from close at hand.'

He saw the underworld and the heavens, he saw the sun amid darkness, and was able to approach the gods. He emerged the following morning and was dressed in an embroidered cloak, and then he stood on a dais, carrying a torch and wearing a crown of palm leaves. A curtain was drawn back that revealed his fellow devotees, and finally he shared a banquet with them. Appuleius said that Lucius (who was probably himself), underwent such initiation on three separate occasions and each time he had to pay certain fees.

Despite the criticism of some historians, the evidence from Dendera, Edfu and Delphi confirms that such chambers did exist, and could be extensive. Plutarch was not only an initiate of Delphi but also served as a priest of these mysteries, so presumably knew a good deal. These rituals were not chronicled because they were not open to non-initiates and Heliodorus of Emesa writing in the third century AD confirmed that the mysteries of Isis and Osiris were 'not made clear to profane people, and those who are skilled in the secrets of nature instruct those who wish to learn these private matters, in their chapels by candlelight.' The Amduat (the 'Book of What is in the Far World') of which the earliest copies date back to 1470 BC, actually has the original title of 'Treatise of the Hidden Chambers'.

The church of St Mary Castlegate in York was found to have an extensive cellar or crypt dating back to Saxon times, which had remained entirely hidden after being blocked off for eight hundred years.[13] So it is not surprising that Egyptian priests could hide the whereabouts of their most secret chambers from prying eyes.

The procedure of initiation was certainly a well-rehearsed one, as the earliest mention of Isis is in the Pyramid Texts of Saqqara dating to the Old Kingdom of 2575-2150 BC. Numerous cats and kittens have been found there, representing Bastet, and one rare lion-cub, with its face painted on linen to represent Sekhmet. Dozens of mummified cats, birds, cobras, and even crocodiles were found there in 2004. Dr. Salima Ikram from the American University in Cairo was thrilled by the finds, saying 'People would make devotional offerings in the form of animals as mummies, and this would have more potency as a blood sacrifice, compared to a stone or wooden image.' Dr Ikram estimated that the finds were from the Ptolemaic period that ended in 30 BC: 'It is one of the most exciting series of finds in the world of animal mummies – ever!'[14]

Appuleius described a procession he saw on the festival day of Isis, with sistrums being shaken and statues of the gods being carried, followed by the priests, each of whom carried something sacred to the goddess, such as lanterns representing light or breast-shaped milk containers for fertility. The High Priest carried a sistrum and a bouquet of roses. Appuleius's story of 'The Golden Ass' is the only Latin 'novel' to survive in its entirety.[15]

The Navigium Isis (Vessel of Isis), was a Roman fesival held on 5 March. It outlived the persecution of the Emperor Theodosius and was still being celebrated in Italy until 416 AD. It consisted of an elaborate procession, with sacred emblems and priests carrying model boats, to the sea or nearest river. There were dancing ladies, encouraged in their efforts by the priests, and a carving of such a celebration shows the presence of the Apis bull, watching the performers. The word carnival almost certainly derives from 'carrus navalis', a naval wagon or float, and it was later appropriated for the Corpus Christi festivals in Spain and Portugal.[16]

The Emperor Theodosius closed all Pagan temples in 380 AD, but Isis was not so easily silenced. Her worship continued at her temple at Philae on the Nile, until it was finally closed by order of Justinian in 529 AD.[17]

The temple of Isis at Pompeii has an inscription over the entrance that reads:

Numerius Popidius Celsinus, son of Numerius, when the temple of Isis had collapsed in the earthquake, restored it from the ground up, at his own expense and the town council in return for his generosity, although he was only six years old, enrolled him into their order without (the customary) fee.[18]

It appeared that Numerius Ampliatus the boy's father was a freedman and therefore not eligible for high political office personally. The generosity he showed in his rebuilding of the Isis temple gained him a voice on the town council through his son. Ampliatus would also dedicate a statue to Osiris/ Bacchus, which was displayed on the rear wall of the temple. The Popidii family appear to have also been patrons. The name of Popidius Ampliatus appears among the 'attendants of Augustus' or the Augustales, who tended to be either slaves or ex-slaves. So this was probably a way that the family could advance in local politics despite its original slave status.

It is believed that in the period between the earthquake and the volcanic eruption (63-79 AD) the cult of Isis was far more popular in Pompeii than the original Roman gods. Its worship had the support of many elite families, making it politically important. Certainly, Isis worshippers seemed to be very interested in political matters, and several painted electoral slogans were found on the temple's external walls when it was excavated.

'All the followers of Isis call for Gnaeus Helvius Sabinus as Aedile.'[19] 'His client Posidius Natalis and all the followers of Isis call for Cuspius Pansa as Aedile'[20]

The Isis temple is one of the most well preserved in the town, and the one which most clearly gives us a picture of its use. It is on a small site, against the city's Large Theatre and had only just been completely rebuilt after the earthquake when the eruption of Vesuvius destroyed the town. It was hidden from the street by a high wall with a large wooden door. It led into a small courtyard and the temple stood in the centre of this, with living quarters for the priests and a good-sized meeting room behind. The building was made of brick and stone with the outside walls stuccoed and painted over. The inner walls of the courtyard were also painted with frescoes. The whole area would have been bright with colour but was not intended for the gaze of passers-by. It also had a good-sized dining room and kitchen, along with sleeping spaces. Fifty-eight terracotta lamps were found in a storeroom at the back. The altar was outside in the courtyard and a smaller building opposite the temple contained a sunken pool. In theory, the initiates bathed themselves in water from the Nile.

Isis had an advantage over purely Roman gods in that her temple was not only opened on holy days. There were two services each day, one at dawn and another in the afternoon. At the morning ceremony the sun was honoured, to which the resurrection of Osiris was connected. The afternoon service was one of blessing and offering of the waters, as an essential part of life. Pictures show priests, white-robed, blessing the water with music and chanting and the burning of incense.

The kitchen at the rear of the temple held eggs and fish on the stove when it was excavated, along with a bowl of lentils which were presumably for the priest's meal. Behind the kitchen there was the skeleton of a man who had been trapped on a narrow staircase, and near to him lay an iron mace, with which he appeared to have tried to break through the wall of ashes collecting around him. Other priests had already left the temple and reached the Triungular Forum before they were crushed by falling columns. They were carrying a statue of the goddess, a sistrum and a silver plaque showing the holy rites. Ceremonial vessels, statuettes and a sack of coins were also found. The man who had been carrying the coins, presumably the temple bursar, had held onto them until the last moment.[21]

Bacchus

The European eighteenth-century Age of Enlightenment was closely engaged with the Classical world, not only through the Grand Tour for rich men's sons and the loot they brought home to embellish their galleries, but also through the ideas they absorbed. The cult of Bacchus was one likely to gain their attention, as it was neither gentle nor boring.

The Greek word 'entheus' means being possessed by a god – hence our own word 'enthusiasm' – and both possession and enthusiasm were prevalent in this deity's followers, said to have been enticed by debauchery.

Bacchus was known as 'the traveller god' and was often shown with wild animals, sometimes riding in a quadriga drawn by four tigers, sometimes actually riding on a tiger, and he was also said to have conquered Libya. The cult had suggestions of cross-dressing, homesexuality due to its men-only parties, and elements of unleashed passions, thoughts and the strange ideas which were expected in their communal gatherings. Women were allowed to take part in some of these, but that didn't sit well with

Roman ideals. Romans, with their Paterfamilial society, preferred their women well under control, safely at home, and not being allowed to indulge in drinking and all the excesses that intoxication produced. In the early Republic, a man technically had the right to kill a wife who drank wine, which led to licentiousness. Many a Roman man may have been licentious himself, but he did not expect to find it at home.

Rome already had a god of wine in Liber, and the growing new Bacchus cult was disliked by some men and by the authorities, not only for the possibility of Roman women drinking, but also for the free mixing of the sexes. Livy said of it: 'When they were heated with wine, and with the nightly liaisons of men and women, debaucheries of every kind commenced,'[22] always a worry. In 186 BC, the Senate banned the worship of Bacchus and this 'Senatus Consultum Bacchanalibus' said that unless you had a special reason, and specific permission from the Senate, a Bacchanalian festival could not be held on your property, nor could you build a shrine to him, he could not be worshipped either in public or in private, either within the city walls or out in the countryside.[23]

When members of the elite had begun to participate in the cult, information was put before the Senate by Publius Aebutius and his lover, the prostitute Hispala Faecenia. The Consuls Spurius Postumius Albinus and Quintus Marcius Philippus were informed of the type of meetings which were taking place and made their report to the Senate. The cult was of general concern because of the belief that it could pose some potential threat to Rome, and inspectors were appointed, rewards offered for information, and legal processes put in place in order to suppress it.

Livy made a great deal of the secret carryings-on, during which only the initiated could indulge themselves in the feasting and drinking, and in the 'coarsest excesses of most unnatural vices'. Young girls and youths were apparently being seduced, all modesty set aside, and 'every kind of vice found its full satisfaction.' Not only that, but poisonings and assassinations were said to be a by-product of the rites, and 'all protests were drowned out by the deafening sounds of drums and cymbals.'[24]

The priestess Paculia Annia was credited – or discredited – with having altered the original rites and also the frequency of the celebrations. She demanded that no man over the age of twenty years should undergo the ten-day initiation ceremony into the cult, as those below the age were thought most fit for seduction and all sensual pleasures. She also changed the original three celebrations per year into five days in every month, thereby in Livy's view 'holding gods and nature in contempt'. He also claimed that seven thousand cult leaders and their followers would ultimately be arrested and executed, with 'many committing suicide to avoid indictment ... there were far more executions than imprisonments.'

Rome was certainly concerned, wild orgies were not encouraged and any suggestion of a woman, or several women, having control over their impressionable young men was something to be eradicated. The organisational aspect of the rites was, however, the most frightening part to Roman society, who imagined that large numbers of their young men would be 'lost' to the cult, as well as the implication of a state within a state, which might undermine Rome's own authority.[25]

There was an element to the Bacchus worship which emphasised the importance of keeping on the deity's right side, of not offending him. He could be a good friend, but he could also be an implacable enemy. The presence of females at the meetings put them on a very different level of sexual immorality than mere drinking parties, and there was something of a moral panic among the authorities. The worship spread nevertheless, and later Roman generals became allied to the god in order to pursue their ambitions, and their involvement made it into what was almost an ancient form of freemasonry. Marc Antony issued a coin with Bacchus on its reverse, probably intended to suggest that he had the support of the god. However, his involvement with Cleopatra and his stance against Rome would have brought no credit to the cult – rather the reverse – and merely confirmed to respectable people the dangers of its membership. Even when drinking was encouraged, it was often used by Rome to keep conquered nations under control and in a subservient position, so they certainly did not want to see their own youths contaminated by addiction to it.[26]

As far away as Georgia, in Eastern Europe, a villa has been discovered with a magnificent mosaic floor in the triclinium or dining room, the central feature of which is of particularly exquisite workmanship and shows Bacchus surrounded by his followers. He was enormously popular in the middle east and was worshipped at Jerash in Jordan until the fourth century AD, in a magnificent temple complex devoted to him alone.

At Paphos in Cyprus there are four late Roman villas, all large and elaborate, named the Houses of Theseus, Dionysus, Orpheus and Aion. All have beautifully preserved mosaic floors, and the House of Theseus was probably the official residence of the Roman governor. It has an intricate mosaic of Theseus dated to 300 AD, while the House of Aion shows Hermes cradling the infant Bacchus on his lap, and the divinity of the young Bacchus is shown by him wearing a halo. Kneeling alongside are three figures said to be 'similar to the three wise men' who are adoring the young Bacchus, as the wise men would later adore the infant Christ.

Bacchus's worship had several of these similarities with the later Christ worship – he was fathered by a god (Zeus), he had a mortal mother (Semele), and miracles were attributed to him as well as to the later Christ. Both were killed (Bacchus by Titans) and both were later resurrected. On Cyprus the Bacchic followers were said to have hit back at what they believed was Christian 'copying' of their traditions by appropriating Christian symbolism in their turn.

Bacchus was considered to be a bringer of life after death and was known as the 'Saviour of Mankind' due to his sexual potency, while later followers of the Christ would use the same title in a spiritual sense only. Bacchus was also known as 'the true vine' far earlier than the Christian use of the same term, his appellations being merely transferred to the newer cult.[27]

Modern scholars tend to be rather sceptical about Livy's rather sensationalist descriptions of frenzied orgies, sexually violent initiation ceremonies for both sexes, and the allegations that the cult was merely a cover for conspiracies against the state. However, it is undeniable that the cult was frowned upon by the usually tolerant Romans, as the Senatus Consultum Bacchanalibus of 186 BC shows, although this was most likely a political rather than a religious decision, coming as it did after the Second Punic War, and appearing to be a reminder to any politician or populist that the Senate's collective authority superseded all others. Though the Senate's official response was tinged with a moral panic, so there was certainly something in it to cause alarm in the conservative elite.

It did survive, and the frescoes at the Villa of the Mysteries at Pompeii are presumed to show depictions of an initiation into the cult, so it apparently suffered no permanent damage and some elements of it are said to still be followed in Greece to the present day.[28]

Cybele or Magna Mater

The worship of the Phrygian mother goddess was adopted in Rome in 204 BC, towards the end of the Punic Wars. The struggle with Carthage had been long and difficult, and on consulting the Sibylline Books the Romans were told that the invader would be driven out of Italy if the goddess was taken to Rome. Ambassadors were sent to Cybele's sacred city of Pessinus, in Phrygia (Central Anatolia), to persuade the goddess to relocate.[29]

However, many Romans were surprised when she did arrive to find that instead of the goddess figure they were expecting, she was represented only by a large black stone! She would later be depicted in feminine form, but her arrival was not straightforward and the legend of it is connected to the important matter of female chastity.

A married woman named Claudia Quinta had been accused of unchastity and had declared her innocence. To prove herself to be innocent, after the ship carrying the Phrygian goddess had become stuck on a sandbar, she said that she would draw the ship up the river to Rome. She repeated this vow to the goddess and prayed for her help, then single-handedly managed to tow the ship free. This miracle proved not only that Claudia Quinta was innocent of the charge against her, but also that the goddess was willing to move into Rome and become the patron of the city. Shortly after her arrival, Rome had an excellent harvest for the first time in several years, and the Punic Wars were also brought to an end with the defeat of Hannibal. The miracles and the accompanying legends were the founding of the goddess's festival of the Megalensia.[30] The pageants of that festival, along with the story of Claudia Quinta, would later be used to promote the worship of the goddess as an upholder of traditional Roman values as well as an upholder of the status of Rome's ruling families.

In the Republican period, Cicero offered up Claudia Quinta's reputation for 'pudicitia', or sexual virtue, to accentuate the failings of the Clodius clan, which whom he was at odds. The Emperor Claudius would also later claim Claudia Quinta as an ancestress, and promoted the cult of her confirmed virtues alongside that of Magna Mater's own consort, the god Attis. Claudia had at least one public statue erected in her honour, in the vestibule of the temple of Magna Mater on the Palatine, and several plaques and reliefs show images of her pulling the goddess's ship to safety.

It is assumed that Attis arrived in Rome along with the goddess Cybele. He was a Phrygian god of crops and vegetation who, in Ovid's 'Metamorphoses' had transformed himself into a pine tree.[31] He may well have been less welcome to the Romans than his miracle working wife, as he brought with him the Galii, the eunuch priests of the foreign cult, and these men also came as a bit of a shock to Rome. They were described as shockingly effeminate, distinctly un-Roman, and seemed particularly obnoxious due to their habit of self-castration. They wore female garments and had a fashion for growing their hair long and dousing it, and themselves, with heavily scented ointments.

However, the worship of Magna Mater did spread, and her legend grew. The goddess was said to have been abandoned to die as a child, but instead of tearing her to pieces, the panthers and lions nurtured her. She would later often be depicted riding in a chariot drawn by four huge lions. She was also said to have invented several musical intruments along with magical medicines which were used to heal sick animals and children. She fell in love with Prince Attis, but he was then only a mortal, and her affection was too much for him to cope with, so he castrated himself and died of it. Cybele, driven mad by grief, roamed about, seeking her lost love, while Attis became associated with Dumuzi and Tammuz and other resurrected gods.

The cult was a noisy, tumultuous business, with priests castrating themselves in front of the statue of the goddess, not a ritual likely to appeal to Roman men. However, it still attracted many women, and only women and castrated males were allowed to attend the main celebrations in the goddess's honour. These quickly gained the reputation of being wild orgies, and there was a great deal of disapproval from Roman males about the indecency of the cult in general and its debauchery in particular. There appears to have been a specific law passed, in relation to the cult, which is known from the writing of Dionysius of Halicarnassus who stated, 'no native-born Roman walks through the city dressed in bright clothes, begging for alms, and accompanied by flute-players, nor does he worship the goddess with wild Phrygian ceremonies.'[32]

This legislation was probably a part of the acceptance of the cult in the second century BC, but even then, it was to be firmly controlled. The priests and priestesses of the cult were segragated and inaccessible to Roman citizens, and their public activities were confined either to the temple, or to a single procession, from which Roman citizens were excluded. Romans did, however, privately set up 'sodalities' or companionships in the goddess's honour, where the leading nobles would dine together.

No Roman citizen was permitted to join the priesthood of Cybele and this regulation may even have applied to their slaves, although it is doubtful whether the Roman male, always so conscious of his masculinity, would be happy to perform the necessary self-castration required.

These after-the-event regulations imply that the Romans had not been fully aware of what the worship of Cybele involved and had not considered its more undesirable elements before asking the goddess to move herself and her priesthood to Rome. It was only later that they realised that the cult was far too 'foreign' to ever really fit in with Roman ideas, and then they did their best to control it. However, under the platform of the temple, excavators have found a cache of simple terracotta images of the god Attis, which might suggest that his own cult had been started in Rome earlier than believed, and that he was being worshipped by some of the poorer people at that time.

Women often slept in the temple, hoping that the goddess would assist them in some way, and many went for healing to the priests who were known to be skilled in medicine. There were priestesses, but they mainly concentrated on the 'mystery' and ecstatic side of the cult, celebrating behind closed doors.

Festivals in the goddess's honour centred on the Megalensia on the 4th to the 10th of April, which involved the ceremony of the Taurobolium, which was the castration and sacrifice of a bull. Earlier, on 25 March was the commemoration of the castration and death of Attis, followed three days later by the Hilaria, when Attis had been resurrected as a god. This connection to the Easter resurrection of the later Christian religion, in which its tenets were copied from earlier eastern beliefs, is again discernible.[33] Eventually the cult diminished, as did so many of the 'mystery' cults, with the exception of the goddess Isis.

Elegabalus

Elegabalus or Elegabal was a Roman-Arabian sun god, initially venerated in Syria. The cult spread to other parts of the empire in the second century AD. The Emperor Marcus Aurelius Antoninus Augustus (r.218-222 AD) was originally the High Priest of the cult in Emesa in Syria, before his accession to the title of emperor in Rome. The foreign sun god would then become associated with the Roman Sol Invictus and a temple known as the Elegabalium was built on the eastern side of the Palatine Hill. This housed a holy stone from Emesa, which consisted of a conical black meteorite. Herodian recorded: 'This stone is worshipped as though it had been sent from heaven. On it are some projecting pieces and markings, that are pointed out, and which the people like to believe are a rough picture of the sun, because this is how they see them.'[34]

The new emperor could hardly have been personally more obscure, and his sudden appearance on the empire's throne was due entirely to the efforts of a woman. The Emperor Caracalla, who died in 217 AD and was the son of the Emperor Septimius Severus, had been hugely unpopular with the Roman people. He had arranged for the murder of his younger brother and co-ruler Geta (in December 211 AD) and despite ordering large public works in an effort to gain popularity, such as the Baths of Caracalla, he had shamelessly curried favour with the military and had ridden roughshod over the civilian population. He was assassinated in April 217 by a man working for Marcus Opellius Macrinus, who was to briefly replace Caracalla, but Macrinus would only reign for just over a year, along with his son and co-emperor Diadumenian. He was the first emperor of Rome to be of the Equestrian class and was also the first emperor never to visit Rome during his reign, due to dealing with conflicts in Parthia, Armenia and Dacia.

He did attempt to make some reforms intended to bring economic and political stability to the city, but while peace was achieved, the cost proved far too high and his fiscal reforms created a great deal of unrest in the military, which had always been his greatest support.

Caracalla's mother, Julia Domna (160-217 AD), had a sister still living, Julia Maesa (165-224 AD). She planned to overthrow Macrinus but briefly retired to Emesa where she came into contact with her grandson, Varius Avitus Bassianus, the high priest of the local sun god Elegabalus. This boy, then only fifteen years old, had a certain resemblance to the deceased Caracalla, and she decided to try to convince the soldiers of the local legion that he was actually his illegitimate son.

Caracalla's reputation of favouring the legions, along with large sums of money provided by Julia Domna, did the convincing, and was enough to have the boy priest proclaimed emperor of Rome. Macrinus bungled an attempt to nip the immature revolt in the bud and fled the field of battle, after which he was killed by a Centurion who had followed him to Asia Minor.[35] His son and co-ruler was later executed.

The boy from Syria then became Emperor of Rome to everyone's surprise except that of his grandmother. Unfortunately, he took his god with him when he travelled to Rome, and became known by the god's name, which he was to make notorious. Earlier Romans may well have found the Cybele religion too foreign for their taste, but Rome's later citizens found themselves with an emperor and a god that were to impose upon them a far more intolerable regime. There was no hope of regulations to limit the excesses of this new cult because its excesses were imposed from the highest level, and the new emperor would prove to be one of the most eccentric and erratic that Rome would ever have to endure. Despite the efforts of the staff inherited from Caracalla, nobody would be able to rein in the boy emperor Elegabalus or oppose in any way the religion he installed.

The palace faction would later be castigated as 'worthless sexual deviants' and the worship of the new god imposed on the Roman people would oust the Roman gods entirely. The new deity became 'Deus Sol Invictus', or god of the undefeated sun, and all other gods, however ancient and traditional, would be placed in subservience to him.

The new emperor, who habitually wore elaborate and costly priestly robes, was to lead dances around the cult's altar. He believed implicitly in Elegabalus and centred everything around him, while the behaviour at the celebrations in the god's honour was to exceed anything attributed to Cybele or Bacchus. Those cults had largely been private, but the new cult of Elegabalus was performed in public, where he demanded adoration, and his imposition on the people was deeply resented, even though regular distributions of food helped to keep the poorer people from rioting.

Considering himself not only the priest of a god, but a god personally, Elegabalus then decided to marry the Chief Vestal Virgin, Aquilia Severa, after divorcing his first wife. He said 'I did it in order that godlike children should spring from me, the high priest, and from her, the high

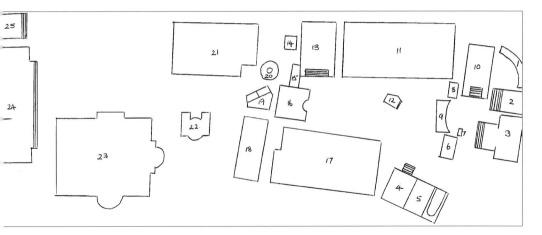

Plan of the Roman Forum

1. Dii Consentes
2. Temple of Vespasian
3. Temple of Concord
4. Curia
5. Secretarium Senati
6. Arch of Septimus Severus
7. Altar of Vulcan
8. Arch of Tiberius
9. Rostrum
10. Saturn
11. Basilica Julia
12. Lacus Curtius
13. Dioscuri
14. Juturna
15. Arch of Augustus
16. Temple of Caesar
17. Basilica Aemilia
18. Antoninus and Faustina
19. Regia
20. Temple of Vesta
21. Domus Vestae
22. Temple of Romulus
23. Maxentius and Constantine
24. Venus and Rome
25. Jupiter Stator

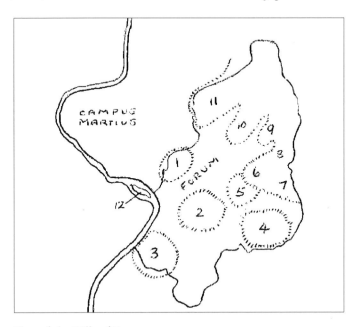

Plan of the Hills of Rome

1. Capitoline
2. Palatine
3. Aventine
4. Caelian
5. Velia
6. Fagutal
7. Oppius
8. Esquiline
9. Cispius
10. Viminal
11. Quirinal
12. Tiber Island

FORTUNA could bring good fortune or disaster. She is often depicted with a gubernaculum a (ship's rudder), a ball or Rota Fortunae (wheel of fortune, first mentioned by Cicero) and a cornucopia. (Inv. 2244, Braccio Nuovo, Museo Chiaramonti: Vatican Museums)

FORTUNA HUIUSCE DEI. This statue of Fortuna of the Present Day is the only one known to have been dedicated to this aspect of the Goddess. (Museo Centrale Montemartini)

Velian Hill in 1932

Above: VENUS AND ROME. This plan (dated 1932) shows the area of the largest temple, built by Hadrian. It was double, with two 'cella' areas back-to-back. Venus Felix faced east and Roma Aeterna faced west.

Right: FORUM OF CAESAR with remains of the Temple of Venus Genetrix.

FORUM OF AUGUSTUS
with remains of the Temple
of Mars Ultor (Mars the
Avenger) commemorating the
deaths of the final assassins
in retribution for the death of
Gaius Julius Caesar.

FORUM OF VESPASIAN.
This once held the Temple of
Peace on the wall of which
the carved map of Rome
hung. The holes in the wall
show its original position.
Now the property of Ss
Cosmo and Damiano.

THE PANTHEON. Built to house the statues of the senior Roman Gods. Just behind this was the Iseum/Serapeum.

THE CIPPI boundary stones of the Pomerium. This dates from the reign of Claudius and is on the Via Pellegrino.

THE WELL OF JUTURNA.
The sacred healing spring where
Romulus and Remus were said to
have watered their horses after the
Battle of Lake Regillus in 495 BC.

Above left: COLUMN FROM ISEUM/SERAPEUM showing Isis priests at their duties. (Vatican Museum)

Above right: VENUS AFTER HER BATH. (Altemps Museum)

Above left: VEILED JUNO said to be a Roman copy of the wooden version brought to Rome from Veii. (Altemps Museum)

Above right: DIANA WITH A HOUND as the Huntress Goddess. (Vatican Museum)

Right: GIRL FLUTE PLAYER. These musicians attended all festivals and sacrifices. (Altemps Museum)

MINERVA WITH HER SHIELD was known as The Aegis. Minerva was Goddess of defensive wars only. (Vatican Museum)

ROMANISED ANUBIS wearing a toga – indicating acceptance of the Egyptian Gods. (Vatican Museum)

SOBEK the Crocodile God representing the Nile. Found in the vicinity of the Iseum/Serapeum on the Campus Martius. (Vatican Museum)

Above right: ISIS WITH SISTRUM. Egypt's premier Goddess wearing Roman dress. (Capitoline Museum)

Above far right: ISIS suckling her son Horus, a powerful symbol of rebirth that was carried into the Ptolemaic period and later transferred to Rome. On the goddess's head is the throne hieroglyph that represents her name. She also wears a vulture head-covering reserved for queens and goddesses. Following ancient conventions for indicating childhood, Horus is naked and wears a single lock of hair on the right side of his head. The faience sculpture dates from c.330 BC. (Metropolitan Museum of Art, AN 55.121.5)

Right: APIS BULL from the Iseum/Serapeum, first century BC. (Altemps Museum)

DANCING LADIES
worshipping at the
Isis Temple for the
Navigidium Festival,
watched by the Apis Bull.
(Altemps Museum)

'LA VESTALE CLAUDIA QUINTA' by Hector Leroux, Paris Salon of 1877. It depicts Claudia Quinta towing the ship bringing the goddess Cybele to Rome in 204 BC. The Salon programme quoted Ovid: 'Injustement accusée d'impudicité, elle prouve son innocence en faisant, seule, entrer dans le Tibre le bateau qui porte la Mère des Dieux. (Ovide, Fastes, 1.IV)

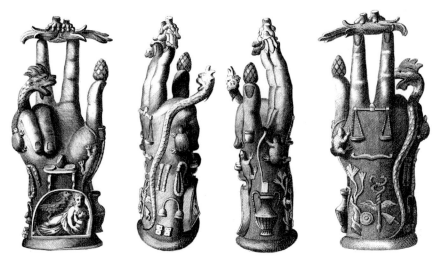

VOTIVE HAND OF SABAZIUS. These are still something of a mystery. There have been a number of archaeological finds of a bronze right hand in the *benedictio latina* gesture. The hand appears to have had ritual significance and may have been affixed to a sceptre. Although there are many variations, the hand of Sabazius is typically depicted with a pinecone on the thumb and with a serpent or pair of serpents encircling the wrist. See page 135.

Above: LARES from the Ludovici Collection. (Altemps Museum)

Right: AESCULEPIUS, God of Healing and Medicine. (Barracco Museum)

Above: MEDICAL VOTIVES of various body parts dedicated at the healing shrine. (Altemps Museum)

Below: FUNERARY PLAQUE showing Salii priest attended by his colleagues, as an honour for his years of service; second century BC. (Altemps Museum)

HEAD OF BACCHUS. God
of vines and winemaking.
(Barracco Museum)

MAGNA MATER (Cybele)
in a quadriga drawn by white
horses. (Barracco Museum)

Above left: BELLONA the Goddess of aggressive wars wearing her helmet. Found at her temple on the Circus Flaminius. (Barracco Museum)

Above right: MERCURY WITH CADUCEUS (Capitoline Museum)

Left: JUPITER OPTIMUS MAXIMUS, the chief of the Roman Gods, his temple dominated Rome from the Capitoline Hill. (Vatican Museum)

Above: TEMPLE OF HERCULES on the Forum Boarium. One of the earliest of Rome's sacred sites. Its shape represents the ancient Roman hut dwellings.

Right: FLORA, Goddess of Flowers, which were used at all festivals and ceremonies. (Altemps Museum)

Left: CORNU PLAYER from a sarcophagus in the Ludovici Collection. Second century AD. (Altemps Museum)

Below: ARA PACIS or Temple of Peace. Built by Augustus to celebrate the connections of the Imperial Family, inaugurated 9 BC. Portraits of the family and of Roma, Tellus, Anna Perenna and other deities. Originally on the northern outskirts of Rome, this temple has been reassembled at the Museum Ara Pacis alongside the Mausoleum of Augustus.

priestess.'[36] He had thoughtfully absolved her of her vows of chastity in order to provide him with these holy children, as he as High Priest had the power to do. The people of Rome were horrified at such sacrilege and Cassius Dio said that the emperor should have been scourged in the Forum, which was traditionally required of anyone who violated the person of a Vestal. The emperor was to do even worse, he removed the head of the statue of Jupiter Optimus Maximus and replaced it with a head presumed to be of Elegabalus, thereby turning Rome's most important temple over to the new god. He removed Vesta's sacred flame and also the sacred shields of the Salii, priests of Mars, adding them to the worship of his own god. This worship then became orgiastic and excessive in the extreme, although he continued to honour his mother and his aunt with the greatest deference, even allowing his mother (Julia Soaemias Bassiana) into the Senate and giving her a seat alongside the Consuls. She and Julia Maesa were depicted on the coinage and his three wives, during their short-lived marriages, appeared on coins also.[37]

He considered that Rome required a Senate of women as well as one of men, and set this up on the Quirinal Hill, although its only known achievement was the making of a complicated code of etiquette for women. He expected all Rome to respect his ideas and worship his god unquestioningly. Once yearly, the holy black stone was carried through the streets of Rome

> ... in a six-horse chariot ... pulled by horses huge and faultlessly white, and wearing costly ornaments, nobody held the reins of these horses, and nobody rode on them or in the chariot, as the vehicle was escorted as if the god was actually the charioteer. Elegabalus walked backwards in front of it, always facing the god, and holding the horses' reins. He made the full journey in this way, looking up into the face of his god.[38]

The Emperor Elegabalus naturally had no interest at all in the routine administration of state business. This was probably just as well, as he was unlikely to have been competent to deal with it. His talents were entirely in the areas of extravagance, and of sexual excesses, where he showed himself to be 'a homosexual pervert of quite abnormal delinquency' and was said to also have prostituted himself. Cassius Dio said of him that he 'performed such acts as I would be ashamed to describe' – but the 'Historia Augusta' did describe them all with avidity, particularly his favouring of several male courtiers who were his lovers.

The imperial household was riven by factions as the relationship between the emperor's mother Julia Soaemias and her sister Julia Mamaea grew more jealous and vindictive, while the clan matriarch, Julia Maesa, could do nothing to reconcile them. Eventually Julia Maesa realised that the emperor and his mother would have to be removed. Fortunately, she had another grandson, a son of Julia Mamaea, and that lady was delighted with the prospect of being an emperor's mother, rather than merely an emperor's aunt. She therefore also cheerfully threw away her reputation by claiming that her son, then known as Gessius Bassianus, was also a bastard of Caracalla, in order to improve his chances of obtaining the throne. Fortunately, this boy, then only eleven years old, was of a different disposition to Elegabalus and was becoming popular with the people and even more importantly, popular with the Praetorian Guards.[39]

It was desirable that the emperor adopt his cousin formally and he was persuaded to do so by the idea of having a relative who would be able to take over the state administration (with senatorial help), leaving him free to concentrate his energies on his god and his private life. The adoption went through – a youth of nineteen adopting a boy of eleven – and even the foolish Elegabalus saw some humour in it, saying 'I seem to have acquired a very large son.'[40]

Bassianus then became Marcus Aurelius Severus Alexander and Elegabalus began to realise belatedly that he had endangered himself and indeed, had signed his own death warrant. He ordered the Praetorian Guards to kill Severus Alexander at the beginning of 222 AD, but they killed Elegabalus instead, along with his mother Julia Soaemias, stripping their bodies and dragging them through the streets of Rome before dumping them both in the Tiber. The Senate then promptly confirmed the accession of the new Emperor Severus Alexander and banished the cult of the alien god back to Emesa, and the worship of Elegabalus in Rome ended violently. The temple of Jupiter Optimus Maximus was re-dedicated as Jupiter Ultor, or Jupiter the Avenger, and the intruder and his cult were obliterated. [41]

Mithras

He came originally from Persia, and the design of his sanctuaries evoked the Persian cave, where Mithras was believed to have killed the bull, which was always represented within the 'cave' sanctuary known as a 'Taurectony'.

Whether painted or presented as a piece of sculpture, the iconography is constant. Mithras kneels on an exhausted bull, holding up its head by the nostrils, and stabs it with his right hand. He looks backwards towards the god Sol, while a dog and a snake reach towards the blood flowing from the wound, and a scorpion attacks the bull's genitals. A raven is also present, either flying or settling itself on the bull. Two torch bearers, one either side, are dressed similarly to Mithras, the one with his torch pointing upwards is Cautes, representing the day, while the other is Cautopates who holds his torch pointing downward, and represents the night or decay. They oversaw the soul's entry and exit from life.[42]

This depiction is not derived from Persian beliefs, it is westernised. It makes much of the foreign origin of the cult, as if to suggest that its authority stemmed from outside of Rome's state religion. Mithras was said to have been born from a rock, sometimes as a child and sometimes fully grown. This miraculous birth was often accompanied by dogs, serpents, lions, dolphins or eagles and sometimes reliefs show the four elements.

One of the more characteristic of the images surrounding Mithras – although poorly understood – is a lion-headed male figure, entwined with serpents. This does not appear to be connected to the animal-headed gods of Egypt, and no exact parallel to the Mithraic leonine figure has been found. This figure has been seen at both Ostia and in Rome.[43]

Like all the eastern religions, there was a need for initiation to make a prospective member one of the official circle of worshippers, and all the mysteries of the religon were barred from outsiders. Only the initiates could commune with the god, thereby forming a closed and secret society. All of these religions promised a better life in the next world and so appealed primarily to the more oppressed sections of Roman society.

The male Senatorial class in Rome did not feature in cults such as that of Mithras before the fourth century AD, when their interest is first noted. No Senators were ever arrested for being involved closely with the cults of Isis, Mithras or Jupiter Dolicherus (who was for a time associated with Mithras and shared his aspect of bull sacrifice.) Later, senior army officials, members of the Equestrian class, and Senators, were certainly involved, although whereas the Isis cult had members among local elites, the Mithras worship remained strongly military, giving that god a more restricted appeal due to its 'male-only' aspect. Its usual locations were army camps, spread throughout the empire, even as far as Carrowburgh on Hadrian's Wall, where a shrine was founded in the third century BC and destroyed by the fourth century AD.[44]

The Romans realised that the cult was relatively young, compared to those of Egypt or Mesopotamia, but its elements of discipline and loyalty made it very attractive to soldiers. Tourists, including the Emperor Hadrian, often visited Egypt to marvel at rhe books of ancient wisdom there, and the temples of Egypt which held texts from the times of the Pharoahs, long before Rome existed. Translations of these were available for sale in Roman times, quite often inaccurate. However, for the Romans these visits were not done to learn from other and more ancient cultures, they were done in a spirit of superiority and the belief that all other cultures should be collected together for Rome's benefit and use, rather than having any intrinsic value of their own.[45]

The Mithraic cult was established in Rome by the second century AD and there is abundant evidence for its continued existence there until the second half of the third century. Up to forty of the sanctuaries for this deity have been identified in Rome, but they were generally out of the way of casual public observation, either within private houses or inside military camps. Likewise, in Ostia, the shrines were off the beaten track, and only two of the ones found were accessible directly from the street. This secrecy and exclusiveness was a fundamental part of its attraction for its members.

Romans still disliked the idea of secret societies just as their ancestors had, always fearing that they might be gathering places for conspirators. Augustus banned clubs of various kinds, due to the Bacchanalian connection to conspiracy, although he must have been fully aware that complete control of such groups was impossible to maintain. Burial clubs under the auspices of a deity were still permitted, as were meetings of a purely religious nature, such as the sodalities formed to worship Jupiter Dolichenus and Mithras, along with societies formed to worship the deceased members of the imperial family.[46]

The structural heirarchy of the Mithras cult with its parallels to army life could also correspond to the lives of slaves and the congregations of the cult appear to have a high proportion of Syrian names, as surviving lists of initiates show. In the cities, for example in Ostia, almost half of the followers of Mithras were slaves or ex-slaves. Some of these people were also associated with the temple of Jupiter Dolichenus on the Aventine.

Romans were predisposed to dislike not only the secrecy aspect of many foreign societies but were even more suspicious of the men who formed the priesthoods of the cults. Those long-haired, highly scented and effeminate men flew directly in the face of Rome's ideals of manhood. They raised questions of gender generally, and that made Roman males uncomfortable. That is not to say that there was no homosexuality in Rome, of course that was not the case, but the Roman male attempted to present the correct image to the world, whatever his private predelictions may have been. Mithras was different to so many of the foreign deities, which tended primarily to be attractive to women – Mithras was the epitome of masculinity, and also represented self-advancement and social mobility, which was desirable, with its promise of transformation in the lives of its worshippers, but in an acceptable form.

Membership of one of these cults did not exclude an individual from membership of others. It was perfectly possible to be a follower of

Mithras, yet at the same time be a member of an Isis temple, or some other eastern cult, and also take part in the normal flow of the Roman state religion at the same time.[47]

The association between Mithras and Jupiter Dolichenus emphasised this ability to share and spread worship, as Dolichenus was an oriental god of the universe and of the heavens. He represented safety and success, particularly in military matters, and was much respected by the army. Shrines to Jupiter in this form were found on the Esquiline and Aventine Hills, although the main cult centre was at Doliche and was sacked by the Persians in the mid-third century BC, after which the cult began to lose favour and support in its native area.

The bull sacrifice aspect of the cult and the Dolichenus worship is also reflected in the Taurobolium of the Cybele followers. From around 225 BC inscriptions refer to the blood of the sacrificial bull, and to the removed testicles, which were caught in a 'cenus' or bowl of several attached cups. This developed into a baptismal rite of blood, with initiates standing in a pit or trench, with slats place above them, onto which the sacrificial victim was led to be killed. Its blood would then pour down onto the people standing below. Many altars commemorating the Taurobolium (or Cribolium if a ram was used) have been found in nearly every Roman province, but especially in Africa, Italy and Gaul.[48]

These rituals were quite different to the process of initiation used in the Mithras cult, where there was a sequence of 'grades' to be accomplished, beginning with the 'Raven' which corresponded to Mercury, then onto 'Nymphus' corresponding to Venus. 'Soldier' was of course for Mars, while the 'Lion' grade represented Jupiter. 'Persian' was for the sun and sometimes called sun-runner, and finally 'Father' corresponded with Saturn. The first of these steps, the Raven, representing as the boundary between the outsiders and the initiates, was called thus as ravens were commonly believed to understand signs from the gods.

Rituals included an initiation banquet, to suggest the meal taken by Mithras after the Cosmic Bull was killed, whose flowing blood was the source of all life on Earth.[49] During the ceremony the Father pointed an arrow at the naked initiate, recalling Mithras firing an arrow at a stone. Another of the rites of the cult was the procession of the Helidromus, or sun runner, which mimicked the sun's journey through the equinoxes and symbolised the journey of the human soul.

Until the end of the fourth century AD, Senators would usually be members of the four priestly colleges of the state religion, but it was also possible for them to be priests of Hecate, Isis or Mithras at the same time. Associating themselves with such cults was a fourth-century innovation, part of the trend towards assimilating these foreign religions into the mainstream state religion of Rome. In any event, the priesthoods were not usually considered to be a full-time occupation in Rome, they would allow time for other duties. Although Hecate was never actually incorporated into the official religious calendar, it is apparent that some elite members wished the priests to be placed within the bounds of normal religious patronage.

In a sanctuary to Jupiter Dolichenus, which had included shrines to Isis and Serapis, there is an inscription stating that 'Apronianus, the civic treasurer, made this at his own expense.' A similar inscription from the same area says that the same man had also paid for statues of Isis and Serapis, so it is clear that it was possible to accept and overcome the differences between the cults, and to be able to support several.[50] Further evidence of this was found at the shrine of Mithras under the church of St. Prisca on the Aventine, which was excavated in 1934. There were representations there of the deities Serapis, Venus, Hecate, Fortuna, Dionysus, Aesculapius and even of Mars. Apparently, the Emperor Septimius Severus had permitted a member of the imperial family to convert the basement of the house, once on the site, into a Mithraeum, probably destroyed in the fifth century.

There are just two Italian tombstones now surviving which mention Mithras, and these are both commemorative of people of the highest level in the cult. It therefore appears that only at the highest level of the Mithraic grades did membership of the religion bestow any social identity on an individual.[51]

Despite the advance of such foreign religions, Rome's own state religion was not fossilised and its temples were largely kept in decent repair. They were continuing to be restored into the fourth century AD by the Prefect of the City, who had taken over the role of the Curator of Sacred Buildings from the earlier empire. In the mid-fourth century one such Prefect repaired the temple of Apollo, while another demolished the small houses that had over time sprung up at the Capitoline end of the Forum Romanum. Once that was done, it was possible to repair the Portico of the Dii Consentes. A little later, the emperor ordered that the temple of Isis at Portus near Ostia be restored, and at the same time it is known that the cult of Vesta in Rome was still alive and flourishing. The last Senatorial priests were attested in the 390s and the latest dedicatory inscriptions, which came from the sanctuary of the Magna Mater on the Vaticano, were in 390 AD. The last known Mithraic inscription from Rome was dated 391 AD. Despite the advances of Christianity, the old religions kept their hold, which was very tenacious.

A Pagan writer travelling from Rome in 402 AD reported having watched a rural Osiris festival, despite earlier imperial bans. A few years later, the old rites were actually resumed officially, during the siege of Rome by the Goths in 408/9 AD, showing clearly that confidence in the 'new' religion of Christianity was lacking for many people and that they did not have faith in its ability to protect them from dangerous enemies. Procopius of Caesarea confirmed that even in his own time, which was the mid-sixth century AD, the Etruscans were still known to be skilled diviners, and that their services as Augurs were still very much in demand.[52]

Sabazius

This deity was originally Phrygian, like the Great Mother Cybele, with whom there were connections, and he was also sometimes associated with Jupiter, having a temple dedicated to Jupiter Sabazius at Caperna, although no others are now known to have existed.[53] In Rome he was believed to be a nomadic deity, associated with horses and wielding a staff of power, sometimes being known as the 'horseman's god'.

The other item most closely associated with his magical or mysterious side was the votive hand. This was usually life-sized, although smaller ones have been found which would have been convenient to carry on the person as a charm. They were believed to have powers of healing and were often made of bronze. One of these was excavated at Tournai in the sixteenth or seventeenth century and is now in the British Museum.[54]

These strange hands, whose ritual meaning has never been fully explained, usually show a right hand, held up in an attitude of benediction. Sometimes a pine cone rests on the tip of the thumb, although on the miniature version it appears as the head of a snake, the body of which curls around the wrist, while another three-headed serpent extends over the back of the hand, and there is a turtle or ram's head in the palm. It is quite likely that the larger versions were intended to be attached to poles to allow them to be carried in processions.

When depicted as a man, Sabazius is a bearded and curly-haired deity, with a ram's head often shown under his foot, and he holds in his left hand a sceptre topped by another version of the hand. Serpents have always been closely connected to the cult, and represent the annual resurgence of nature, connecting the deity to fertility. Serpents in ancient times were a sign of renewal, due to their ability to shed their skins, and it has been suggested that snakes played a part in the cult's rituals, where they were presmably sacrificed.

At Pompeii, the Casa di Biria (Regio II, Insula I), was a place where the worship of Sabazius took place. The long peristyle garden held an altar and was certainly spacious enough to accommodate worshippers. The pillars on either side of the doorway displayed graffiti including the words 'antrum' or 'grotto', which were used by Virgil to describe the dwelling place of the Cumae Sibyl. There was an illustration of a naked priest performing what appears to be a ritual skipping dance while holding a tambourine. Two storerooms were found containing various cult objects, including two of the life-sized bronze hands, with the usual details of decoration. There were two unusual square terracotta vases, with a small bowl on the rim of each one, just above the handle. The house itself had fairly crudely painted pictures of the gods, high up on the sides of the entrance, showing Venus, Mercury, Bacchus and Priapus, with their accompanying symbols, and the walls of the rooms had paintings of baskets of fruit, animals and birds.[55]

There was an interesting head of a bearded male, also found within the house, which appears to be wearing an Egyptian-style headdress of the 'Nemes' type, which were usually made of striped and starched linen, covering the crown of the head and the back of the neck, often shown being worn by Pharoahs. The head is recorded as being of Jupiter/Ammon and is now in the Naples Archaeological Muaseum.[56]

One of the most interesting aspects of the House of the Sibyl is its connection to Pompeii's final weeks and months. Apparently, the City Fathers had become concerned about the rather obvious signs in the area, which suggested that the city was about to suffer another serious earthquake. The previous one in February of 62AD, of a magnitude between 5 and 6, had severely damaged the area and also its neighbour Herculaneum. It is not correct to assume that the people of Pompeii were not aware of the dangers, they were not stupid, and after having their city so badly damaged only sixteen years earlier they knew that problems such as earth tremors, cracked wall plaster, and the sudden breakage of water pipes might mean that there would be another natural disaster to be dealt with. Admittedly, the area had always been subject to sulphurous clouds, and the Fields of Fire outside the city were well known. People with breathing difficulties were often sent from Rome to breathe in the sulphur, which was also good for skin ailments. However, matters had taken a more worrying turn, with the fracturing of water pipes, deviation of flow of the waters into the city, and other signs which could not be ignored.

Questions were certainly raised, and it was decided to ask the local Sibyl, Biria Onomastia, if she knew of any reason for concern. She apparently reassured them, telling the enquirers that, on the contrary, she had had a vision, which showed her that the city would be popular throughout the known world, and would be visited by people from all nations, 'even more than a thousand years from now!' She emphasised that the city was perfectly safe from destruction such as it had suffered sixteen years previously. Satisfied by her assurances, the repair work continued, on the assumption tha the tremors, the jolting of the pavements, and the exodus of wild birds and other wild creatures from the area meant little, and that the land would eventually settle down.

Biria Onomastia was, of course, correct. However, 'the sight' never gives a full picture, and although the area is indeed one of the 'must-see' attractions in Italy and brings in visitors from all over the world, she was not forewarned that the Volcano Vesuvio would erupt, and that the resulting explosion would be catastrophic, or that she would be one of the many victims. Her home, along with the vast majority of Pompeii's buildings, has certainly become popular, and Sabazius did appear to reveal the future to his priestess, but unfortunately in not quite enough detail.

The most extraordinary aspect of the spread of so many 'foreign' gods in Rome was their acceptance by the people and eventually, for most of them, their eventual place as a part of Rome's state religion. This acceptance was sometimes accompanied by doubts of suitability or security, but most of these imported cults would go on to build shrines, attract worshippers, and live amicably with the other varied deities already in existence.

This multifaith attitude was widespread, and there appears to have been little conflict between most of the newer cults and the ones already established, so long as the state religion continued to be respected and the state itself was in no danger from sedition.

The variations of cults must have been quite entertaining to watch, with their colourful processions of priests and priestesses, their costumes, flowers and music. Rome had always been cosmopolitan and there was no difficulty in welcoming the newcomers, so long as they all eventually became Roman, and added to the lustre of Rome, with their loyalties intact.[57]

5

Emperor Worship

The concept of emperor worship began in Rome before there was an emperor to whom worship could be given – and long after the removal of the kings whose reigns had been divisive.

Rome had for centuries prided itself on its Republic, although even that depended very largely on a system of old ruling families continuing to govern, with only occasionally a man of lower birth being able to rise to prominence within the structure. The Romans detested the idea of one-man rule – the idea that, because of an accident of birth, any one man could take possession of the state and do as he wished with it. They despised the countries that still supported monarchies, taking pleasure in the idea that if a man in high office proved unworthy, he could be removed. It was always a 'he', as another thing that could not be tolerated was the idea of a female ruler. Queen Cleopatra of Egypt (Cleopatra VII Ptolemy) was not, to them, someone to be proud of, but a butt of salacious jokes and another opportunity to look down on foreigners for their curious lifestyles.

Rome did have some provision for the rule of one man, however, for in exceptional circumstances some exceptional men had held the position of Dictator. It was an office usually given for six months only, and the man appointed would choose a second-in-command who would be known as Master of Horse. During the time of his appointment a Dictator would have authority over all other officials and could not be prosecuted for any decisions taken. At the end of the six-month period, or at the end of the emergency which had necessitated his appointment, the Dictator would step down, after which the rule of Rome would again revert to the Senate and the Consuls.

Running for political office in Rome was never an egalitarian undertaking. A great deal of money was involved, for bribes and also for the banquets, games and other political ploys that electioneering entailed. Each level of the Cursus Honorum required expenses, to allow a man to consolidate his position at his present level and allow him to aspire to the next.

Occasionally, a man without the necessary 'background' i.e. the necessary high birth or political connections, did manage to breach the walls of that elite band. Gaius Marius did it, but he was possessed of great wealth and had enjoyed a resounding military career. He had also married a woman of high status, a Julia, the aunt of the man who would later begin the destruction of the very edifice upon which they all stood, the Republic. That man would be Gaius Julius Caesar.

Gaius Marius, that successful 'new' man, would go on to become Consul for a record seven times, despite determined opposition from the Patrician establishment, but his huge success rested on the firm base of his military capabilities and his great popularity with the people. He would eventually be superseded by Lucius Cornelius Sulla.[1]

The difficulties faced by Sulla were the opposite of those Gaius Marius had to contend with. While Marius had money but no high birth, Sulla was of the Patrician 'Cornelia' gens, but had no money. Despite early setbacks, he also proved to be an inspirational and capable leader of men, possessing great charisma which endeared him to his soldiers, who even lent him their own money on campaign to fill up his war chest when the Senate proved unwilling to bear the expenses. After returning to Rome, he was obliged to march on the city and defeat Marius and his army comprised largely of slaves, recruited due to promises of freedom if successful, and installed himself as Dictator.[2]

His would be a Dictatorship with a difference. Not for Sulla the restrictions of a six-month rule, he was aware that the problems in Rome would take far longer than that to solve, but he promised to step down when the situation was settled. To be fair to Sulla, often criticised by history, Gaius Marius had left Rome in a state that could not be put right in the short term. In his own time, Sulla was not without solid support, and he had been left without authority or funds on his eastern campaign, while chaos reigned in the Rome of Marius's final years. Sulla's proscriptions on his return were no worse than those of anyone else, notably Gaius Marius, Marcus Antonius, and Caesar himself, who killed unarmed Romans after Thapsus because of their support of Pompeius.

Where Sulla showed greater sense than Caesar was in laying down the Dictatorship when he considered his work was done. He had given Rome a series of laws, wide-ranging and sensible, which had strengthened the power of the Senate.[3] Gaius Julius Caesar was said to have remarked at the time that the retirement showed that Sulla did not know what he was doing, but Sulla was then able to have something like a normal life – albeit briefly – which Caesar would never even contemplate. Sulla had long suffered from a skin ailment which gave him constant pain, and he died at the age of sixty, probably from overuse of the alcohol to which he resorted.[4] Many of his decent and sensible laws were eradicated after his death, returning Rome to its usual merry-go-round with the eventual rise of Julius Caesar, who had a quite different agenda. Whereas Sulla had been rightly called 'The Last Republican',[5] Caesar had no such affinity with Republican sentiments. He believed implicitly in his own right to rule and would work, scheme and fight with that one aim in mind, to become the ruler of Rome – a king in all but name.

Sulla had considered the younger Caesar dangerous and he would be proved right, but Caesar had personal charisma, and many people were too blinded by his great military successes to see his other side. These personal charms and affability won him many friends (both men and women, for he gained a reputation as a notorious adulterer, whose soldiers sang songs about his prowess in the bedchamber with the wives of his colleagues).

These personal attractions covered the fact of his overriding ambition, he would sacrifice anyone in his determination to win powerful allies and achieve his ends. He arranged a marriage between his only daughter Julia and Gnaeus Pompeius Magnus solely because he needed Magnus's support at the time, having had to break off her previous betrothal. However, the alliance did not last, as Julia died in childbirth, and the partnership between her husband and father also dissolved. Caesar would still move onward and upward brushing aside all opposition and gradually reaching an unassailable position.

When he crossed the Rubicon River, to start his own march on Rome, he was reworking Sulla's earlier attempt at political power. Like Sulla, Caesar would make it work, but unlike Sulla he did not, and could not, promise to lay down the authority when his work was done. He knew that if he ended his Dictatorship his many enemies (who had grown tired of his arrogance and hauteur), would tear him to pieces. Not for Caesar the prospect of a retirement with family and friends, however short. He had to hold onto power by whatever means possible, using his military successes, extensions of his authority, and his own forceful personality, finally awarding himself the title of 'Dictator in Perpetuity', which made him almost a king.

When Caesar returned to Rome in August 45 BC, after having put down all major foreign insurrections and proved beyond all doubt the greatness of his military capabilities, the Senate voted him divine honours, and the month of his birth was renamed July. He was also 'offered' the title of Rex or king, which he officially refused, knowing that it would be a step too far and pointlessly alienate his followers; but he didn't need it, having all the power of the position without the crown.[6]

In Rome, opposition to his unprecedented position was becoming stronger. The indifference with which he began to treat the opinions of others had altered the feelings of the Patricians who should have been his greatest supporters. The soldiers and the common people still loved him, but they saw only one side of him, and what the Patricians saw they no longer liked.

Caesar had planned to leave Rome on 18 March 44 BC to lead his campaign against the Parthians. The atmosphere in Rome was tense in the extreme, and the soothsayer Spurinna, who came from Etruria and was highly regarded, with Cicero, Plutarch and Suetonius all later writing of his status, had tried to warn Caesar of impending danger.[7] Spurinna had said that he had found a bull without a heart during the performance of a sacrifice, and had told Caesar to 'beware of the next thirty days'. This was probably less a supernatural prediction than a shrewd reading of the rising heat of the political climate. Caesar should have been, and probably was, aware of the increased tensions, but chose to ignore them. He possibly believed that if he could return to Rome with yet another triumph to celebrate, things would cool down. Time was running out for him. By the Ides of March (the 15th), with him preparing to leave on campaign within three days, there would be a limited window to rid Rome of him permanently. His attendance at the Curia attached to the temple of Pompeius Magnus which topped his Theatre complex on the Campus Martius would provide the final opportunity, although it meant that the act would have to be a public one.

Caesar was seated and apparently poring over some paperwork when he was approached by a group of men, who appeared to intend to present a petition. He was seen to arrogantly wave them away, but one of them grabbed the neck of his toga and Caesar, surprised and affronted, tried to fend him off. Caesar's only weapon was the metal stylus with which he was writing, and he is known to have stabbed his assailant's arm with it, but it was no match for the knives of the many assassins who then clustered around him. Caesar was stabbed with twenty-three dagger thrusts, and was said to have uttered no cry, but only a groan at the first stroke. Some later related that when Marcus Brutus, the son of Caesar's long-term mistress Servilia Caepionis, rushed at him, Caesar had said in Greek 'You too, child?'[8]

As Caesar lay dying, although already beyond speech, he managed to pull a fold of his toga down to cover his thighs, to preserve his dignity. It was also said that he managed to drag another fold over his face, to prevent his killers seeing his expression as he lay powerless and bleeding to death.[9]

The men who actually attacked Caesar were barely half of the total number of Senators who had previous knowledge of the assassination plot. More than sixty men were estimated to have been involved in the conspiracy, and they were adamant that Caesar had effectively signed his own death warrant by ignoring the traditions of the state, and by wielding almost royal power.

The assassins and their supporters would, however, be surprised and dismayed at the backlash which followed the killing. Far from being acclaimed as liberators, as they had presumably expected, they found themselves facing opprobrium and having to hide in a city torn apart by public grief. It was said that they had intended to speak from the rostra to explain their actions, but they found that impossible and instead retreated to the temple of Jupiter Optimus Maximus on the Capitol, in great danger of losing their own lives. At the funeral of the Dictator, Marc Antony further fuelled the anger of the people by his eulogy of Caesar, and the body was burned, not on the Campus Martius, as was intended, but in the Forum itself, by a hysterical crowd.[10]

Marc Antony, Caesar's Master of Horse, became acting head of state, having been chosen as Caesar's fifth Consular partner in the Dictator's continual run of Consulships. Marc Antony was Caesar's second cousin and might have expected to be able to replace him, but there was another contender for power, at that time unconsidered, in the person of Caesar's great-nephew, the eighteen-year-old Gaius Octavius. When Caesar's will was retrieved from the Vestals and read, Antony was to find that Octavius had been adopted by Caesar, becoming in the process not only Caesar's legal son and heir, but also changing his name to Gaius Julius Caesar Octavianus. This young man, although initially dismissed as a nonentity by Marc Antony, was eventually to prove to be a very clever and dangerous adversary.

Born a Plebeian, the son of Gaius Octavius and Caesar's niece Atia (daughter of Caesar's sister Julia and her husband Marcus Atius Balbus), the subsequent adoption in Caesar's will made him automatically a Patrician. It also made him responsible for providing Caesar's funeral games, which would become the 'Ludi Victoriae Caesaris' and would be held in Caesar's honour for ten days from 20 July. It was during the course of these Games that a comet appeared in the daytime sky, which remained clearly visible for several days. This 'Stella Critina', or comet of

Caesar, was one of the most famous of ancient times and is said to have shone brightly for seven days in a row.

Roman writers were amazed at the size and brilliance of this comet, and made detailed reports of its appearance, as did Korean astronomers also, whose earliest mention of it claimed that it had appeared in the western sky on 18 May 44 BC with a 'tail' 8-10 degrees long! Chinese astonomers would also report that its tail was 10-15 degrees long, and that it travelled northwards. Modern astonomers suggest that it had a parabolic orbit and could by now be 800 AU from the sun – the AU or astronomical unit is derived from the Earth's orbit, and the distance between the Earth and the Sun is only 1 AU.[11]

This 'Sidus Julium' or Julian Star was as visible as Venus on its journey across the sky, and may well have been the brightest daylight comet in history. In 44 BC it was hailed as being Caesar's spirit, flying home to its residence with the gods. Octavianus certainly welcomed the manifestation and used it as a propoganda tool, as an indication not only of Caesar's new divinity but also that the gods, including the new Divus Julius, were his supporters. When Octavianus eventually became Augustus, he issued a coin (19-18 BC) showing the comet. On the obverse is a Laureate head and the words 'Caesar Augustus' and on the reverse is the Star, with eight rays and its tail pointing upwards. The wording there is 'Divus Iuliu(s)', a reminder of the Julian dynasty's divine connections. The comet's official number is C/-43K1.[12]

The thirteen years from the murder of Julius Caesar to the Battle of Actium – which changed everything – were not easy. Rome's leadership had suffered fractures beyond repair, but it limped along under a Triumvirate consisting of Gaius Octavianus, Marcus Antonius, and Marcus Aemilius Lepidus. Initially, Antonius was very much the dominant partner, although around 37 BC this had mutated into a greater equality between him and Octavianus. The Triumvirate had reinstated the proscriptions and Antonius, in particular, showed himself to be the most enthusiastic in shedding blood, making the irreplaceable Cicero one of his victims. Cicero's scathing criticisms had made an enemy of Antonius, who had him tracked down and murdered on 7 December 43 BC. As Appian was to record...

Cicero was proscribed, along with his son, his brother, his brother's son and all his household and his friends ... the Centurion drew his head out of the litter and cut it off ... he also struck off the hand with which Cicero had written the speeches against Antony as a tyrant... Antony was delighted beyond measure and the head and hand of Cicero were suspended from the rostra in the Forum, where he had formerly made his public speeches.

It is said that even at his meals, Antony would place Cicero's head upon the table until he became satiated with the horrible sight.[13]

Brutus and Cassius had rallied some support in the east in order to challenge the Triumvirate and had recruited many of the troops that had once fought for Pompeius. They were soundly defeated by Octavianus and Antony in the summer of 42 BC at Philippi in northern Greece. Antony had covered himself in glory there, but Octavianus had taken to his tent with 'an illness' shortly after the action commenced, and escaped just before Brutus's troops overran his camp.

To be fair to Octavianus, he knew that he was useless as a fighter, although he was certainly brilliant as a political leader. As time progressed this knowledge was to result in the appointment of Marcus Vipsanius Agrippa, who was more than capable of taking over the fighting, while Octavianus did the thinking. Together they would make a team formidable enough to beat anyone. In 41 BC, Antony was to meet Queen Cleopatra and become her lover, taking his first steps towards his downfall. His passion for Cleopatra and his life with her in Alexandria appeared to be appalling and scandalous in every way to the Romans, and Octavianus cleverly played on the scandal, destroying Antony's credibility and creating an image of him as someone who would rule Rome as a foreign potentate, with the Egyptian Queen at his side, if given half a chance.[14]

Meanwhile, in Antony's absence, Octavianus had brought some order to Rome, assisted by Agrippa, who improved the water and sewage systems. Octavianus projected the image of himself that was to endure throughout his long life, that of the ideal Roman man, youthful, energetic, handsome, capable in every way and a good husband to the ideal Roman woman, Livia Drusilla. They were the very model of what Romans should be and a direct and deliberate contrast to the supposedly licentious lifestyle of Cleopatra and the presumably debauched one of Antony, whose residence in the east had ruined him completely in the eyes of Rome.

Octavianus had made a move to seize power by 32 BC, and the Triumvirate was scheduled to come to its end in 31 BC. Octavianus's move was in the Senate House, not on a battlefield and he had somehow obtained a copy of the will of Marc Antony (held by the Vestal Virgins in Rome), and he read it aloud to the astonished and disgusted Senators. It confirmed that Antony intended to move the capital to Alexandria, and that he intended to leave Rome to sink to a very secondary position. It was certainly the final straw for those who had watched Antony's growing dependence on, and unfortunate subservience to, the Egyptian Queen, and it led to the final showdown.

Antony and Cleopatra had intended to invade Italy in the summer of 31 BC, but Octavianus then showed his brilliance as a tactician by having Antony's supply lines cut, while Marcus Agrippa dominated the sea. Food ran out and disease began to spread and by September of 31 BC Antony's fleet was trapped on the Ambracian Gulf on the western coast of Greece. His army was camped on an unhealthy marsh near to Actium, while Octavianus watched their every move.

Their only salvation was to fight their way out. Antony did make a desperate bid to fight but was no match for Marcus Agrippa and while the Battle of Actium raged Cleopatra ordered her ships away. Antony saw her breaking free of the blockade, heading home for Alexandria. He followed her, leaving Octavianus master of the Roman world. Within a year Octavianus had entered Alexandria and Antony and Cleopatra both committed suicide to escape further humiliations. Octavianus was later to remark: 'The whole of Italy, unprompted, swore to obey my commands, and asked me to be their leader in the war that I won at Actium.'[15]

Octavianus returned to Rome in 28 BC and the general expectation was that he would consolidate his role as a Dictator. However, he renounced those powers, on the Ides of January 27 BC. The alarmed Senate immediately urged him to at least remain as Consul, to which he – with a becoming show of reluctance – agreed, and he was then named 'Augustus' as he described in his 'Res Gestae':

In my sixth and seventh Consulships, after I had extinguished civil war, and by universal consent had power over all things, I transferred the Republic from my power to the control of the Senate and People of Rome. For this meritorious service, I was named 'Augustus' by the Senator's decree and the door posts of my house were publicly wreathed in laurel, and a civic crown (oak leaves) was fixed above my door. A golden shield, placed in the Curia Julia, was given to me by the Senate and People of Rome for my courage, my clemency, my justice and my piety, as stated on the inscriptions upon it. After that time I excelled in authority all other men, even though I had no greater power than the rest, who were my colleagues in the magistracy.[16]

Augustus certainly 'excelled in authority' all other men from that time, but it is not true that he had no greater power than the rest, or that he had transferred power back to the Senate and People of Rome. He clung onto absolute power and the Senators were fully aware who was now pulling the strings. He was the one who made the laws and could not be brought before any court, although he still claimed to be only the first among equals, or 'primus inter pares'. He had every right to be pleased with his successes, and also pleased with the new title of Augustus (illustrious one), and he would use careful restraint over his frightening powers – but the powers were still there, however carefully he used them.[17]

The comments of a contemporary, Velleius Paterculus, are worth reading:

> After twenty years the civil war was ended, foreign conflicts buried, peace recalled, the fury of arms stilled, the rule of law restored along with the authority of the courts and the majesty of the Senate... husbandry returned to the fields, respect to religion, security to mankind with each man safe in the possession of his property. Existing laws were usefully amended and new laws introduced, for the health of society. The Senate was reformed without harshness, but not without severity. The leading men – those who triumphed and held the highest positions, were urged on by the Princeps to ornament the city.[18]

The praise from Paterculus may have been rather fulsome (he was a partisan), but there must have been a general feeling of relief that the conflicts that had dragged on for far too long were finally ended. Paterculus also mentions the title 'Princeps', which was the title Augustus chose to be known by. Princeps Senatus had always referred to the most senior of the members of the Senate, but for Augustus it was to mean even more. He refused to be called 'Dictator' and no doubt thought that Princeps sounded rather milder, but it still gave him, effectively, all the power that Caesar had held.

The Republic was gone and could not be revived. The thirty-five-year-old Octavianus had become Augustus and was the true ruler of Rome. It was the culmination of the years since Caesar's murder, after which Octavianus had taken Caesar's name and declared that he was to be 'Divus Filius', or son of the god. He did not claim divinity for himself, and his achievements, although described in rather vainglorious terms in his 'Res Gestae', were indeed impressive.

The newly named Augustus was head of state, and he intended to rule with the help of Marcus Agrippa and Gaius Cilnius Maecenas, who were both friends of his without actually being friendly towards each other. Agrippa, the successful soldier, had been Consul in 37 BC and again (with Augustus) in 28 and 27 BC. Maecenas had never held public office and was a wealthy patron of the arts, so these men were total opposites and it would take Augustus's own implacable will to blend the two together.[19]

The Ara Pacis, or altar of peace, would be built after Augustus's campaigns in Gaul and Spain. It was commissioned by the Senate in 13 BC and completed four years later. It was originally positioned so that the shadow of the huge obelisk, then on the Campus Martius, would fall onto it on the date of Augustus's birthday. It was made entirely of white marble, which was originally painted in bright colours, and shows a procession of the Imperial Family which had taken place in 13 BC. All the members of the imperial family are identifiable, along with Marcus Agrippa who was then the heir apparent and the husband of Augustus's only daughter, Julia. The altar was intended to be used only once a year, for a sacrifice on the anniversary of its inauguration. This exquisite monument is now displayed in a specially commissioned building next to the newly opened Mausoleum of Augustus.

Caesar had sensibly refused the title of king, as did Augustus, but Augustus would eventually transform the old title of 'Imperator', used by soldiers on the field of battle to acclaim a successful general, into something very different. Augustus ruled an empire which would grow larger and more powerful still, with an imperial family at the top of the social pile, but his changes would also give new opportunities to Romans and also the Roman state religion. As well as the usual pantheon, some indigenous and some adopted, there would also be an Imperial cult, and temples would begin to be built to Augustan Fortune, or Augustan Concord, which connected the ruling family to the gods and eventually made them into deities also. What had started with Caesar's comet, the Stella Critina, the appearance of which had begun the cult of Julian divinity, would end with many of the emperors believing that they were gods even during their lives.

The inhabitants of any Roman town consisted of free-born, freed, and slaves. The ability to take any part in political matters was the distinguishing factor, as only free-born male Roman citizens could hold office. A freedman (freed slave), could vote in elections, own a businesss, and have resources, and could participate in the various religious cults, and he could even become a priest in the cult of the Emperor, the position of an 'Augustalis'.

Being an Augustalis was important, and free citizens and freed slaves were able to join the 'college' of priests involved in the worship of the Emperor. Freedmen, who were denied participation in any other public offices, were particularly eager to vie for the honour of becoming an Augustalis. These were appointed by a town's councillors and were obliged to pay a fee to the public purse. They then could demonstrate their loyalty to the emperor while increasing their own social status within their community. They could also receive honours given by their town, as in Pompeii where Gaius Calventius Quietus and Gaius Munatius Faustus both received honorific seats (known as 'bisella') for their use at public performances.[20]

Citizenship would depend on the status of one's mother. Any child born to a freed-woman was also born free, but a child born to a slave woman – even if the father was a free citizen or a freed slave – was still a slave. The male child of a freed-woman was able to aspire to high public office, but there are also examples of freedmen using their own free-born children to acquire political influence locally, something that would be denied to them personally.

Again, in Pompeii, we have already seen that the six-year-old son of the freedman Numerius Popidius Ampliatus was admitted to the town council, despite his tender years, when his father paid for the rebuilding of the temple of Isis after the earthquake of 63 AD. It would naturally be the father who benefited from the honour awarded to the son.[21]

Another example of the rise of freedmen and their families is the tomb of Publius Vesonius Phileros, which is outside Pompeii. The inscription on it records his free status, and that he was an Augustalis. The word 'Augustalis' had been inserted into the text after the original insciption was made, showing that he had gained the office later, and he proudly wanted it to be included. 'Publius Vesonius Phileros, freedman of a woman, Augustalis, built this monument for himself and his family while they were still alive, and for his patron Vesonia, daughter of Publius, and for his friend Marcus Orfellius Faustus.'[22]

This particular tomb is interesting, not only because the builder had included a friend alongside his family, but because he and that friend later fell out, and so a second inscription was added. There was a legal dispute between them, and the anger of Vesonius is still obvious:

> Stranger, if it is not too much trouble delay for a while and you will discover what you should avoid. This man, whom I thought was my friend, produced informers against me and a lawsuit was begun. I thank the Gods and my own innocence that I am free from all trouble, and I hope that neither the household Gods, nor the Gods of the Underworld, receive the man who lied about our dealings.[23]

Women could also be prominent in the Imperial cult, and in Pompeii the wealthy and well-known woman named Eumachia was a public priestess, which was another way of describing the role. She was married to Marcus Numistrius Fronto, and she built the large Eumachia building in the town's Forum out of her funds and dedicated it to Augustan Concord and Piety. Her statue shows her veiled, as a priestess, representing her own piety and womanly virtues. The inscription reads:

> Eumachia, daughter of Lucius, public priestess, in her own name and that of her son, Marcus Numistrius Fronto, built at her own expense

the chalcidium (porch), crypta (covered pasageway) and porticus, and dedicated them to Augustan Concord and Piety.[24]

Eumachia's tomb, outside the Nuceria Gate of the town, records that she built it for her family and herself at her own expense. Prominent people often had their tombs provided for them at public expense, or they might be built on donated public land. Given that Eumachia's status as a public priestess was so great, it seems strange that she paid for it herself. It is the largest outside Pompeii, consisting of a terrace, a seating area, and an enclosure to hold the burials. A frieze shows Amazons fighting and there were inscriptions for the deceased members of her household.

One public priestess at Pompeii who did have her impressive tomb built on land donated by the town council, was Mamia, whose services to the town are largely obliterated on her inscription, which was found in the Forum. It appears that she was responsible for the construction of some temple to the Genius (divine spirit) of something which is now unreadable. One suggested was that it had originally been on the other side of the Forum, close to the Eumachia building, and had been wrongly designated as a temple of Vespasian.[25] Her inscription reads: 'To Mamia, daughter of Publius, public priestess, a burial place was given by the decree of the town councillors.'[26]

One public honour bedstowed on Gaius Munatius Faustus was the bisellum, or seat, at the Theatre. When he died, he was buried in a simple tomb, built by himself, outside the Nuceria Gate. His wife Naevoleia Tyche inherited his property and business and then promptly built another tomb, intended for her own use and also for her freed slaves. This was larger and more expensive than that of her late husband. This altar-style tomb, outside the Herculaneum Gate, was inside a raised enclosure, with carvings showing her husband's ship and his bisellum, and with a heavily decorated inscription topped by her own portrait. Inside were several glass cremation urns, each with a lamp. The inscription reads:

Naevoleia Tyche, freed-woman of Lucius, set this up for herself and for Gaius Munatius Faustus, Augustalis and country dweller, to whom on account of his merits, the town councillors with the approval of the people decreed a bisellum. Naevoleia Tyche built this monument for her freedmen and freed-women and for those of Gaius Munatius Faustus, during her lifetime.[27]

The Augustales in the town were obviously a thriving group, and it has been suggested that Eumachia's own impressive building on the Forum may have been used by them for their meetings and their feasts. This is implied by the similarities with the Basilica of Herculaneum, which seems to have been connected to the Augustales in that town.

We do know from inscriptions that the Augustales were wealthy people and wealth was always necessary for anyone fulfilling a priestly office, as the position could prove a very expensive one to maintain. However, it was still a high honour and gave freedmen and freed-women recognition that they were proud of. The Imperial cult appears to have gradually become connected to other religious groups, particularly to those of Maia and of Mercury and to the Public Lares.

Although a state cult of the emperor still appeared to be generally unacceptable, there were many privately funded temples and shrines set up in sanctuaries and other prominent places, sacrifices dedicated to the living Augustus, and statues for other members of his family. Within these cults a social rise could be combined with showing one's personal loyalty to the emperor, but this respect was for a living being, and was not exactly the same as the worship given to a deity. Augustus would not be deified until his death in 14 AD, and Livia's political stability at that time depended heavily on the fact that she had been married to a man who became a god. She also found herself officially adopted by Augustus in his will dated 3 April 13 AD. This adoption meant that his wife suddenly also became his daughter, and her name was then changed from Livia Drusilla to Julia Augusta. She also found that she was then a priestess of the Imperial cult of the deified Augustus. This must have been accepted by her in a spirit of realpolitik, underpinned by a strong dose of cynicism. She had been married to Augustus for over fifty years and knew perfectly well that he was all too human. However, the continuance and extension of the Imperial cult required her to accept her late husband as a deity, for if he was divine then she also could become divine by association, although her own deification was not confirmed until the reign of her grandson, the Emperor Claudius.

This acceptance of her deceased husband's new status was matched by Livia's gift of one million sesterces, which was a reward given to the Senator Numerius Atticus, who had claimed that he had seen the new god, Augustus, actually ascending into heaven![28]

Gaius Julius Caesar had always claimed divine descent for the members of the gens Julia, from their supposed ancestress Venus Genetrix. He had built a temple to that goddess in the Forum Julia and Augustus had acknowledged the connection by putting busts of Livia Drusilla, and his own sister Octavia, alongside the statue of Venus there.

Augustus's own deification – apart from the award of divinity to Caesar, due in large part to the very convenient appearance of the Stella Critina, which the quick-thinking Augustus made political capital from –

was a totally un-Roman idea. It arose from the eastern customs of royal families, their final 'trump card' to set them apart from ordinary people, and also to give them an aura of sanctity which made them more secure and untouchable.[29]

As the eastern rulers had included their female relatives in the general family deification, so did Augustus, showing great honour to his wife and his sister during their lifetimes. Although no official deification came to Augustus and his relatives during their lives in Rome – that would have been altogether too much for Romans to accept at that time – in the east the situation was different. Livia was only in her thirties, accompanying Augustus to the eastern empire, when the Ionian city of Teos issued coins showing her as divine, after which event her personal cult gained momentum.

Ovid reported having received a gift from his friend Cotta Maximus, a silver statuette of Livia Drusilla showing that her face was by then already familiar enough and that respect given to the Imperial family was more open, and more inclined towards religious feeling, in areas abroad.

Cassius Dio related the situation immediately after the death of Augustus, when things had become very different. 'At that time, the Senate declared Augustus to be immortal, assigned to him sacred rites and priests to perform them, and appointed Livia … to be his priestess. They also authorised her to be attended by a Lictor whenever she exercised her sacred office.'[30]

Germanicus was given the role of Chief Priest of the new Augustan cult, and Livia had received another unprecedented honour, as the Lictor who was assigned to accompany her was used only by Magistrates and the Vestal Virgins, that small group of six very special women whose personal sanctity was the very lifeblood of the Roman state. Livia's Lictor would give her a status and prestige that no other Roman woman had ever been granted. Livia accepted her new role and along with her son Tiberius, the new Emperor, decided to build a temple to Augustus in Rome. Livia was fully aware of the benefits she would accrue from the divine honours given to Augustus, and that her own new position of 'Priestess and daughter' of Augustus (as she was called by Velleius Paterculus), would give her an honoured role in the Rome ruled by her son. She was to dedicate Augustus's image in her house on the Palatine, and she staged festivals in his honour.

Tiberius also benefited as he was the adopted son of Rome's new deity. This further connection between Livia and Tiberius did not make their personal relationship any easier, and in the years before Livia's death the Emperor Tiberius retired from Rome to spend most of his time in Capri. One of his explanations for the move was his desire to escape from his mother! Despite this friction, they both fully understood their mutual dependence. They could not know that their personal difficulties would fade into insignificance beside those of their successors.

Livia Drusilla was seventy-two when Augustus died, and the changes she was faced with were accepted and dealt with in accordance with her personal common-sense and stern moral outlook. Augustus's 'Ges Restae,' carved onto large bronze plaques, would list his version of the events and achievements of his life. By the end of her own life, Livia was a very wealthy woman and the owner of a great deal of valuable property – so much so that she could afford to leave in her will fifty million sesterces to the man who would be the future Emperor Galba.[31]

She died in 29 AD at the advanced age of eighty-five or eighty-six, and Tiberius did not see her at the end, remaining in Capri and pleading pressure of work. He sent Caligula to deliver the funeral oration before she joined Augustus in his Mausoleum on the Campus Martius. Tiberius vetoed the award of any divine honours for his mother, and also cancelled the fulfillment of her will.[32]

Robert Graves in his 1934 novel *I, Claudius* suggested that Caligula was at the deathbed of his grandmother and took pleasure in terrifying the old lady by telling her she would not become a goddess – she needed the promotion to protect her from punishment after death for all the evil acts she was supposed to have done during life. Unfortunately, Graves was therefore responsible for the destruction of her reputation, by making her accountable in the modern public mind for various murders and all kinds of evil deeds. There is no evidence that the real Livia Drusilla was anything like his fictional one, on the contrary she was revered as being the perfect wife for the great Augustus, and also as being the ideal Roman matron.

The 'Consolation to Livia' described her as 'one woman who has given so many benefits through her two offspring.'[33] The Senate wanted to create her 'Mother of her Country' while worshippers in a western province acclaimed her as 'Mother of the World'. There is no reason to place the guilt of assorted crimes upon her, as like the vast majority of Roman women at that time she was largely defined by her relationship with the men of her family. She certainly played her part in the successes of her husband, but she was subservient to him in a way that later, and more scandalous, empresses would have scorned. Augustus demanded complete control of all aspects of his sovereignty, along with complete personal loyalty from those close to him. However, he did not always reciprocate. He was perfectly capable of ruthlessness, so one must suppose that all events during his reign had at least his tacit approval.

Not until thirteen years later, in 42 AD, were Livia's full honours restored to her and her deification completed by her grandson Claudius. She was then officially named Diva Augusta and an elephant-drawn chariot would carry her image to all the public games. A statue of her was then also placed in the temple of Augustus, alongside his, and races were held in her honour. Women began to invoke her as a goddess, as she and her husband were finally reunited as deities together.

The Augustales who were originally formed to perform public services and acts of devotion on behalf of Augustus would continue after his death. There are records of the Sodales Flavii, and of Hadrianales, of Aeliani and of Antonini, but the Flamines Augustales were appointed during the lifetime of Augustus, which made them different. However, both Suetonius and Cassius Dio confirm that this 'during life' form of worship was confined to the provinces, as was the issue of coins bearing the head of Livia. It was not a practice in Rome actually to worship Augustus during his lifetime.

Many Romans believed that gods had all once been mortal and had only achieved immortality after the death of their physical bodies. This made the Caesar cult, formed after his funeral with the appearance of the Stella Critina as a heavenly focus, not too difficult for most people to accept. Likewise, with the cult of Augustus, its formation only after his death in 14 AD was acceptable.

Later emperors, particularly those whose grip on mental stability was a little shaky, tended to a different view on divinity. Livia's son by her first husband, Tiberius Claudius Nero, who became the Emperor Tiberius after the death of his stepfather Augustus, was known as 'Tristissimus Hominum', or the gloomiest of men. He appeared to have a good deal to be gloomy about, as the Imperial family had already begun to be chaotic. He had been obliged to divorce his wife Vipsania, of whom he was very fond, in order to marry Agrippa's widow Julia, who was Augustus's only child. Although this would give Tiberius that closer connection to the family, Julia already had a depressing reputation for promiscuity and would eventually be exiled by her father. The forced marriage brought Tiberius great unhappiness – it was said that he once saw his beloved Vipsania accidentally, and 'followed her with tears in his eyes and intense unhappiness on his face… precautions were then taken to ensure that he would never see her again.'[34]

Even though Tiberius had known Julia all his life and had been brought up with her as step-siblings, they had never been close, and their marriage was a sham. Tiberius's brother Drusus had died of a riding accident at the age of only twenty-nine, leaving their mother Livia more distraught than anyone had ever seen her. The death also greatly affected Augustus, and

Suetonius claimed 'He felt so deep a love for Drusus that, as he admitted to the Senate on one occasion, he considered him to be no less his heir than were Julia's sons (his grandsons), whom he had adopted.'[35]

After the death of Augustus, four Roman legions stationed on the Rhine and three on the Danube staged mutinies. Tiberius's son Drusus dealt with the Danubian mutiny swiftly, but the German one was more serious. Germanicus's men murdered several brutal centurions and there were demands that Germanicus should sieze power, which he refused, but the suggestion brought his leadership into question. At one point, he threatened suicide, drawing his sword, but a soldier then contemptuously drew his own sword and offered it to Germanicus, claiming it was sharper. Despite his lack of ability as a commander, Germanicus played a key role in the Imperial Julio-Claudian family, and he and his wife Julia Agrippa had nine children, six of whom survived. One of these children would become the Emperor Caligula while another would become mother of the Emperor Nero. Germanicus fell ill and died in Syria in 19 AD.

The rule of Tiberius became tyrannical and the emperor did not have Augustus's ability to draw people to him. He had a poor relationship with the Senate, whom he derided as 'men fit only to be slaves.'[36] The Imperial family became fractured and the only two heirs left were the teenaged sons of the deceased Germanicus, Nero and Drusus, although their mother, Agrippina the Elder, disliked Tiberius and held him responsible for the death of Germanicus her husband. Finally sick of the lot of them, Tiberius had her sons banished to the island where Augustus had once kept his wayward daughter Julia, and retired to his villa on Capri in disgust in 28 AD. That left Caligula.

Even though Tiberius had serious doubts about Caligula's fitness to rule, his accession was inevitable. In 37 AD Tiberius died and Rome fell into the hands of the new Emperor, Gaius Caligula. Oddly enough, he had seemed to be a breath of fresh air after the miserable rule of Tiberius. Caligula was initially greeted with great enthusiasm, but it was not to last. Caligula's formative years were spent with the sons of eastern rulers on Capri, and he very much liked their imperious behaviour, as well as their attitude towards women. He had an affair with at least one of his sisters, and possibly with all three, and was totally unsuited to being given absolute power.

He already believed firmly that he was a god – but a living one – and that his divinity gave him the right to do just as he liked. He enjoyed watching people being tortured on any pretext and liked to make sexual assaults on women at parties. He left Rome to campaign in the north, which was a fiasco, but made his soldiers collect seashells as proof of his victory over his fellow god, Neptune. He fully intended to make his favourite horse the famous Incitatus into a Senator, but the human Senators acted first, and while Caligula was watching a gladiatorial show a Tribune of the Imperial Guard stabbed him to death. It taught future emperors only one thing, which was always to keep on good terms with the Praetorian Guards. Petronius wrote of him with disgust: 'Up to this point I have written as if about a Princeps, everything else I write concerns a Monster.'[37] It must have all seemed a far cry from the sensible rule of Augustus.

The Guards who had killed Caligula knew that he would have to be replaced, but they wanted someone malleable. They decided on Caligula's uncle, Claudius, who was the son of Drusus and Agrippina. Augustus had banned him from appearing in public, and he was described as 'sickly in his body, so that his head and his hands shook slightly.'[38]

Claudius married four times, but two of those ladies were Messalina and Agrippina the Younger, so he was probably to be pitied. His other wives were Plautia Urgulanilla, whom he was obliged to divorce for adultery, and Aelia Paetina, who was also divorced. His full disabilities also included a club foot, and possibly cerebral palsy. However, he had a love of history, although very little political acumen. He had been regularly humiliated by the dreadful Caligula, but he succeeded better with the army and managed to invade Britain, which even Caesar had failed to do successfully. He also had the common sense to employ very efficient and well-educated freedmen as secretaries of state, to ensure the Empire's smooth running.

He was far less fortunate in his personal life and had no control at all over his third wife, Messalina, who once competed with a notorious whore to discover which of them could service the most men in one night. Even that behaviour he ignored, until she decided to marry herself to one Gaius Silius, a Senator who had ambitions to replace Claudius on the throne, not only in Messalina's bed. They were betrayed by a loyal freedman of Claudius's and were killed on the emperor's orders. He finally married his own niece, Agrippina the Younger, who was already the mother of Nero, who moved into the royal household with her. Claudius's own son and daughter stood no chance at all against their awful step-brother, just as Claudius stood no chance against his new wife. His son Britannicus was to die from poisoning, while Claudia Octavia was married to Nero. After her father's death and Nero's accession, the unfortunate girl was divorced, then falsely accused of adultery, found automatically guilty and ordered to commit suicide.

While Claudius was alive, his wife Agrippina was fast becoming her son's best teacher, for she was to kill her husband/uncle with poisoned mushrooms, in order to clear the way for Nero to become emperor.

Suetonius observed: 'Even if Nero was not the instigator of the Emperor Claudius's death, he was at least privy to it, as he openly admitted, for he afterwards used to laud mushrooms, the vehicle by which poison had been administered to Claudius as 'the food of the gods' as the Greek proverb has it.'[39]

As a food of the gods it had certainly sent Claudius to join his divine ancestors, and in 54 AD he was succeeded, as Agrippina had intended, by Nero, twenty-seven years old. The new emperor much preferred to leave the running of the Empire to others but resisted all attempts to control his private life. He believed that he was a great actor and musician, and also a great lover, combining his pleasure in the theatre with the pleasures of cutting a swathe through the women of the Senatorial class.

Nero considered himself to be on quite a different level to everyone else. Eventually tiring of his mother's interference, he decided to rid himself of her, and planned her murder. He arranged for her to visit him at the Bay of Naples, and while she was there he treated her with surprising consideration, but the boat he arranged for her to travel back in had been sabotaged. The stern, where she would sit, was designed to collapse. However, Agrippina proved to be a strong swimmer and did not drown. Nero then concocted a plan suggesting that she had tried to kill him, and sent a detachment of guards to put his mother to death by the sword in March of 59 AD.[40]

Meanwhile, he had tired of his wife, Claudia Octavia, the daughter of Claudius. He divorced her to replace her with Poppaea Sabina and then, apparently with Poppaea's connivance, he falsely accused Claudia of committing adultery. He demanded that she kill herself, and she obediently cut her wrists, but her death took too long for the impatient guards who had been sent as witnesses to confirm that she was dead. They apparently bound her, and cut her arms and legs, so that she would bleed out more quickly. She was only nineteen years old when her 'suicide' was forced on her on 8 June 62 AD.

Finally, the Empress Poppaea Sabina, Nero's second wife, also fell foul of his temper. She had an argument with her unloving husband in the year 65 AD, and he kicked her to death while she was pregnant. After the event he appeared remorseful and gave her a magnificent funeral. Ironically, her own mother, Poppaea Sabina the Elder, had also lost her life due to the aggression of one of the imperial family. Famed for her great beauty, she had become a victim of the Empress Messalina, the wife of Claudius. There were several versions of this story of greed and jealousy, one of which concerns a lovely pleasure garden called the Gardens of Lucullus, owned by Decimus Valerius Asiaticus. Messalina wanted to own the gardens, and accused Asiaticus of committing adultery with Poppaea, threatening them with imprisonment, and she harrassed them both so much and made their lives so miserable, that they suicided.

The more popular story is that Poppaea had become the mistress of the actor Mnester, who was very handsome. Messalina wanted him for herself, but he was in love with Poppaea, and refused the Empress. Messalina hounded him, to no avail, until she persuaded her husband Claudius to order Mnester to 'do her bidding in all things' which he finally did. He became the Empress's lover at her order and Poppaea Sabina killed herself in despair.

Mnester was also to die due to his connection to Messalina, as he was one of the reluctant witnesses to the idiotic marriage she contracted with Gaius Silius, and was arrested with the others. He pleaded with the Emperor Claudius that he had had nothing to do with any conspiracy, and had merely been obeying Messalina 'in all things' as Claudius had instructed him to do. However, his pleas fell on deaf ears and he was killed, along with the rest of the unfortunate wedding guests.[41]

Nero's great fire of Rome had taken place in 64 AD and even though Nero was not actually present at the time, he showed no particular interest in the burning of the city, nor in the welfare of the inhabitants, many of whom lost their lives, while others lost homes and businesses. The conflagration had started on the night of 19 July at merchants' shops close to the Circus Maximus and it spread rapidly. For Nero, it proved to be the perfect opportunity to use part of the subsequently cleared areas to build his magnificent Domus Aurea, or Golden House, the pleasure grounds of which would spread halfway across the city. The beauty and luxury of the palace would be unrivalled, although the homeless Romans would be less than impressed by its wonders, which were said to include walls adorned with gold and mother of pearl and ceilings that could shower guests with flowers or perfume, and which was surrounded by gardens including lakes and woods containing wild animals.

Nero would travel to Greece for the Olympic Games (which had to be re-scheduled to suit him), and while there he was awarded several prizes, returning home in triumph and expecting the Romans to rejoice and admire his successes. However, in his absence a serious conspiracy was being formed. The army was not as powerful as it had formerly been, but Nero had lost any control over it. Galba, the Governor of a Spanish province, was to declare himself Emperor. On 9 June 68 AD, the Praetorian Guard declared for Galba and Nero was officially deposed by the Senate. He fled the city, heading for the house of a freedman named Phaon, not realising that Phaon would betray him. Hearing the approach of soldiers, Nero stabbed himself, crying 'Oh, how great an artist dies in me!' He was then thirty-one years old.[42] Galba's accession would bring to an end almost a century of rule by the Julio-Claudian dynasty, which had derived from Augustus and Livia, but would not replace it with anything secure or lasting.

The vacuum, opened up by Nero's early death, was to create civil war rather than the hoped-for peace. Tacitus said of Galba, 'He seemed greater as a private citizen, when all would have agreed that he was capable of ruling ... if only he had not done so!'[43]

A series of short-lived emperors were to make Rome's situation worse, rather than better. Galba reigned from October 68 AD to January 69 AD. Otho who followed him reigned from January 69 AD to December 69 AD.

Vespasian would reign for ten years, (69-79 AD), and actually worked hard for Rome. He demolished Nero's extravagant Golden House and built the great Amphitheatre of the Colosseum where Nero's landscaped lake had been. He tried to emulate Augustus in the manner of his lifestyle and also in his method of ruling. When he died, however, he claimed something that Augustus had never actually done, divinity, by exclaiming 'I think I am becoming a god!'

All accounts agree that Vespasian's belief in horoscopes was profound. He did not fear murder plots, even though there had been several, because he knew that his sons would succeed him. He is said to have dreamed of a pair of scales bearing Claudius and Nero on one side and himself with Titus and Domitian on the other. This apparently became a true prophecy, as the two families were destined to rule Rome for equal lengths of time.[44]

Titus was graceful, dignified and good-looking, with winning ways which made him popular. His reign would be marked by the catastrophe of the eruption of Vesuvius and the destruction of Pompeii and Herculaneum. Titus would visit the stricken area twice, and he also spent large amounts of his personal fortune in attempting to help the survivors. Unfortunately for Rome, his reign was short, only two years (June 79-September 81 AD) and when he finally succumbed to a fever and died at the age of forty-two, he was genuinely mourned.

His successor, his brother Domitian, was far less likely to become popular. His imperial grandeur offended people; he demanded to be addressed as 'Master and God'. He pursued what he professed to believe were sex scandals, and one of his inquisitions resulted in two of the Vestal Virgins being buried alive, yet his own conduct was far from being beyond reproach. When he first became emperor, it was reported that he spent hours alone, catching flies and stabbing them with a needle-sharp stylus. When once asked whether there was anyone with the emperor, Vibius Crispus replied quickly 'Nobody – not even a fly!' Lucius Junius

Quintus Vibius Crispus was a Roman Senator, three times a Suffect Consul and a companion at the emperor's court, known for his wit and quick-thinking.[45]

Domitian would become known for his fondness for extravagant entertainments, for chariot races, mock battles, hunts of wild beasts and all kinds of gladiatorial shows, sometimes even with women taking part. He allowed the crowd to call for a combat between two pairs of gladiators, who were men from his own court, and who would be obliged to enter the arena still wearing their court finery. He took his self-divinity very seriously indeed, as when holding a festival in honour of Jupiter, which consisted of music, gynmastics and horsemanship, and was held every five years, when he would wear a gold crown engraved with the images of Juno, Jupiter and Minerva, while beside him would sit the Priest of the Deified Flavians and the Priest of the Capitoline Jupiter, both dressed alike, and also wearing gold crowns – but theirs would also be engraved with Domitian's image as a god. This was, of course, to emphasise that he was the equal of the Capitoline Triad. Not for him the usual courtesy of waiting for his death before apotheosis.

He did restore the temple on the Capitol Hill, which had again burned down, but would allow no names except his own to be engraved upon it. He cancelled the traditional grain dole and added two new teams of chariot drivers (purple and gold) to the existing four (red, white, green and blue), apparently equating the games with the people's need for free food. He forbade actors to perform on the public stage and yet allowed plays for his own entertainment in private. All castrations were strictly forbidden, which meant that the unfortunates still in the hands of the slave-dealers would be worth far more, but then prohibited any rise in their values. He started a campaign to improve public morals (ignoring his own shortcomings in that respect) and expelled one ex-Questor from the Senate because the man was overfond of acting and dancing. He forbade women of presumed bad character from inheriting legacies or using litters in the city, and he struck a knight from the jury-roll because he had divorced his wife for adultery, but then relented and taken her back.

He took a very dim view of any presumed (though unproven) lack of chastity within the Vestals, and decided on execution, although he reverted to the traditional punishment of them being buried alive. The Vestala Maxima, Cornelia, who had been acquitted at a first trial, was tried again and sentenced to be buried alive, while her supposed lover was clubbed to death in the Comitium.

Domitian's own cruel streak became apparent quickly, with the execution of a boy merely because he was a pupil of the actor Paris, and resembled him. The emperor put to death many Senators, some being accused of conspiracies, and others on trivial charges. One of these was Aelius Lamia, who lost his life over some harmless witticisms he had made at Domitian's expense. The emperor had decided on an entirely new form of questioning in such cases, which involved the scorching of the prisoner's genitals and the cutting off of people's hands. He once summoned a palace steward to dine with him, much to the man's delight, but had his victim crucified the following day.

His financial extravagance soon resulted in him running out of money, so he resorted to extortion. Any charge made against a person could result in a confiscation of that man's property, and he instigated a merciless tax on the members of the Jewish community, whether they still practised their religion or not. Suetonius wrote of this: 'As a boy, I remember once attending a crowded court, where the Imperial agent had a ninety-year-old man examined in public, to establish whether or not he was circumcised.'[46]

On his accession he had boasted to the Senate that he, personally, had conferred the imperial power on his predecessors Vespasian and Titus, and now had merely taken it back. On having divorced his wife Domitia Longina, and had then taken her back, he said that he had 'recalled her to my divine bed'. He was generally hated and feared. Finally, 'friend and favourite freedmen conspired to murder him, with the connivance of his wife Domitia.' He executed, on a trivial pretext, his own cousin Flavius Clemens. He lived in terror of assassination himself, and firmly believed that he knew the exact day and date of his own impending death.

During the final few months of his life, there had been many violent storms, and by midnight on the night before his due date of death he was so terrified that he jumped out of his bed. At dawn he condemned to death a German soothsayer who had told him that the lightning storms foretold a change of government. He then asked his freedman what the time was, and the man told him 'The sixth hour,' untruthfully, knowing that he feared the fifth hour. Domitian was greatly relieved, believing that the prophecy was proved wrong, and went to take a relaxing bath. Shortly afterwards, he was informed that an important messenger needed to see him, so believing himself to be then safe, he returned to his bedchamber and was killed there.

A boy attendant, who was in the room at the time attending to the household gods, later said that he had witnessed everything. He reported that on receiving the first blow, Domitian had called for a dagger that he kept beneath his pillow, but it had no blade and he found himself locked inside the room. He apparently struggled for his life for some time and attempted to grasp the attacker's dagger with lacerated fingers and even attempted to claw out the man's eyes, but he was killed at last. His body was carried away on a common litter by the public undertakers, as if he were a pauper. It was then cremated by his old nurse Phyllis, in her own garden, after which she took his ashes secretly to the temple of the Flavians, to be mixed with those of his niece Julia, daughter of his brother Titus. He had once been offered her in marriage, but had refused her, because of his then infatuation with Domitia Longina, and his niece had married another. However, when her husband died, Domitian had seduced her and 'demonstrated his love for her so openly and so ardently that she became pregnant by him. She was then to die as a result of an attempted abortion which he forced her to undergo.'[47]

The people of Rome showed clearly that they were quite indifferent to his death, but his troops wanted to avenge the man they called 'Domitian the God'. The Senators, long abused by him, had his votive statues and shields hurled down, decreed that all the inscriptions to him be defaced and that all records of his reign should be obliterated.

The Flavian dynasty ended and took its dreams of divinity with it. It heralded the succession of what would later be termed 'the five good emperors', which started with Trajan in 96 AD and ended with the death of Marcus Aurelius in 180 AD. Then the kakistocracy would begin again, with the accession of Commodus who assumed rule after the death of his father but could only maintain it for three years. During that time, he concentrated on his pleasures, leaving ruling to others, to Rome's deprivaton. Cassius Dio said of Commodus:

This man was not naturally evil, but he was as simple as any person who has ever lived. His stupidity, together with his cowardice, enslaved him to his companions, and it was through them, at first, that he missed out on the better life and was led into cruel and wasteful ways.[48]

Commodus's sister received many slights from him and plotted his assassination. His abject terror at the idea of such an outcome caused one Tigidius Perennis to insinuate himself into a posititon of trust with the emperor, and this man effectively ruled a Rome dominated by his brutality. Commodus's own debauchery foiled any attempts at sensible government and his arrogance and self-belief increased. Commodus considered that he was the god Hercules, and imagined himself to be a great gladiator, killing many men in the arena due to his unjust choice of weapons. After riots in the Circus Maximus, organised by his mistress Marcia and a man named Eclectus, a cubicularius (freedman personal attendant) with whom she was having a relationship, Marcia and Eclectus took over the government.

However, the end was then close, and in the autumn of 192 AD Commodus staged a display in the Amphitheatre where he – dressed as the god Hercules – slaughtered several handicapped people who were dressed as enemies of the gods. After this display of barbarity Marcia made her own attempt on his life, and poisoned him. When it seemed that he might actually recover from the resulting illness, she had the wrestler Narcissus strangle him.[49]

He was followed by Pertinax, an elderly ex-Consul who lasted all of two months before being murdered; then by Didius Julianus who did slightly better with a reign of three months. Then there was the reign of Septimius Severus, who arranged to be adopted back into the family of Marcus Aurelius, thereby connecting himself to authority and a claim that Commodus had been his brother. However, Severus preferred, perhaps sensibly, to stay out of Rome, and spent several years in the provinces. This was not appreciated either, as Cassius Dio was to relate:

> Severus said that he had acquired a great country (Mesopotamia), and had provided a bulwark for Syria, but the facts proclaim otherwise. It has been the cause of constant wars for us, and an enormous cause of expense. It yields very little, and it costs a very great deal and reaching out to people who are closer to the Medes and the Persians means that we are – in some ways – fighting their wars.[50]

The two sons of Severus, Caracalla and Geta, were rivals who hated each other, and although Severus on his deathbed in February 211 AD pleaded with them to 'live in harmony with each other, enrich the soldiers and despise everyone else,' it should have been obvious even to him that they could not work together. They even divided the palace between them, walling off the two halves. Geta, being the younger and less well connected, was at a disadvantage to Caracalla. He was summoned to a meeting by his brother in December 211 AD where he was murdered. The murder concluded with a general massacre, which was said to have claimed as many as 12,000 lives.

Caracalla nevertheless wanted acclaim. He spent time in the circus, driving a chariot and tried to show that he was in accord with the people. He conferred citizenship on all free-born men of the Empire in 212 AD by the 'Constitutio Antoniniana' but the old protections given by holding citizenship had long been eroded, and Cassius Dio cynically remarked that the 'Constitutio' was merely a device for collecting more taxes.

Caracalla never won over the Roman people, and even the lavish Baths of Caracalla, (completed in 216 AD) which could accommodate 1,600 bathers at one time, failed to gain him any popularity. In Alexandria in

215 AD, his response to insulting chants about the death of his brother led to another massacre, when he set his troops on the crowd. His attempts to align himself with earlier emperors and any kind of good government were all miserable failures.

In April of 217 AD, while viewing the ruins of Carrhae (in modern Turkey), he dismounted to relieve himself near to the temple of the goddess Luna. He was attacked there by one Marcus Oppellius Macrinus, a prefect of the Praetorian Guards, who ran him through with his sword.

After some discussion, Macrinus was then declared emperor, lasting in power from April 217 to June 218 AD, and only managed to hold onto power that long by bribing the military. He came up against Julia Maesa, the aunt of Caracalla, whose mother Julia Domna (wife of Septimius Severus) had recently died. Julia Maesa plotted against Macrinus in favour of her teenaged nephew Varius Avitus Bassianus, the chief priest of the Syrian god of the sun, Elegabal. Because there was a resemblance between this youth and the late emperor Caracalla, she claimed that Bassianus was actually Caracalla's son, and the army, already thoroughly sick of Macrinus, fought him. Macrinus fled the field but was pursued and beheaded.

The new emperor's formal name became Marcus Aurelius Antoninus, in an attempt to join him to memories of better times, but he so completely identified himself with his strange and alien god, that he was better known as Elegabalus. His reign from June 218 to March 222 AD did the Flavian dynasty no favours at all and he was only nineteen years old when he was killed, although it was considered that his reign of around four years had been quite long enough.

His installation of his god as the principal deity in the Pantheon, giving it the name of 'Deus Sol Invictus' or god of the undefeated sun and his leading of the dances around its altar, often wearing a woman's gown, along with his regular identification of himself as Venus, were disliked, but even more disliked was the fact that he declared that all the traditional Roman gods were from then on subservient to Elegabalus. (See pages 127–130.) 'Who could tolerate an emperor who indulged in unnatural lusts of every kind, when not even a beast of this sort would be tolerated?'[51] The emperor's eccentricities quickly became intolerable, and scandals of all kinds were repeated with horror. His marriage to the Chief Vestal Aquilia, after magnanimously freeing her from her vows, disgusted the Romans, who could not tolerate the violation of one of their most valuable religious beliefs. His household was equally chaotic, with the Emperor's mother, Julia Soaemias and her sister Julia Mamaea at odds with each other. Cassius Dio was to report that the emperor had said to Aurelius Zoticus, 'Don't call me Lord, for I am a Lady!' and also that Elegabalus had enquired of the doctors whether it was possible to have an incision made in order to create a vagina.[52]

To the Romans the young man to whom they apparently owed allegience was anathema, and even the clan matriarch, Julia Maesa, could do nothing to control his foolish impulses. Details of the end tend to be as confused as everything else about that reign, but it appears that the Praetorians killed both Julia Soaemias and her son the Emperor. Their bodies were stripped and violently abused in the Forum Romanum, and then dragged through the city and dumped into the Tiber – that general mark of extreme disrespect, denying any decent form of disposal.

The next heir was Severus Alexander, a son of Julia Mamaea, aged only eleven at his accession. His reign would also be short, in 235 AD both he and his mother would be murdered in a mutiny at Mainz, in Germany, led by a junior officer named Maximinus Thrax. He then declared himself to be the emperor, although he would never even set foot in Rome. So it went on, with the one blessing for Rome's exhausted population being that the religion imposed by Elegabalus died with him, and the Senate banished all mention of the alien god. Unfortunately for Rome, it would not be the last time that a Roman Emperor favoured a deity based on the worship of a Semitic mountain god.[53]

For later emperors it was clear that murder came as part of the package and the purity of purpose intended during the early part of the Empire was long gone. The religious aspect of the deified emperors also changed, from the useful and well-intentioned Augustales which had provided opportunities for freedmen and a concept of public service to the state, to the eventual line of deranged emperors who believed that they were gods by birth, many of these behaving in so extreme a manner that they could only be removed by violence. The Imperial cult had once acted as a focus of loyalty towards the emperor, but all Romans had an ambivalent attitutude towards the idea of any living man being revered as a god, and even Caesar's divine honours would have caused offence during his life.

The downward slide from the shining dream of Augustus after the victory at Actium eventually resulted in the mire of Elegabalus, and the infighting of so-called 'soldier' emperors resulting in the tearing apart of Rome, like dogs fighting over a bone. There were glimpses of light – Aurelian, Diocletian and Constantine would stem the tide for a while, but the rot had set in, the rewards were too great and the pickings too easy.

It had become clear that very few of the emperors had been worthy of worship after all.

6

Divination

When Spurinna, the soothsayer from Etruria, warned Caesar that he should be careful of himself, it was something that most Romans would have taken seriously. Spurinna was known to be a specialist in divination, and his success rate with prophecies had earned him great respect. The Etruscans, in general, were considered to have knowledge of such skills, so the well-known Spurinna was a man whose merest utterances would usually be heeded.

Caesar, however, was by that time gripped by such hubris that he probably believed no 'earthly' dangers could threaten him. His course was set and he intended to pursue it. He was also, at that time, most likely thinking ahead to the campaign he was due to start within days, and that once out of the city, he would leave all trivial problems behind him. He expected further military success and knew that he would be well protected by his devoted legions, and his position within Rome would be strengthened rather than otherwise.

Due to his wide-ranging concerns, both military and political, and to the enormous good fortune he had already enjoyed, he was less likely than most men to show submission to any changes of fortune. Everything could be dealt with, he had gained so much, and he clung to his belief in his own personal destiny. He had, however, trodden on a great many toes in his rise to prominence, and he had also assumed powers which many people did not think he was entitled to. While still having the loyalty of his legions and the approval and admiration of the common people, he was losing the support of many in the Senate, who resented his assumption of absolute power. The fiction of 'primus inter pares' or first among equals had long since withered, and the situation within Rome was far more dangerous for him than he had realised.

> Not only did he accept excessive honours, such as the life-Consulship, and a life-Dictatorship, a perpetual Censorship, the title 'Imperator' put before his name, and the title of 'Father of the Country' appended to it, also a statue standing among those of the ancient kings, and a raised couch placed in the Orchestra at the Theatre, but he took other honours which, as a mere mortal, he should have refused. These included a golden throne in the Senate House, and another on the Tribunal. He had a ceremonial litter for carrying his statue to the religious processions around the circus and he had temples, altars, and divine images. He also had a priest of his own cult, a new College of Lupercals to celebrate his divinity, and the renaming of the seventh month as July. Few, in fact, were the honours which he was not pleased to accept, or assume.[1]

Once, when a soothsayer reported that a sacrificial beast had been found to have no heart, a very unlucky omen indeed, Caesar said 'The omens will be more favourable when I wish them to be; meanwhile I am not surprised that a beast should lack a heart, which is the organ which inspires the finer feelings.'

His discourtesy towards the Senators included not rising to greet them, and on the occasion of the Latin Festival a member of the crowd put a laurel wreath bound with the white ribbon of the royal diadem on the head of his statue. When two Tribunes ordered its removal Caesar reprimanded and deposed them both, so from that day he was suspected of having tried to resume the kingship. This was exacerbated when, at the Lupercalia Festival, Marc Antony the Consul made several attempts to crown Caesar with a white ribbon (the original royal diadem). Caesar refused it and sent the crown away to the temple of Capitoline Jupiter. However, at the next meeting of the House, Lucius Cotta (a relative of Caesar's mother Aurelia), announced a decision of the 'Fifteen', the men who had charge of the Sibylline Books, which claimed that 'only a king can conquer the Parthians,' suggesting that the title be conferred upon Caesar for the forthcoming campaign.

In Rome, warnings abounded, quite apart from those of the soothsayers. Someone wrote on the pedestal of the statue of Lucius Brutus (the deposer of the last king of Rome), 'If only you were alive now!' On the pedestal of one of Caesar's own statues was the sentiment, 'Brutus was elected Consul when he sent the kings away, Caesar sent the Consuls packing, Caesar is our king today.'[2] (This was possibly originally translated from the Latin rather neatly in rhyme by Robert Graves in his *The Twelve Caesars*.)

Again, during a sacrifice the Augur Spurinna warned Caesar that danger threatened him and that it would not come to him later than the Ides of March. He did not actually tell Caesar to 'beware the Ides of March' but had certainly warned him of dangers threatening his safety for the thirty days ending with the Ides of March. On the day before the Ides (the fifteenth day), a little bird, known as the king bird, flew into the Hall of Pompeius Magnus on the Campus Martius, holding in its beak a small sprig of laurel. It was pursued by a swarm of different birds, which then tore it to pieces.

On the night before the Ides, it was reported that Caesar had dreamed that he was soaring above the clouds, and then shaking hands with Jupiter. Even more worrying, his wife Calpurnia reported that she too had dreamed – in her case that the gable ornament on their house, resembling those on temples which had been one of the honours given to Caesar, had fallen down and that Caesar lay stabbed in her arms. She then begged him not to attend the Hall of Pompeius on that day, but Caesar dismissed her fears.

He did not, however, set off for the meeting of the House until around 10am, when the Senate had been gathered for some time and was waiting for him. He had been persuaded to attend by Decimus Brutus, who argued that he should not disappoint the Senate.

As he went to the Campus Martius a man approached and pressed a warning note into his hand. Caesar did not read it, merely transferred it to his left hand, along with various petitions he had not yet read. Several victims were sacrificed on his arrival, but in each case the omens were not favourable, although Caesar disregarded this, stepping forward to enter the House with Spurinna watching him. It was reported that Caesar turned to Spurinna and said 'The Ides of March have come!' intending to deride the prophecy, but Spurinna replied sadly 'Yes, they have come, but they have not yet gone!'

When Caesar took his seat, Lucius Tullius Cimber approached him, apparently to offer a petition regarding the recall of his brother from exile. Caesar waved Cimber away in his usual impatient fashion and as described briefly earlier, Cimber angrily grabbed at the shoulder of Caesar's toga, pulling it down from his neck. Caesar then cried out in amazement 'Why – this is violence!' and a man named Servilius Casca stepped forward and stabbed him. This was immediately followed by others, all joining in. Caesar suffered twenty-three stab wounds and in the struggle some of the conspirators, eager to take a turn, stabbed each other. About sixty Senators had known about the plot, and Marcus

Antonius had been warned the previous evening, though while outside the House he had allowed himself to be drawn to one side, as if by someone wishing to speak with him, as Caesar entered the Hall.[3]

When Caesar finally fell to the ground, it was supposedly against the plinth supporting the statue of Gnaeus Pompeius Magnus, which had been re-erected within the Hall that he had built. A huge statue, purported to be the same one, is now in the gardens of the Palazzo Spade in Rome. When the victim fell to the ground, the watchers fled. Marc Antony, who had by then reappeared, prevented the body of Caesar being thrown into the Tiber as the usual mark of disrespect, and he would also prevent the family property from being confiscated.

Caesar had certainly had sufficient time to change the course of his day, and had had several of the types of warnings that, in his time, would and perhaps should have been taken seriously, such as the sacrifices showing bad omens, the flight of the birds into the hall, the dreams of both the victim and his wife and even the warnings of well-wishers, all of which were disregarded. It is now easy to say that Spurinna's warning, despite him being a famous Haruspex and diviner, was most likely based on sheer common sense. Anyone with some political awareness should have been able to see that the situation in Rome was becoming very unstable and that Caesar's attitude towards those with whom he had to work had become extremely arrogant, causing resentments. Because he refused to alter his day, it could be said that he walked into his own sacrifice as the 'willing victim' that the gods liked to accept.

All the portents at the time, signs, omens, prophecies, and the casual behaviour of birds and animals were all recognised signs of the will of the gods. The Romans were a very superstitious people and even the 'enlightened' and better educated among them would hardly be likely to ignore so many unpropitious omens all manifesting at the same time.

Caesar's neglect of these signs may have been his proud rejection of the beliefs of his fellow Romans, although his cry of surprise when he was attacked suggests that he had not considered that Lucius Tullius Cimber was likely to assault him, and that he was merely amazed at what he considered to be the man's presumption in daring to take hold of his clothing.

As a young man, Caesar had been made a priest, being appointed to the position of Flamen Dialis by Gaius Marius, during the civil war of 87/86 BC. The position of this senior Flaminate was a very important one but was so hedged around with taboos that few people would wish to suffer it for their lifetime. The appointment had been construed as an act of jealousy and spite. Gaius Marius, that famous old soldier, had married Caesar's paternal aunt. Marius was seeing his own powers fade as he aged, and although he would cling on to the bitter end, through more Consulships than anyone had ever had, he still did not want this promising young man ever to have the chance to eclipse his amazing successes. Marius's marriage had certainly advanced him socially, but his own abilities had given him his military reputation and his devoted admirers.[4]

When Marius was gone and Rome was in Sulla's hands, Caesar's mother Aurelia Cotta had enlisted the help of the Vestala Maxima to help her plead with Sulla for her son's release from the confining position which would always prevent him from being a military commander. Sulla had agreed to this, although reluctantly, with the remark about the young man, 'In him I see many Marius's!' It was hardly a compliment, as Marius had eventually torn Rome apart. Sulla was right in seeing the potential of Caesar, but he could also understand why Marius had thought it necessary to clip Caesar's wings.

The lifestyle restrictions of the position of Flamen Dialis – which also restricted the life of his wife, the Flaminia Dialis – were stultifying, and to a modern eye some were ridiculous. He was not allowed to touch iron, or to view a body recently dead. He could not spend more than one night at a time outside the city, he could not swear any oath, nor could he have any dealings with soldiers, could not have his hair cut except by a free citizen, touch goats, uncooked meat, ivy or beans, or eat any type of leavened bread. He could not have buckles on his shoes or boots and could use only bronze tools to shave with or have his fingernails trimmed. He had to be a Patrician, married to a Patrician woman, and their parents had to have been still living at the time of their marriage. It was a lifetime position and also a double one, for if the Flaminia died, then the Flamen would have to resign.

The life of the Flaminia was almost as restricted as that of her husband and her clothing, like his, was dyed woollen, with a cap of ivory topped by a pointed apex held on by a band of wool. They had to marry by the old-fashioned rite of Confarriatio, which was almost indissoluble, and the Flaminia was bound by the same restrictions but was also forbidden from having her fingernails cut on an unlucky day, or ever mounting stairs or a ladder of more than three steps, possibly to prevent her ankles being seen.[5]

Religious positions were usually held by prominent people in political life, with the exception of the Rex Sacrotum, and the Flamen Dialis, whose lives were defined by their position. Any priesthood was usually considered a social distinction, and also a useful political lever. Cicero was proud to be appointed an Augur, even though he had his doubts about religion in general, and about augury as a useful science. What it meant in real terms was that anyone who wanted to be anyone had to be prepared to at least pay lip service to the state religion.[6]

The late Republic and the early Empire had four chief colleges of priests, responsible for the religious life of the city and the performance of the official rites. There were sixteen Pontifices, along with sixteen Augurs, fifteen men known as 'sacris faciendis' (for conducting sacrifices) and ten Epulones, or organisers of feasts. These were a college of male priests, established in 196 BC, to take over the task of organising feasts from the Pontiffs. There had originally only been three, but Sulla had increased the number to seven and Caesar had increased it again to ten, although they continued to be named the 'Septemviri' Epulones, or seven feast-organisers. They arranged the feast of Jupiter, all public banquets and the feasts associated with various other festivals and games.[7]

The members of the priestly colleges were all of equal status, but the Pontifices and the Augurs were considered to be rather more distinguished than the others. All priesthoods could be held for life, once elected, and since there were only around sixty priesthoods of the major religions, and around two to four hundred public men vying for the honours of election, it was unusual for any man to hold more than one of them.

However, Julius Caesar did, when he was elected as Pontifex Maximus and also as an Augur. Strictly speaking, he then had three official priesthoods, as he had been freed from the role of Flamen Dialis, but no other man could hold it while he lived, so the rites and rituals had to be performed by the Pontiffs on his behalf.

Only the later emperors could be members of all of the colleges, as Augustus recorded in his 'Res Gestae'.[8] This could mean very long delays before any hopeful candidate could gain election, if he gained one at all. Cicero, who was Consul in 63 BC, had to wait a further ten years before he became an Augur, although Pliny the Younger congratulated himself on doing rather better, as he was a Consul in 100 AD and became an Augur in 103 AD.

In earlier times, the members of the four colleges had been co-opted, but this tended to produce a 'closed-shop' situation, with family members and close friends being honoured. In 103 BC, popular pressure eventually instituted a different system, whereby existing members put forward a number of nominees for vacant positions. The final decision would then be made by an assembly of seventeen out of Rome's thirty-five tribes, and a successful candidate would have to undergo the usual ceremonies to ensure the approval of the gods. This method was also used under the Empire, however the emperor might consider himself empowered to make the final selections, and these would then be agreed by the Senate.

The senior college was that of the Pontifices, the 'bridge-builders'. They were certainly involved in the sacred duties for the maintenance of the bridges, as well as having taken over responsibility for general control of the state religion. Over the years, a manual, the 'Commentaries of the Pontifices' had been compiled, and this was consulted on points of procedure. This manual could advise what to do if a sacrifice went wrong, or if the auguries were particularly ominous. The Pontifices had authority over the religious calendar and were ruled by the Pontifex Maximus, who was elected, not chosen from among the existing Pontifices. Originally, all the priests were required to be of Patrician birth, as with the Flamen Dialis and his Flaminia, but by 300 BC a Lex Ogulnia stipulated that half of the members of the College of Pontifices should be of Plebeian birth.

The Pontifex Maximus, as head of Rome's religious life, was also an advisor to the Magistrates on any religious matters. This position was probably originally an invention of the earliest part of the Republic, as the Rex Sacrorum (a title once held by the kings of Rome), had then been the chief priest.

When the monarchy was abolished with the founding of the Republic in 509 BC, the new rulers of Rome, the Senate, created a new priestly role, with a status superior to that of the Rex Sacrorum, and this position took the title of Pontifex Maximus. He was to be elected in order to reinforce the statesmanlike aspect of his office. He was to supervise all the members of the priestly colleges, the Pontifices, the Augurs, the Fetiales, and the minor priests, along with the Vestal Virgins.[9] In Republican times, he had occupied the Domus Publica which was shared with the Vestals, albeit with entirely separate accommodation. The official headquarters of the Pontifex Maximus was then the small Regia building in the Forum, which had altars within in, and the status of an official temple.[10]

The Flamines were the priests of certain named gods, with the three major ones representing Jupiter (the Flamen Dialis), Mars (the Flamen Martialis) and Quirinus (the Flamen Quirinalis). There were twelve minor Flaminates, of Flora, Pomona, Furrina, etc, but because they were more 'professional' and technical, being concerned with the worship of a particular god who was more obscure, these were not sought-after positions for men who were also engaged in a political career. Some of these Flaminates, including the strange restrictons which surrounded the life of the Flamen Dialis, show that these priesthoods were relics of Rome's ancient past, as was the Rex Sacrorum, or king of ceremonies.

During the monarchy the kings had held both temporal and spiritual power, and when they were gone the new Republican Magistrates took over most of the temporal powers, along with some of the spiritual ones. What was left over became the concern of the Rex Sacrorum who, nominally, took precedence at religious ceremonies, as a sign of respect for the antiquity of his position. However, in reality, most of his original functions had been delegated to the Pontifices, and by the late Republic his title was an honour but carried little real power.[11]

The 'Quindecimviri sacris faciendis' or Fifteen Men were the guards of the Sibylline Books and on rare occasions were required to consult them, if Rome was facing extreme danger or suffering from some other unusual problem. They were also responsible for 'translating' the mysterious verses into some form understandable to the general public, in order to give a lead in answering whatever problem had prompted the consultation. As this was not often done, they were also made responsible for the general supervision of the 'foreign' cults in Rome. They had the unusual task of washing the black stone, which represented the Phrygian goddess, Magna Mater, and this goddess, who had been brought to Rome at the height of the Punic Wars on the recommendation of the Sibylline Books, was always considered to be too different from Rome's own gods to be entirely trusted. For two centuries after the arrival of the black stone, it was treated with extreme care and suspicion, and apart from the Quindecimviri priests, no other Romans took any active part in the cult of the goddess.[12]

Astrology was always enormously popular in Rome, and it was quite usual to have a child's horoscope read shortly after birth to attempt to determine what sort of person the child would turn out to be, as well as learning about the main events of its life. Not everyone was a believer and Cicero, despite being an Augur himself and taking great pride in the fact that he had been elected to that honour, generally disbelieved in such things and in divination particularly. He went so far as to write a book about it, in which he attempted to disprove its claims.[13] Tacitus went down the same road, when he said that astrologers were 'a breed of men who betray the powerful and deceive the hopeful, and that although they were constantly being banned from Rome, they were equally constantly to be found there.'[14]

Yet, for the ordinary people of Rome, who did not converse with the intellectuals who had the leisure to ponder such questions and were able to scoff at the hopes and fears of the disadvantaged, the astrologers and seers of various kinds provided a needed reassurance that their lives might get better, at least a little easier, giving them hope. Almost every excavation in Italy unearths hundreds of amulets, charms, curses and so on, upon which someone had once pinned their faith.

However, not all intellectuals were opponents of astrology. The Stoic attitude was rather different to that of the practical Cicero, or the cynical Tacitus. Apuleius told of a young and innocent boy who could be put into a trance either by music or by the fumes of herbs, so that he 'forgets the present and returns to his own nature, which is immortal and divine, and so can, by a kind of instinct, foretell the future.'[15]

Astrology had spread from Babylon and from Egypt, and in its basic form was incompatible with the Roman state religion. This was because it held that fate predominated, and that all that could happen was determined by the heavenly bodies. Suetonius said that the Emperor Tiberius was 'careless about the gods and about religion, because he was addicted to astrology and believed that everything was pre-ordained.'[16]

Valens was similarly fatalistic:

It is impossible for any man, by prayer and sacrifices, to overcome what is fixed from the beginning, or to alter his tastes. What has been assigned to us will happen, without our praying for it, and what is not fated for us will not happen, however much we pray for it.[17]

Not everyone believed that things were so rigidly controlled. If the stars could control or foresee the events of the future, it was only because the gods chose it to be so. Divination, when official, was not disreputable and never became a matter of merely reading horoscopes. Its function was more serious and far more important, it concerned the well-being of Rome rather than the desires of individuals. It was intended to provide the answers to questions such as 'What does this tell us about the gods?' or 'What course of action would be approved of by the gods?' Because there were relatively few people qualified to find the answers to those questions, the Augurs and the other professionals were there to advise and explain, to interpret rather than to dictate. The rules were carefully formalised, and the questions and answers were designed to advise and benefit the state as a whole, in order to secure the co-operation of the gods.[18]

Two main types of signs, by which the gods could make their intentions known, were those which were deliberately requested before a course of action was to be taken, which were known as 'impetrativa', and those which were sent by the gods without being asked for, known as 'oblativa'. These could apply to private or public affairs, but the public side of the business is far better recorded.

Before any major decision was taken by the Magistrates, the approval of the gods had to be asked for. If two or three ranks of Magistrates were present, only the most senior could make the request. The usual signs from the heavens came, logically enough, from the flights of birds. This was known as 'auspicia' from which the word 'auspices' is derived. The officiating Magistrate would designate a part of the sky which he intended to watch, and he would take a seat in the open air to wait and see what passed by his field of vision. He would have a man nearby to record any sightings and there would usually be a member of the college present to help him to interpret the movements of the birds. Clouds would also be taken note of, and certainly lightning or thunder would be taken as an omen to be recorded. By the time of Augustus there was a good deal of literature available to help to interpret the meanings, even though the methods of the Augurs were supposed to remain secret. The books would give the traditional explanations, taking away the guesswork and making augury a well-organised science. The first Augurs had been created by King Numa Pompilius (715-673 BC) and even in 509 BC there were still only three, one for each of the tribes then in existence.

If lightning should appear to a Magistrate who was taking the Auspices before a public assembly it would mean that no meeting could be held that day, and all business would have to be suspended due to the inauspicious occurrence. However, this could also be open to human failings, and sometimes sheer abuse. In 59 BC, the Consul Bibulus was greatly at odds with his opposite number, the Consul Julius Caesar, and opposed the legislation which Caesar intended to have passed by the Senate. Bibulus announced that he intended to retire to 'watch the sky' (servare de caelo), which meant that all public business had to stop, and the measure that Caesar was trying to push through would have to wait. Bibulus made sure that his sky-watching lasted a very long time, so long in fact that he was successful in preventing Caesar from passing the legislation he wanted.[19] It was later said that if Bibulus looked hard enough for inauspicious lightning, then he would certainly eventually see it!

As lightning was the prerogative of Jupiter, it was the most important of all the signs. When a Magistrate settled himself down with his assistant and his secretary in order to 'see the lightning' on first taking office, he would invariably claim to have seen a flash of light in the sky on his left, as this was considered to be a fortunate omen. Of course, claiming to have seen a brief light in the sky was far easier to fabricate, when necessary, than a claim of having seen a flight of birds.

Thunder, also of course connected to Jupiter, was studied and a calendar survives which gives details of the significance of the various sounds to be alert for, and also the days of the year on which it might be expected. For example, thunder on 3 December could mean 'a shortage of fish will make people eat meat' or if thunder was heard on 19 August it could foretell that 'women or slaves will commit a murder.'[20]

Outside of Rome these ceremonies might have to take place without an Augur being present, although the various 'signs' in the sky, as well as the flight patterns of birds, their songs, the pitch intonation or frequency of their songs or movements, could become very complicated.

Livy considered that by his own time people had become negligent about their relationship with the gods. He made a point of carefully recording everything he heard about the signs and omens, although he did not attempt to interpret them. For the year 169 BC he recorded that 'at Anagria a torch was seen in the sky, and a cow spoke.' At Menturnae the sky had appeared to be on fire for a time. At Reate it had once rained stones. At Cumae the statue of Apollo wept real tears for three days and nights. In Rome a crested snake was seen within the temple of Fortuna Primigenia. A palm-tree had grown in the courtyard of the temple of Fortuna and it had rained what appeared to have been blood. A further omen, not officially recognised, claimed that at Fregellae a spear blazed with flames for over two hours without being consumed by it.[21]

Before the Battle of Pharsalus, the army of Pompeius Magnus saw many unfortunate omens. These terrified the troops and convinced them that their venture was likely to be a disaster. They claim to have seen thunderbolts, fireballs and meteors, and Lucan reported that the 'whole sky appeared to be setting itself against their march.' The standards, which were usually displayed standing upright, could not be pulled from the ground and were made so heavy by the amazing swarms of bees that had settled on them 'that the Aquilifers (standard bearers) could not lift them.' A bull that was intended for sacrifice in order to ask the help of the gods on that day kicked over the altar and ran off. As no replacement could quickly be found for it, the sacrifice could not be made. All of these portents put the troops into a very fearful frame of mind, and they would then have good reason to have no confidence in the coming battle. This proved to be the case, for despite having a far larger army at his command Pompeius Magnus was soundly defeated by Caesar on that day, 9 August 48 BC.[22]

The recognition that such natural signs and omens could be taken as approbation or warnings from the gods was so important that in Rome there were special sites dedicated to the art. The Auguraculum was a small roofless building, officially a temple, oriented to the cardinal points, in which augury could be practised. The portions of the sky to be watched were designated by stones marking out the ground. The building could be a small hut, but in Rome there were three permanent ones, on the Citadel, on the Palatine, and on the Quirinal Hill. Festus claimed that originally the Arx itself, the hill next to the Capitol, was used as an Auguraculum, as it faced east, which was considered to be on the Augur's left, lucky side.[23]

Any Magistrate serving as a military commander also took the Auspices daily, and part of the camp on a campaign would be made a Tabernaculum Augurale. This Augural tent would be the centre of religious and legal proceedings while the army was in camp. So important was this procedure considered to be, that when – in 99 BC – one Tiberius Claudius Centumalus built a house in Rome which obstructed a clear view from the Auguraculum, he was forced by the Magistrates to demolish it.[24]

Another form of omen to which great attention was paid was the chance remark, spoken by a person in innocence of its hidden meaning, yet which could give the answer to a problem. In 386 BC, after Rome had been sacked by the Gauls, the Magistrates discussed whether or not to move the capital elsewhere, in case the area of Rome had become an unlucky place. While the debate was still raging, a troop of soldiers marched into the marketplace, and was halted there by their commander with the shouted words 'Let us stop here!' His words were believed to have been divinely inspired and therefore the decision to stay where they were, in Rome, was made for them. They discussed it no more and proceeded to rebuild their city where it was.

Auguries depended heavily on the time of the year, the seasons, and so on, while disputes did certainly arise, and one of them was the famous one between Romulus and Remus, when they were decided where to build their city. Augury was decided on to solve the problem, and they separated, each with his own Augur, and when they returned to show their findings, Remus claimed he had seen six vultures in the sky, whereas Romulus claimed that he had seen twelve! Naturally, it was helpful if the watcher and his Augur were in accord.

A later development regarding the habits of birds was to study how and what they ate. Special chickens began to be kept for this purpose, and they were cared for by licensed chicken handlers. This was far more convenient on campaign when wild birds might not be available and presumably time was of the essence. To use these birds, a cage containing some of them would be opened, and pieces of bread or cake would be thrown in front of it. It was considered favourable if they rushed for the food and ate it eagerly, with crumbs falling from their beaks. An unluckier sign would be for the birds to refuse to leave their cage, or flap their wings and cackle, or even worse to try to fly away. However, even in its own time it was seen as an unreliable method, far too dependent on whether or not the birds were hungry, or relaxed, or had been stressed by a journey. In the First Punic War, when Appius Claudius Pulcher needed a speedy answer and the birds were proving uncooperative by refusing to eat, he threw them all into the Tiber, saying 'Then let them drink!' He had good reason for his temper, as the birds' refusal to assist had jeopardised the expedition on which he had been determined – which was later to prove disastrous for him.

Such omens and portents were watched for by most Romans, and many people genuinely believed that the gods made their will known by such signs. Modern readers might despise such beliefs, but how many will still walk around a ladder, rather than under it? How many, when seeing a single magpie, will not look around for its partner, in the hope of turning potential 'sorrow' into potential 'joy'?

Even Tacitus, usually the most sceptical of Roman writers, recounted that on the day that the Battle of Bedriacum took place, in 69 AD, a strange bird settled in a wood near to Regium Lepidum and would not be chased away. Otho, the defeated emperor, killed himself at the end of that battle, after which the mysterious bird had vanished. Tacitus remarked: 'It is undignified for an historian to presume to discredit the truth of this apparition.' He was equally convinced by the flock of ill-omened birds which darkened the sky when Vitellius contemplated fighting at Mevania a little later on.[25]

Few people were able to behave like the elder Marcellus, who was an Augur and always travelled on campaign in a litter with the blinds drawn, so that he did not have to see any signs; the very antithesis of circumspect. The majority of people would be keen to know and learn, or would at least be afraid to miss a warning of danger. Like Augustus, they would have been pleased and proud to hear that a dying oak had been revived as soon as the Emperor had set foot on the Isle of Capri.

As, however, it was often very difficult to understand what the gods were trying to tell mortals, if a sign was given unasked for to a Magistrate, it was up to him whether or not to take any notice of it. So possibly Marcellus was correct in not allowing his day to be troubled by extraneous signs about which he could probably do nothing, and it certainly made life easier. However, if such a sign revealed itself to an Augur, and he announced it 'nuntatio', then it would have to be respected and dealt with. If a sign revealed itself to a private citizen, he could report it to the Pontifices, who would be able to decide whether or not it was worth dealing with, after which it would become their responsibility, not his.

Certain signs were said to be often reported, such as talking cows or bloodied rain. These acquired conventional meanings that elicited a standard reply. The Pontifices would look at a previous occurrence and decide whether the action taken on that occasion would also serve in the present instance. If in doubt, they could then consult with the Augurs, but if the sign had never previously occurred, they might be in doubt how to respond. If the Augurs ruled that the gods were angry about something, how could they possibly be appeased if nobody knew what had caused their anger?

When ordinary measures failed, the last resort was the reading of the Sibylline Books. These oracles were kept in a stone chest, underground, beneath the temple of Jupiter on the Capitol Hill. When the temple was burned down and totally destroyed in 82 BC they were eventually replaced by a new collection garnered from Italy, Greece and the East. The newer books, written in Greek as verses, were re-copied and housed in two gold chests in the temple of Apollo on the Palatine, on the order of Augustus.

Like the Augurs and the Pontifices themselves, the College of Fifteen Men, the Quindecimviri, who alone had the right to consult them, were not actually priests but men in public life. Tacitus, surprisingly, was one of them and to be elected to that college was considered a social distinction. If instructed by the Senate, the Quindecimviri would see what the Sibylline Books had to say, although we are not sure of the actual process used. Were the leaves loose and one extracted at random? Whatever the official procedure used, the Sibylline Books were so highly regarded that their recommendations were generally followed.[26]

These books became responsible for the acceptance of several Greek religious cults, quite a far-sighted policy in fact, as the interest and excitement of something new could always distract the fearful citizens at times of crisis. They had been responsible for the adoption of the 'Lectisternium', which was the display of the statues of the gods, reclining on couches at feasts, as if present in person. For this, the Sibylline Books had been consulted in 400 BC after an amazingly severe winter during which the roads into the city were blocked by snow and the River Tiber froze over. That dreadful time was followed by an equally dreadful summer, which in contrast was hot, sticky and unbearable. At the same time Rome was engaged with one of the worst parts of the war against the people of Veii. When the books were consulted in despair, it was recommended that the correct relationship with the gods could only be restored by having them present on feast days. The huge prestige of the books and the total confidence in their predictions lasted throughout the Republican period.

In 56 BC, they declared that an army should not be sent to Egypt, and thus deprived Pompeius Magnus of the command he greatly desired. Later they would signify approval for Augustus to hold the Saecular Games in Rome, which were to commemorate a century – or Saeculum – in the life of Rome, in 17 BC.

That these prophecies and announcements could quite easily be manipulated to provide the answer most suited to the state's requirements did not escape the notice of the people. It did not, however, disturb them in the way a modern people might be disturbed, with real feelings of resentment towards their rulers at the connivance. For Romans, their religion was concerned far less with personal integrity than with what was right for Rome, and therefore connected to Rome's security and success. If the recommendations appeared to work in Rome's favour, then that was surely sufficient proof that it was correct.

Cicero had said that in private life no important step was taken without ascertaining the will of heaven,[27] but by the time of Augustus it was very doubtful whether most people were so punctilious, even if Augustus was. Before any long journey he would notice whether there had been heavy dew, for if so, it meant that the gods favoured the journey, and would allow him a safe return. For most people, the taking of the Auspices would gradually be restricted to the major occasions of life, for instance observing the flight of birds for a marriage. Catullus was to refer to Julia being married to Manlius Torquatus as being 'with the blessing of a bird'.[28] Other events of importance would be the coming of age of a son, and his donning of his first toga. The head of the family would be responsible for such an important occasion, for observing the omens and also interpreting them. Horace gives the impressions that this element of 'private' divination was quite widespread, but he explains his own feelings on the matter with cheerful cynicism:

> Whereas others attempt to predict the outcome of a journey by the hooting of an owl, the sight of a wild wolf running across a field from Lanuvium, or the appearance of a pregnant dove or fox, while others might be deterred by a snake crossing their path and frightening the horses, or by the flight of a woodpecker or a crow... I only have to look at the threatening waves to know the dangers that my mistress is running if she goes on this voyage.[29]

His common sense was commendable, but it could not be shared by everyone and for the most the exchange between the gods and their worshippers, even if conducted largely by mysterious signs and signals, was still a lot better than having no contact at all.

There was more to it, for a man could demonstrate the correctness of his own political stance by showing that he was acting in accordance with divine will. This was shown in the dispute between Cicero and Publius Clodius Pulcher in 56 BC, when Cicero, after a year of exile, had returned to Rome to find that his property had been taken over by the dreadful and vindictive Clodius, and had been dedicated to the gods. Cicero's subsequent restoration of his house was accompanied by strange noises and disturbances, which were attributed to the anger of the gods at the destruction of the shrine (ironically to Liberty), which Clodius had put on the site. Each man would defend his position vigorously and each believed that he was doing what was right. Both were calling on the gods to confirm their sacred contract, but the response was very vague, as might be expected.

The parade of one's 'association' with the gods on a personal level raised the question of just how close an association it could be, and for what amount of time. Magistracies and military commands could never be other than temporary and even a man awarded the all-important Triumph for his achievements was only dressed to represent Jupiter in his glory for the length of the celebration. The slave who rode behind him in the triumphal chariot constantly reminded him that he was 'only a mortal', even at the moment of his greatest importance. What then could be the connection for the ordinary man, anxiously watching the skies and perhaps hoping for good omens to brighten a difficult life, but needing an interpreter even for that?

Cicero reported that there had once been a decree passed to encourage the art of Haruspicy within the leading families of the Etruscan cities.[30] If this was indeed passed in the second century BC, there would be a revival of these necessary skills and Livy did record that Haruspices had an increasing importance at that time. The membership of the three most senior priestly colleges is well recorded for the late third and early second centuries BC, certainly better than for any other period during the Republic.

The important priesthoods were monopolised by the elite families, and even when quite young a nobleman could hold one of the priesthoods. Cicero noted that elite men could hold both high political offices alongside priesthoods. These would in any case be 'shared out' among the important families, diffusing the honours, powers and responsibilities throughout the group.[31]

Conflicts arose from time to time between the priests, or between priests and Magistrates. They turn on points of religious law, the priests usually resisting some practical proposal on the grounds that it was against established custom. For instance, the Pontifices in 222 BC prevented Marcus Claudius Marcellus from adding the cult of Virtus to an existing temple to Honos. This was on the grounds that each deity would need to have his own chapel, for in the event of a lightning strike, or some other manifestation, it would be impossible to know which deity was offended, and to whom sacrifices of appeasement should be made. The result was that Marcellus was obliged to build two chapels instead of one.

Despite the usual keen competition for priestly positions among the elite families, two of these important positions were difficult to fill. The restrictions on the life of anyone appointed as Flamen Dialis (see page

169) might well be expected to put anyone off wanting the position, and it had been vacant from 87 BC until Augustus, as Pontifex Maximus, had it filled in 11 BC. The accompanying restrictions on lifestyles had caused problems between the Flamines and the Pontifex Maximus more than a hundred years earlier, and Augustus made certain changes to the rules, or at least 'altered certain relics of a primitive antiquity to the modern spirit'.[32] We do not know the full details of these changes, but it appears that the Flamen was to be allowed to spend more time outside of the city, and there were changes regarding the restrictions on his wife, the Flaminia. In 22 AD, one Flamen Dialis argued that he should be allowed to go abroad to govern a province, although Tiberius argued against such a radical change. He did, however, agree to lift the ban on any other than a 'Conferreatio' marriage for the Flamen and Flaminia, and would ease further some of the restrictions on the Flaminia's lifestyle. The Emperor Domitian would go so far as to allow the Flamen Dialis to divorce his wife, without having to lose the position, thus breaking the ancient 'double' tradition of the priestly function.[33]

These changes had been very long in coming but could be instituted more easily when the emperor held the position of Pontifex Maximus, although debates over the restrictions on the Flamen Dialis had continued throughout the reign of Augustus. Appointment to any priesthood often depended upon the patronage of whichever emperor happened to be in power. Augustus – and later emperors – being members of all four of the priestly colleges, could and did influence the outcome of the priestly elections; in any case there would be no doubt in whose gift the office lay. In an early letter addressed to Trajan, Pliny explicitly asks the emperor for the gift of priesthood. He specified 'the office either of Augur or of Septemvir, both of which are now vacant.'[34]

A Septemvir was one of seven men appointed to execute commissions. They could perform either secular or religious services and were one of the most influential of the groups in Rome. The Septemvir Epulones were the men responsible for the preparing of the feasts held in honour of the gods.

The other important position which, over time, became more difficult to fill, was surprisingly that of the Vestal Virgins. On one occasion, when a Vestal Virgin died Augustus found that Senators were reluctant to offer their daughters (usually chosen between the ages of six and ten years). Suetonius claimed that Augustus had sworn that if any of his own granddaughters had been the right age, he would happily have offered them, but he increased the privileges of the Vestals, including giving them special seats at the Theatre, and they would later sit with the distinguished Imperial ladies.[35] It is not clear whether these small measures were enough to encourage the Senatorial families to give up their daughters, although things did improve under Tiberius, probably due to his offer of a grant of two million sesterces to any new Vestal, in addition to her usual salary. Tacitus claimed that under Tiberius two Senators vied with each other to have their daughters chosen as Vestals, and the office retained its high prestige throughout the third and into the fourth centuries AD.[36]

The importance of the position of Vestal Virgin had to be weighed carefully by any family. Although accusations of unchastity and subsequent executions may have been mercifully rare, they were not unknown, and the women concerned would bear the brunt of the resulting downfall and disgrace and their families with them, if the tide ever turned against the Domus Vestae. It hardly seems credible that Vestals, knowing the penalties, would behave foolishly with men as many times as they had been accused, so it is tempting to assume that they were largely innocent of the accusations and became scapegoats when things went wrong for Rome. It was a part of the position and had to be accepted as its downside along with the far more pleasant respect and enormous privileges they were given.

This was shown in 114-113 BC when the daughter of a Roman of Equestrian rank was struck by lightning while riding on horseback. She was found with her tongue sticking out and her dress pulled up to her waist. This was declared to be a 'prodigy' and was interpreted by the Etruscan Haruspices as an indication of a scandal involving the Vestals and the Knights. As a result of that 'explanation', in December 114 BC according to tradition three Vestal Virgins were tried for unchastity and one of them was sentenced to death. In a reaction against the acquittal of two of them, Sextus Peducaeus, a Tribune of 113 BC, carried through a Bill in the Popular Assembly in order to institute a new trial, this time with the jurors of the Equestrian rank and a specially appointed Prosecutor, the ex-Consul Lucius Cassius Longinus. This new trial resulted in the death penalty for the other two Vestals previously acquitted.[37] That these unfortunate women were perfectly innocent of the death of the daughter of the Equestrian was not relevant to the Romans. The gods spoke to mortals through such 'accidents of nature' and culprits had to be found, therefore the Vestals had to pay the price.

Some of the reports of consultations with the Haruspices make it clear that there was no actual 'college' in Rome until the end of the Republican period, and that Etruscan Haruspices were specifically summoned to Rome when needed, from Etruria, to give advice on 'prodigies'. These prodigies were events such as the death of the Equestrian's daughter that were considered to be in some way unnatural.

This use of Etruscans in the priestly function did not necessarily mean that the men themselves were foreigners, merely that they were trained in a skill that had been foreign. Although modern studies show that Etruria and Rome were close, to the Romans the religious traditions of the Etruscans were very different and seemed quite alien. For this reason, they were respected for the unusual power they represented.[38]

The Haruspices particularly used the interpretation of the signs given in the entrails of sacrificial animals, and most often used the liver for this. This would be carried out at almost all public sacrifices, whether in Rome or elsewhere. The entrails would be carefully examined as to their colour, markings, shape and also for the appearance of the gallbladder. There are many images of Haruspices performing these rites.

A bronze model of a liver was found at Piacenza in Italy in 1877 engraved with lines dividing it into forty-two sections. These probably related to the sky, with the name of the ruling deity written in Etruscan on each section. The example found is believed to date from the third century BC.[39]

The sacrifice of animals was the central ritual for most religious occasions. The victim would first be examined to establish its suitability for the offering, and precise rules controlled the type of animal, its age, sex, size and colour, all in relation to the occasion. If it did not pass this inspection, it would be rejected without hesitation. A manual was available to deal with procedures, and if the sacrificial animal proved in some way unsuitable its owner would be expected to take it back to its seller and find another that was hoped would be more acceptable. Nothing but a perfect specimen was good enough to be offered to the gods, whether that sacrifice concerned a pair of doves, a sheep, a goat, or a bull. It was also essential for the victim to appear to go to its death willingly and the perfect ending would be when the creature bent its head in submission to the god just before its death. To this end, the animals were generally drugged before the rites began, to make them more docile. However, the drugging of a large and recalcitrant animal is a very risky business as well as an inexact science. It was not unusual for the creature to struggle with its captors, or sometimes even to excape and run away. This is actually mentioned in the manual, so must have happened enough times for the response to such an event to be tackled officially.

Assuming that the victim was bought, cleaned, made attractive with flowers or gilding, and drugged sufficiently to make it tractable – but not so much that it fell asleep – there was then the procession to the altar, where prayers were said, and the divine recipient of the sacrifice was named. The creature would then be blessed and made sacred by the placing of a little wine and meal on its head. It was believed that this was the moment when the gods would miraculously transform the creature's entrails, to make them show either acceptance or rejection of the offering. Incidentally, if an animal should die, or even be stolen, before the scheduled sacrifice, it would count as if it had already been sacrificed and had been consecrated to the god.[40] If the sacrifice contained any errors, or went wrong in any way, it was considered inauspicious.

The victim could, if large, be stunned with a hammer first, but it was preferable for it to be killed by only one blow. Once it was dead, the liver was examined and if all appeared to be in order it would be considered to have been accepted by the deity involved, butchered, and then cooked and eaten.[41] However, if the entrails in any way indicated that the sacrifice was not acceptable, then more victims would be needed until the matter was clear and 'litatio' had been achieved, which meant that the sacrifice was accepted. The word 'litatio' represented not just the sacrifice itself, but also the successful completion of it and its acceptance by the deity. Even the butchering required a certain special knowledge, with a 'sacred' vocabulary for the various cuts of meat, in order to differentiate between what was offered to the god, and those parts which would later be offered to the worshippers. Mortals were forbidden to eat the parts intended for the gods, although the whole procedure was intended to reinforce the connection between mortals and their gods, as part of the worship – and acceptance of that worship – that formed the sacred contract.

During the Imperial period, a sacrifice was withheld from the gods following the death of the Emperor Trajan, as it was believed that the gods had not performed their part of the contracted bargain, which was to keep the emperor safe for a stipulated length of time. His death within that 'agreed' time had broken the contract and therefore the god did not deserve to enjoy the offering.

When some doubtful point arose, particularly in the interpretation of the entrails, whether it was a private or a public sacrifice, the Haruspex would be required to give his opinion. Of course, he would expect payment for this service, as would everyone else concerned with the ritual of the sacrifice, even if something caused it to be aborted. The Popa who used the stunning hammer and the cultrarius who used the knife to kill, were usually slaves or freedmen and were together known as the Victimarii. They and the flute player, an essential figure, would all require their fees, whether the sacrifice was considered to have been successful or not. If it was deemed unsuccessful, the sacrifice could become a rather costly and wasteful business, and certainly so if several victims had to be sacrified to achieve the desired result.[42]

There were a large number of what might be considered 'unofficial' Haruspices, and these were people who had picked up enough of the subject to be able to get by, without actually having the full training. Most of the emperors would do very little without having a Haruspex in attendance, although having one on the staff was not always enough. The Haruspex of the Emperor Vitellius (a man named Umbricius) warned him that there was a dangerous plot against him within the palace. He was rather slow with his prediction, for Vitellius was murdered that same day, without having time to do anything about the danger.[43]

While Haruspices were primarily concerned with the reading of the entrails of slaughtered animals, they were also often consulted on other matters, and could be asked to give advice on any kind of divine manifestations, such as earthquakes.

Many prominent people consulted them regularly, and the Tribune Gaius Sempronius Gracchus appears to have had a Haruspex in regular attendance, as a permanent part of his household. Almost two hundred years later, the Advocate and Senator Marcus Aquilius Regulus also regularly sought the advice of one of them, although the faith placed in them could sometimes be misplaced. Although well known, Marcus Aquilius Regulus was reprehensible in his dealings with other people. Pliny the Younger told a story about him coveting a large legacy which a rich and sick woman of his acquaintance was likely to leave. Regulus visited her and assured her that she was not likely to die in the near future, and that if she altered her will in his favour she would have plenty of time to change her mind. He backed this up by telling her that the conjunction of the stars at her birth proved that she would live many more years, and even had the Haruspex consult the entrails at a sacrifice that Regulus had specifically arranged. The reading of the entrails confirmed all that he had claimed regarding her supposed life span, so with relief the woman did change her Will in Regulus's favour. She was to die shortly afterwards, leaving him the inheritor of a substantial legacy. [44]

Juvenal, always rather cynical, also had several stories describing the gullibility of the public and how the fashionable people would flock to popular Haruspices for their advice. Opinions differed as to the benefits to be gained from listening to these men, and Cicero quoted a remark made by the Elder Cato, who had wondered how one Haruspex could look at another without laughing.

Lucius Junius Moderatus Columella (born in 16 AD) referred to 'the Haruspices and soothsayers who fleece the ignorant in return for idle superstitions.' Even more celebrated was the earlier retort of Hannibal, when King Prusias refused to allow him to begin a battle, because the entrails had seemed unfavourable. He asked the king sarcastically 'Do you place more faith in a slice of veal, that in an experienced general?'[45]

Such ridicule, however, did not impress everyone and the Haruspices would continue to be consulted so widely that the Emperor Tiberius was forced to attempt to regulate their profession by insisting that all consultations should be held in public, and before witnesses, to attempt to minimise the possibility of fraud.

Despite the obvious problems and the potential manipulation of the clients, the Haruspices and the soothsayers and all other people engaged in the practice of foretelling the future continued to have great support. The practice of divination by using the liver of an animal was defended by the philosopher Epicetus and remained one of the most widely used methods of private augury.[46]

There were other variations of divination:

Geomancy – the art of divining by means of the lines formed when earth was thrown onto a surface.

Aeromancy – the casting of sand or dirt into the wind and studying the shape of the resulting dust cloud.

Pyromancy – divination by fire, or by the signs derived from the flames.

Libanomancy – when incense was placed on the flames and their subsequent colour and shape was studied.

Hydromancy – the art of divining by water is not fully understood, although dark water was used for 'scrying' or using it as a crystal ball, to look into to see shapes or signs. Likewise, a mirror was often used, a highly polished metal surface, and this would include the use of a soldier's shield, which was known as 'Catoptromancy'.

Since the deity was assumed to be present at any such reading, he or she would convey the omen, although it may still have been the duty of a priest to be able to fully interpret it.

A very common type of prophecy was through dreams. Many civilisations have regarded them as being a means of communication with a higher power. Even in modern times there are many books which claim to interpret dreams, and pre-cognitive dreams have been authenticated, suggesting that the ancient belief in such matters may have some foundation.

The Elder Pliny, who was famously unimpressed by most of the divination methods, did believe that some dreams could have significance. He was to investigate a case of a soldier, who, having been bitten by a dog and suffering greatly from a resulting infection, was completely cured after a remedy was applied that had been suggested to him in a dream. In this dream, the man's mother appeared to him, to tell him of the correct remedy to use, although she was in Spain at the time.[47] Pliny was fascinated by such things and was a great collector of facts or anecdotes, always ready to record anything of interest that he came across. Most people were far less able to look objectively at unusual occurrences and were happy to continue to believe that all unusual phenomena came directly from the gods.

According to Suetonius, Julius Caesar had dreamed that he slept with his mother Aurelia Cotta and disturbed by this asked an interpreter for an opinion. Caesar was told that it meant that he would rule the world, for one's mother is the symbol of the earth itself. Cicero criticised the theory of dreams, as experience tells us that not all dreams come true. A Stoic might argue that not all of a dream can usually be remembered, therefore we are unable to interpret them correctly. Cicero dismissed this argument by asking why the gods, caring and benevolent as some were supposed to be, would not spell out clearly the answers for the dreamers. Most people have senseless and confusing dreams; perhaps only a wise man could dream in a clear and meaningful way? Neither side was completely wrong, for in antiquity if a certain type of dream was desired, a technique could teach people how to prepare themselves, with prayers, meditations and so on, in order to have the sort of dream they desired.

The Emperor Augustus at the Battle of Philippi in 42 BC had retired to his tent due to an illness. While he slept he had a dream that his camp was about to be overrun, so he left just in time, as his dream proved correct and his life was saved by it. From that time, he was known to pay great attention to such prophetic dreams. He was not the only Roman to feel that way, as dreams were taken very seriously by both Virgil and Livy, as well as by the general public.

Livy told of one Tiberius Latinius who had a dream in which Jupiter told him that he disapproved of a prelude-dancer who usually opened the Games, he also told Latinius that he should convey this disapproval to the Magistrates. Although Latinius was a devout believer in the gods, he was also a Plebeian and was afraid to approach the Consuls. He did nothing for some time about the strange dream but was reminded by the god through a series of untoward incidents that beset him. Latinius grew more and more afraid as he also began to suffer from fearsome nightmares, and he eventually decided that the regular incidents of his days, and the awful dreams of his nights, would need to be shared. He finally reported his recurring dream to the Senators, and to his astonishment those important men immediately believed his story. In order to appease Jupiter they ordered that the Games should be repeated, but without the presence of the offending prelude-dancer. After this was done, Latinius's life returned to normal, and his faith in the gods was fully confirmed. Livy's retelling of that story was recounted in all seriousness, and with every assumption of the credibility of the prophecies.[48]

Reliance on the foretelling power of dreams was widespread and even Suetonius is reputed to have attempted to put off a civil case, in which he and Pliny were involved, because he had had a bad dream about it.[49]

Lucretius (Tiberius Lucretius Corus 39-65 AD) attacked the idea that dreams were derived from any divine inspiration. Yet he had to return to the subject repeatedly owing to the strength of the superstitions surrounding them. The interpreters of dreams continued to enjoy a flourishing trade despite all his efforts. The main force of the anxiety over such things was, of course, the desire to have clearer communication between mortals and gods. It was obvious that the gods were difficult to approach or understand, yet all human success and happiness depended upon their goodwill and on their approval of human actions.

The Romans, in so many other ways a pragmatic and practical people, would not have gone to all the trouble they did if they did not believe that such rituals of appeasement could work. In their eyes they did everything they possibly could to earn the benevolence of the gods, and their prayers often state a claim to a god's goodwill, addressing the deity by name, as when Mopsus prayed to Apollo saying, 'Phoebus, if I have worshipped you and still worship you, then grant my request.'[50] This claim to the attention of the god is not usually based on any particular moral worth of the suppliant, but entirely on his devotion to the deity, his 'pietas'. It was this devotion, this regular worship, along with occasional sacrifices and the deep-down belief in that god's power and ability to assist if he or she chose, that mattered. The morality of the suppliant mattered not at all, his personal goodness or otherwise was irrelevant.

The Romans connected prayer and sacrifice in two different ways. Prayer was a straightforward request, accompanied by either an offering, or a promise of one. That is the form used in both Cato's and Augustus's prayer: 'Be favourable and propitious to me, to my house and to my household ... for all these causes be increased by the sacrifice of a sucking pig, a lamb and a calf.' It is the form that was followed on all ordinary family occasions, when prayers and sacrifices were offered either at mealtimes or at festivals. This type was offered as a free goodwill gesture, an offering of devotion to the deity concerned without any attempt to blackmail that deity into agreeing to anything.[51] It was a relationship based on trust and a giving of the best one had while relying on the god's divine favour.

There was another way in which sacrifice could be used, and that was to vow that if – and only if – the god played his or her part in acceding to a certain request, then a certain offering would be made in return. This vow was totally dependent on the contractual relationship and the resulting sacrifice was not a free or goodwill offering, given in a spirit of trust, but something that formed an intrinsic part of any legal contract, essential even today: offer, acceptance, and consideration. 'Consideration' in legal terms is the price paid for goods or services, in this case the sacrifice.

It was not a relationship which was in any way intended to degrade the power of the deity invoked, nor did it turn the deity into a puppet. As can be seen by the thousands of surviving inscriptions which record the performance of such vows, the predominant tone is still one of great humility, with a note of gratitude. The sacrifice itself was chosen with every attempt made for it to be pleasing to the deity.

A slave who vowed for his freedom said of this type of contract that it was 'vowed as a slave, paid for as a free man' (servos vovit liber solvit)[52] and within his obvious pride and gratitude there is a great deal of religious feeling, coupled with self-confidence and dignity. It was not a relationship that had reduced either party.

In the making of such a private vow, the man would write his request, and the promised offering, on a wax tablet and then tie it to a statue of the god concerned. At that stage it was considered that he was on trial for his vow. If the prayer was not answered, then nothing further needed to be done. If, however, the prayer was answered then the grateful recipient would pay for the vow and also set up some a small memento of the happy outcome, as the freed slave did. There are many such inscriptions which simply give the name of the god, the name of the person making the request, and the letters 'V.S.L.M.' which stand for 'votum solvit libens merito' and means that the person concerned had willingly paid the vow to the god.

Public vows naturally tended to be more impersonal and perfunctory. Several of the vows made for the emperor are preserved in the inscriptions recording the activities of the Arval Brethren and a typical one, made in 80 AD, uses the standard formula:

Jupiter Optimus Maximus, if the Emperor Titus Caesar Vespasianus Augustus, Pontifex Maximus, holder of Tribunician power, Father of his Country, and Caesar Domitian son of the deified Vespasian, of whom we deem that we are speaking, should live and their house be safe on the next first day of January that comes to pass for the Roman people, the Quirites, and for the state of the Roman people, the Quirites, and you preserve that day and them safe from all dangers (if there are, or shall be, any before that day), and if you have granted them a felicitous issue in the manner that we deem we are speaking of, and you have preserved them in that present condition, or better, and may you so do these things, then we vow that you shall have, in the name of the College of Arval Brethren, two gilded oxen.

When Appius Claudius, Consul of 296 BC, in the middle of a desperate battle, raised his hands to the heavens and cried 'Bellona, if you grant us today the victory, I vow to dedicate a temple to you!' then the vow was certainly less formal, but probably more heartfelt than the rather stilted phrases of the vow of the Arval Brethren.

These Arval Brethren, or 'Fratres Arvales', were a college of priests in Rome whose chief original duty was to offer sacrifice for the fertility of the fields. The brotherhood was of great antiquity and was almost forgotten during Republican times, but Augustus revived it and it then probably lasted until the time of Theodosius I. It consisted of twelve members elected for life from the highest ranks, and during the principate they included the Emperor. There are few literary allusions to them, but ninety-six of their Minutes (or 'acta') have been discovered inscribed on stone in the Grove of the Dea Dia near Rome.[53]

The Arval Brethren did not lose their status even if they were exiled. According to Pliny the Elder, their sign was a white band with a chaplet of sheaves of grain.[54] The Brethren assembled at the Regia in the Forum Romanum, and their task was the worship of Dea Dia who was an ancient goddess of fertility of the fields. On the three days of her festival, in May, they would offer sacrifices and chant secretly inside the goddess's temple. The master of the college would personally select the three days of the celebration (by a now unknown method), and her dates are now believed to have been 27, 29 and 30 May.

The first of these days was always spent in Rome, while on the second the celebration would be transferred to a sacred grove just outside the city, and the third day would be again celebrated in Rome. The Brethren's duties included the ritual of the Ambarvalia, which was the sacrifices done at the borders of the city of Rome at the fifth milestone of the Via Campana or Salaria, which is now on the Monte delle Piche on the right bank of the River Tiber.

The sacrificial victim would be led three times around a field of grain, where farmers and their slaves danced and sang praises to Ceres. The blood of the victim would feed the fields and encourage the crops to grow and the victim's entrails would be examined in the usual way, to ensure that the offering was acceptable to the gods. They also had archaic prohibitions, which included the use of iron being forbidden, and they used olla terra, which was a jar of unbaked earth, another reminder of their ancient origins.

Although relatively obscure, these men played their part in the Roman people's close contact and dependent relationship with the gods, ensuring that the fields would remain fertile, that Rome would continue to be prosperous, and that all Rome's people would be fed and kept secure.[55]

7

Magic

Although the Romans commonly used auguries, the interpretation of dreams, and the advice of a Haruspex in everyday life and everyday worship of their gods, magic was considered to be a different thing altogether. Unlike the carefully controlled ceremonial of the sacrifice, or the government-approved watching of the flight of birds, or the respect from all classes given to the results of dream interpretations, the performance of the rites of magic was something secretive, random, dangerous and often frightening. It could allow one person to control another against their will, or even to control a group of other persons. It could be a love potion, or it could contain a curse, but to the superstitious Romans it always meant the possibility of being at the mercy of another.

So, does that mean that the Romans did not use magic? No, of course not, for they were just as willing to curse an enemy, steal a lover, or try to change their fate for the better as anyone else. From the earliest times, and despite occasional prohibitions, they continued to consult the practitioners of magic, or indeed practise it themselves as enthusiastic amateurs. The possibilities that it might just work were simply too tempting to ignore.

In its most basic form, magic is potentially the great equaliser, giving hope to those people to whom fate had been less than kind, and seemed (or indeed still seems, for magic is still widely practised), to be the way to achieve for oneself the blessings and successes that fate withheld. Some people go through their lives apparently in possession of every advantage, with beauty, intelligence, sufficient wealth to ensure comfort and sufficient status to give them the respect of others. People whose lives are less easy may admire them, even love them, but the element of resentment is usually also there. Why wasn't I born with beauty, health, intellect or wealth enough to win me the admiration of other people? Why can't I have some of that for myself?

The first recourse is usually prayer, to ask whatever god one has faith in to grant some of those blessings. Such prayers generally remain unanswered, and then the suppliant has to look elsewhere. Magic is the next resort, to attempt to control one's private world by the use of outside and unseen forces, using rituals and ceremonies which have prehistoric roots. There is good reason to believe that it all goes back to the original cult of the great Earth Goddess, who is most easily seen in the very ancient temples on Malta, where the worship of the all-powerful Mother Goddess was supreme.[1] This goddess was to be eventually worshipped – under different names – for thousands of years. She became Ge, Gaia, Demeter, Ceres, Terra Mater, Bona Dea, Cybele, Ishtar or Atargatis, with the female and reproductive element always predominating.

It is common to many of the most ancient beliefs that the use of iron is banned, particularly for knives to be used in rituals. Its ban continued in the prohibitions surrounding the lives of the Flamen Dialis and other priests. The Greeks had a new interpretation for the existing Mother Earth sanctuaries, for example the one at Delphi, where they added Apollo. This attempt to impose a newer religious figure alongside the older one raised inevitable conflict, and this may explain why the uses of magic were suspect, even feared, within the Greek world.

The witches Medea and Circe are portrayed as being both evil and dangerous, capable of taking away a man's will, and reducing him to animalistic status, but not only could Circe transform anyone into a beast, she could also predict the future, which was seen as yet another magic power. The witches may have been the goddesses of an earlier religious tradition, or the priestesses of a Mother Earth cult, and their knowledge of herbs and healing plants, along with the uses of mushrooms and other less pleasant things, may well have also played a part in their early priestly training. There again, a new civilisation took over an older one, debasing its rituals and beliefs. This was also to happen when Christianity took over from the earlier Pagan religions and began the eradication of what had existed for thousands of years, down to its later hunting out of presumed witches in an attempt to destroy the remnants of the still surviving Pagan cults.

The word 'Magic' is derived from 'Magoi', an early tribe or caste recognised in Iran as being specialists in rituals and religious knowledge. The word 'Shaman' is derived from a priest and medicine man. To become one of these priests required strict training and harsh asceticism, with isolation from the community, fasting, long sessions of prayer and meditation, the learning of the uses of drugs, and even monotonous exercises such as whirling, which helped to produce a state of trance or delirium during which visions might be expected.[2]

Theocritus (310-250 BC) is mainly known for his pastoral poetry, but he also wrote a number of pieces which describe everyday life in Alexandria. One of these was entitled 'Pharmakeutria', the feminine form of Pharmakeutes, which means witch or sorceress – also derived from 'pharmakon' meaning a drug, potion, or spell. Any herb or chemical could come under that heading. The poem concerns a young woman whose lover has deserted her, and she collects together the necessary items to perform a ritual whereby she hopes to draw him back to her.

She uses barley groats, bay leaves, bran and wax and liquids such as wine, milk and water for libations, with coltsfoot and pulverised lizard. She also has part of the fringe from the lover's cloak, as in religious beliefs anything belonging to the person concerned has absorbed his or her 'essence', whether it be clothing, fingernails, hair, semen, or some item that was of value to them. This made the personal item itself into a magical object and one that was very useful in the preparation of a spell.

By the end of the last century BC, Hellenistic magic was already fully formed and all the occult practices that we know of, whether astrology, daemonology or whatever else, had become sciences that could be taught to others. Much of this instruction was very likely carried out in secret, with small groups studying with a teacher. Egyptian priests were supposed to be the holders of many great mysteries, which they never shared with outsiders and unfortunately, that means that we have little idea of what these apprenticeships or training periods consisted. There are, however, many handbooks on the more technical side of the sciences, such as alchemy and astrology, plus a great many formulae of practical use, in the magical papyri. A trend towards specialisation continued as the sciences became more complex, and although some who called themselves sorcerers tried to dabble in several, in reality it would be very difficult to master more than one properly, so those who claimed wider knowledge were usually amateurs or plain charlatans.

The magical papyri show the type of power that people desired to have over others, and the amulets which were often worn give some idea how they attempted to protect themselves from such magical forces being used by others. The first of these papyri were brought to Europe by Johann d'Anastasy, a Swedish Vice-Consul in Cairo from 1828 to 1859. They contained formulae for love magic, exorcism, and curses and their importance should not be underestimated. The Great Magical Papyrus, now in Paris, consists of thirty-six sheets covered on both sides in writing, a total of 3,274 lines of text.[3]

What is now available, however, is only a very small part of the wealth of magical literature once in existence. We know that the early Christians were sedulous destroyers of these ancient treasures. St Paul made many Ephesians burn their books, which were extremely valuable, as Ephesus was one of the centres of ancient lore.[4] This short-sightedness was only one of the many incidents of bigotry by which an important accumulation of ancient knowledge, perhaps containing many important cures as well as spells, was lost to posterity.

Magical ostraca were a cheaper version of the papyri, and the material used for these was usually terracotta pots. These range from the fourth century BC to Byzantine times, and they operate in the same way. One love spell from Oxyrhynchus was designed to break up a woman's marriage and draw her affections towards the socerer instead, and may have been typical of many others. Amulets could, of course, be worn to deflect such magical work, including curses, the evil eye and all other evil powers. These were often made of cheap materials, but precious stones were also believed to have their own powers, and thousands of carved gemstones have survived, being more durable than terracotta pots. These also had an ornamental function alongside the magical one, and were worn on the body as necklaces or as rings. The word 'amulet' is derived from 'amolitum', which means something that repels or deflects; amolior means remove or carry away. A follower of any religion could safeguard themselves by wearing one of these attractive and protective pieces of jewellery.[5]

However, the ancient world was full of magical powers and people may have felt themselves always under some kind of threat. They might then decide to take action of their own to forestall any evil coming their way rather than remaining passive, when an amulet might not be thought sufficient protection on its own. Much black magic may have been performed as a precaution, on the theory that if someone was putting a curse on you, it might be better to strike first and put one on them.

A magician's equipment was discovered at Pergamon, probably dating from the third century AD, consisting of a bronze table and base covered with magical symbols, plus a dish, also decorated with symbols, a large bronze nail with letters inscribed on its flat sides, two bronze rings and three polished black stones inscribed with the names of supernatural powers. Some attempt was made by the discoverers to establish a connection between the symbols found in three concentric circles around the edge of the dish with the twenty-two cards of the Tarot.[6]

The Roman historian Ammianus Marcellinus[7] described a type of ancient Ouija board used in a séance in 371 AD with unfortunate results. It consisted of a metal disk, the rim of which was engraved with the letters of the Greek alphabet. One had to hold a ring, suspended on a light linen thread, and after certain prayers and incantations had been addressed to the 'deity of divination' (perhaps referring to Apollo) the ring was expected to swing from one letter to another, forming words. On that occasion, two very dangerous questions were asked of it. One was 'When will the Emperor die?' and the other, 'Who will the next Emperor be?'

The oracle began to swing, spelling out a name which appeared to be the start of 'Theodorus' but before the name could be completed, one man in the room lost his nerve and stopped the séance. The authorities somehow learned of it, and all those involved were arrested, tried and executed – including the unfortunate Theodorus, who had not been present and knew nothing about his name having been mentioned. Seven years later, it became clear what the oracle had intended to tell the group, as the Emperor Valens was then killed and the next Emperor was called Theodosius.

Magic words were deemed to be very powerful, although the word Abracadabra is not attested to before Serenus Sammonicus in his work 'Res Reconditae' (Secret Matters), in 212 AD. The magic word 'Abraxus' is often found on ancient gemstones and the Greek historian Herodotus claimed that the priest-magicians of Egypt used it in magical chanting to enable the great blocks of stone to be lifted when the pyramids were being built.

Ancient hieroglyphs describing the rituals usually begin with the words 'djed medu', which means 'the words to say' and gives the priest the exact formula he is to recite. The pyramid texts are the oldest known religious texts in the world and first appeared in the pyramid of King Unas who reigned around 2,350 BC. However, even their appearance in his pyramid at Saqqara does not mean that they were composed at that time, and their use of grammar indicates that they had even earlier roots, perhaps having been written on materials that have not survived, such as wooden coffins or linen shrouds. The fact that they begin with the words 'djed medu' implies an oral tradition rather than a written one, similar to ancient poetry which was composed long before such things became inscribed on stone.[8]

What does emerge is the permanence and universality of magic as used in the ancient world and that the same types of magic were being practised from the earliest times, right through to the Roman Empire.[9] One of the earliest forms involved herbs and throughout history mankind has benefited from the use of plants; for food of course, clothing, shelter, cosmetics, medicines and perfumes. They can be used as insect repellents, for strewing on floors, or for scenting linen, for washing or for embalming of the dead. Thyme, which today is largely a culinary herb, (although also an excellent insect repellent), was used by the Egyptians for embalming. Sage, also now used mainly as food flavouring, was commonly used against snake bites, as a hair tonic and for whitening the teeth. Belladonna carries its function in its name, as Mediterranean women used to squeeze the juice of the plant into their eyes, which hugely dilated the pupils, hence 'bella donna', or beautiful woman. However, its more formal name of Atropa Belladonna gives it other functions, where it can be used in medicines as a sedative, a diuretic, and a narcotic – it can be used to kill.[10]

Like the gods, many plants are generally multi-functional with a good side and a bad side, available for either purpose. The stately and beautiful Monkshood (Aconium Nepellum) is used in Chinese medicine for heart diseases and uterine cancer, and it is also useful as a local anaesthetic – it is also a deadly poison. Likewise, the innocent looking Henbane, useful for asthma, colic, as a sedative and a painkiller, is also the source of Hyoscyamine, Atropine and Scopolamine, and is also deadly poisonous. It is hardly to be wondered at that these naturally occurring plants would at some point be used for their more dangerous qualities, rather than their helpful and healing ones, when temptation arose and the means were ready to hand.

Flax was the source of linen, which came in different grades like everything else. Linen was the main textile product of Egypt and some spells actually specified that a particular grade of linen should be used. As a plant, it had a meaningful relationship with the agricultural cycle, and was imbued with great symbolic value. Its production was the one thing in Egypt that the Pharoah did not own, being in the control of the priests.

Only 'pure' linen, meaning bleached, or at least undyed, could be used for any religious ritual, including the mummification of humans and sacred animals. The priests were always dressed in fresh, pure linen, and they wrapped the statues of the gods in it within the sanctuaries. This clothing, like that of the priests, would be replaced daily. The clothing of the gods was royal linen, a product of the workships attached to the temples.[11]

The significance of the linen also gave it a place in spell-binding, which literally means the tying or binding of knots into strips of linen, by which a magician could create an effective amulet. Knotted cloths could have magic drawings on them, and a series of knots made one after the other, along with the spells spoken at the same time so that the knots captured and held them, locked the incantation into the linen.

Among the recommendations for preventing a threatened miscarriage was a spell to be recited while knotting a piece of cloth, which was then to be inserted into the vagina. Knotting a similar cloth around someone's head could prevent recurring headaches, while on tomb or coffin paintings some people are shown performing religious rites with similar cloths around their heads, perhaps to indicate status, or the bonds may have given them some protection while the ritual was performed.

The magic of knotting spells could also be performed with materials such as yarn, coloured or uncoloured threads, or with human hair. Some textual amulets were written on a piece of clean papyrus (which is a piece not previously used, as scribes habitually erased earlier texts and reused the papyri), and some spells were beautifully copied out in their entirety, along with instructions for their use. They could then be folded into a tiny, tight roll or little bundle, tied into a knotted cord and worn next to the skin.

In Egypt, as in Rome, being a priest was not necessarily a full-time occupation. Priests normally came from local leading families as there were no restrictions on them having wives and families; quite the reverse, the position was often handed down within the family circle, for not only was a reasonable social status a requirement but also some formal education and priestly training.[12]

The position was often combined with other responsibilities, such as owning and managing an agricultural estate. Large temples tended to divide the priesthoods into groups so that they worked in rotation, with each group attending to the temple rituals for three or four months of the year, as a contrast to the Roman tradition, whereby senior positions were lifetime posts. Though priests were also expected to be called upon at any time, and particularly so if one had acquired a reputation as a healer, or an accomplished magician or seer. The Egyptians believed that in the beginning, everything had been perfect and any later fall from that state of perfect harmony was due to the imperfections and greed of mankind. The duty of the Pharoah was to be the guarantor of Ma'at, or truth, and the main thing asked of the people was that they live in Ma'at and help to reconnect the physical world with the perfect harmony of the Cosmos.

After death, everyone travelled from the physical world to the Duat, or Farworld. This did not hold any concept of heaven or hell, but existed simultaneously with the physical world, occupying the same space, yet eternal. Therefore, the world of the dead was always very close, concurrent with that of the living, and was available to be communicated with, as were the gods. Therefore, all temple rituals were specifically intended to maintain that universal harmony.

Every priest would have some contact with magic in the course of his duties, but only a few were likely to have specialised in it, either in Rome or in Egypt, except for one goddess whose priesthood was famous for their magical expertise. The wab-priests (meaning pure and clean), of the Goddess Sekhmet were a relatively low-ranking priesthood, but Sekhmet had power over all kinds of ailments with no obvious physical cause. These were the infectious diseases caused by bacteria, viruses, and parasites. Supernatural causes were the ancient explanation for such afflictions, and the priests of Sekhmet were fully equipped to deal with such problems due to their particular knowledge of hygiene.

As we have seen, the religion of Isis and Serapis was very strong in Rome as well as in many cities outside it. The Egyptian gods were believed by Romans to be particularly useful in all magical matters, and the Goddess Sekhmet was represented in the Isis/Serapis complex on the Campus Martius by large numbers of more than life-sized statues of this lion-headed goddess of healing, many of which are now displayed within the Vatican Museum, along with a larger number of other Egyptian deities.[13]

There is a charming story regarding Sekhmet, who was released onto a disobedient world by the God Ra, her father. Ra was tired of the humans and their misbehaviour, their lack of respect and their disharmony, so he sent his daughter to punish them. However, Sekhmet is easy to unleash but very difficult to control, and she set about killing the humans with enthusiasm and was deaf to all entreaties to stop. Even her Great Father Ra could not get through to her, until the idea came to the other gods that great jars of beer could be coloured red, to look like blood, to attract her away from the carnage. These were then poured onto the ground, and Sekhmet who was thirsty eagerly lapped them all up, becoming drunk and sleepy – and so humankind was saved. There was some sympathy in Rome for a powerful and excitable goddess who shared the Roman military trait of 'having no reverse gear' and being difficult to control.

While the Egyptian priests were famous for their love of clear and life-giving water, so, too, were the Romans, with their wonderful aqueducts, fountains, and pipework that took water into their cities, providing healthy drinking water even to those people who were too poor to afford to have piped water taken into their homes. There were cheap and sometimes free days at the baths, public fountains and water troughs throughout Rome, and other cities such as Pompeii and Herculaneum, and they shared the Egyptian belief that clear and flowing water had magical and healing properties.

The connection with Anna Perenna's fountain in the Paroli district of Rome, where spells and curses had been left in the water, where the flow of clear springwater would invigorate the words, has already been mentioned. In Egypt, also, the flow of clean water was believed to have power to both absorb and carry a spell or curse along with it.

The Metternich Stela was set up by a priest named Nesu-Atum in around 350 BC. Its use was intended for healing of people who visited the temple at Heliopolis, which was an area sacred to the Mnevis Bull. The stela is 35 inches high (89cm) and is inscribed closely throughout with beautifully detailed spells, along with images of the god Horus, pictured as a child standing on a crocodile and surrounded by other deities. The combination of these images and the spells were essential to the magic powers of the Stela, and water poured over the stone would absorb the magic words. Anyone who subsequently drank the water would be imbued with the magic, which would enter the body to produce a cure. As with any healing statue, it was intended to be seen from all angles, which was also a part of its power. The word for remedy was 'pekher', which meant to encircle or go around, and is the same word used for magical enchantment. The Metternich Stela serves as a model for the use of clean water not only for cleansing, but also for carrying the 'goodness' of healing with it.[14]

In Rome, the water nymph Egeria was worshipped by pregnant women in the hope that she would give them an easy delivery. Egeria was also believed to be the spirit of a sacred spring that flowed from the roots of an equally sacred oak tree. From the earliest societies, the ruler was responsible for the fall of the life-giving rain and the fruitfulness of the earth, and this belief is held worldwide, with the regular fall of rain being of enormous importance.

The early kings of Rome may have acted as rain-makers, with the king imitating Jupiter and pretending to make thunder and lightning. This ceremony appears to have formed part of the ritual of Jupiter Elicius, who drew lightning and rain from the clouds and there could be nobody more fitting to perform such a ceremony than the king, who was the representative of the sky god.[15]

Philosophers who were interested in magic described themselves as Theurgists. According to Plotinus, Theurgy aimed at establishing sympathy with the universe and used the forces that flow through all things in order to be in touch with them. The term 'Theurgist' appears to have been introduced by Julianus, a Hellenised Chaldean who lived in the reign of Marcus Aurelius and Theurgists would form a late Pagan religious sect. They not only discussed the gods, like theologians, but also performed certain actions which they claimed actually affected the gods. They included mediums and used those people to attempt to influence the gods, or to force them to appear. The Theurgists were an educated and respected group of men and women, quite different to the low-rent sellers of curses and spells. The Emperor Julian gives some impression of their ritual: 'Voices and noises, calls, stirring music, heady perfumes, doors that appeared to open by themselves, luminous fountains, moving shadows, mists and statues that appeared to come to life.' How such effects were produced is not known, although they seem to be similar to the repertoire of any fake medium, omitting only the ectoplasm. They are also fairly similar to some of the initiation ceremonies required by the more exotic religions.

It has been suggested that the Emperor Julian may have been affected by the use of some drug, either ingested or inhaled, to produce the altered state of consciousness necessary for the effects to appear real to him.[16]

Iamblichus wrote:

The Theurgist, by virtue of mysterious signs, controls the powers of nature. Not as a mere human being, or as one who possesses a human soul, but as one of a higher rank of gods, he gives orders that are not appropriate to the condition of man. He does not really expect to perform all these amazing things but by using such words he shows what kind of power he has, and how great he is, and that because of his knowledge of the mysterious symbols he is obviously in touch with the gods.[17]

It would appear that even Iamblichus, who was a believer in Theurgy, did not quite believe everything he saw, and is aware that much of the 'smoke and mirrors' effect is done to produce a certain ambience in order to prepare the followers to accept whatever is shown to them, with regard to visions or other manisfestations, all designed to impress.

Virgil, at the end of Book Four of the *Aeneid* describes the hero Aeneas's meeting with Queen Dido, who has just begun to build Carthage. She falls in love with Aeneas and hopes he will stay with her as her consort, but he leaves her to found an empire of his own, resulting in her love for him turning into a bitter hatred. She then hoped to destroy him and prepared a sacrifice to the powers of the Underworld. Finally, realising that no love magic is going to bring him back to her, she kills herself and becomes, by her death, a curse.

It was believed that all suicides, victims of murder, men killed in battle, and people who died young or while still children – in other words all those who had died before their allotted time – could and possibly would unleash enormous destructive power.[18] The opening of the Mundus in Rome, on certain days of the year to allow the dead to return to earth, was always considered dangerous. The shades of such people who had died before their time could be particularly vengeful and harbour great resentment against other people who were fortunate enough to be able to enjoy their full span of life. Propitiatory gifts and prayers would be given in the hope that the dissatisfied shades would take no revenge upon the living.

Pliny preserved many religious and magical beliefs alongside his other notes. He did not believe in all of the magic arts and felt that most of the claims of magicians and sorcerers were simply false, or at best exaggerations. If there was any real truth in such practices, then the Emperor Nero, who studied magic with the best teachers and had access to all the best books on the subject, should have been formidable due to his magical powers – but wasn't.

However, sensibly, Pliny advised caution. He said that although magic was both ineffective and infamous, 'intestabilis', it still contained 'shadows of truth', especially regarding the art of making poisons. It was the drug itself which worked, rather than the spell that went with it. However, Pliny still said, 'There is nobody who is not afraid of spells,' and he kept an open mind about the amulets and charms which so many people wore to protect themselves. A large part of Pliny's interest was in the preparation of drugs and remedies to cure illnesses, and that interest was primarily in folk medicine, which has a long history of effective cures. Many physicians were then experimenting with the uses of drugs in conjunction with diet, exercise and baths in mineral springs, producing what would now be considered a nature cure. Pliny does frequently recommend one natural product, both for inside and outside of the body, and that is honey. Very sensible of him, for honey is an ingredient whose healing properties are well recognised in both ancient and modern times.[19]

Pliny the Elder recorded several thousand recipes for drugs and other remedies, and even mentions drugs which were concocted by the Magi, although he does not recommend those and appears to positively dislike them. He considered such people to be merely sorcerers. According to him, the arts of the Magi covered three main areas: 'medicina' 'religio' and 'artes mathematicae', or astrology. Many professional magicians at that time were also healers who performed various rituals and addressed prayers to the deities. Pliny's reference to 'religio' does not mean the same as 'religion', as he means superstition rather than religious faith.

He disliked and distrusted those professionals and called them 'frauds and charlatans', yet he still admitted that the best of them did have some skills. 'People agree that by merely smearing menstrual blood on the doorposts, the tricks of the Magi, those worthless quacks, can be rendered ineffective – I would certainly like to believe this!'[20]

Professional sorcerers were consulted by many types of people, but their most regular clients were culled from the performers at the theatres or at the Circus. These people were not only particularly superstitious by nature, but they also had to be aware of the undercurrents around them, which might mean that they were overtaken by rivals, or even prevented from doing their best work due to some spell or curse laid upon them by a malicious competitor. There was a general fear of evil and of supernatural forces being unleashed, whether deliberately being aimed at someone or being released randomly due to an incompetent magician making a mistake.

Psychokinesis is defined as being the moving of objects without direct physical contact, and the home where the future Emperor Augustus was born was believed to be inhabited by a 'poltergeist' type of force. When a new owner of the property decided to sleep in a certain room, he found himself ejected, mattress and all, by 'a sudden and mysterious force'.[21]

Cases of possession have been reported since the earliest times and in one sense the Oracle at Delphi – a woman who spoke in a trance with a voice not her own – was a case of possession. Her state of consciousness was autosuggestively induced but by whom, or what? She apparently had very little control over it and cases like this were usually assumed to be in the control of some deity, or even a daemon. Not everyone proved suitable to serve as a medium, but it was said that 'young and unsophisticated persons' were the best candidates.[22]

How these people were put into their trances we cannot know, although hypnosis was also practicsed in antiquity and the technique of inducing such a trancelike state or making one susceptible to external suggestions is a very old one, and may even have been handed down from the sanctuaries of Egypt. In ancient times, the Greek word 'ekstasis', meaning 'stepping outside of oneself', was used to describe such trance states, whether they were spontaneous or deliberately induced.

The Corpus Hippocratum dating from the late fifth or early fourth century BC specifically attacks shamans and others who attempted to treat epilepsy. Because the nature of this ailment was not understood, its treatment was left largely in the hands of priests and practitioners of magic. These people, often somewhere between real priests and folk healers, filled a void and made their living in a dark area where no cure could be forthcoming, yet the sufferers and their families still needed some hope. They were attempting to treat a disease which had natural causes by using appeals to supernatural forces and Hippocrates was famously very critical of their methods:

> The truth about the so-called 'sacred' disease is this – in my opinion it is no more divine or sacred than any others, but has a natural cause ... because of their ignorance and its strange character it is unlike any other disease, so people thought of it as having a divine origin. They

are unable to understand it and continue to believe in its divine nature; at the same time their simple-minded therapies, purifications and incantations prove the opposite ... or should we consider it divine just because of its strange nature? In that case there would be many 'sacred' diseases, not just one, for I can show that other diseases can be no less bizarre or amazing, and yet no-one calls them 'sacred'.[23]

Hippocrates was forward-thinking in his awareness of the natural causes of epilepsy, the so-called sacred or falling disease. Unfortunately, few people were so rational, and even Pliny the Younger described how in Rome, at the time of the Games, people would bring suffering relatives to the Colosseum in the hope of being able to get them a cup of warm blood from a freshly slaughtered or mutilated gladiator, preferably while it was still flowing from his wounds. This was thought to invigorate the sufferer and breathe new life into him, to the easement of the disease.

Relatively modern doctors had no reason to feel superior, or to be dismissive regarding these ancient beliefs. In the nineteenth century AD, although belief in possesson by a daemon was commonly rejected, an even firmer belief had taken its place. Nineteenth-century doctors firmly believed that fits caused by epilepsy were brought on by excessive masturbation and various remedies were attempted to prevent it, believing that it led to blindness, madness and general debility. These ranged from spiked rings to prevent an erection to encasing the unrepentant masturbator's hands in plaster! The final solution, to avoid the sufferer spending his life in a straitjacket, was of course full castration; rather drastic and nothing whatever to do with his probable epilepsy. For women, also, drastic measures were recommended and clitorectomy was usually carried out. Mr Baker Brown, a Fellow of the Royal College of Surgeons, cheerfully stated that he preferred to 'simply use scissors' for this, and a number of Victorian female epileptics were mutilated in this way, suffering horribly.

Theophrastus, in his 'Portrait of a superstitious person' wrote at some length, and not without humour, when describing a person who was prey to fears of the supernatural, and how likely such a person was to become the victim of the charlatans and fake diviners who would flock around him:

The superstitious person is one who will wash his hands at a fountain and then also sprinkle himself from a temple font, to fully cleanse any imagined pollution. He will take a laurel leaf into his mouth and walk around like this all day, or at least until he had thrown three stones across the road. When he sees a snake he will invoke the god Sabazius, if it is a red snake – but if it is the sacred snake he will at once establish a shrine on the spot. Whenever he passes a pile of shiny stones at the crossroads, he will pour oil from his flask onto them, and will fall on his knees and worship them before he continues on his way. If a mouse gnaws a hole in a barley sack in his house, he goes to an 'advisor' and asks him what to do about it. If the advisor tells him to take the sack to a cobbler and have it stitched up, he will pay no attention to this sensible advice, but will go his own way and prefer to offer a special sacrifice. He is capable of purifying his house quite often, saying that it has come under a spell from Hecate. If he startles an owl as he walks along, he may be frightened and shout 'Glory be to Athena!' before he can continue. He will never walk on a flat tombstone or come near to a corpse, or to a woman who has just given birth, saying that it is better for him not to be polluted. On the fourth and seventh days of the (last ten days of) the month, he will order his servants to mull wine, while he goes out to buy myrtle wreaths, frankincense and smilax – when he comes back to his house he will put wreaths on the busts of Hermaphroditus all day long! Whenever he has had a dream he will consult the interpreters of such dreams, the seers and the augurs, to find out to which god or goddess he ought to pray. He will also go to the 'Orphic' priests in order to be initiated. This is the kind of person who will sprinkle himself thoroughly with seawater every month, along with his wife, or if the wife is busy, along with the nursemaid and the children. Whenever he sees someone at the crossroads who is crowned with garlic he will go hastily away, pour water over his head, and call the priestesses of Hecate and make them carry a squill, or a puppy, around him for purification. If he sees a madman, or an epileptic, he shudders and spits into his bosom.[24]

Other people found nothing funny in the subject and the following Roman spells are from three different periods. The first is from the second century BC; the second is from the first century BC and the third is rather later, around the fourth century BC.

If something is out of joint, it can be set by the following spell – take a green reed, four or five feet long, split it in the middle, and let two men hold it to their hips. Begin to recite the following formula – 'moetas vaeta daries dardaries astataries dissunapiter' until the parts come together. Put a knife on top of it and when the two parts come together and touch each other, grip them with your hand and make a cut left to right, tie it onto the dislocation or fracture, and it will heal. But you must recite every day for the dislocation, the formula 'haut haut haut istasis tarsis tardannabou dannaustra.' (Cato – 'On Agriculture')

Stolo smiled and said 'I will use the same words that he wrote down, or rather the ones I heard from Tarquenna, whenever someone begins to feel pain in his feet, you can heal him. When you think of him, say 'I think of you, heal my feet, let the earth retain the illness, let health remain here in my feet. He prescribes to recite this formula twenty-seven times, to touch the earth, and to spit. It must be recited sober. (Varro – 'On Agriculture')

To be recited sober and touching the relevant part of the body with three fingers, the thumb the middle finger and the ring finger, the other two being stretched out. Say 'Go away, no matter whether you were born today or earlier, created today or earlier, this disease, this illness, this pain, this swelling, this redness, this goitre, these tonsils, this abscess, this tumour, these glands and the little glands, you call forth and I lead forth, I speak forth, through this spell, from these limbs and bones.' (Marcellos Empiricus – 'De Medicamentis')

These spells show that folk medicine did not change substantially over time. Cato the Elder distrusted doctors, and as the owner of an estate would be required to attempt first aid for his servants. Varro's is more 'magical' as it involves the invocation of a supernatural power. Marcellus was a professional physician and in his opinion one has to quote the appropriate part of the body, or its ailment, to make the spell work. In the last two examples, sobriety is recommended for anyone performing a religious or magical ritual.[25]

The adopted son of the Emperor Tiberius, Julius Caesar Germanicus, died rather mysteriously in Antioch in 19 AD. According to Tacitus, workmen who searched the residence found objects, secreted under the floor and between the walls, which seemed to have been placed there by someone who wished Germanicus ill. He had two main enemies, despite being generally popular, and these were Gnaeus Calpurnius Piso and his wife Plancina. While dying, Germanicus said that he believed that Piso or Piso's wife had poisoned him, but his distraught friends suspected black magic. Piso was later prosecuted by the Senate and eventually committed suicide. His wife first escaped condemnation, but was prosecuted later and then also killed herself. Tacitus gives no opinion on whether murder by poison or by the dark arts was held responsible, but he lists some fairly incriminating material found in Germanicus's house:

The terrible impact of his illness was intensified by Piso. Under the floors and between the walls of his house, the remains of human bodies were found and dug up. There were also spells and curses and lead tablets with the name 'Germanicus' engraved, and furthermore half-burned ashes, smeared with blood and other tools of evil magic, by which it is believed souls can be handed over to the divinities of the Underworld.[26]

An inscription from the first century AD refers to a city (Tuder/Todi) being in grave danger because of a curse laid on certain members of the city council. By making the curse known it was, of course, possible to frighten all the other councillors. The man who set up the inscription, Lucius Cancrius Primigenius, made a vow to Jupiter Optimus Maximus that he would set up the inscription in the temple if more details came to light, especially the names of the intended victims. This did happen, and the details were recorded. The names of the intended victims had been written on tablets and buried close to some tombs. This was always a way of increasing the strength of a curse, by adding to it the adulterating qualities of the dead. The perpetrator turned out to be a slave owned by the city. This slave, whose grievance is not noted, was not identified by name, but he was convicted of sorcery and duly executed. The inscription placed in the temple of Jupiter Optimus Maximus reads:

> For having saved the city, the city council and the people of Tuder, Lucius Cancrius Primigenius, freedman of Clemens, a member of the Committee of Six Men in charge of the worship of the Augustans and the Flavians, the first to be honoured in this way by the order, has fulfilled his vow to Jupiter Optimus Maximus because through his divine power he has brought to light and protected the names of the members of the city council which, by the unspeakable crime of a worthless communal slave, had been attached to tombs, so that a curse could be put upon them. Thus Jupiter has freed the city and the citizens from the fear of danger.[27]

Another such curse, this time more personal, is from North Africa in the third century AD. It was found in a tomb and its victims are two teams of charioteers. The four teams were known by the colour of their uniforms: Reds, Blues, Whites and Greens. The person laying the curse must have had rather a lot of money on his preferred teams, the Blues and the Reds, because he condemns the Greens and the Whites to be carried off by a daemon. He uses the name of the Jewish deity Yahweh, by variants of the name, in order to strengthen his curse:

> I conjure you, daemon, whoever you may be, and order you to torture and kill, from this hour, this day, this moment the horses of the Green and White teams. Kill and smash the charioteers Clarus, Felix, Primulus

and Romanus, do not leave a breath in them. I conjure you by him who has delivered you, at the time, the god of the sea and of the air – Iao, Iasdao, Oorio and Aeia.

It is a pity that we cannot know the outcome of this curse and whether the offending teams suffered any injury, or whether they remained entirely unaware of this man's exhortations.[28]

One section of the Great Magical Papyrus is concerned with love magic. The 'magician' has to make two dolls, one for himself and the other representing the woman who is desired. The doll representing the female must be pricked or stabbed with thirteen iron needles, at certain points, with formulas recited as it is done. The intent is obvious and concerned with the female becoming helpless with desire for the man involved. It is a form of female subjugation, an exercise in control, and is designed to conquer the woman and reduce her to sexual slavery. The woman had presumably refused the attentions of the man, who felt resentment towards her as the cruel and vindictive tone of the spell makes clear. The recitation of prayers, formulae and various rites may well have been expensive, as the magician would have been fully employed with it for some time, including making the doll, inserting the steel pins, and performing the recitations.

The lengthy recitation is tedious and repetitive in the extreme but is also disturbing in its increasingly hysterical and controlling tone. It is worth giving it in its entirety despite its length, in order to show the kind of thing that people were prepared to pay large sums of money for, and also to elict sympathy for the woman, its intended victim, who was the reluctant object of this man's fevered and dangerous affections.

> Take wax or clay from a potter's wheel and form two figures, one male and one female. Make the male look like Ares in arms, holding a sword in his left hand and pointing it at her right collarbone. Her arms must be tied behind her back and she must kneel. Fasten the magical substance on her head and neck. On the woman's figure write 'Isee iao ithi oune brido lothion neboutosoualeth'. On her right ear 'Ouer mechan' and on her left 'libaba oimathotho.' On her face write 'amounabreo' and on the right eye 'orormothio aeth' and on the other eye write 'choboue'. On the right shoulder 'adeta merou' and on the right arm 'Ene psa enesgaph' and on the other 'melchiou melcheda.' On her hands write 'Melchamelchou ael' and on her breast write the name, on her mother's side, of the woman you want to attract. On the heart write 'balamin thoouth' under the abdomen 'aobes aobar' and on her sexual organs

'blichianeoi ovoia'. On her buttocks put 'pissadara' on the sole of her right foot 'elo' and on the other 'eloaioe'.

Take thirteen bronze needles and stick one in her brain while saying 'I am piercing your brain (NN).' Stick two in her eyes, two in her ears, one in the mouth, two in the midriff, one in the hands, two in the genital organs, two in the soles, saying each time 'I am piercing such and such a member of (NN) so that she may remember me (NN) alone.'

Take a lead tablet and write on it the same formula. Tie it to the two creatures with thread from the loom, after making 365 knots, saying as you have learned 'Abrasax hold her fast!' As the sun is setting you must place it near the tomb of a person who has died untimely, or died a violent death, along with the flowers of the season.

The formula to be written and recited 'I am handing over this binding spell to you, Gods of the Underworld, Hyesemigadon, and Kore Persephone, Ereschigal and Adonis, the Barbaritha, chthonic Hermes, Thoouth Phokentazepsu, Aerchthatoumi sonktai Kalbanachamre and to mighty Anubis Psirinth, who has the keys of the Underworld. To men and women who have died before their time, to young men and women, from year to year, from month to month, from day to day and from hour to hour. I adjure you all the Daemons of this place to assist this Daemon. Arouse yourselves for me, whoever you are, male or female, and enter every place, every neighbourhood, every house, and attract and bind. Attract (NN) daughter of (NN) whose magical substance you have. Make (NN) daughter of (NN) be in love with me. Let her not have sexual intercourse with any other man, neither from pleasure nor from behind. Let her not have any pleasure with another man, only with me (NN) so that she (NN) is unable to eat or drink, to love, to be strong, to be healthy, to enjoy sleep, (NN) without me (NN) because I adjure you to be faithful, the awesome name, at whose sound the earth will open and the name at whose terrifying sound the Daemon will panic, the name at whose sound rivers and rocks will explode. I adjure you, Daemon-dead, male or female, in the name of Barbaritha Chenmbra, in the name of Abrat Abrasax Sesengen Barpharages, and in the name of Marmareoth Marmarauoth, Marmaroth Marechthana Amarza Maribeoth. Listen to my commands and the names. Just arouse yourselves from the repose that holds you whoever you are, male or female, and enter every place, every neighbourhood, every house, and bring her (NN) to me and keep her (NN) from eating and drinking, and let her (NN) not enjoy the attempts of any other man only my own (NN). Yes! Drag her (NN) by her hair, by her heart, by her soul, to me (NN) every hour of her life, night and day, until she comes to me (NN) and let her (NN) remain inseparable from me. Do this and bind her, for all time and for all of my life, and force her (NN) to be my servant. Let her not flutter away from me even for one hour of her life.

'If you accomplish this for me I will let you rest at once. For I am Barbar Adonai who hides the stars, who governs the bright splendour of the heavens, I am the Lord of the World, Aththouin Iathouin Selbiouoth Aoth Sarba Thiouth Iathrierath Adonai ia Roura Bia Bi Biothe Athoth, Saboath ea Niapha Amarachthi Satama Zsuaththere Serpho Ialada Iale Sbesi Iaththa Maradtha Achil Ththee Choo Oe Eacho Kansaosa Alkmouri, Thyr Oso Mai. Attract her, bind her (NN), make her love me, desire me, yearn for me, (NN) because I adjure you Daemon-dead, in the name of the terrible, the great, Iaeo Baph Renemoun Othi Larakripha Eueai Phirkiralithon Yomen Er Phaboa to bring her (NN) to me, to join head to head, glue lips to lips, join belly to belly, approach thigh to thigh, fit the black together with the black, and let her (NN) perform sexual acts with me (NN) for all eternity.'[29]

On reading this unhinged harangue, the first instinct is to wonder whether the object of this man's affections was worth all the bother and expense he had undoubtedly been put to. The second, unfortunately, is to fully understand why the woman he wanted rejected him in the first place, as his obsessive desire to own her, body and soul, suggests that in more modern times he would probably have been arrested and given over to the care of a psychiatrist.

Fortunately, most rejected lovers did not go to such extremes, although another papyrus from the collection, also now in Paris, calls on Eros to help him to attract the woman of his dreams, with the usual demands that she be brought to him, with discomfort as the penalty for her refusal.

Let her not sit, if she is talking to someone let her not talk, if she is looking at someone let her not look, if she is kissing someone let her not kiss, if she is enjoying something pleasant let her not enjoy it... Do not enter her through her eyes, nor through her sides, nor through her nails, but through her soul and settle in her heart and burn her guts, her breast, her liver, her breath, her bones, her marrow, until she comes to me ... inflame her guts and rip them out, shed her blood, drop by drop, until she comes to me.[30]

It does not seem to occur to these dangerously obsessive men that a rather different, perhaps gentler approach might have produced a better result. Their sexual demands and their need for the total subjugation of the women they profess to love, and their desire to go to any lengths to get their own way, makes them sound like wilful children, and as such it is no wonder that they had difficulty in finding a willing partner. Any averagely sensible young woman would run for the hills at the sight of them. One can only assume that these spells, however time-consuming and expensive they were to prepare, were total failures. Though they did provide a good living for the magicians.

Apart from love spells, curses and strangely prophetic dreams, the world of the ancients was populated by all kinds of spirits. Communicatiom could certainly be established with them in various ways, but the ancients believed that the 'unquiet dead' – those who had died untimely, were the most readily available and the most willing to involve themselves in the spells and curses of mortals. They would have plenty to still be angry about and so the magicians were able to use them.

The dead of the family were 'fed' at various times, with oil, honey and water being poured into, or onto, the grave. Often the living family would have a meal close to the grave or tomb, and the deceased would be invited to share that meal. This ensured that the shades never felt left out of normal family life, and that they were still consulted on family matters and formed a part of that family. This was to ensure that they did not begin to feel any bitterness towards their relatives for neglectful treatment.

Necromancy is the art of predicting the future by means of communicating with the dead. As a technique it falls within the sphere of magic as practised by witches or magicians, and its use is very ancient.[31] The shades of heroes formed a special class among the dead and were considered to be especially powerful after their death because of the power they had held during life. Alexander the Great was an example of this, and the worship of deceased Roman emperors was a form of such hero worship. It was believed that the shades of someone famed for his powers in life could protect his local area after his death and that while usually benevolent, he could also turn into a Daemon and cause epilepsy or mental illnesses.[32] Stories about haunted houses were as popular in Rome as they are now, and there was a strong belief that spirits could remain to haunt their place of death.[33]

Black magic is the technique of summoning up one of the lower daemons, and of arousing its natural anger, then directing that anger towards a victim in the hope of doing them harm. This could be a very risky operation, and the magician involved would need to take extra precautions for his own protection. No ordinary magician would attempt to influence the higher gods, but the 'lower' daemons, who may have once enjoyed great prestige as deities, were believed to have fallen in status and become sufficient for the needs of an ordinary magician, without him having to expose himself to the far greater dangers of tackling the stronger powers.

Plato, in his 'The Republic' mentions guardian daemons that accompany people through their lives, know their innermost thoughts and feelings, or their most secret actions. Once a person dies, they are then able to act as their advocates, or even accusers, before the final judgement. Aristotle – who was called the father of scientific daemonology – had a theory regarding subordinate or lesser gods, who inhabited the planets. Many ordinary people had a firm belief in evil spirits, which were able to affect the behaviour of humans against their will and better instincts, although others thought that this was merely an excuse used to explain their own shortcomings and lack of control.

Plutarch assigned some of the functions of gods to the daemons, but unlike the gods, daemons would eventually grow old and die, which is how he explained the decline of the great oracles of the ancient world. He suggested that daemons, rather than gods, had been in charge of them, but had eventually lost their powers and had died off. [34]

Daemons could become visible but more usually showed themselves by sign. Philostratus in his 'Life of Apollonius of Tyana' tells of the ghost of an Ethiopian satyr who pursued the women of a particular village, making a terrible nuisance of himself. Apollonius set a trap for him, consisting of a trough full of wine to slow down his amorous inclinations, and although the satyr did not become visible, his presence was shown by the wine being seen to diminish as he drank it, so he later became inebriated and fell asleep. Even though the early Christians did believe in the powers of the Pagan gods (why else would they be so determined to be rid of them?) they considered them all to be evil, which can't have made the newly neglected deities behave well, but the followers of the new religion knew those powers were present and that in certain circumstances people could be at their mercy. Exorcism was practised quite often, and the 'Rituale Romanum' still includes the official handbook of the Catholic Church in such matters, *De Exorcismis et supplicationibus quibusdam* (Typis Polyglottis Vaticanis, 1999, 2013).[35]

There were, however, always non-believers and Lucien in his 'Lovers of Lies' enjoyed making fun of those people who believed in the supernatural world and tried everything to protect themselves from it.[36] The Christian church, as well as the Pagan, acknowledged that there was certainly 'something' outside of the normal order of things, and made much of being able to exorcise cases of what they called daemonic possession. This attests to the general climate of fear and the belief these other-worldly powers could take over one's body or mind and bend them to their will.

St Benedict (480-543 AD) was usually considered by the church to be the best of the exorcists available to fight the supernatural forces, and medals with his image can still be found. These were used in exactly the same way as the Pagan amulets had been, to offer personal protection for the wearer against evil spirits.[37] Whether these amulets show the image of St Benedict or Isis, the intention not only to protect but to give a measure of good health, good fortune, success and prosperity was the same. Most were cheaply made of stone or base metal, and some were designed to hold the scraps of paper or papyrus which could be rolled or folded inside, to be worn next to the skin.

The point of wearing such things where they would touch one's skin is that all human fluids, including sweat, were valuable in the search for extra power. All human 'debris', such as hair, fingernail or toenail clippings, even the first stubble shaved from a young man's face, all formed a part of the life force. The spell, blessing, prayer or charm (all amounting to the same thing) they contained would perform the same function as the wearing of an image of the Eye of Horus, or the later crosses and holy medals. The opinions of the educated and cynical in these matters, when common sense becomes blunted by the sheer fear of the unknown, were unlikely to influence the feelings of ordinary people. Most had little if any leisure time in which to ponder the mysteries, and life was hard enough without some outside force making things more difficult, so the easiest response was a quick trip to the nearest magician or amulet maker in the hope of deflecting the worst of the surrounding malignity.

Even so innocuous an item as an amulet, an item supposed to represent 'white' magic, could be used otherwise. Once any amulet had been made, a ritual of consecration could intoned over it. This was not always necessary, as most of them would have been bought in the marketplace and made in bulk, to be worn immediately, often on a thong of donkey leather. In certain cases, the carving of some design, or the addition of certain letters or words, might be considered an act of consecration. The very act of writing or carving anything could, to an illiterate person, imply the use of some esoteric magic which was available only to the initiated, that is someone more educated.

Some Greco-Egyptian amulets clearly express a wish to do harm to another person and may have been intended only for such use during a ritual or formal curse ceremony. The chariot races and other sporting events provide examples of the use of these amulets containing curses. At these times, the hopes and feelings of the spectators were strongly engaged, and they might also have bet more money than they could afford on the outcome, making both the charioteers and their horses (as we have already seen) the victims of curses. To counteract this, even the horses would often be hung with protective amulets and the people who drove them, who were already superstitious, would wear their own.

There are frescoes and sculptures which show many scenes of the Circus in which the horses are wearing little bells on their harness, which serve the same function, that of driving away evil spirits or malign influences. Bells have always been used for this purpose, from church bells to cow bells, but failing owning a bell, any metallic object would do the same job, hence the horse brass.[38]

Plutarch, who witnessed the rapid growth of the cult of Isis during his lifetime, clearly considered that even the 'good' deities of that pantheon appeared daemonic. They must certainly have looked very strange to people who were accustomed to gods and goddesses in purely human form who behaved the way that normal humans did, only with greater powers and sometimes shorter tempers. The animal-headed deities of Egypt would have taken some getting used to, but the Romans adapted them as they adapted almost everything else, to make them more easily acceptable. They harnessed their powers and qualities into a recognisable Roman viewpoint, resulting sometimes in an even stranger combination of animal-headed people wearing togas. Even the element of magic within the Egyptian religion could be adapted and added to the magical practices already well established and flourishing in Rome.[39]

One practice that fitted well into both religious traditions was casting horoscopes. According to Ptolemy, the art of medical astrology was first developed in Egypt with the physician-astrologer examining the patient and casting his nativity at the same time. This would give him additional information about the patient's state of health and the stars could warn of weak points to be watched out for. If the physician was hesitating between two forms of treatment to be used, the stars could indicate the best route to take. The ancient astrologers made an effort to determine, as closely as possible, the moment of the client's or patient's birth. This could be vital, as the nature of the universe changed from second to second and meant that normal methods of measuring time were not accurate enough to give a reading, only an astrolabe would do.

The term 'astrolabe' originally meant 'star-taking' and in Ptolemy's time the astrologers not only observed the sky but used charts, observations of nature and kept records of unusual celestial phenomena to define the 'astral time' of a person's birth, in relation to the lapse of time since the mose recent phenomena were recorded.[40]

Mars and Saturn were usually considered to be 'bad' planets to be born under, but their influence could be weakened if they were in more favourable positions at the time of a birth, for instance if Mars were in Aries, or Saturn in Aquarius. If both were in hostile signs at the time of the child's birth, it might suggest that the person would be destined to be a criminal. Saturn allied to Mars in 'honourable' positions could forecast outspoken people, who were obnoxious, boastful, pitiless or harsh and quarrelsome. In the opposite positions, Saturn and Mars could suggest robbers, pirates, profiteers, lawbreakers, thieves, perjurers, or even murderers.

With the Sun in the same house as Mars, it could create athletes who were daredevils anxious to please their audience, or tellers of obscene jokes who were likely to grow old in foreign lands and be buried among strangers, and whose lives would provide as much low-class entertainment as their arts.[41]

The Roman, Vettius Valens, an astrologer of the second century AD, felt that it was his duty to tell his clients the truth about what the future held for them, as well as trying to help them to face it and deal with it. Most people, however, were not willing to face an unpleasant forecast, and preferred to cherish vain hopes. People are always eager to believe that things will not be as bad as predicted, and then resort to prayers to foster new hopes of deliverance. These frantic prayers are likely to be in vain, and Valens refers them to

... the professional actors who play their roles and leave the stage when the plot demands their exit, as during life we must play the part assigned to us by Fate, and try to make the best of it, even if we do not like it very much... Fate had decreed for every human being the unalterable realisation of his horoscope, fortifying it with many causes of good and bad things to come. Because of them, two self-begotten goddesses Hope and Chance, act as the servants of Destiny. They rule our lives and by compulsion and deception make us accept what has been decreed ... some find a part of their expectations fulfilled, so put up higher stakes and wait for a permanently favourable outcome, without realising how unstable things are, and how quickly accidents can happen. Some who are disappointed in their expectations, not just occasionally but again and again, surrender body and soul to passions and live dishonoured lives and are disgraced, or else they exist as slaves of fickle chance and treacherous hope, and are never able to achieve anything in life ... it is impossible by prayers or sacrifices to overcome the foundation that was laid in the beginning, or substitute another one more to one's liking. Whatever is in store for us will happen even if we do not pray for it and what is not fated will not happen, despite all our prayers ... we must act the character that Fate has assigned to us and adapt ourselves to what happens in any given situation, even if we do not agree. For if one refuses, he will suffer it anyway and then get no credit.[42]

This fatalistic attitude is certainly a hard road to follow, yet for anyone who is able to give up personal satisfactions in order to be a willing part of an overall plan, it would certainly mean a great saving in sacrifices, prayers, gifts to temples, or vain hoping for rewards.

Alchemy, the forerunner of modern chemistry, was an occult philosophy which attempted to connect the universe more closely with humans and it contained elements of astrology, religion, theosophy and mysticism. Much of ancient alchemy is highly technical and special apparatus was constructed in a similar way to modern research methods. The ultimate goals, however, were not scientific as we would understand the term. Although some discoveries were made, they tended to be accidental or unrecognised, even forgotten in the greater aim, which was the attempt to turn base metals into silver and gold, or to find some elixir to prolong human life far beyond its normal span, or even the creation of a human being by some means other than the obvious method. It was firmly believed that enormous wealth and power would result from such discoveries, but they ignored the enormous amounts of money and other resources which were used up while they experimented, wasted.

The oldest extant tract on alchemy, the Papyrus Ebers, a 68-foot-long roll discovered at Thebes, is sometimes referred to as 'the oldest book in the world'. It concerns the uses of chemistry, or alchemy, for medicinal purposes. It contains over eight hundred prescriptions for remedies, which were carefully guarded and were believed to have been based on divine revelations.[43] The Papyrus Ebers was purchased in Luxor during the winter of 1873-1874 by Georg Ebers. It dates to around 1,500 BC and has been translated and published, while the original is in the library of the University of Leipzig.

Alchemists worked on drugs to restore health and prolong life, but they also developed dyes for fabrics. We know that the famous Tyrian purple which was much in demand by the wealthy of the Roman Empire was a secret of the Tyrians, and so long as they retained their monopoly over it, their profits were enormous. Alchemists attempted to compete by making similar dyes, and these were cheaper to produce and to a certain extent they succeeded. Some mummies have been found with wrappings of an indigo dye which is still fresh and unfaded today.

Cosmetics, particularly in Egypt, along with perfumes, lotions and creams, were exported for great profits. They knew of processes such as oxidation, solutions, reduction, smelting and alloying and both mercury and sulphur could show amazing effects and proved very popular regarding colour changes. Distillation of spirits may also have been discovered by Egyptian alchemists towards the end of the antique period, but the fermentation of barley into beer had been used for thousands of years, along with the fermentation of grape juice to make wine from ancient Greece.[44]

Egyptian technology reached a high level early, with a flourishing industry which could produce aromatic oils, perfumes, and blends of incense for domestic use and for export. Blended oils were used both on the living and on the dead and could also serve as medications. Jars have been found containing residues of perfumes intended not only for personal use, but also to be burned as sacrifices to the deities. The anointing oil and the sacred incense which were described by Moses were psychoactive or capable of altering a person's mental state and these enabled the priests to both 'see' and 'hear' the gods.

Some years ago, the ruins of a building were found at En Boquet near the Dead Sea. From the vegetal matter found there it is possible that this was an early alchemical laboratory, specialising in the production of aromatic essences. Plutarch described Queen Cleopatra on her barge, surrounded by her servants, and wearing fantastic robes. He especially remarked on the 'wonderful scents from many perfumes' which emanated from them.[45]

Many of these great achievements bordered onor suggested the magical, particularly if their recipes were kept secret. An important example, much used in warfare and to great effect, was Greek fire. This was a highly combustible mixture which had proved enormously useful in naval engagements, as it continued to burn while on water. Its exact formula is now lost to us, although some historical sources believe it was probably based on naptha and quicklime. The Byzantines would use it as an incendiary weapon, thrown from small terracotta pots, like a hand grenade. It could also be 'fired' from a tube, to give the effect of a simple flame-thrower. One of its names was 'sticky fire' as it adhered to clothing, skin or armour and was almost impossible to put out. Dousing with water had no effect on it, and while burning it did horrendous damage. However, it could only be used on a calm sea with favourable wind conditions, or it could be blown back onto the user. Later Muslim countries would counter this problem by covering themselves with hides soaked with vinegar, and it was also said that urine had a dousing effect, having an effect on the chemical reaction.

Armies who captured this astonishing concoction found that they were unable to recreate it for themselves, which added to its mystique and the fear it engendered. Julius Africanus, writing in the third century AD, records a mixture that ignited spontaneously from heat or intense sunlight, which was generally used for thrown grenades and night attacks.[46]

To anyone on the wrong side of it this strange compound, it must have seemed to have come direct from the infernal regions. Livy, in the early first centuryAD, described the priestesses of Bacchus dipping 'fire' into water, 'which did not extinguish the fire, for it was made of sulphur mixed with lime.'[47] However sensibly one tried to explain its composition, its effects were terrifying and highly successful.

The mystical side of alchemy is well documented. Many alchemic operations may be considered as 'sacrificial offerings' and were only to be attempted once the alchemist concerned had been initiated into the higher mysteries. The ultimate goal of this – as in the mystery religions – was personal salvation. Alchemy could be used for more than a science, becoming a way of life in exactly the same way as did magic or religion. The alchemist would continue to study, pray, distil and meditate and perhaps might even make an important discovery, but the search for perfection would continue.[48]

Weather magic was performed regularly and was an aspect of the arts which had great practical importance. It could determine feast or famine as well as affecting the daily lives of people who largely lived out of doors.

The concept that bad weather was caused by malicious daemons lived on, hence the necessity of banishing them from time to time, which became the responsibility of the weather conjurors. The belief that such things as thunderstorms and lightning along with other natural phenomena were manifestations of the gods also held firm, requiring the usual placatory sacrifices. Dolichenus, associated with Jupiter, was a sky and weather deity, as was Tempestates, a Roman goddess of weather who had a temple outside the Porta Capena in Rome. This temple had been vowed by Lucius Cornelius Scipio, Consul in 259 BC, after he had been a survivor of a great storm off Corsica during the First Punic War.[49]

The Poplifugia, held in July, commemorated the 'flight of the people' to Goat's Marsh on the Campus Martius. At that time, young women, originally maidservants but later including free-born women, dressed in their finery and staged a mock combat there, followed by feasting and working at magic close to an ancient fig tree. These rites were believed to be connected with the weather and they survived until the end of the Republic. The details were handed down by Plutarch but had also been recorded in many earlier works.[50]

Rites associated with weather magic were, from time to time, officially prohibited, but they survived to continue into medieval times. The magicians involved in this type of magic were believed to have the power to raise or prevent storms and were subsequently feared. For that reason, they were included in the general bans and prohibitions such as those of Sulla's 'Lex Cornelia Sicariis et Veneficiis' of 81 BC, which was still in effect in the early Empire.[51] This Lex Cornelia regarding the use of magic came down firmly on all occult practices:

It is agreed that those guilty of the magic arts, be inflicted with the supreme punishment i.e. to be thrown to the beasts, or crucified. Actual magicians, however, will be burned alive. (Section 17)

No one is permitted to have these books of the magic arts in their possession. Anyone in whose possession they are found will have their property confiscated and the books publicly burned. They themselves shall be deported to an island. Not only is the profession of this art, but also its knowledge, to be prohibited. (Section 18)

The Christian church would later go to great lengths to suppress all forms of Pagan magic, if only to replace them with its own versions, but belief in the supernatural and in powers that could be cajoled or controlled, in potions, spells, herbs and all kinds of charms and bewitchments concerning love and health, have continued. For many medieval churchmen, the continued hold of the 'old' gods along with their rites, charms, divining, alchemy and everything else connected to them, was condemned as idolatrous, devil worship, or a way of controlling the feeble-minded, even while they produced their own versions of the same. Paul called the old beliefs 'sins' and ordered even medical treatises to be burned, and also the amulets upon which people had depended, yet these amulets were replaced by holy medals and eventually by pilgrim badges, so what was the difference? Either could produce the same amount of faith or effect.

The old beliefs, while certainly including charlatans and the money-hungry as do all beliefs, were open and inclusive and each person had freedom of choice. This aspect would be eroded and replaced by a mandatory acceptance of the teaching of the new cult, along with suspension of freedom of thought and oppression of women, who generally came to be considered as merely vessels of sin. The new cult would also usher in the persecution of non-believers such as the Jewish people, who had always lived peacefully in Rome, and the attempted extermination of anyone (although more often women), who was accused of continuing to dabble in what were then described as 'the black arts'.

Alongside the persecutions, the new church developed its own 'occult' rituals, including Christian curse-tablets or 'tabellae defixionum', while a casting-out rite, which could be used against anyone who had been condemned as anathema, continued to be used. The old Roman forms of 'Damnatio' 'Devotio' and 'Exsecratio' lived on in Christian guise, as is shown by the Pontificale Romanum, the church's book of ceremonies which Bishops may perform.[52] This book not only describes the performance of the sacraments but includes the rites of damning or casting out (Damnatio) with a formal curse (Devotio) and Exsecratio, which is the power to perform such a curse. These powers are not always limited to Bishops, but according to current Latin Catholic Canon Law can, in certain circumstances, be used by others, including abbots and rulers of dioceses or quasi-dioceses who may not have been ordained as Bishops.[53]

This ability to call down greater powers in order to curse or condemn – however rarely the powers might actually be used – is no different from recourse to the magic that the church professes to abhor. Despite many efforts at suppression and the use of fearful and inventive punishments, even after the countless occasions when dabbling in the occult rites has failed to produce the required results, the desire to try again has never faded.

This human need to have contact with something else outside the realm of ordinary human experience, something that can command unusual powers and perhaps produce extraordinary effects for those who believe firmly enough, is still with us, despite the real advances of the modern age – and every effort to eradicate the fascination of the mysteries has been superfluous.

8

The Calendar of Festivals

The Roman calendar of official festivals was both extensive and complicated. Over time many of the festivals had lost their agricultral origins, which left them at odds with an increasingly urban populaton. Some others had merely lost popularity and although they were still celebrated, they had become the kind of religious occasion where a priest celebrated on behalf of the people, and the vast majority of those people allowed them to pass without active participation.

There were nevertheless plenty left and many of these remained popular and well attended, particularly the festivals which promised some kind of excitement, such as a chariot race. As the Romans did not have a Sabbath these festival days were times of relaxation and release for many, but the concept of 'non-working' days was still alien. Work continued for most people unless they were actually attending some festival or taking part in one, and there was always the preparation of food and the selling of wines. Nobody was obliged to join in, and for some people the only acknowledgment of the event would be to stop work briefly as a procession passed by. The sight of people working was considered inauspicious as well as being disrespectful towards the priests. There were enough 'unlucky' days already without tempting fate by offending any god unnecessarily, and the unfortunate days were well known by most people, even though they might not be marked on the calendars. They would certainly be avoided for the start of any new venture or important family occasion.

The Kalends was the first day of every month, but the Nones and the Ides changed slightly, depending on whether it was a thirty-one-day month or not. The thirty-one-day months were March, May, July and October, in which cases the Nones would be on the seventh day of the month and the Ides on the fifteenth. On the thirty-day months, the Nones would fall on the fifth day of the month, with the Ides being on the thirteenth day.[1]

The days immediately following the Kalends, the Nones or the Ides were all considered to be unlucky generally, but for the highly superstitious person the fourth day before the Kalends, Nones or Ides would be added to the list. The days when the Mundus was opened on the Palatine, which were August, 5 October and 8 November, were very unlucky indeed, as were the days when the families remembered their dead – the Parentalia from 13 to 21 February, and the Lemuria on 9, 11 and 13 May. These were all days when the ghosts of the dead might be expected to walk.

More than eighty days in any one year had some unlucky taint and whole chunks of time were considered inauspicious for any important new beginnings such as marriages. The whole of the month of May was one of these, as was the first half of June. No marriage should take place on the Kalends, the Nones or the Ides of any month, because the following day, the unlucky one, would be the first day of the bride's new life. Roman armies were not expected to engage when the Mundus was open, or during the Latin Festival (the Feriae Latinae), which was a moveable date early in the year. Saturnalia, originally on 17 December, was also proscribed, as was any date which was the anniversary of a Roman military disaster.[2]

For the public life of the state, the Nundinae was important. This was the market day, originally the eighth day of each week but called 'Nundinae' or ninth day, because in early Rome when days were counted the two terminal days at each end were included. One period of Nundinae to the next was the Nundinum and the days were spoken of as 'the Nundinae' or the day before the Nundinae and so on.

The interval between the first and the third of three successive Nundinae (which, when counting both terminal dates would be a period of seventeen days in total), was known as a 'Trinundinum' and a number of public functions had to be performed on three successive Nundinae, for instance the publication of the candidates for public elections or the announcement of a bill which was to be brought before a public assembly. In early Rome, the names of debtors and often details of their arrest were publicly exhibited for that period, to give friends and relatives an opportunity to bail them out.[3]

The increase in astrology during the mid- to late Republican period did a great deal to familiarise Romans with a week of only seven days. When each day felt the influence of a particular planet, then the superstitious – and there were many – would want to know which planet it was, and which were the unlucky days connected with it.

During the time of Augustus, Saturn's Day (Saturday), was considered particularly unlucky for starting on a long journey. Though the lecturer Diogenes always spoke in Rhodes on Saturdays, and even at the request of the Emperor's stepson, Tiberius,[4] he refused to change his day.

The first public record in Rome of the change to the seven-day week is from a calendar dated between 19 BC and 14 AD. It came from the Sabine area, although the names of the days are not given. The first column merely marks the seven days of the week, while the second column shows the eight days of the usual Nundinum. Another fragmentary calendar from the time of Augustus marks the days of a seven-day week, as does one from the early days of the Empire.[5]

Inscriptions from Latinum and Campania that show the different market days in different towns, have the names of the towns and the names of the seven days of the week. On some of these there are holes against the town names and the days, so that a marker could be inserted to indicate when the next market day would be in each town. With a planetary week of only seven days, but a market week still using eight days, the day of the market would move forward by one day for each successive week. If held on a Tuesday on one week, it would fall on the Wednesday in the following week, and so on.

A graffito at Pompeii records a date in the year 60 AD in the fullest possible way, saying 'In the Consulship of Nero Caesar Augustus and Cossus Lentulus, eight days before the Ides of February, on a Sunday, the sixteenth day of the Moon, the market day at Cumae – five days before the market day in Pompeii.'[6] This confirms a statement by Josephus that by the second half of the first century AD everyone was becoming familiar with the seven-day week. Cassius Dio, writing in the early third century, said the same and Juvenal suggested that by the early second century AD schools followed the seven-day timetable, and on a certain day each week recitals took place, like the lectures of Diogenes in Rhodes a century earlier. When Avidius Cassius was Governor of Syria in the early second century AD he gave his troops a full military exercise 'every seventh day' – once a week.[7]

The moneylenders in Rome were especially busy on the Kalends, Nones and Ides of each month, for on those days interest on borrowed money was due to be paid. The Kalends of January and July were also the dates when rents were to be paid. Cassius Dio stated that it was unlucky for the public life of the state if the Kalends of the first month of the year (originally March but later changed to January), should fall on the Nundinae. It was also thought unfortunate if the Nones of any month coincided with the Nundinae and the public disasters of 78 BC and 52 BC were attributed to the clash of these dates.[8]

These deaths and rebellions could, of course, have happened at any time but at a time of general unrest it is convenient to blame the troubles of the state on the unlucky aspects of the dates concerned, or on a poor conjunction of the planets.

The Roman religious year had both fixed and moveable dates and in the Republic there were forty-five regular Festivals or 'Feriae Publicae' that had the same day each year. This would actually amount to fifty-eight festival days if you include the Ides of each month, which were sacred to Jupiter, and the Kalends of March, which were sacred to Mars. These were festivals whose expenses were paid for by the state, mainly for the sacrificial offerings and these days were also usually the anniversaries of the dedication of some temple or altar to that divinity whose festival it was. Jupiter was the god most greatly honoured, followed by Mars. Why these festivals did not usually fall on the even days of the months, except for the Regifugium (24 February) and the March Equirra which was on the 14th, we cannot be sure, though the odd numbered days were generally considered to be more fortunate than the even, so that may have been sufficient reason.

The Calendar of Festivals is essentially constructed around agriculture, despite the urban lives of the majority of the people by the time of Augustus. In April there were festivals to avert diseases for the plants, and to encourage their fertility. In June, September and November the farmers would be hard at work, so there were fewer festivals, but in February and December, when the farmers had more time to spare, there were many more.

Even the army had fixed seasons. Fighting was vital to Rome's survival, certainly in the early days, and levies were held and conscripts were called up in March. So it was in March that the shields of Mars were taken down by the Salii priests, and Mars was honoured by a series of festivals. He was also honoured again in October, which usually marked the end of the fighting season.[9]

The moveable feasts were fixed and announced each year by the Consul or Praetor, or by one of the priestly colleges. These festivals were named the 'Feriae Conceptivae' and the most important of these was the three- or four-day-long Latin Festival, which took place early in the year, the consequence of the old tradition of Consuls commanding the armies on campaign, which would have meant that the festival would need to be completed before they left Rome. This method of dating the festival continued even when the Consuls were no longer expected to command the armies personally in the field. The Compitalia at the end of December or in early January was also on a date fixed by the authorities, as were several other 'Feriae Conceptivae', which had once been of agricultural significance.[10] The Compitalia was for one day only, but extended to three during the Empire. It was usually selected by the Praetor for a date in late December or early January.

The Sementivae, which took place on two days in January, separated by a seven-day interval, had its dates chosen by the Pontifices. It was a festival of spring sowing with offerings made to Tellus on the first day and Ceres on the second. These offerings included cakes made of spelt flour and a pregnant cow. The oxen used for ploughing the fields would be garlanded and it meant a general holiday for the farmers. Masks and puppets hung from the trees in celebration and Ovid equated it with the Paganalia. The Paganlia was essentially a village festival and the work Pagan meant 'villager' originally. The festival was connected to the Sementivae which was held in January usually on the 24th to the 26th, with offerings to Tellus and Ceres. The date was fixed by the Magistri Pagi.

The Ambarvalia took place on three days at the end of May. This was a rite of purification and involved a procession around the fields. It was essentially beating the boundaries to drive away evil spirits. Sacrifices would be offered at various points during the procession and all agricultural work ceased for the duration.

The Augurium Canarium, which took place on a date selected by the Augurs, usually took place when the corn was in ear, before the harvest. This rite involved the sacrifice of a red-coloured dog.

The Fornacalia or Feast of the Ovens was held on a day in February which was fixed by the Curio Maximus for each Curia. These Curia were citizenry groups, eventually numbering around thirty, and every Roman was presumed to belong to one or another. They designated an Assembly, or Council, where official and religious matters were dealt with. The Fornacalia would be arranged on the understanding that those people who missed their Curia's chosen date, or didn't know to which Curia they belonged, could celebrate instead on 17 February, which was also known as the Feast of Fools.[11]

There were more. The Feriae Imperativae were days of honouring the gods when all businesses, paticularly lawsuits and the dealings of the courts, were suspended. These were the days which were held 'on demand' when special celebrations or expiations were called for. These were often held in response to a particular event, or some catastrophe or natural phenomena which might mean the displeasure of the gods. It could also be a day of thanksgiving if a threatened crisis had been averted. They could include the day of a successful general's Triumph, when the victorious man was honoured by a day of celebration, also on a date fixed by the Magistrates, on his return to Rome. This type of celebration initially only lasted for one day but by the end of the

Republic the Triumph days had multiplied. Fifteen full days were granted to Caesar at the end of his Gallic campaign in 57 BC. Twenty further days were granted to him only two years later. By then Julius Caesar had Rome over a barrel and the Magistrates, whose powers depended on him, were only too eager to placate him.

Cicero proposed a 'Supplicationes' of fifty days in 43 BC after the Battle of Mutina, which was granted by the Senate and Augustus was also to allow Supplicationes on fifty-five other occasions, at an average of sixteen days each time, totalling around eight hundred and eighty days. These Supplicationes were days of public prayers, either asking for aid or giving thanks for aid received. They could also be ordered in response to the appearance of some 'prodigy' or unusual and inexplicable happening. The people wore wreaths of flowers and leaves, attended sacrifices and visited temples. There was no comparable inflation for the normal Triumphs, which remained at one or two per year or quite often none at all.

The Empire did bring in some new celebrations, both official and unofficial, when the imperial birthdays were added to the usual list, along with the dedications and imperial consecrations, which added thirty-two new festivals to the already extensive list between 45 BC and 37 AD.

Each new emperor was eager to add his own 'special' days, for family birthdays, anniversaries of various kinds and their own Games. Most of these died out once that particular emperor was dead or replaced by a new one, but the Ludi Augustales, which became an annual event in Rome under the Emperor Tiberius, was eventually to go on for a full ten days, from 3 October to 12 October.

The memory of Gaius Julius Caesar, by then considered to be a god due to the brilliant propaganda-skills of Octavianus (later Augustus), along with the ever-popular Germanicus, were still celebrated by the army long after they were dead; and the imperial ladies had their own days of respect. The oriental cults which had grown popular in Rome added their own dates of celebration and when Gaius Caligula sanctioned the worship of Isis (Aset) there was a seven-day festival which started on 28 October and culminated in a three-day long 'ecstasy' from the 1st of November to the 3rd. Isis also had the 'Navigidium Isis' in the spring (the Romans continued to use the Greek version of the goddess's name, rather than the Egyptian one), and this festival opened the sailing season on the fifth day of March.

The Great Mother, introduced at the end of the Second Punic War, only had one celebration day on 27 March when her statue was washed, and her days only extended with the Taurobolium in the second century AD. This was due to the general discomfort regarding her rites and the greater popularity of Isis and Magna Mater.[12]

Mithras also grew in favour, due to the Emperor Aurelian's devotion to this sun god and to the erection of a great temple to Sol Invictus in 274 AD. When such imported religions received official recognition, their main festivals became Dies Feriati, or official festival days. If they did not become an official part of Rome's state religion their own followers would continue to worship them, observing their own dates.

This is not to say that everyone spent every spare moment in running off to one temple or another. Most people had to work and many had no particular religious affiliations anyway. Others, like Cicero, never really observed religious festivals except to use the day's name in his usual correspondence, otherwise remaining indifferent to the religious days and their ceremonies. Cicero stated that the festival days gave free men a respite from quarrelsome litigation as the law courts were closed on important dates, and he preferred to enjoy restful days off in the country. Shops did not shut, nor did workmen down tools except to avoid 'polluting' a religious procession by their work continuing. A crier usually went ahead of any important procession to give warning of its approach.

Slaves usually had a holiday at the Compitalia (2 January) and the army was known to be particularly fond of the festival of Saturnalia, which also became a holiday of sorts for slaves, with masters and slaves exchanging places briefly.[13]

A small number of festival days did mean a full day's holiday for certain groups of workers. May 15 was when Rome's merchants did honour to Mercury, their particular patron. This was the date on which his temple was founded, and they would sprinkle water there and also upon their bodies as an act of purification, probably hoping that the previous year's sharp practices would be forgiven and that they could have plenty of new customers to fleece in the future.

The fishermen had their own Games, the Ludi Piscatorii, on 7 June, in the Trastavere area of Rome, which was also the day of the Vestalia for women, dedicated to Vesta, when the bakers and millers had a festival and their donkeys and millstones were decorated with violets and small loaves.

The flute-players holiday on 13 June has already been mentioned, which culminated in a feast at the temple of Jupiter on the Capitol. There they usually became very drunk and then roamed the streets of the city, wearing masks and making a nuisance of themselves. It was a time when all decent citizens locked their doors and kept out of the way of the marauding gangs of musicians.

The Neptunalia was on 23 July, a celebration for the bargemen and dockhands who worked on the River Tiber. They celebrated the

Portunalia also, which fell on 17 August. Portunus was originally a god who protected doors (porta), but who became the protector of harbours and had his own Flamen, the Flamen Portunalis, and a beautiful little temple still surviving on the Forum Boarium. The Neptunalia was one of Rome's oldest festivals, sacred to Neptune the god of water. He also became associated with horses and the god Consus, and there was a temple in the Circus Flaminius within the Campus Martius. As well as on 23 July, Neptune had a festival on the first day of December.[14]

Marcus Aurelius attempted to curtail the vast number of festival days by trying to ensure that two hundred and thirty days were left free of such celebrations, in order to allow the businesses and litigation courts to continue. The eminent Prof. J. P .V .D. Balsdon emphasised the point that business went on during festivals, hoping that, '...in the distant future, no scholar happening upon an Italian calendar, in which every day is a saint's day of one sort or another, will suggest that the Italians never did any work!'[15] The average Roman did work much as usual, perhaps only showing interest in the most important festivals and letting the others pass him by.

As the action of Marcus Aurelius showed, there was some disruption to the normal working day when the Dies Nefasti interfered with the sitting of the law courts. These were days when no political assembly was permitted, and it was not permissible to initiate any legal business of a civil nature, although such business could continue if a sacrifice was made first. Such days were determined by the Pontiffs and were shown as being marked with an 'N' in the calendars. There were fifty-eight such days in the pre-Julian calendar, and fifty-nine days marked 'NP' on calendars, which meant 'Nefasti Publici', days when assemblies and legal business were certainly not permitted. This was probably because they coincided with major festivals.[16]

The public business of the state was conducted on Dies Fasti, usually marked 'F' on the calendars, and on Dies Comitiales, marked with a 'C'. Public assemblies could not meet on any day which was a Dies Comitialis, unless that day also happened to coincide with the Nundinae, or the celebration of one of the moveable feasts, or with a Feriae Imperativae. Public meetings could not be held on the Dies Fasti, for these days were reserved exclusively for the judiciary. Legal transactions could and did take place also on the Dies Comitiales on which a public meeting was being held – so long as it was not also a day of Feriae Conceptivae or Imperativae – confused? You should be! Probably most other people were also confused, or more likely just got on with their lives and ignored the complications. Only those people directly involved in state or legal business needed to be aware of the routine of permitted or forbidden days.

The number of useful working days had certainly become rather small, and Julius Caesar added a further ten days, when he changed the calendar in 46 BC (the ancient usage date for this being 708). He made them all into Dies Fasti, because he believed that the number had to be enlarged to permit sensible practices to prevail.[17] By this and other small changes, the number of proper working days rose to fifty-two and Augustus is said to have altered the designation of thirty other days, in order to make the number of available days larger still. [18]

In the second century AD, Marcus Aurelius made further changes, as the earlier days set aside by Caesar and by Augustus had been encroached upon by new festivals, many in honour of the imperial family. He was to institute Dies Iudiciarii to the original Dies Fasti, making available new dates which were intended for legal and public business, thereby increasing the total to 230 days in the year. Even this was barely enough as during the time of Julius Caesar the total had been 243 days set aside for such business.

A further 106 days of the Republican calendar had been given over to Nefasti, which were days not available for any public business. Of these, forty-five were the festivals already referred to, but the rest would also have some religious significance. Even in ancient Rome there could be confusion over the meaning of the word 'Nefastus' as strictly speaking it denoted a day on which public business could not be conducted, but this did not imply that the day was actually inauspicious. In everyday parlance, it came to mean a black or unlucky day.

When the Emperor Nero killed his mother Agrippina in 59 AD, one Senator proposed that in future the anniversary of her birthday should be regarded as a Dies Nefastus. It might have been more logical to make the date on which she gave birth to Nero into a Dies Nefastus, but in any case, it was an incorrect use of the term. [19]

During the Republic it had been perfectly in order for the Senate to meet on any date, even on festival days or the so-called unlucky days. After the passing of the Lex Pupia (date unknown), meetings on any Dies Comitiales were forbidden, or perhaps only on a Dies Comitialis when a public assembly was held. Senators were not prevented from meeting on a Comitial day once the meeting of the Assembly had broken up, and in any case a dispensation could always be granted to the Senate by its own resolution, provided that no Tribune intersposed his veto. There has been some speculation on the date of the Lex Pupia itself, and also on the definite nature of it, unfortunately without conclusive result.[20]

From 153 BC onwards, when the first day of January was the beginning of the civil year, January, February and March had the greatest amount of Senatorial business. The Tribunes who entered office on 10 December and the Consuls, who took office on the first day of January, all had legislations to introduce. In February, the foreign embassies were heard, and in March the provincial governors were appointed. After that there would be recess from early April to mid-May, when Senators were free to leave Rome, when they usually took the opportunity to visit their villas or their estates in Campania. In Cicero's time (except for the two years of public crisis in 44 and 43 BC) there are no known meetings of the Senate between 5 April and 15 May.[21]

Senators would return to Rome for the elections of the Magistrates, which were held in July, the month when the election of Tribunes had always taken place. Unfortunately, the holding of the elections at a time when farmers were busy with harvests and threshing and (in the time before Gaius Marius) the citizens on their military service were also unavailable, gave a disproportionate weight to the urban vote. Likewise, during the Republic, the Senators were not supposed to leave Italy, but their villas would probably only be a few miles outside Rome. In theory, again during the Republic, they might have been compelled to attend the Senate if they were resident in the city. When Marcus Antonius threatened to have Cicero brought to the Senate by force on 1 September 44 BC, there was no precedent for him to force such attendance, and despite all his threats he did not actually hold any such power.

The business of the courts, as with the business of the Senate, was transacted as far as possible during the first eight months of the year, despite the usually extreme heat of July and August in the city. By the extortion law, the Lex Acilia of 123 BC, Praetors were banned from accepting new cases for trial if the application was not brought before 1 September. Even then, April tended to have already been largely earmarked for Games, which made it something of a holiday for the law courts. Augustus also took into account the fact that in September and October large numbers of members would wish to be out of the city, on their estates, so lots were cast and only those selected by chance were obliged to attend during those two months.[22] It was always taken for granted that attendance during December was very likely to be poor.

The effect of the usual interrruption during public festivals and the Games of court proceedings was evident during Cicero's prosecution of Gaius Verres, who was a Magistrate notorious for his misgovernment of Sicily. Cicero was already campaigning for the Consulate and feared that many nobles would oppose him, but in the event he was successful in his endeavours and the opposition was restricted to his usual rivals, Gaius Antonius (the uncle of Marc Antony), and Lucius Sergius Catalina, both of whom already had tarnished reputations. However, Cicero had been under great stress at the time and feared that Verres's defender Quintus

Hortensius would be able to use the proliferation of holidays and Games around that time to drag out the case until the end of the year.[23]

Perhaps the best way to demonstrate how the religious calendar worked is to list the main celebrations in date order – so far as they are known – along with an explanation of their form and intended function. It must be remembered that despite the proliferation of holy days, the Romans simply enjoyed a procession and a bit of a show just as much as anyone else, particularly if it was followed by a dole of free food and wine. A good crowd might follow a procession in the hope of some entertainment or a free meal. A smaller ritual for a less popular deity, or one which only concerned the priests, would very likely be ignored.

January

Originally, the Roman year began in March with the onset of spring. However, for administrative purposes it was put back to the first day of January, when Julius Caesar reformed the calendar in 45 BC. The Julian calendar was then in use until the Gregorian calendar replaced it in 1582 AD and had been instituted because the Roman civic calendar had crept three months ahead of the solar calendar.

Caesar, advised by the Alexandrian astronomer Sosigenes, introduced the Egyptian Solar year as 365¼ days. The year was divided into twelve months, each with thirty or thirty-one days, except for February, which usually had only twenty-eight days, with an extra day added every fourth year. There was no February 29 in the Julian calendar in Roman 'leap' years as they simply repeated 23 February. To align the civic and solar calendars Caesar had added several extra days to 46 BC so that it eventually contained 445 days. However, due to misunderstandings the smooth working of the revised calendar was not actually achieved until 8 AD.

The first important event in the month of January was the procession and sacrifice for the new Consuls, the two men who took up their year's duty on that date. The solemn procession went along the Via Sacra to the Capitol Hill, where white bulls were sacrificed to Jupiter, in payment for the continued security of the state.

The **Compitalia** was the next event, usually taking place from 3 to 5 January. At the end of the Republic, it followed the Saturnalia and took place at the end of December, or sometimes in early January, but during the Empire it became fixed in date. This was a particularly Roman festival, which marked the end of the corn sowing and on country estates it still had many features in common with the Saturnalia. Slaves would be given extra rations – often including wine – and the estate bailiff, or

Vilicus, and his wife would dine with the estate workers. In this way, he represented the master, who may originally have shared the celebration with his field workers, but later he was less likely to be based on the estate itself, having become more urbanised.[24] The Saturnalia and the Compitalia would later be attacked by Christian writers (from the second century AD onwards) but the celebrations survived intact into the fifth century AD. They had been a reasonable way to allow servants to have a little freedom and to receive some small rewards for their work.

By the late fourth century onwards it was the Kalends (first day of each month), that Christians disapproved of, as in January of each year it had developed into a five-day festival (1-5 January), including the three days of the Games, the Ludi Compitales. It had become a very boisterous event, even more so than the Saturnalia and the Compitalia, which had originally been intended to honour the Lares Compitales, when shrines were erected where four roads intersected. The shrines were open on all sides to allow the Lares from neighbouring farms free passage. The farmers hung up their small woollen dolls – one for each free member of the household, with a woollen ball for each slave. Altars were set up and sacrifices made, and each day would end with general feasting. It was a good opportunity for masters and servants to let off steam in amity.

Augustus would transform this Lares worship within Rome, so that it became a public cult rather than a purely private one and the sacrifices were then conducted by a state priest. It was always a riotous affair and due to this rowdiness was twice suppressed, but Augustus wished it to be continued because it encouraged a sense of identity within Rome. He also used it to provide a truly 'Roman' festival, in the face of the encroachments from imported foreign religions.

The New Year celebrations were also a time for decorating the doors of houses with laurel wreaths, and having family horoscopes done, to find out what the coming year had in store.[25]

Agonalia fell on 9 January, in honour of Janus. This god with two faces represented beginnings and endings, not just of the year but of all old and new, looking at the past and forward into the future. There was usually a scramble at that time to ensure that debts were paid and other business matters completed. Janus was a varied deity and could refer to one's mindset in getting over problems, learning to live with difficulties or defeats and of keeping as optimistic an outlook as possible, always hoping for better things. He was one of the oldest of Rome's gods and the attitude of enthusiasm and confidence encapsulated the Roman spirit. As the god of all new beginnings, Janus was always mentioned first in any list of prayers to be said, and the first month of the year bore his name. It was customary to give small gifts to friends and relatives at that time, with lamps being especially popular, as they lighted the way into the New Year to come.

Janus was also honoured on 17 March, 21 May and 11 December, along with other deities, when the Rex Sacrorum sacrificed a ram at the Regia, and he often also shared celebrations with Liber Pater, Vediuvis and Sol Indiges.[26]

The **Carmentalia** was from the 11th to the 13th of January and was the festival of Carmentis, a goddess of childbirth. She also had a gift for prophecy (one of the meanings of the word 'Carmen' is oracle) and was popularly supposed to have lived an amazingly long life of one hundred and ten years. When she finally died, she was buried at the foot of the Capitol Hill close to the Porta Carmentalis. A minor Flamen was assigned to her, the Flamen Carmentalis, who would invoke her by one of two names, either Postuerta (feet first) or Porrima (head first) signifying the positions of a foetus.

It was said of her that she had once refused to attend a sacrifice at the Ara Maxima after Hercules had invited her, but after her regusal he then banned women from ever attending his festivities, making him a solely masculine deity. The 13th was also the Ides, always sacred to Jupiter.

The **Paganalia** was a festival of village communities and was equated by Ovid with the Sementivae. Pagamus meant a villager and the celebration was conducted by the Magistri Pagi who decided its moveable date, usually around the 24th to 26th of January. It appears to have been held on two days with a seven-day interval between them, and concerned spring sowing of crops, or the protection of such crops that had been sown in the autumn. Offerings were made to Tellus on the first day and to Ceres on the second, and these would include a cake of spelt flour and a cow in calf. Masks and puppets, known as 'oscilla' may also have hung from the trees at this time.[27]

February

This takes its name from 'februm', which was an instrument of purification. The first day, the Kalends, was followed by the **Amburbium** on 2 February, to cleanse the city of Rome. A corresponding Ambarvalia held in May would purify the fields.

The **Parentalia** was otherwise known as the Dies Parentales and was the festival of the dead. It was held between the 13th and the 21st of the month, and the last day was one of public ceremony, while the preceding ones were for private remembrance of the family's deceased relatives, particularly one's parents. During this sacred time, all marriages were forbidden and all the temples were closed. Magistrates did not wear their toga praetexta, their official garment, or any other sign or insignia of office.

The rituals involved libations of wine, milk, or blood at parental tombs, with food being presented to the ancestors in order to revive them and prevent their spirits, the Manes, from fading away completely, or even worse, disturbing the living. Groups of mourners would be seen going outside the cities to feast at family tombs, where a share of the food and wine was offered to the spirits of the ancestors. Some of the larger tombs had a dining space in which the family could sit to share this meal with the deceased. For poorer people, it might be only a matter of pouring a beaker of one of the approved liquids into a jar or other receptacle which was buried halfway into the ground above the grave. Failure to perform this basic service of respect towards one's dead could have very unfortunate consequences, if the relative should return to complain of being neglected.

This was not the only celebration during that nine-day period. It was always a busy time as other rites also had to be performed, which were quite different in tone. The 13th was the Ides, sacred to Jupiter, and the 15th of the month was the festival of the **Lupercalia**, a very boisterous occasion. This was not just for purification, it was also was a fertility rite. It had been originally a shepherd's festival in honour of Lupercus, a pastoral god, and was very ancient, so much so that there was dispute about which god was being honoured, as some cited Faunus, who was associated with Pan.

Worshippers would gather at the Lupercal, a sacred cave at the foot of the Palatine Hill and there the priests would sacrifice several goats and a dog. There would also be an offering of sacred cakes. Two teams of young men of noble families were smeared with the blood of the animals, which was then wiped off with wool dipped into milk. While this was going on, they were obliged to laugh aloud, and then they feasted. The highlight of the day for the public was when the two teams of young men, dressed in nothing but the strips of hide from the slaughtered animals, ran into the Forum Romanum and through the assembled crowds, whipping young women of childbearing age with strips of the goat skin, which was presumed to promote fertility.

In 44 BC Marc Antony had led one of these teams, stirring up popular support for Julius Caesar (his second cousin), but practically exposing himself due to the skimpiness of his costume, which caused a minor scandal. The fake screams of the young ladies and the general delight of the crowd did not hide the fact that, also on that day, Marc Antony tried to tie the white ribbon of the diadem around Caesar's head, which did not find favour with the crowd in the Forum, so

Caesar pretended to be annoyed and ordered that the ribbon be offered to Jupiter.[28]

It was at such festivals that the general rules of respectable behaviour were temporarily suspended. It gave people a chance to let off steam, to enjoy themselves and then resume their normal lives with no harm done. The festival of the Lupercalia was always immensely popular and when the church took over in Rome they found it impossible to suppress this ancient Roman festival. It was only under Pope Gelasus I, in 494 AD, when the date of the Lupercalia was given to the Purification of the Virgin Mary, that the event was finally robbed of its energy, probably due to the total contradiction of the spirit of the day to its original purpose of promoting fertility.

Quirinalia was held on 17 February and honoured Quirinus, a member of the original Capitoline Triad who had probably originally been a Sabine war deity. He was absorbed into the state religion and the Flamen Quirinalis officiated for him. The temple on the Quirinal Hill was one of Rome's oldest, having been dedicated in 293 BC, possibly on the site of an even earlier shrine. The temple was built by Lucius Papirius Cursor and was struck by lightning in 206 BC, then burned down completely in 49 BC. It was rebuilt by Augustus in 16 BC to become one of Rome's largest temples. It stood until at least the fourth century AD. The feast of Quirinus was known as the Feast of Fools.

The **Feralia** on 21 February was dedicated to the gods of the Underworld and was held on the final day of the Parentalia, when food offerings were taken to the family tombs. It was marked as Nefasti Publici in imperial calendars, and as Fasti in the 'Fasti Antiates' which was a calendar dated to 70 BC.[29]

The **Terminalia** was a festival held on 23 February to honour Terminus, the deity of boundaries and marker stones. His own boundary was actually inside Jupiter's main temple on the Capitol Hill. (See page 108.) When a boundary marker was placed, a short ceremony and a sacrifice were performed, with the blood of the sacrificial victim along with ashes from the fire and other offerings placed in the bottom of the hole dug to receive the boundary stone. Each boundary was considered to have its own minor deity, and these were worshipped along with Terminus at the Terminalia.[30]

The **Regifugium** was sacred to Jupiter and held on 24 February. During the Republic this was considered to be a day of freedom, as it celebrated the dethronement of the last king of Rome, King Tarquinus Superbus, in 509 BC. It was not, however, considered to be a particularly lucky festival as it fell on an even-numbered day. The meaning of its name is disputed, appearing to refer to the king's flight from Rome[31] and the sacrifice of the Rex Sacrificulus, whose concern was religious (otherwise known as the Rex Sacrorum).[32] For the Romans it represented freedom from oppression along with hopes of a newer and freer future.

March

The first day of March was, of course, the Kalends, sacred in this case to Mars. As the year originally began on the first day of March, and although sacred to Mars, it was generally a month of renewal and awakening. It not only had aspects of fertility which were connected to the coming spring, such as the popular festival of Anna Perenna, but it was also concerned with cleaning, renewing and a fresh start.

It was the month when Vesta's sacred fire was re-lit (on the first day of the month), by the rubbing together of sticks. The Vestal storehouse was opened, which had been kept closed and guarded all the year, with only the Vestals and the Pontifex Maximus allowed entry. It housed the sacred elements for later rituals, including the ashes for the Parilia, and a statue of Athena which was said to have been rescued from the burning city of Troy.

During March the streets were busy with the dancing priests, the Salii, who were divided into two colleges (or sodales) each of twelve men, known as either the Palatini or the Collini, and these men danced in procession during the festivals for Mars. They were pre-Republican in origin, one of the minor priesthoods and chosen for lifetime appointments, but they could resign if they obtained a major priesthood or a magistracy. They were from the Curia Saliorum on the Palatine (the Palatini) or from the Curia on the Quirinal (the Collini).

They were in charge of the ancilia, the sacred shields of Mars, and their major duty was to sing and dance on several days in March and October, the start and finish of the fighting season. For processions they wore suits of archaic military armour and they performed ritual dances at various locations throughout the city. Their chants were also ritualised and their meanings largely forgotten, even in Cicero's time. Over their armour they wore an embroidered tunic, and they carried swords. Each night during their festivals they lodged at a different house, where they were feasted. The climax of the lengthy festival was on 19 March, with the performance of the Quinquatrus, when they processed through the streets in the heart of Rome, in the presence of the Pontifex Maximus. It ended on 24 March, after which the sacred shields were returned to their storage place within the Regia.[33]

The **Equirria** on 14 March was a chariot race which took place on the Campus Martius. The month was generally sacred to the god Mars and he had many different aspects throughout the Roman world, including agricultural origins. He was known as Mars, Maris, Mamors, Marmor or Mavors. The Ara Martis, his altar on the Campus Martius, was served by the Flamen Martialis and Mars also had temples on the Via Appia and the Circus Flaminius.

The Via Appia temple was the place where the army would assemble before leaving Rome on campaigns. It was outside the Porta Capena and between the first and second milestones from Rome, in an area known as the 'Ad Martis'. The special sacrifice of the Suovetaurilia (the bull, the ram and the boar), could be offered to Mars and his main temple, outside the Porta Capena (the southeastern gate close to the Circus Maximus), was believed to hold images of wolves, which were associated with him. Julius Caesar is said to have planned to build a huge temple to Mars on the site of the lake he dug for mock sea battles, the naumachiae, but the plan was abandoned and the site was eventually used for the Parthenon instead.[34]

The Ides of March (the 15th) was sacred to both Jupiter and Anna Perenna. Anna Perenna had her festival on the first full moon of what was once the first month of the year. Her name is recorded in the prayer 'ut annare perennaresque commode liceat', which meant 'for leave to live in and through the year to our liking'. Her worship took place in a sacred grove on the Via Flaminia in Rome. When the Plebeians seceded from Rome and fled to Mount Sacer (Sacred Mountain), Anna Perenna provided them with food sufficient to prevent a famine among them, and for that action of kindness and sympathy she became a deity after her death.

Anna Perenna's festival was a joyful occasion, a festival of song, dances, drunkenness, and also casual sex, all of which took place in the open at her Grove, and it was a general holiday for the Plebeians. It was generally rather looked-down upon by the Patricians, who considered it a time of extreme licence and bawdiness. Each person in attendance at the festival was supposed to drink one cup of wine for each year of life desired from that day onward, resulting in drunkennesss. However, those who frowned upon the atmosphere of promiscuity which was part of the celebration are missing the point, whether they were the Patricians of their own time, or the historians of our own.

To a Pagan the sex, which was an ingredient of the festivities at that time, was not merely a by-product caused by excessive drinking (which might well have been expected to have the opposite effect) but was an intrinsic part of the worship of Anna Perenna. The fertility aspect was paramount in that spring season and the general coupling 'fed' the earth and also fed the gods of fertility in a way no other offering could. The young people who had taken part then found their way back into town, often in a tipsy procession which scandalised their more strait-laced neighbours.[35]

The **Liberalia** on 17 March was the festival of Liber Pater and his consort Libera. Liber the Father was a fertility deity with an important cult on the Aventine Hill. He does not appear to have had a temple entirely to himself as he shared that of Ceres. During a famine in 496 BC the Sibylline Books recommended that Demeter, Iacchus and Kore (who were Greek gods associated with the Eleusinian Mysteries), should be identified with Ceres, Liber and Libera, so these were then worshipped together. The Liberalia was a time of sacrifices, crudity and song, along with a general relaxation of behaviour, when masks hung on trees. There may originally have been Games performed, but these had stopped by the time of Ovid.[36]

The Agonalia could be held on 17 March, as well as 9 January, 21 May and 11 December, when it shared with the Janus worship as noted above. On each occasion a ram would be sacrified at the Regia in the Forum.

The **Quinquatrus** on 19 March (which by Roman reckoning was the fifth day after the Ides of March), came to be recognised as the start of the five-day long festival and holiday in Rome which was known as the Greater Quinquatrus. It was the chief festival of Minerva, with the first day being her birthday and the other four days being days on which the Circus held Games. Minerva, goddess of defensive war only, not offensive conflict, had temples on the Aventine and Caelian Hills.[37]

The **Tubilustrum** was held on 23 March and was the ceremony of purification of the trumpets (tubae), which were used in religious rituals. It was held on the last day of the Greater Quinquatrius and would be repeated on 23 May. It also involved the sacrifice of a ewe lamb and was held in a building known as the Atrium Sutorium. It was a festival of Mars, but also later dedicated to Minerva. There was also a festival of Vulcan on the same day, which was linked with the Tubilustrum by the belief that Vulcan had actually made the sacred trumpets.

March 23 was also considered a day of mourning, as the 24th was a Dies Sanguinis, or Day of Blood. Priests of some of the foreign sects flagellated themselves and even held a Taurobolium, which was the killing of the bull when the blood was intended to fall over the worshippers. This had originated in Asia Minor and the Archigallus, who was the head of the Galli, the eunuch priests of the goddess Cybele, killed the bull over a pit or platform, through the planks of which the blood would pour over the people beneath. Sometimes a similar ceremony was held but with a ram as the sacrificial victim, in which case it was known as a Cribolium.

April

This was a very busy month and on the first day, working-class women were allowed to use the men's public baths and while there they would pray to Fortuna Virilis for success with men in the coming year. On the fourth day of the month the Ludi Megalensis began, which lasted until the tenth day. These Games were held in honour of Magna Mater. From the 12th day to the 19th was Ludi Cerealis, Games held in honour of Ceres, although their original rural beginnings tended to be forgotten by the urban population of later Rome. The Ceriales also honoured Liber and Libera and was held on the final day, rounded off the Games. The Ides on the 13th was sacred to Jupiter Optimus Maximus.

The **Fordicitia** was another agricultural festival, this time in honour of Tellus, when a pregnant cow was sacrificed in each of the thirty wards or Curiae of the city. The unborn calves were burnt and their ashes would be used by the Vestal Virgins during the Parilia festival. The Fordicitia was held on the 15th day.

The **Parilia** on 21 April was Rome's own birthday, the festival of Pales, and was marked by an ancient purification rite for sheep and the shepherds. Milk and cakes were offered to Pales and the shepherds washed themselves in the early morning dew and drank sheep's milk. They later leaped through a bonfire on which sulphur had been thrown to purify the flocks by its smoke. The blood from the sacrificial October Horse along with the ashes from the unborn calves killed at the Fordicitia would also be used at that time to help to fumigate the flocks.

Vinalia on 23 April was the first of two festivals connected with the production of wine. Originally celebrated in honour of Jupiter, it also became associated with Venus. The April celebration was known as the Vinalia Priora and was a time when casks filled the previous autumn were opened and a libation offered to Jupiter.

A temple to Venus Erucina was dedicated on 23 April 181 BC outside the Colline Gate and it became a day when Venus received her tributes from Rome's prostitutes, for whom she acted as a patron. Her temple was also dedicated on the Capitoline – one of a pair – the other being for Mens (right-thinking), after the disaster of the Battle of Lake Trasimene in 217 BC.[38]

Robigalia on 25 April was for Robigus, a deity whose gender was always unclear but who was believed to prevent mildew, red rust and blight on the crops. A red or rust-coloured dog was sacrificed on that day, together with a sheep. This took place at the fifth milestone on the Via Claudia, which had once marked the end of Roman territory. This sacrifice was to prevent the blight and mildew spores from entering the territory of Rome and adversely affecting the vines and cereal crops. The officiating priest was the Flamen Quirinales.[39]

The Ludi Floriales were Games held in honour of the flower goddess Flora from 28 April to 3 May. These were celebrations and games, including races, in the Circus Maximus. The **Floralia** was held to ensure that the crops blossomed well and bore sufficient fruit. The Games held at that time were the responsibility of the Plebeian Aediles, and they eventually stretched to last for six days, beginning with theatrical performances and ending with Games where hares and goats were set loose in the Circus, while beans and lupins were scattered on the spectators to represent fertility.

The Floralia, while cheerful and attractive as a celebration, involving the wearing of colourful flower garlands and brightly coloured clothing, came to be regarded as a prostitute's feast. The strip-tease type of plays which were performed in the theatres showed it to be representative as much as a flowering of sex as of the plants, and respectable people often complained that the crowds of prostitutes and their clients made it an even more salacious occasion than the Saturnalia. It had certainly become more licentious as time went on and Cato the Younger famously walked out of one of the theatrical performances in protest at its content, being disgusted by it. He was however a firm traditionalist and could not bring himself to suggest that the celebrations, however bawdy they had become, should be banned.

Flora's temple was on the Aventine, near to the Circus Maximus, and had been built by a recommendation of the Sibylline Books after a severe drought in 241 or 238 BC that had caused a great deal of crop damage. Its dedication date was 28 April.

The **Feriae Latinae** was a far more serious occasion, being a very important festival due to its joining together of the Romans and the Latins at a temple on the Alban Mount. It was usually held at the end of April, on a date decided earlier that year by the incoming Consuls. The festival had originated when Alba Longa, not Rome, was the chief city of Latium. A libation of milk was offered to Jupiter and the surrounding towns brought agricultural produce, while puppets in human shapes known as 'oscilla' were hung from the trees and a white heifer, specifically one that had never been yoked, was the victim of the sacrifice, and was later eaten in a communal meal intended to bring together two areas which had so often been antagonistic towards each other.

It was treated as a general holiday and was important enough for the Magistrates to be obliged to attend it in person, representing the amity hoped for. It was a time of seeing friends and of mutual co-operation. If there should be any flaw in the proceedings, they would have to be repeated to ensure that there was no offence to the gods. After the one day of religious observances, there were two days of Games for the entertainment of the people. Towards the end of the Republic its importance increased, probably due to the fairly recent Social War and even that confirmed sceptic Cicero refused to allow his daughter Tullia's engagement to take place on either of the two days following the Feriae Latinae, as they were considered 'religiosi.'[40] The festival remained very significant and its continued performance and popularity lasted for over a thousand years.

May

The **Lemuria** on the 9th, 11th and 13th of May was dedicated to ghosts, especially those who had died young, therefore before their time and who might be expected to be resentful of luckier people who enjoyed a full span of life. Ovid described the private ritual in which a man washed his hands, spat nine black beans from his mouth and recited the words 'with these I ransom me and mine' and then re-washed his hands while avoiding looking behind him. It was always considered sensible to avert the eyes at any religious duty, or when at a sacrifice, or in any possible dealings with the Underworld.[41] The Roman attitude towards death was expressed by Cicero who said of it 'That long night, when I shall cease to exist, troubles me more than this brief life, which yet seems too long.'[42]

The 15th was the Ides and as always, sacred to Jupiter. Also on that day the Vestals retrieved the small rush puppets which resembled old men from the twenty-seven Sacra Argeorum shrines in the city, where they had been displayed. These puppets were then thrown into the Tiber and these 'argei' may have represented very early human sacrifices. Towards the end of March these small dolls had been set up in the shrines (thirteen of these twenty-seven shrines have now been identified) and had been left there until the Ides. A procession which included the Flamen Dialis and his Flaminica, along with the Vestal Virgins and the Praetor Urbanus, stopped at the Bridge of Sublicius and threw the dolls away.

The Agonalia on 21 May was celebrated by the Rex Sacrorum by the sacrifice of a ram at the Regia. This event may have honoured Vediovis, as there was a temple to this deity on Tiber Island. Originally a deity of swamps and volcanic movements, he was later to become identified with Apollo. Another temple was vowed by Lucius Furius Purpurio in 198 BC where the cult statue of Vediovis was found. It had been of colossal proportions, and similar in design to the images of Apollo.

Tubilustrum on 23 May was sacred in this case to Vulcan. The 23rd also saw Flora's Festival of Roses. The **Ambarvalia** was probably celebrated on 29 May, to purify the fields outside the city. This involved beating the boundaries to drive evil from the fields and the worship of Mars, Jupiter, Janus and Ceres. All work ceased for the occasion and sacrifices were offered at the various sites. It was one of the days upon which a full Suovetaurilia (consisting of the sacrifice of an ox, a ram, and a boar) could be offered.[43]

June

Vestalia was on 9 June and was sacred to Vesta. On the fifth day of the month the married women were allowed into the Vestal's storehouse to take food and offerings, this day also being a baker's holiday. A fresco from Pompeii shows a miller's donkey wearing garlands of flowers for this celebration, along with little cakes in honour of the day.

On 11 June was the **Matralia** for Mater Matuta, the festival of Mothers. The wife of a first marriage decorated the statue of Matuta at the temple between the Forum Boarium and the Forum Romanum, just inside the Porta Carmentalis. This was discovered in 1937 under the church of St. Ombono and much votive material regarding children was then found there. The Ides on the 13th was the festival of the guild of flute-players, involving all the noise and distractions of their rowdy behaviour.

On 15 June the Vestals swept out their storehouse, and all the rubbish they collected from it was carried to the Tiber and thrown into the river. This clearance marked the end of an 'unlucky' period that had begun in early May, after which life could return to normal.

The **Fors Fortuna** took place on 24 June, and on the far bank of the Tiber were two shrines to Fortuna where slaves could attend her celebrations alongside free persons.[44] This holiday was open to anyone who wished to attend, as people of all degrees were just as likely as any other to be affected by adverse fortune at some time in their lives.

Cicero described a scene of people pouring out of the city on that day in order to attend the very popular sacrifices at the shrines to Fortuna. He painted a pleasant word picture of the river area looking very festive and with many small boats racing each other on the water.[45]

July

Poplifugia opened the month with the Festival of the People's Flight. This ancient festival was held on the Campus Martius and the fact that it was held before the Nones was highly unusual, possibly referring to its connection with the Regifugium, or flight, or the deposed king. Poplifugia means 'flights or rout of the people' and may have meant the flight of most of the Romans when attacked by the people of Fidenae after the Gauls sacked Rome. The festival was held on the 5th, although there may have also been another celebration on the 7th, which was known as the Nonae Caprotinae.[46]

The eventual victory for Rome was celebrated by a feast in honour of Juno Caprotina. The day following was the Vitulatio, which marked the Pontiff's thank offering for the event. It was said that Romulus then celebrated the 7th as a continuance of the ancient events.[47]

The **Ludi Apollinares** were next, on the 6th to the 13th. These Games in honour of Apollo had great popular support although – or perhaps because – they had largely lost their religious flavour. Cicero commented on them: 'It is indeed something for one's mind to relax, both at the spectacle and at the impression of religious feeling,' although over time an impression of religion was about all it amounted to.[48]

The Ides on the 15th were for Jupiter as usual. From 304 BC for a time, but more regularly after Augustus, a mounted procession of the Equites Equo Publico went through the city from the Forum to the Capitol Hill, known as the Transvectio Equitum. This parade of young men of the Equestrian class was in honour of Castor and Pollux and it commemorated the victory of the Battle of Lake Regillus in 496 BC. Augustus revived the ceremony and developed it further, making it into an interesting and well-attended spectacle.

The **Lucaria** was from the 19th to the 21st and had lost its original meaning but possibly in early times had been the propitiation of woodland spirits when the forests were originally cleared. It was celebrated in a large grove between the Via Salaria and the River Tiber.

The **Ludi Victoriae Caesaris**, or Caesar's victory games, were, like all games, very popular indeed, being held from the 20th to the 30th. The **Neptunalia** on the 23rd was celebrated by the lighting of bonfires, into which small live fish were thrown as an offering to Neptune.

The **Furinalia** which took place on 25 July was a quite obscure festival. It was dedicated to an ancient goddess of springs and streams, who had a sacred grove at the foot of the Janiculum Hill. Her own priest, the Flamen Furinalis, celebrated for her, but by the end of the Republican period that even was largely forgotton.

August

The month opened on the 3rd with the rather gruesome spectacle of the 'Supplicia Canem' or the Punishment of the Dogs. This commemorated the failure of the city's guard dogs to warn the people when the Gauls arrived. It involved suspending dogs on crosses, or forked poles, before sacrificing them. The Sacred Geese of Juno had given the necessary warning, so a goose was at the same time lauded, being carried through the city in honour.

The 5th of the month was for Salus, a goddess of health and during the Empire the occasion was called the Salus Publica Populi Roman,i or public health of the Roman people. [49]

On the 12th the Praetor offered a heifer to Hercules in his temple on the Forum Boarium. The was a deity very popular with businessmen who offered a tithe of their profits to him. This entirely masculine god was never attractive to women, and female worshippers were not welcome.

Diana was celebrated on the 15th and as slaves could attend her festival it became a holiday for them.

The **Portunalia** was held on the 17th, for the deity who guarded ports and dockyards. This festival was celebrated by all those who worked on the docks or the ports or were in any way connected with sailing.

Vinalia Rustica was on 19 August and this festival may have started, or perhaps merely blessed, the grape harvest. The first grapes were broken from the vine by the Flamen Dialis and, due to its early celebration, may have been too soon for the harvest itself. It was associated with Jupiter and later also with Venus, as was its counterpart the Vinalia Prioria. However, being a country festival, it lacked the rather rowdy and unrestrained connotations of the other and was an altogether more respectable event.[50] It was also the time when gardeners took their holiday.

Consus was celebrated on the 21st, the god of the granaries and vital to Rome's continued prosperity. Consus was worshipped in an underground barn beneath the Circus Maximus and in popular legend his festival was connected to the Rape of the Sabine Women. However, due to that position within the Circus, he soon became associated with the racing of horses, either with chariots or without. Sacrifice was held there before the racing began, when the priest of Quirinus went with the Vestals in procession. The Vestals were among the very few women allowed front-row seats at the Games, although in the Circus Maximus itself they had always been allowed to sit with the men.[51]

The **Vulcanalia** was on the 23rd and little is known of this festival, although Maia and Hora, who were believed to be his consorts, were also honoured with him on the day.

Opiconsivia was on the 25th. The festival of the goddess Ops, the guardian of abundance, whose title Consiva meant 'sower' or 'planter', took place at her shrine inside the Regia in Rome, although she would also later have a temple on the Capitoline Hill. She may originally have been a Sabine deity and while the festival on the 25th was for her alone, she was also honoured on 19 December at the Opalia and worshipped during the Vulcanalia on 23 August.

Volturnalia on 27 August was for the obscure god Volturnus, who was possibly an early Etruscan river god. His cult dwindled during the later Republican period, although he had his own Flamen, the Flamen Volturnis, and he was regarded as the father of the water deity Juturna.[52]

September

This month had few purely religious festivals, but the 5th to the 19th of the month saw the Ludi Romani, or Roman Games, which always attracted huge crowds with people travelling into the city from nearby towns and from the countryside.

On the 13th was the anniversary of the dedication of the temple of Jupiter Optimus Maximus, which had been rebuilt several times, but the anniversary of 507 BC was the one which was celebrated. A white heifer was sacrificed by that year's Consul, followed by a procession and a banquet. On this occasion the statues of Jupiter, Juno and Minerva joined the guests, carried in to attend. They were beautifully dressed and were surrounded by musicians playing pipes and harps and with clowns. This most likely took place on the most important day of the Games, the 15th.[53]

October

The **Meditrinalia** on 11 October was in honour of the new vintage and libations of it were offered to the gods in general on the day. **Augustalia** on the 12th was for Augustus, and to celebrate the whole imperial family. These Augustan Games had a sacrifice in the temple of Augustus at the Porta Capena, which celebrated and commemorated his safe return to Rome from Asia Minor.

Fontinalia was on the 13th and was for Fons or Fontus, the god of wells and springs, and at this time fountains were decorated with flowers in his honour. The family of the Fonteia gens clamed descent from Fontus, just as the Julians did from Venus and the Aurelii did from Sol Indiges.

The real focus of of October was the horse racing, with the chariot races on the 15th. The most important chariot race took place on the Campus Martius, where the left-hand horse of the victorious team was sacrificed to Mars by the Flamen Dialis. This was done at the Ara Maxima, or altar of Mars, to ensure good crops. Despite the great importance of this day and the importance of its sacrifice, which required the absolute best that was available to the god, it was not actually marked on any calendar. It started in the sixth century BC at an unknown location on the Campus Martius, when two chariots, each pulled by the fastest horses, were raced. The winning, nearside, horse was then killed with a spear and its head and tail (with genitals attached), were taken to the Regia so that the blood could drip onto the sacred hearth. The head was then fought over by two teams for the honour of displaying it, these were the Suburans (of the Subura district), and the Sacravienses (of the Sacra Via area).

The tail and genitals were then burned by the Vestals, and the ashes mixed with some of the blood, to be kept by the Vestals until 21 April, when it was mixed with the ashes of the unborn calves killed with their mothers six days earlier at the Fordicitia. It would then be used for the purification of the fields at the next Parilia.[54]

Armilustrum on 19 October was for Mars and was held on a square, which was also called the Armilustrum, on the Aventine Hill. This marked the closing of the campaign season and the Salii may have cleaned and purified the sacred armour at that time, which was then put away until the following year.

The Ludi Victoriae Sullae were held on the 26th of October to the 1st of November, were Games to celebrate the victories of Lucius Cornelius Sulla, named in honour of the goddess Victoria. These had been established in 81 BC to mark Sulla's victory at the Battle of the Colline Gate, when he finally defeated a large army of Samnites who had been a thorn in the side of Rome for a very long time.

November

This was a fairly quiet month, enlivened only by the Plebeian Games, or Ludi Plebei, which were held between the 4th and the 17th. These were in honour of Jupiter and featured more chariot racing in the Circus Maximus. They had probably been established in 220 BC by Gaius Flaminius when he was Censor, and were second only in importance to the Ludi Romani. Their performance was the responsibility of the Plebeian Aediles.

On the 13th of the month Jupiter's Ides were also celebrated, during the Ludi Plebei.[55]

December

The festival of **Bona Dea** was all-important during this month, with the ceremony of 'Putting the goddess to sleep' for the winter, which took place on the 3rd day. The festival was significant for Rome's security, and its performance was confined to women. No men were allowed to intrude, not even slaves, male children or male pets. This was connected with the scandal of Publius Clodius Pulcher, who had gatecrashed the ceremony at the house of Gaius Julius Caesar (then the Pontifex Maximus) in 62 BC.

Juvenal said that the worship was 'only confined to drunks and perverts anyway', as the men liked to imagine the women getting up to all kinds of salacious behaviour on this day. However, as they could not attend, they could not know, and their sour-grapes attitude received a shock when the festival had to be celebrated again in its entirety, due to Publius Clodius Pulcher's sacrilege. It led to a court case in 61 BC in which he was prosecuted by the state, with Cicero acting as a prosecution witness.[56]

The Agonalia on the 11th was in honour of Sol Indiges when another ram was sacrificed by the Rex Sacrorum at the Regia. The Ides on the 13th were for Jupiter, and were followed by the **Consualia** on the 15th, which was for Consus. This was possibly to celebrate the autumn sowing, as the August one had celebrated the harvest. Horses and asses were garlanded and allowed to have a day's rest. The altar at the Circus Maximus may also have been opened for the festival during December.

The **Saturnalia** was started on the 17th of the month, and eventually this celebration would last for several days. It opened with a sacrifice at Saturn's temple in the Forum Romanum, followed by a public feast which anyone was allowed to attend. All the shops would close, along with the schools and the law courts, while the whole population dressed in whatever holiday clothes they could afford. Slaves were given special privileges and sometimes even swapped places with their masters for a short time, while parents gave their children gifts of toys and friends gave candles to each other. It was a time of friends and families gathering together and visiting each other, a season of goodwill.

However, not everyone enjoyed it. Pliny the Younger retired to a private room for the duration of the festival [57] and Seneca said that it 'should be observed with frugal contemplation', perhaps the original complaint about the commercialisation of religious observance? Most people had a good time and enjoyed the relaxation of the usual rules, while looking forward to a fresh start.

Opalia on 19 December was in honour of Ops and was her second major festival, also associated with Saturn.

Divalia on 21 December was for Angerona and was performed at the shrine of Voluptia in Rome, with a sacrifice at the Curia Acculeia, probably an unroofed enclosure which was for the observation of divine signs in the sky. The shrine, which was possibly at the foot of the Palatine, held a statue of Angerona, with her mouth bound as a sign of her sacred silence.

The **Larentalia** on 23 December again honoured Jupiter, along with Larentia. It consisted of funeral rites performed at the supposed tomb of Acca Larentia and was celebrated by the Flamen Quirinalis and the

Pontiffs. The goddess was fairly obscure but appears to be connected with the original founding of the city. In one legend, she married a wealthy Etruscan named Tarutius who died young and left her substantial estates, which she later bequeathed to Rome. It justified Rome's claim to be the owner of certain territories. Another legend about her claimed that she was the wife of the shepherd who found the twins Romulus and Remus and adopted them. She was reputed to have had a dozen children of her own, and the Twelve Arval Priests were founded in their memory. These were the oldest priestly college, extinct by the time of the late Republic but restored by Augustus, and the subsequent emperors were always Arval Priests. They were originally concerned with fertility, especially that of the fields, for which they sacrificed. The word 'Arvum' meant a ploughed field.

Their shrine and cult centre was at the fifth milestone outside Rome, at La Magliona beside the Tiber. After the deification of Augustus, the Arval Priests became responsible for certain aspects of the Imperial cult, although the only evidence of their existence during the Republic is from Varro, who attempted to explore the origins of the Roman race, but most of whose works are unfortunately now lost.[58]

The continuance of public respect for the gods, percolating down from the highest levels, is shown by the action of the Emperor Domitian in ordering the destruction of the tomb of a young man, which had been built by one of his own freedmen for that man's son.

Unfortunately, the stones used for it had been intended for the temple of Jupiter on the Capitol, and Domitian made a firm example of the offender and showed his personal disgust that the stones earmarked for a sacred place had been used for a base purpose, thereby giving grave offence to the god. Domitian had the young man's tomb destroyed and the body thrown into the Tiber. He made several remarks on the subject, clarifying that he did not want anyone in the future to imagine that such sacrilege could go unpunished, and the disrespect shown to the deity should not be repeated.[59]

The Emperor Marcus Aurelius summed up his own religious feelings:

> To them that ask thee, 'Where has thou seen the Gods?' I answer first of all ... that they are in some manner visible and apparent ... neither have I seen my own soul, yet I respect and honour it. So then, for the Gods, by the daily experience that I have of their power and providence, towards myself and others, I know certainly that they are – and therefore I worship them.[60]

Conclusion

One of the greatest benefits of Rome's state religion was its inclusivity. Gradually, 'new' religions became accepted and had their shrines built. Their worshippers could attend their rituals in peace and, with only a few exceptions, they welcomed everyone. Nobody was obliged to become a member of any of the cults, no shrines were wilfully destroyed, and toleration was the norm.

I can almost hear you say, 'But what about the Christians?' I have not devoted a particular section to Christianity within the scope of this book, because it was a case apart.

Those unfortunates who died in the arena usually did so because they were criminals or enemies of the state (apart from gladiators). They did not die there for purely religious reasons, as in Rome the various religions worked more or less alongside each other. Nobody was killed simply for following a particular religion and the Christians who were executed suffered that punishment not because they chose to follow a rather obscure leader, but because they became a threat to the Roman state itself.

The Egyptian, Jewish or Syrian religions did not actually threaten the security of Rome. Although some of the imported religions may have been looked at askance, due to curious rituals, celibate or even eunuch priests or other strange ideas, they usually managed to co-exist alongside the indigenous religion. The Christians did not do that.

They believed themselves to be the only 'true' religion, and that they were always right, which in the Roman world was intolerable. It eventually created an explosive situation that Rome could well do without, particularly in view of its aspect of Emperor-worship. The Christians refused to accept the divinity of the Roman Gods, let alone that of the Emperor, and it was this determination to deny the pre-eminence of Rome itself that turned the worship of a foreign political leader turned mystic from a minor religious cult into a criminal act.

As Professor Mary Beard in her book *The Colosseum* rightly pointed out:

> There are no genuine records of any Christians being put to death in the Colosseum ... it was only later that the Christians invested heavily in the Colosseum as a shrine for martyrs ... there are no accounts of this punishment for religious divergence before the fifth century AD, by which time Rome was already Christianised. Therefore the retrospective claims to such martyrdoms are a later fabrication.[1]

Any Christians killed were executed not for religious reasons but for political ones, in that they had denied the authority of the Emperor and the Roman state.

The strange Christian desire to be seen as 'martyrs' was one that the Romans simply could not relate to. To the modern mind, also, it seems a very strange method of promoting one's religion, as any fanaticism surely lacks common sense, and is off-putting to others rather than otherwise.

St Ignatius Bishop of Antioch, in the early second century AD, was one such – a man who actually begged for such a death. While he and a few like him may have wished to be 'ground beneath the teeth of wild beasts to make of himself a pure loaf for Christ', for the majority of people such immoderacy is incomprehensible and abhorrent. It is also exactly the kind of religious posturing that the Romans most disliked and it created political problems, as irrational speech of that kind so often tips over into irrational behaviour. The setting up of an alternative form of authority was seen as prejudicial to good order. Political opponents were naturally firmly dealt with, and Ignatius eventually got his wish, being killed by two lions during the reign of the Emperor Trajan. Martyrs claimed to see in such violent deaths 'a union with Christ in suffering,' but neurotic obsession with drawn-out and painful death cut no ice with more sensible people, who preferred to live their lives rather than throw them away.

In the fourth century AD, Constantius, son of Constantine, passed a law forbidding Pagan sacrifices (in 341 AD) and subsequently all the temples were cleared and all images removed or destroyed, to be replaced by images relating to the new Christian cult. It has been claimed that at the beginning of the Christian era, there were still 424 temples, 304 shrines, 80 statues of gods in gold or silver, and 64 statues of deities in ivory; this plus 22 equestrian statues, 36 triumphal arches and 3,785 statues in bronze, and the remains of Imperial palaces, baths, aqueducts, circuses and 28 public libraries. A nice haul, particularly if it could be claimed in the name of religion.[2] Most of all this wondrous treasure was wilfully destroyed, as was shown by the Theodosian Code, promulgated by the Emperor Theodosius II (401-450 AD) which orders: 'The temples shall be closed in all places, and in all cities, so that access to them is forbidden so as to deny to all abandoned men the opportunity to commit sin.'

Regarding not wishing to worship according to Christian rites, it states:

> We adjudge them demented and insane, and shall sustain the infamy of their heretical dogmas, their meeting places shall not receive the name of churches, and they shall be smitten – first by divine vengeance and secondly by the retribution of our own initiative, which we shall assume in accordance with divine judgement... If any person should be proved to devote their attention to Pagan sacrifices, or to the worshipping of images, we demand that they be subjected to capital punishment.[3]

This shows not only that there were sufficient backsliders to need the new rules putting into effect, but also that the new cult was far less tolerant than the previous state religion it replaced. The upheaval was certainly not done with the approval of the majority of the Roman people, but was an arbitrary decision imposed from above.

Many favourite rites and festivals continued despite all the bans, and the new religion would have difficulty in eradicating the old. New rituals were devised to suit the newly puritanical atmosphere, including that of 'churching' a woman forty days after she gave birth, in order to 'purify' her from the contamination of childbirth. This was based on Mosaic law and would have both baffled and disgusted the Romans, with its suggestion that a woman had to be spiritually 'cleansed' from the sin of sex and giving new life, turning a time of natural renewal and family joy into something darker, unclean and sinful.[4]

The new ideas would, in fact, expand on the idea of the sinful aspect of all sexuality, forcing the majority of women into becoming little more than brood mares with sinister overtones, eventually blaming them for being temptresses whose rampant drive seduced 'innocent' men, despite the many instances of male on female abuse. There would develop a demonisation of women in general, believing them to be sources of vice and disease, which did nothing for their personal freedoms and greatly encouraged misogynistic attitudes which lasted for centuries.[5]

The result was an erosion of the joy of life, with suspicion of personal happiness and oppression of personal freedoms, coupled with a dangerous watchfulness for occasions of sin, and a subsequent eulogising of the celibate and religious way of life. These attempts to superimpose one cult above another cannot have fooled everyone, and reluctance to comply in the early stages was met with force, which became stronger over time, ensuring obedience regardless of preference. Not only were temples and images removed, but persecution took place from the fourth century AD.

In 386 AD, Libanius appealed to the Emperor Theodosius I for toleration to be shown after attacks by Christian monks who, he claimed, 'hasten to attack temples with sticks and stones and bars of iron ... the priests there must either keep quiet or die ... this scattered rabble congregates and they feel themselves in disgrace unless they have committed the foulest outrages.'[6] Unfortunately, such intolerance has continued throughout the centuries and over time great efforts have been made to suppress archaeological and other evidence suggesting that things were not originally as Christians had been led to believe by their teachers.[7]

Even that most fundamental item of Christian dogma, regarding the death and resurrection of the Christ, was copied from the legends of Osiris, and recent discoveries regarding the family of the Christ have been ridiculed, although they throw grave doubts upon the accepted viewpoint.[8]

The destruction of Rome's incomparable heritage of monuments has proceeded apace for centuries and these depredations were not only caused by the incursions of enemies – who tended to avoid the remains of the Roman buildings – but primarily by successive Popes, who not only permitted but encouraged the burning of the ancient, high-quality marbles to produce lime. This vandalism has continued until relatively recently, with an attitude of staggering indifference towards the unique cultural legacy that Rome had given the world. Illustrations of Rome, even from the late 19th century, show many beautiful buildings that had somehow survived for two millennia but are now no longer in existence.[9]

I believe Christianity shares with the other Monotheistic religions – who like to call themselves the 'People of the Book' – a mindset of superiority, particularly towards the female half of the population. This attitude has no justification and these religions share little understanding or co-operation between themselves, which has led to abuses in both personal and political areas. They have stood in judgement over non-believers with such actions as would be intolerable, were the false vindications of religious righteousness not being used as an excuse for bigotry. People of all religions need to be aware that their views cannot, and must not, negate any other person's equal right of denial.

Conclusion

As Helmut Koester wrote, 'Only dogmatic prejudice can assert that the canonical writings have any exclusive claim to apostolic origin and thus any historical priority.'[10] The Romans deserve great respect for their achievements, their culture and their tolerance of the many different religions of others which formed part of their Empire. New Pagan beliefs are also returning, as people prefer to explore for themselves and live within a less repressive framework. Religion, like history itself, changes with expanding knowledge, but the old adage still holds true:

'The gods do not die while ever their names are spoken.'

Endnotes

Abbreviations

C.I.L. – Corpus Inscrptionum Latinarum
I.L.S. – Inscriptiones Latinae Selectae
J.R.S. – Journal of Roman Studies

Introduction

1. J.P.V.D. Balsdon 'Life and Leisure in Ancient Rome'
2. R.M. Ogilvie 'The Romans and their Gods'
3. Cicero 'De Natura Deorum'
4. Pliny the Elder 'Natural History'
5. Servius Sulpicius Rufus (106-43BC)
6. Virgil 'The Aeneid'
7. Aulus Gellius 'Noctis Atticae'
8. Roger Goodburn and Helen Waugh 'Roman Inscriptions in Britain'
9. R. M. Ogilvie 'The Romans and their Gods'
10. Polybius 'The Histories'
11. Pliny the Elder 'Natural History'
12. J. P. V. D. Balsdon 'Life and Leisure in Ancient Rome'
13. David Wadkin 'The Roman Forum'
14. Pliny the Elder 'Natural History'
15. Cicero 'Letters to Atticus'
16. Horace 'The Complete Odes and Epodes'

1 Faceless Gods

1. Seneca 'De Brevitate Vitae'

2. Virtue – Virtus; Truth – Veritas; Faith – Fides.
3. Sol Indiges was a sun deity and Tellus was an earth deity, Liber Pater was associated with fertility and the vine.
4. J. P. V. D. Balsdon. 'Life and Leisure in Ancient Rome'
5. Plutarch's Lives – 'Camillus'
6. Piero Treves. 'Brennus, Gallic Chieftain'
7. Livy 'History of Rome'
8. Pliny 'Natural History'
9. H. H. Scullard. 'Festivals and ceremonies of the Roman Republic'
10. David Wadkin. 'The Roman Forum'
11. The term 'punic' is from the Latin 'punicus' meaning Carthaginian.
12. David Wadkin. 'The Roman Forum'
13. Horace 'Odes'
14. The 'Res Gestae' of Augustus gives a personal account of his achievements. See 'Res Gestae divi Augustae' Cambridge University Press. (2009)
15. Boatwright, Gargola and Talbot. 'The Romans – from village to Empire'
16. Ovid 'Fasti'
17. Varro, Marcus Terentius. Known as Varro Reatinus to distinguish him from his younger contemporary Varro Atacinus.
18. Mary Beard. 'The Triumph'
19. Livia Drusilla, wife of Augustus, her name later became Julia Augusta.
20. Under Augustus the social qualification was lowered and by 5 AD they had to accept the daughters of freedmen. Initially only nobles were eligible.
21. Tacitus 'Annals'
22. Mary Beard et al. 'Religions of Rome'
23. R. M. Ogilvie. 'The Romans and their Gods'
24. Ibid
25. Mary Beard et al. 'Religions of Rome'
26. Plutarch 'Moralia'
27. Livy 'Ab Urbe Condita Libre' (On the founding of the City).
28. Polybius 'The Histories'
29. Adrian Goldsworthy. 'Cannae – Hannibal's Greatest Victory'
30. Livy 'Ab Urbe Condita Libre'
31. The Sibylline Books were the work of the Cumae Sibyl, collections of prophecies and warnings. Much was lost during the Social War in the Republic.
32. Adrian Goldsworthy. 'Cannae – Hannibal's Greatest Victory'
33. Pliny the Younger 'Epistulae'
34. David Wadkin. 'The Roman Forum'
35. Ovid 'Fasti'

36. Frontinus, Sextus Julius 'The Aqueducts of Rome'
37. Plutarch – Lives. 'Pompeius Magnus'
38. S. B. Platner. 'A Topographical Dictionary of Ancient Rome'
39. C. E. Schultz. 'Women's Religious Activity in the Roman Republic'
40. Ibid
41. Plutarch – Lives. 'Julius Caesar'
42. J. P. V. D. Balsdon. 'Roman Women'
43. Cicero 'Letters to Atticus'
44. W. Jeffrey Tatum. 'The Patrician Tribune'
45. C.I.L. VI. 68
46. R. M. Ogilvie. 'The Romans and their Gods'
47. Ovid 'Fasti'
48. Antony Kamm. 'The Romans – an Introduction'
49. Allison L. C. Emmerson. (Article) 'Re-examining Roman Death Pollution' J.R.S. Volume 110. (2020)
50. Pliny. 'Natural History'
51. R. M. Ogilvie. 'The Romans and their Gods'
52. David Wadkin. 'The Roman Forum'
53. Cassius Dio 'History of Rome'
54. The Black Stone (Lapis Niger) was discovered by Giacomo Boni in 1899 close to the Arch of Septimius Severus in the Forum Romanum.
55. Livy 'Ab Urbe Condita Libre'
56. David Potter. 'Emperors of Rome'

2 Female Gods

1. Livy 'Ab Urbe Condita Libre'
2. Quintus Ennius (239-169 BC) considered the father of Roman poetry. His epic poem 'Annales' is now largely lost.
3. Robert Burn. 'Ancient Rome and its Neighbourhood. An Illustrated handbook to the ruins of the City and of Campagna.'
4. Ovid 'Fasti'
5. Macrobus 'Saturnalia'
6. Superintendenza Speciale Archeologia Belle Arti e Passagio di Roma.
7. Gwyneath McIntyre and Sarah McCallum. 'Uncovering Anna Perenna, a focused study of Roman Myth and Culture'
8. Adam Bilstein (Article) 'Instability and Impermanence', Society for Classical Studies, December 2015.
9. Lynda Telford. 'Sulla, a Dictator Reconsidered'
10. Nicholas Horsefall. 'The Cultural Horizona of the Plebs Romana'
11. Ovid 'Fasti'
12. Sir James Frazer. 'The Golden Bough'

13. Hendrik Wagenvoort. (Article) 'Diva Angerona' in 'Selected Studies in Roman Religion'
14. Varro – Marcus Terentius
15. Georges Demezil. 'La Religione Romana arcaica con un'appendice sulla religione degli Etruschi'
16. Mary Beard et al. 'Religions of Rome'
17. Thomas Wiederman. 'The Fetiales – A Reconsideration'
18. W. D. Harris. 'War and Imperialisation in Republican Rome'
19. H. H. Scullard. 'From the Gracchi to Nero'
20. Lynda Telford. 'Sulla, a Dictator Reconsidered'
21. Ibid
22. Virgil, Publius Vergilius Maro 'The Aeneid' 'The Georgics' and 'The Eclogues'
23. Livy 'Ab Urbe Condita Libre'
24. Vitruvius 'On Architecture'
25. Cato the Elder 'On Agriculture'
26. Ovid 'Fasti'
27. Andrew Lintott. 'Violence in Republican Rome'
28. Livy. 'Ab Urbe Condita Libre'
29. Valerie Flint et al. 'Athlone History of Witchcraft and Magic in Europe, Ancient Greece and Rome' Volume Two.
30. Cicero 'In Verram.'
31. Barbette Stanley Spaeth. 'The Roman Goddess Ceres'
32. W. Warde Fowler. (Article) 'Mundus Patet' J.R.S. Volume Two (1912)
33. Plutarch's Lives – 'Romulus'
34. Juvenal 'Satires'
35. Jason Linn. (Article) 'The Roman Grain Supply' Journal of Late Antiquity. Volume Five. (2012)
36. Now in the Museo Archaeologico in Naples.
37. Homer (800 BC to 701 BC). Credited with writing the 'Iliad' and the 'Odyssey'
38. The religion of 'Strengheria' is a form of witchcraft with southern European roots, sometimes referred to as 'La Vecchia Religione', or old religion. The Sicilian 'Strega' was often a useful witch, arranging marriages, concocting potions and casting out devils, much like the 'cunning women'.
39. Ovid 'Metamorphoses'
40. Ovid 'Fasti'
41. Ibid
42. Juvenal 'Satires'
43. Sallust 'Bellum Catilinae'
44. Ovid 'Ex Ponto' (Letters from the Black Sea)

45. P. Allison. 'The Insula of Menander at Pompeii – Volume III, The Finds'
46. Plutarch's Lives – 'Gaius Marius'
47. Cicero 'In Verram'
48. Eleanor W. Leach. 'Fortune's Extremities – a Roman Consul and his Monument'
49. Livy 'Natural History'
50. Lynda Telford. 'Sulla, a Dictator Reconsidered'
51. The ancient 'diadem' was not a jewelled tiara as we know it, merely a long white ribbon, fastened over the crown of the head and tied at the back. It is shown on ancient coinage quite clearly, especially that of Cleopatra VII.
52. Ovid 'Fasti'
53. Ibid
54. The Curia Calabra was a shrine used for the observation of the new moon. Its exact location is unclear, but it was possibly on the Capitol. However, Servius identified it with the Hut of Romulus on the Palatine.
55. Rome's three virgin goddesses were Diana, Vesta and Minerva.
56. T. Corey Brennan. 'The Praetorship in the Roman Republic'
57. Pomerium restrictions were strict. For example, Magistrates holding Imperium did not have full power inside it; only the Lictors of a Dictator could carry the fasces within the Pomerium boundary; no dead could be buried inside (but Trajan's ashes in 117 AD were placed at the foot of his column). Provincial Magistrates could not enter without loss of their Imperium and a general could only enter on the day of his Triumph. Even the Comitia Centuriata had to meet on the Campus Martius, outside the boundary. The Theatre of Gn. Pompeius Magnus, in the Curia of which G. Julius Caesar was killed, was outside the boundary, which allowed Senators to attend who could not cross the boundary without losing Imperium; weapons were prohibited inside the Pomerium, but daggers were often carried beneath the toga, so as Caesar was assassinated outside the boundary, the conspirators did not commit sacrilege.
58. Hesiod 'Theogony'
59. Jeremy R. Rutter. 'The Three Phases of the Taurobolium' Phoenix. Volume 22. No.3. (1968)
60. Ovid 'Fasti'
61. Mary Beard. 'The Roman Triumph'
62. Lynda Telford. 'Sulla, a Dictator Reconsidered'
63. Ariadne Staples.'From Good Goddesses to Vestal Virgins'
64. The Servian Walls (built by Servius Tullius) were built from large blocks of volcanic tufa and are documented as being up to ten metres high. Part of the wall is visible near Rome's Termini Station. During

the Republic the walls were largely abandoned, but in 270 AD Aurelian rebuilt them larger and stronger, his walls being 18 km long, 3.5 metres thick and enclosing approximately 3,500 acres. Roman citizens were utilised to help build them, incorporating the Pyramid of Cestius and the Claudian Aqueduct within their structure.

65. Suetonius 'The Twelve Caesars – Nero'
66. Mary T. Boatwright. 'Hadrian and the City of Rome'
67. Cassius Dio 'Roman History'
68. Plutarch's Lives – 'Sulla'
69. Vitruvius 'Ten Books on Architecture'

3 Male Gods, Joint Festivals, Divine Locations

1. Suetonius 'Augustus'
2. Pliny the Elder 'Natural History'
3. T.W. Potter (Article) 'A Republican healing sanctuary at Ponte di Nona near Rome, and the classical tradition of votive medicine.' J.B. Archaeological Association. No. 138
4. L. Vagnetti. 'Il deposito votivo de Campetti a Veio'
5. The Hippocratic Corpus. Kaplan Classics of Medicine. The works of Hippocrates make interesting reading. As part of the Oath, Hippocrates insisted on doctor and patient confidentiality, and that doctors should be held criminally responsible for errors of judgement. He remarked that no disease is any more divine than any other, and also observed that 'Physicians are many in title, but are very few in reality.'
6. R. A. Adkins. 'Dictionary of Roman Religion'
7. M. J. Green. 'Dictionary of Celtic Myth and Legend'
8. Livy 'Ab Urbe Condita Libre'. Livy's monumental work on Rome's history covered the earliest legends before the traditional foundation of the city in 753 BC. It went right through to the reign of Augustus, in Livy's own lifetime. Titus Livius (64/59 BC to 12/17 AD) was on familiar terms with members of the Julio-Claudian dynasty and was a personal friend of Augustus.
9. Ibid
10. M. Terentius Varro 'Res Rusticae'
11. Vitruvius 'On Architecture'
12. Panonia the Province was bounded by the River Danube, and covered western Hungary, eastern Austria, northern Croatia and parts of Serbia, Slovenia and Bosnia-Herzogovina.
13. Romano-British jewellery, the Snettisham Hoard. British Museum, carved intaglio (1986 0401.193)
14. Sarah B. Pomeroy. 'Spartan Women'

15. Cicero 'Against Verres'
16. Plutarch's Lives – 'Pompeius Magnus'
17. L. Richardson. 'The New Topographical Dictionary of Ancient Rome.' The Forma Urbis Romae was a huge marble map of the city, dated between 203 and 211 AD, based on property records. It originally measured 60 ft wide and 45 ft high, made of 150 marble slabs. It was mounted on an interior wall of the Temple of Peace, in the Forum of Vespasian. It was so detailed it showed the floor plans of every temple, bath house and insula in the centre of the city. Around 200 fragments of this map are now in the Ara Pacis Museum.
18. Tertullian 'De Spectaculis'
19. Ibid
20. Spokesman from the Archaeological Team, Scavi di Pompeii, 2018.
21. C.I.L. 1-326
22. Varro 'On Agriculture'
23. C.I.L. VI-180
24. David Potter. 'Emperors of Rome'
25. Cassius Dio 'Roman History'
26. L. Richardson. 'The New Topographical Dictionary of Ancient Rome'
27. Ibid
28. Ibid
29. Mary Beard et al. 'Religions of Rome'
30. Lesley and Roy Adkins. 'Dictionary of Roman Religion'
31. E. Nash. 'Pictorial Dictionary of Ancient Rome' Volume One.
32. Suetonius 'The Twelve Caesars – Life of Augustus'
33. Joanne Berry. 'The Complete Pompeii'
34. J. P. V. D. Balsdon. 'Roman Women'
35. Livy 'Ab Urbe Condita Libre'
36. Sidonius Apollinaris 'Epistulae'
37. J. P. V. D. Balsdon. 'Life and Leisure in Ancient Rome'
38. H. H. Scullard. 'Festivals and Ceremonies of the Roman Republic'
39. Mary Beard et al. 'Religions of Rome'
40. Ibid
41. H. H. Scullard. 'Festivals and Ceremonies of the Roman Republic'
42. L. Richardson. 'A New Topographical Dictionary of Ancient Rome'
43. Ibid
44. H. H. Scullard. 'Festivals and Ceremonies of the Roman Republic'
45. David Potter. 'Emperors of Rome'
46. C.I.L. X-809
47. Mary Beard et al. 'Religions of Rome'
48. L. Richardson. 'A New Topographical Dictionary of Ancient Rome'
49. E. Nash. 'Pictorial Dictionary of Ancient Rome' Volume Two.

50. J. Fergusen. 'The Religions of the Roman Empire'
51. M. Baigent, R. Lee and H. Lincoln. 'The Holy Blood and the Holy Grail'. Hardly the most trustworthy source, but in this case correct.
52. L. Richardson. 'A New Topographical Dictionary of Ancient Rome'
53. Lesley and Roy Adkins. 'Dictionary of Roman Religion'
54. H. H. Scullard. 'Festivals and ceremonies of the Roman Republic'

4 Foreign Gods

1. Boardman, Griffin and Murrey (Editors). 'The Roman World'
2. Lesley and Roy Adkins. 'Dictionary of Roman Religion'
3. Lynda Telford. 'Women of Ancient Rome'
4. Joanne Berry. 'The Complete Pompeii'
5. William McQuitty. 'Island of Isis'
6. Ibid
7. C.I.L. VI-30915
8. C.I.L. VI-2234 and VI-32462
9. Apuleius XI. 26
10. C.I.L. VI- 8707
11. C.I.L. VI-354
12. Filippo Coarelli. 'I monumente dei culti orientale in Roma – questione topographiche e cronologiche' in Bianchi and Veermaseren (Editors) 'La Sotoriologia dei culti Orientale nell'Imperio Romano'
13. Jeffrey Iverson. 'More Lives than One – the evidence of the Remarkable Bloxham Tapes'
14. The Guardian – Archaeology. 23 November 2019. Article by Ruth Michaelson.
15. Apuleius 'The Golden Ass' and 'Metamorphoses'
16. Andrew Afoldi (Article). 'A festival of Isis in Rome under Christian Emperors of the Fourth Century.' J.R.S. Volume 28. (1938)
17. William McQuitty. 'Island of Isis'
18. C.I.L. X-846
19. C.I.L. IV-787
20. C.I.L. IV-1011
21. Marcel Brion. 'Pompeii and Herculaneum'
22. Livy 'Ab Urbe Condita Libre'
23. C.I.L. I-2-581. The intaglio containing this decree was engraved on bronze and was discovered in 1640 at Tiriolo in Calabria. The original is now in the Kunsthistoriches Museum in Vienna.
24. Livy 'Ab Urbe Condita Libre'
25. Bettany Hughes. 'Bacchus – Ancient God of Ecstasy' on BBC TV in 2018.
26. Ibid

27. Erich S. Gruen. 'Studies in Greek Culture and Roman Policy'
28. P. G. Walsh (Article). 'Making a drama out of a crisis – Livy on the Bacchanalia' in Greece and Rome 43. (1996) Jstor. 643095.
29. Mary Beard et al. 'Religions of Rome'
30. Ovid 'Fasti'
31. Ovid 'Metamorphoses'
32. Mary Beard et al. 'Religions of Rome'
33. Lyn E. Roller. 'In search of God the Mother – the Cult of the Anatolian Cybele'
34. Herodian. 'History of the Roman Empire'
35. David Potter. 'Emperors of Rome'
36. J. P. V. D. Balsdon. 'Roman Women'
37. Elegabalus first married Julia Cornelia Paula, then the Chief Vestal Julia Aquiilia Severa, then thirdly Annia Faustina.
38. Cassius Dio 'Roman History'
39. J. P. V. D. Balsdon. 'Roman Women'
40. Herodian 'History of the Roman Empire'
41. David Potter. 'Emperors of Rome'
42. David Ulansey. 'Origins of the Mithraic Mysteries'
43. CIMRM. 222 from Ostia and CIMRM. 369 from Rome
44. Guy de la Bedoyere. 'Gods with Thunderbolts'
45. David Potter. 'Emperors of Rome'
46. Mary Beard et al. 'Religions of Rome'
47. R. M. Ogilvie. 'Romans and their Gods'
48. Lesley and Roy Adkins. 'Dictionary of Roman Religion'
49. David Potter. 'Emperors of Rome'
50. Mary Beard et al. 'Religions of Rome' quoting I.L.S. 4381
51. I.L.S. 4270 = CIMRM 511 (Rome); CIMRM 708 (Milan)
52. Procopius of Caesarea 'The Gothic Wars'
53. E. N. Lane. 'Corpus Culti Jovi Sabazii'
54. British Museum Votive Figure – 1895-0621.4
55. Wilhelmina F. Jashemski. 'The Gardens of Pompeii and Herculaneum and the Villas destroyed by Vesuvius'
56. Naples Archaeological Museum. Inventory Number 10473
57. J. P. V. D. Balsdon. 'Life and Leisure in Ancient Rome'

5 Emperor Worship

1. David Potter. 'Emperors of Rome'
2. Arthur Keaveney. 'Sulla, the last Republican'
3. Lynda Telford. 'Sulla, a Dictator Reconsidered'
4. Ibid

5. Arthur Keaveney. 'Sulla, the last Republican'
6. David Potter. 'Religions of Rome'
7. Barry S. Strauss. 'The Death of Caesar'
8. Suetonius 'Life of Caesar'
9. Christian Meier. 'Caesar'
10. Richard Holland. 'Augustus'
11. J. T. Ramsey. 'The Comet of 44 BC and Caesar's Funeral Games'
12. The Comet's Numerical Designation is C/-43K1.
13. Appian of Alexandria 'Historia Romana'
14. David Potter. 'Emperors of Rome'
15. Octavianus/Augustus. 'Res Gestae Divi Augusti' (Achievements of the Divine Augustus)
16. Ibid
17. Richard Holland. 'Augustus – Godfather of Europe'
18. Velleius Paterculus. 'Compendium of Roman History – Book II'
19. David Potter. 'Emperors of Rome'
20. Joanne Berry. 'The Complete Pompeii'
21. Ibid
22. Inscription Pompeii – AE. 1986 – 166A
23. Inscription Pompeii – AE. 1964 – 160
24. Eumachia Building, Pompeii. Inscriptions C.I.L. X.810 and C.I.L. X.811
25. Joanne Berry. 'The Complete Pompeii'
26. C.I.L. X. 998
27. C.I.L. 1030
28. Cassius Dio 'Roman History'
29. Matthew Dennison. 'Empress of Rome – the Life of Livia'
30. Cassius Dio 'Roman History'
31. Matthew Dennison. 'Empress of Rome – the Life of Livia'
32. Suetonius 'Life of Tiberius'
33. Anthony A. Barrett. 'Livia – First lady of Imperial Rome'
34. Suetonius 'Life of Tiberius'
35. Ibid
36. Tacitus 'Annals'
37. Suetonius 'Life of Caligula'
38. Cassius Dio 'Roman History'
39. Suetonius 'Life of Nero'
40. Anthony A. Barrett. 'Agrippina, Sex, Power and Politics in the Early Roman Empire'
41. Tacitus 'Annals'
42. David Potter. 'Emperors of Rome'
43. Tacitus 'Histories'
44. Suetonius 'Life of Vespasian'

45. Suetonius 'Life of Domitian'
46. Ibid
47. Ibid
48. Cassius Dio 'Roman History'
49. David Potter. 'Emperors of Rome'
50. Cassius Dio 'Roman History'
51. Historia Augusta 'Life of Elegabalus'
52. Cassius Dio 'Roman History'
53. David Potter. 'Emperors of Rome'

6 Divination

1. Suetonius. 'Life of Julius Caesar'
2. Ibid
3. Plutarch 'Life of Julius Caesar'
4. Marc Hyden. 'Gaius Marius, the Rise and Fall of Rome's Saviour'
5. Aulus Gellius 'Noctis Atticae'
6. R. M. Ogilvie. 'The Romans and their Gods'
7. Lesley and Roy Adkins. 'Dictionary of Roman Religion'
8. 'Res Gestae Divi Augustus'
9. John Hazel. 'Who's Who in the Roman World'
10. David Wadkin. 'The Roman Forum'
11. R. M. Ogilvie. 'The Romans and their Gods'
12. Marcus Annaeus Lucan – 39-65 AD.
13. Cicero 'On Divination'
14. Tacitus 'Histories'
15. Apuleius 'Apologia'
16. Suetonius 'Life of Tiberius'
17. Vettius Valens. A writer of astronomy in approximately 150 AD.
18. R. M. Ogilvie 'The Romans and their Gods'
19. Marcus Calpurnius Bibulus (d. 48 BC) was in oppositon to Caesar regarding the Agrarian Land Law. Bibulus was a convinced Republican and despised Caesar's takeover of the Government. When he was forcibly prevented from vetoing the land law, he 'retired to watch the heavens' for omens, and spent so long in doing it that all further legal business was blocked, which was of course his intention.
20. R. M. Ogilvie. 'The Romans and their Gods'
21. Livy 'History of Rome'
22. Lucan 'Pharsalia VII'
23. Festus 'Summary of the History of Rome' – commissioned by the Emperor Valens.
24. R. M. Ogilvie. 'The Romans and their Gods'

25. Tacitus 'Histories'
26. R. M. Ogilvie. 'The Romans and their Gods'
27. Cicero 'On Divination'
28. Catullus 'Complete Works'
29. Horace 'Complete Works'
30. Cicero 'On Divination'
31. Mary Beard et al. 'Religions of Rome'
32. Tacitus 'Annals'
33. Plutarch 'Roman Questions'
34. Pliny the Younger 'Letters'
35. Suetonius 'Life of Augustus'
36. Tacitus 'Annals'
37. Livy 'Summaries'
38. Mary Beard et al. 'Religions of Rome'
39. Lesley and Roy Adkins. 'Dictionary of Roman Religion'
40. Cicero 'On Divination'
41. Gregory S. Aldrete (Article). 'Hammers, Axes, Bulls and Blood – some Practical Aspects of Roman Animal Sacrifice. J.R.S. 104. (2014)
42. Jack J. Lennon (Article). 'Victimarii in Roman religion and society.' Papers of the British School in Rome.
43. R. M. Ogilvie 'The Romans and their Gods'
44. Pliny the Younger 'Letters'
45. King Prusias I, King of Bythinia, gave refuge in 188 BC to the fugitive Hannibal and employed him as his Admiral.
46. Epictetus (55-135 AD) was a Stoic philosopher from Phrygia.
47. Pliny the Elder 'Natural History'
48. R. M. Ogilvie. 'The Romans and their Gods'
49. Pliny the Younger 'Letters'
50. Ovid 'Metamorphoses'
51. R. M. Ogilvie. 'The Romans and their Gods'
52. C.I.L. X-1569
53. On the Via Portuensis, known as the Lucus Deae Diae, about five miles south of Rome. Her cult dates back to very earliest history but was re-introduced by Augustus.
54. Pliny the Elder 'Natural History'
55. R. M. Ogilvie. 'The Romans and their Gods'

7 Magic

1. Prof. Sir Themistocles Zammit. 'The Pre-historic Temples of Malta and Gozo – a Description'

2. Georg Luck. 'Arcana Mundi – Magic and the Occult in the Greek and Roman Worlds'
3. 'The Greek Magical Papyri in Translation' edited by Hans Dieter. Known as the Greek Magical Papyri and written in Greek, from Graeco-Roman Egypt. The materials date from the 100s BC to the 400s AD. One of the best known of these texts is the Mithras Liturgy.
4. Acts – 19:18-20
5. Pliny the Elder 'Natural History'
6. Georg Luck. 'Arcana Mundi'
7. E. R. Dodds (Article). 'Supernatural Phenomena in Classical Antiquity' Proceedings of the Society for Psychical Research, Number 55 (1971)
8. Christina Riggs. 'Ancient Egyptian Magic'
9. Georg Luck. 'Arcana Mundi'
10. Jenny Linford. 'A Concise Guide to Herbs'
11. Robert K. Ritner. 'The Mechanics of Ancient Egyptian Magical Practice'
12. Christina Riggs. 'Ancient Egyptian Magic'
13. Sekhmet is the Goddess of War, but also of healing. Some daemons were sent by Sekhmet to carry disease, war and strife into the world, but she also has her caring side, even if she could be changeable, very much like the Roman Goddess Fortuna, with whom the Egyptian Gods were closely allied in the shape of the Isis and Fortuna pairing at Praeneste.
14. Christina Riggs. 'Ancient Egyptian Magic'
15. Sir James Frazer. 'The Golden Bough'
16. Georg Luck (Article). 'Witches and Sorcerers in Classical Literature' in Witchcraft and Magic in Europe. Volume Two. (1999).
17. Iamblichus. 'On the Mysteries of the Egyptians, Chaldeans and Assyrians'
18. Virgil 'Aeneid'
19. Pliny the Elder 'Natural History'
20. Ibid
21. Suetonius 'Augustus'
22. Iamblichus 'On the Mysteries of the Egyptians, Chaldeans and Assyrians.'
23. George Luck. 'Arcana Mundi'
24. Theophrastus 'Characters – Portrait of a Superstitious Man'
25. Georg Luck. 'Arcana Mundi'
26. Tacitus 'Annals'
27. C.I.L. 11.2. 4639
28. A. M. H. Audollent. 'Difixionum Tabellae'
29. PGM. IV. 297-408. Great Magical Papyrus. Paris.

30. PGM. IV. 1495-1546. Great Magical Papyrus. Paris.
31. Georg Luck. 'Arcana Mundi'
32. The rituals surrounding the worship of these heroes appears to have been different to the normal worship of the dead. Unlike the Immortal Gods, they had obviously lived and then died, and were worshipped at their tombs, rather than in any temples dedicated to them.
33. Pliny the Younger 'Letters'
34. Plutarch 'De Defecto Oracularum'
35. The 'Rituale Romanum' is still used for states of daemonic possession, and for the ritual of exorcism.
36. Lucien of Samosata. 'Lovers of Lies' – also known as 'The Doubter' – is a satire making fun of those people who believed too easily in the supernatural. In 'The Works of Lucien of Samosata'
37. Georg Luck. 'Arcana Mundi'
38. C. Bonner (Article). 'Studies in Magical Amulets, Chiefly Graeco-Egyptian' in University of Michigan Studies. (1950)
39. Mary Beard et al. 'Religions of Rome'
40. Ptolemy (Claudius Ptolomaeus) 'Tetrabiblus'
41. Manetho 'Apotelesmatica' edited by J. L. Lightfoot.
42. Vettius Valens 'Anthologiae'
43. Georg Luck. 'Arcana Mundi'
44. Ibid
45. Plutarch 'Life of Anthony'
46. Julius Africanus 'Cesti – The Extant Fragments'
47. Livy 'Ab Urbe Condita Libre'
48. Georg Luck. 'Arcana Mundi'
49. Lesley and Roy Adkins. 'Dictionary of Roman Religion'
50. Noel Robertson (Article). 'The Nones of July and Roman Weather Magic' (1987)
51. Justin J. Meggitt. 'Did Magic Matter? The Saliency of Magic in the Early Roman Empire'
52. Pontificale Romanum. The liturgical book containing the rites and ceremonies usually to be performed only by Bishops.
53. Canon Law is the system of the laws and legal principles enforced by the heirarchical authorities to regulate the church's external organisation and government, and to order and direct the activities of its followers. It is the oldest functioning legal system in the Western World.

8 The Calendar of Festivals

1. J. P. V. D. Balsdon. 'Life and Leisure in Ancient Rome'
2. Ibid

3. A. K. Michaels. 'The Calendar of the Roman Republic'
4. Suetonius 'Life of Tiberius'
5. C.I.L. I – 220
6. C.I.L. IV- 4182
7. Gaius Avidius Cassius (130-175 AD) was popular in Syria where he was Governor. He was a native of Syria and Suffect Consul under Marcus Aurelius. He commanded the army under Verus in the Parthian War of 162-165 AD, leading to the conquest of Mesopotamia. However, he had delusions of grandeur and in 175, on hearing false news of Aurelius's death, proclaimed himself Emperor. He ruled the east for only three months and six days, and Marcus Aurelius, who had survived an illness, ordered Cassius killed by a Centurion in 175 AD. No coins bear his image from his very brief attempt to rule.
8. The year 78 BC was the year Lucius Cornelius Sulla died and Lepidus attempted to overthrow his Constitution. Pompeius Magnus crushed a rebellion in Gaul the same year. There was trouble in Etruria when Veterans taking over land allotments met with strong resistance from local farmers. The year 52 BC saw Milo killing Publius Clodius Pulcher and duly being exiled to Massilia. There was also a rebellion in Gaul that year, led by Vercingetorix.
9. J. P. V. D. Balsdon. 'Life and Leisure in Ancient Rome'
10. Ovid 'Fasti'
11. Ibid
12. A .K. Michaels. 'The Calendar of the Roman Republic'
13. Tacitus 'Histories'
14. Lesley and Roy Adkins. 'Dictionary of Roman Religion'
15. J. P. V. D. Baldson. 'Life and Leisure in Ancient Rome'
16. Lesley and Roy Adkins. 'Dictionary of Roman Religion'
17. J. P. V. D. Balsdon. 'Life and Leisure in Ancient Rome'
18. Suetonius 'Divus Augustus'
19. Tacitus 'Annals'
20. A. K. Michaels. 'The Calendar of the Roman Republic'
21. J. P. V. D. Balsdon. 'Life and Leisure in Ancient Rome'
22. Suetonius 'Divus Augustus'
23. Cicero 'Against Verres' (In Verram)
24. J. P. V. D. Balsdon. 'Life and Leisure in Ancient Rome'
25. The Compitalia was suppressed in 64 BC and remained banned until 58 BC. It was suppressed again in 45 BC due to what was then termed 'political exploitation'.
26. Lesley and Roy Adkins. 'Dictionary of Roman Religion'
27. Ovid 'Fasti'

28. At the Lupercalia the young women of child-bearing age put themselves in the path of the nearly-naked young men, hoping to be 'whipped' by their favourites, perhaps as much to catch the young man's eye and have the thrill of seeing him almost unclothed, as much as to wish for a child.
29. H. H. Scullard. 'Festivals and Ceremonies of the Roman Republic'
30. N. G. L. Hammond and H. H. Scullard (Editors) 'The Oxford Classical Dictionary'
31. Varro 'De Lingua Latina'
32. Livy 'Ab Urbe Condita Libre'
33. H .H. Scullard. 'Festivals and Ceremonies of the Roman Republic'
34. Ibid
35. J. P. V. D. Balsdon. 'Life and Leisure in Ancient Rome'
36. Ovid 'Fasti'
37. Lesley and Roy Adkins. 'Dictionary of Roman Religion'
38. H. H. Scullard. 'Festivals and Ceremonies of the Roman Republic'
39. Lesley and Roy Adkins. 'Dictionary of Roman Religion'
40. Cicero 'Letters to his Brother Quintus'
41. R. M. Ogilvie. 'The Romans and their Gods'
42. Cicero 'Letters to Atticus'
43. J. P. V. D. Balsdon. 'Life and Leisure in Ancient Rome'
44. The right of slaves to attend this festival was a huge concession, as normally the presence of an enslaved person would pollute a religious ceremony. One statue of the God Mars is known to have had a notice placed on it, which said 'This statue is not to be touched by any slave.' However, the Wheel of Fortune could affect everyone and anyone, therefore Fortuna's festival was considered to be a holiday for all.
45. Cicero 'De Finibus V'
46. Tertullian 'De Spectaculis'
47. Sir James Frazer. 'The Golden Bough'
48. Cicero 'Letters to Atticus'
49. H. H. Scullard. 'Festivals and Ceremonies of the Roman Republic'
50. Ibid
51. The Circus Maximus was originally built by King Tarquinius Priscus before the start of the Republic. It filled the whole of the Vallis Murcia, between the Palatine and Aventine Hills. Only Roman citizens were admitted, and in Republican times there is a possibility that freedman were reclassified as 'slaves' for the occasion, which was possibly done to prevent seats being taken up that full and freeborn citizens required.
52. H. H. Scullard. 'Festivals and Ceremonies of the Roman Republic'

53. Augustus took the credit, in his 'Res Gestae', for restoring the couches on which the statues of the gods of the Capitoline Triad were placed for these occasions.
54. Paul Jacobs and Diane Atnally Conlin. 'Campus Martius – the Field of Mars in the Life of Ancient Rome'
55. J. P. V. D. Balsdon. 'Life and Leisure in Ancient Rome'
56. Juvenal 'Satires'
57. Pliny the Younger 'Letters – II'
58. Varro (Marcus Tarentius) 'La Lingua Latina'
59. Suetonius 'Life of Domitian'
60. Marcus Aurelius 'Meditations'

Conclusion

1. Mary Beard and Keith Hopkins. 'The Colosseum'
2. 'losttreasures-intolerance-greed.com'
3. 'Codex Theodosianus' – the laws of Theodosius II, published in 438 AD.
4. Lynda Telford. 'Women in Medieval England'
5. Ibid
6. Libianus 'Pro Templis' from 'Orations'
7. Michael Baigent and Richard Leigh. 'The Dead Sea Scrolls Deception'
8. Simcha Jacobovici and Charles Pellegrini. 'The Jesus Family Tomb'
9. Rudolfo Lanciani. 'The Destruction of Ancient Rome'
10. Helmut Koester. 'Ancient Christian Gospels – Their History and Development'

Bibliography

Primary Sources

AFRICANUS Julius. 'Cesti – The Extant Fragments'. Translated by William Adler. De Gruyter (2012)

APPIAN 'History of Rome'. Loeb Classical Library Harvard University Press (1912)

APULEIUS 'The Golden Ass' Penguin Classics, (1999)

APULEIUS 'Metamorphoses' Bloomsbury Academic (2018)

APULEIUS 'Apologia' Harvard University Press (2017)

AUDOLLENT A. M. H. (Editor) 'Difixionum Tabellae' Pranava Books Reprint (2020)

AUGUSTUS 'Res Gestae Divi Augustae'. Edited by P.A. Brunt and J. M. Moore. Oxford University Press (1969)

AULUS GELLIUS 'Noctes Atticae'. Schoningh im Westermann (1977)

CASSIUS DIO 'Roman History' Penguin Classics (1987)

CATO THE ELDER 'On Agriculture' Prospect Books (1998)

CATULLUS 'The Complete Works' Everyman (1995)

CELSUS 'Selected Letters' Penguin Classics' (1986)

CICERO 'Selected Letters' Penguin Classics (1986)

CICERO 'On Divination' Oxford University Press (2007)

CICERO 'De Natura Deorum' Penguin Classics (1978)

CICERO 'In Verrem' Penguin Classics (2004)

DIODORUS SICULUS 'Library of History'. Translated C. H. Oldfather, Harvard University Press. (1989)

DIONYSUS OF HALICARNASSUS 'Roman Antiquities' Translated by Ernest Cary, Harvard University Press (1950)

FESTUS 'Summary of the History of Rome' – Commissioned by the Emperor Valens, completed around 370 AD.

FRONTINUS Sextus Julius, 'Aqueducts of Rome' Cambridge University Press (2004)

GREEK MAGICAL PAPYRUS – In translation, edited by Hans Dieter Betz, University of Chicago Press (1985)

HERODIAN 'History of the Roman Empire – from the death of Marcus Aurelius to the accession of Gordian III'. University of California Press (2021)

HESIOD 'Theogany and Works and Days' Penguin Classics (2000)

THE HIPPOCRATIC CORPUS Kaplan Classics of Medicine, Kaplan Trade (2008)

HISTORIA AUGUSTA translated by David Magie, Loeb Classical Library (1921)

HORACE 'Odes and Epodes' translated Niall Rudd, Harvard University Press (2004)

IAMBLICHUS OF CHALCIS 'On the Mysteries of the Egyptians, Chaldeans and Assyrians' translated by Thomas Taylor, Create Space Independent Publishing Platform, (2015)

JUVENAL 'Satires' Cambridge University Press (2016)

LIBIANUS 'Pro Templis' (Oration 30) Harvard Univerity Press (1977)

LIVY 'Ab Urbe Condita Libre' translated by B. O. Foster, Loeb Classical Library (1919)

LIVY 'History of Rome' Loeb Classical Library (1989)

LUCIEN OF SAMOSATA 'Lovers and Lies' (also known as The Doubter) in 'The Works of Lucien of Samosata'. Forgotten Books (2007)

MACROBIUS 'Saturnalia' translated by Ludwig von Jan, Gottfried Bass (1852)

MANETHO 'Apotelesmatica' edited by J. L. Lightfoot, Oxford University Press (2020)

MARCUS AURELIUS 'Meditations' J. M. Dent (1904)

MARTIAL 'Liber de Spectaculis' translated by Roger Pearse. Ipswich (2008)

OROSIUS Paulus, 'Seven Books of History against the Pagans' Liverpool University Press (2010)

OVID 'Epistilae – Ex Ponto' Cambridge University Press (2014)

OVID 'Fasti' Penguin Classics (2000)

OVID 'Metamorphoses' Penguin Classics (1955)

PATERCULIS Velleius, 'Compendium of Roman History Book II' Harvard University Press (1989)

PLINY THE ELDER 'Natural History' Penguin Classics (1991)

PLINY THE YOUNGER 'Epistulae' Penguin Classics (2003)

PLUTARCH 'Moralia' Harvard University Press (1936)

PLUTARCH 'On Isis and Osiris' Create Space Independent Publishing Platform (2014)

PLUTARCH 'Lives' J .J. Chidley (1843)

PLUTARCH 'Roman Questions' Harvard University Press (1938)

PLUTARCH 'De Defectu Oraculorum' (On the Ceasing of Oracles) Apostle Horn (2018)

POLLIO Marcus Vitruvius, 'Ten Books on Architecture' translated by Morris Hicky Morgan, Adamant Media Corporation (2005)

POLYBIUS 'Histories' translated by W. R. Paton, Harvard University Press (1922)

PROCOPIUS OF CAESAREA 'The Gothic Wars' Conflict (2015)

PTOLEMY (Claudius Ptolemaeus) 'Tetrebiblus' Harvard University Press (1940)

'RES GESTAE DIVI AUGUSTAE' Cambridge University Press (2009)

RUFUS Gaius Musonius, 'Lectures and Fragments' Create Space Independent Publishing Platform, (2015)

SALLUST 'Bellum Catilinae' Kessinger Publishing (2010)

SENECA THE YOUNGER 'De Brevitate Vitae' Cambridge University Press (2008)

SENECA 'Natural Questions – the Complete Works' University of Chicago Press (2010)

STRABO 'Geography' translated by H. L. Jones, Harvard University Press (1917)

SUETONIUS 'The Twelve Caesars' Penguin Classics (1957)

TACITUS 'Histories' translated by C. H. Moore, Harvard University Press (1925)

TACITUS 'Annals of Imperial Rome' Penguin Classics (2003)

TERTULLIAN 'De Spectaculis' Harvard University Press (1960)

THEOPHRASTUS 'Characters' Routledge (2018)

VALENS Vettius, 'Anthologiae' Andrea Gehrz Inc. (2016)

VARRO Marcus Terentius, 'De Lingua Latina' Palala Press (2015)

VARRO 'On Agriculture' Loeb Classical Library, Harvard University Press (1934)

VARRO 'Res Rusticae' Good Press (2021)

VIRGIL 'The Aeneid' Penguin Classics (2003)

VITRUVIUS 'On Architecture' Dover Publications Inc. (1998)

Secondary Sources

ADKINS, Lesley and Roy 'Dictionary of Roman Religion' Oxford University Press (2001)

AFOLDI, Andreas. (Article) 'A Festival of Isis in Rome under Christian Emperors of the Fourth Century AD' reviewed by Thomas A. Brady. J.R.S. Volume 28 (1938)

ALLISON, P. 'The Insula of Menander at Pompeii – Volume 3 – The Finds' Oxford University Press (2006)

ALDRETE, Gregory S. (Article) 'Hammers, Axes, Bulls and Blood – Some Practical aspects of Roman Animal Sacrifice' J.R.S. Volume 104 (2014)

ALTHEIM, F. 'History of Roman Religion' (Translator H. Mattingly) Methuen (1938)

ALVAR, Jamie. (Article) 'Egyptian Goddess spread from Egypt to England' National Geographic (19 March 2020)

ANDO, Clifford. 'The Matter of the Gods' University of California Press (2008)

ARYA, Darius Andre. 'The Goddess Fortuna in Imperial Rome – Cult, Art and Text.' Thesis and Dissertation, University of Texas (JSTOR) (2006)

ASHBY, Rev. Thomas. 'A Topographical Dictionary of Ancient Rome' Oxford (1929)

BALSDON, J. P. V. D. 'Roman Women' Bodley Head (1962)

BALSDON, J. P. V. D. 'Life and Leisure in Ancient Rome' Phoenix (2002)

BARRETT, Anthony A. 'Agrippina – Sex, Power and Politics in the Early Roman Empire' Yale University Press (1996)

BARRETT, Anthony A. 'Livia – First lady of Imperial Rome' Yale University Press (2002)

BEARD, NORTH and PRICE 'Religions of Rome' Volumes One and Two, Cambridge University Press (1998)

BEARD, Mary. 'Pompeii' Profile, (2008)

BEARD, Mary and HOPKIN, Keith 'The Colosseum' Profile (2011)

BEARD, Mary. 'The Roman Triumph' Harvard University Press, (2009)

BECK, Roger. (Article) 'The Mysteries of Mithras and a new account of their Genesis' J.R.S. Volume 88 (1998)

BEDOYERE, Guy de la. 'Gods with Thunderbolts' Tempus (2002)

BERRY, Joanne. 'The Complete Pompeii' Thames and Hudson, (2007)

BETTINI Maurizio and SHORT William Michael (Editors) 'The World through Roman eyes – Anthropological Approaches to Ancient Culture' Cambridge University Press (2018)

BILLINGTON, Sandra. (Article) 'Fors Fortuna in Ancient Rome' in 'The concept of the Goddess' Routledge (2002)

BILSTEIN, Adam. (Article) 'Instability and Impermanence – Uncovering Anna Perenna' in 'Society for Classical Studies' 14 December 2015

BOARDMAN, GRIFFIN and MURRAY (Editors) 'The Roman World' Oxford University Press (1996)

BOATWRIGHT, GORGOLA and TALBERT 'The Romans, from Village to Empire' Oxford University Press (2004)

BOATWRIGHT, Mary T. 'Hadrian and the City of Rome' Princeton University Press (1987)

BONNER, C. 'Studies in Magical Amulets – Chiefly Graeco-Egyptian' University of Michigan Studies (1950)

BRENNAN, T. Corey. 'The Praetorship in the Roman Republic' Oxford University Press (2000)

BRION, Marcel. 'Pompeii and Herculaneum – the Glory and the Grief' Elek Books (1960)

BURN, Robert. 'Ancient Rome and its Neighbourhood – an Illustrated Handbook to the Ruins of the City and Campagna' Bell/London (1895)

BURNS, Jasper. 'Great Women of Imperial Rome – Mothers and Wives of the Caesars' Routledge (2006)

CARETTONI, G. (Article) 'Excavations and Discoveries in the Forum Romanum and on the Palatine in the Last Fifty Years' J.R.S No 50 (1960)

CLAUSS, Manfred. 'The Roman Cult of Mithras, the God and his Mysteries' Routledge (2000)

COARELLI, Filippo. 'I Monumente dei culti orientale in Roma – questione topografiche e cronologiche' in 'La Sotoriologia dei culti orientale nell'Imperio Romano' Leiden (1982)

COARELLI, Filippo. 'Rome and Environs – an Archaeological Guide' University of California Press (2014)

COCCO, Gianpaolo de. 'Alle origini del'Carnevale – Mysteria Isiaci e miti Cattolici' Florence, Pontecorboli (2007)

CORNELL, T. J. 'The Beginnings of Rome – Italy and Rome from the Bronze Age to the Punic Wars' Routledge (1995)

DUMEZIL, G. 'La Religione Romana Archaica – con un appendice sulla Religione degli Etruschi' Johns Hopkins University (1996)

DENNISON, Matthew. 'Empress of Rome – the Life of Livia' Quercus (2011)

EDWARDS, Catherine. 'The Politics of Immorality in Ancient Rome' Cambridge University Press (1993)

EMMERSON, Allison L. C. (Article) 'Re-examining Roman Death Pollution' J.R.S. Volume 110 (2020)

FERGUSON, J. 'The Religions of the Roman Empire' Thames and Hudson (1970)

FLINT, Valerie et al. 'Athlone History of Witchcraft and Magic in Europe – Ancient Greece and Rome, Volume Two' Continuum International Publishing Group (1998)

FLOWER, Harriet. 'Ancestor Masks and Aristocratic Power in Roman Culture' Clarendon Press (1999)

FLOWER, Harriet. 'The Dancing Lares and the Serpent in the Garden' Princeton University Press (2017)

FOWLER, W. Warde. 'The Roman Festivals' MacMillan (1899)

FOWLER, W. Warde. (Article) 'Mundus Patet' J.R.S. Volume Two (1912)

FOWLER, David Hugh. 'Oxford Dictionary of Saints' Clarendon Press (1978)

FRAZER, Sir James. 'The Golden Bough' Wordsworth (1993)

FUTRELL, Alison. 'The Roman Games' Wiley-Blackwell (2006)

GAUGHAN, Judy E. 'Murder Was not a Crime – Homicide and Power in the Roman Republic' Universtiy of Texas Press (2010)

GOODBURN, Roger and Waugh, Helen. 'The Roman Inscriptions of Britain' Sutton Publishing (1983)

GRADEL, Itta. 'Emperor Worship and Roman Religion' Oxford University Press (2008)

GREEN, M. J. 'Dictionary of Celtic Myth and Legend' Thames and Hudson (1992)

GRUEN, Erich S. 'Studies in Greek Culture and Roman Policy' University of Chicago Press (1996)

GUIDOBALDI, P. Soprintendenza Archeologica Di Roma, 'The Roman Forum' Electa (1998)

HAMMOND, N. G. L. and SCULLARD, H. H. (Editors) 'The Oxford Classical Dictionary' Oxford University Press (1970)

HARRIS, W. D. 'War and Imperialism in Republican Rome' Oxford University Press (1979)

HAZEL, John. 'Who's Who in Ancient Rome' Routledge (2001)

HOLLAND, Richard. 'Augustus – Godfather of Europe' Sutton Publishing (2004)

HORSFALL, Nicholas. (Article) 'The Cultural Horizons of the Plebs Romana' in Memoirs of the American Academy in Rome, University of Michigan Press (1996)

HYDEN, Marc. 'Gaius Marius, the Rise and Fall of Rome's Saviour' Pen and Sword (2017)

IVERSON, Jeffrey. 'More Lives than One' Souvenir Press (1976)

JACKSON, Ralph. 'Diseases and Death in the Roman Empire' British Museum Publications (1988)

JACOBS, Paul W. and CONLIN, Diane Atnally. 'Campus Martius – the Field of Mars in the Life of Ancient Rome' Cambridge University Press (2014)

JASHENSKI, Wilhelmina M.F. 'The Gardens of Pompeii and Herculaneum and the Villas destroyed by Vesuvius' University of Maryland Press (1979)

KAMM, Antony. 'The Romans – an Introduction' Routledge (2008)

KEAVENEY, Arthur. 'Sulla, the last Republican' Routledge (2005)

KNEALE, Matthew. 'A History of Rome in Seven Sackings – from the Gauls to the Nazis' Atlantic (2018)

KOESTER, Helmut. 'Ancient Christian Gospels – Their History and Development' SCM Press (1999)

LANE, E. N. 'Corpus Cultis Jovi Sabezii' Brill (1989)

LEACH, Eleanor W. (Article) 'Fortune's extremities – Quintus Lutatius Catulus and Largo Argentina Temple B – A Roman Consul and his Monument' Memoirs of the American Academy in Rome, Volume 55 (2010)

LENNON, Jack J. (Article) 'Victimarii in Roman Religion and Society' Papers of the British School in Rome, Volume 83 (2015)

LEVICK, Barbara. 'Julia Domna – Syrian Empress' Routledge (2007)

LINFORD, Jenny. 'A Concise Guide to Herbs' Parragon (2007)

LINN, Jason. 'The Roman Grain Supply' in Journal of Late Antiquity Volume 5 (2012)

LINTOFF, Andrew. 'Violence in Republican Rome' Oxford University Press (1999)

LUCK, Georg. 'Magic and Occult in the Greek and Roman Worlds' Johns Hopkins University Press (2006)

LUCK, Georg. (Article) 'Witches and Sorcerers in Classical literature' (in Witchcraft and Magic in Europe, Volume Two, Ancient Greece and Rome) University of Pennsylvania Press (1999)

MacMULLEN, Ramsey. 'Paganism in the Roman Empire' Yale University Press (1981)

MacQUITTY, William. 'Island of Isis – Philae, Temple of the Nile' MacDonald and Jane's (1976)

MATYSZAK, Philip. 'Ancient Magic – a Practitioner's Guide to the Supernatural in Greece and Rome' Thames and Hudson (2019)

McINTYRE, Gwyneath and McCALLUM, Sarah (Editors) 'Uncovering Anna Perenna – a Focused Study of Roman Myth and Culture' Bloomsbury Academic (2019)

MEGGITT, Justin J. (Article) 'Did Magic Matter? The Saliency of Magic in the Early Roman Empire' Journal of Ancient History (2013)

MEIER, Christian. 'Caesar' Harper Collins (1995)

MIANO, Daniele. 'Fortuna, Deity and Concept in Archaic and Republican Italy' Oxford University Press (2018)

MICHELS, A. K. 'The Calendar of the Roman Republic' Princeton University Press (1967)

MOSER, Claudia and KNUST Jennifer (Editors) 'Ritual Matters, Material Remains and Ancient Religions' University of Michigan Press (2017)

NASH, E. 'Pictorial Dictionary of Ancient Rome' Zwemmer Volume One (1962A) Volume Two (1962B)

NIELSON, Inge. (Article) 'The Temple of Castor and Pollux on the Forum Romanum – Excavations 1983-1987' Acta Archaeoligica (1989)

NORTH, J. A. (Article) 'Conservatism and Change in Roman Religion' Papers of the British School in Rome No.44 (1976)

NORTH, J. A. (Review Article) 'These He Cannot Take' J.R.S. 73 (1983)

NOCK, A.D. 'Conversion' Clarendon Press (1933)

OGDEN, Daniel. 'Greek and Roman Necromancy' Princeton University Press (2001)

OGILVIE, R. M. 'The Romans and their Gods' Pimlico (2000)

ORLIN, Eric. 'Foreign Cults in Rome – Creating a Roman Empire' Oxford University Press (2010)

PELLEGRINO, Charles and JACOBOVICI, Simcha. 'The Jesus Family Tomb' Harper Element (2007)

PHARR, C. (Article) 'The Interdiction of Magic in Roman Law – Magic in the Twelve Tables' Classical Quarterly, Cambridge University Press (2002)

PIRANOMONTE, Marina. (Article) 'Il Santuario della musica e il Bosco Sacro di Anna Perenna' Electra Roma (2002)

PIRANOMONTE, Marina. (Article) 'The Discovery of the Fountain of Anna Perenna and its Influence on the Study of Ancient Magic' Archeopress Oxford (2016)

PLATNER, Samual Ball. (Revised by Thomas Ashby) 'A Topographical Dictionary of Ancient Rome' Oxford University Press (1929)

POMEROY, Sarah B. 'Spartan Women' Oxford University Press (2002)

POTTER, David. 'Emperors of Rome' Quercus (2008)

POTTER, Timothy. 'Roman Italy' Ithaca (1982)

POTTER, T. W. (Article) 'A Republican healing sanctuary at Ponte di None, near Rome, and the Classical tradition of votive medicine' Journal of British Archaeology Association, Number 138 (1985)

RAMSEY, J. T. 'The Comet of 44 BC and Caesar's Funeral Games' Scholars Press (1997)

RICH, J. W. (Article) 'Augustus's Parthian Honours, the Temple of Mars Ultor and the Arch in the Roman Forum' Papers of the British School at Rome No.66 (1998)

RICHARDSON, L. 'New Topographical Dictionary of Ancient Rome' Johns Hopkins University Press (1992)

RIDAT, Pauline. 'Roman Women, Wise Women and Witches' Phoenix (2016)

RIGGS, Christina. 'Ancient Egyptian Magic' Thames and Hudson (2020)

RITNER, Robert K. 'The Mechanics of Ancient Egyptian Magical Practice' University of Chicago Press (2004)

RIVES, James B. 'Magic in Roman Law' University of California Press (2003)

RIVES, James B. 'Religion in the Roman Empire' Wiley Blackwell (2006)

ROBERTSON, Noel. (Article) 'The Nones of July and Roman Weather Magic' Museum Helviticum Volume 44 (1987)

ROLLER, Lynn E. 'In search of God the Mother – the cult of the Anatolian Cybele' University of California Press (1999)

ROSE, H. J. 'Ancient Roman Religion' Hillary House (1948)

RUPKE, Jorg. 'Religion of the Romans' Polity Press (2007)

RUTTER, Jeremy B. (Article) 'The Three Phases of the Taurobolium' Classical Association of Canada Volume 22 (1968)

SPAETH, Barbette Stanley. 'The Roman Goddess Ceres' University of Texas Press (1996)

SPAETH, Barbette Stanley. 'From Goddess to Hag – the Greek and Roman Witch in Classical Literature' Oxford University Press (2014)

SCHEID, John. 'Introduction to Roman Religion' Indiana University Press (2003)

SCHULTZ, C. E. 'Women's Religious Activity in the Roman Republic' University of North Carolina Press (2006)

SCULLARD, H. H. 'Festivals and Ceremonies of the Roman Republic' Thames and Hudson (1981)

SCULLARD, H. H. 'From the Gracchi to Nero' Routledge (1982)

SCULLARD, H. H. and CARY Max. 'A History of Rome Down to the Age of Constantine' Palgrave McMillan (1980)

STAPLES, Ariadne 'From Good Goddess to Vestal Virgins – Sex and Category in the Roman Religion' Routledge (1998)

STEINBY, Eva Margareta. (Editor) 'Lexicon Topographicum Urbis Romanae' (five volumes) Rome (1993-1999)

STRATTON. Kimberley B. 'Daughters of Hecate, Women and Magic in the Ancient World' Oxford University Press (2014)

STRAUSS, Barry S. 'The Death of Caesar' Simon and Schuster (2016)

TATUM, W. Jeffrey 'The Patrician Tribune – Publius Clodius Pulcher' University of North Carolina Press (2010)

TAVENNER, Eugene. 'Studies in Magic from Latin Literature' Kessinger (2003)

TELFORD, Lynda. 'Sulla, a Dictator Reconsidered' Pen and Sword (2014)

TELFORD, Lynda. 'Women in Ancient Rome' Amberley (2022)

THOMAS, Teresa Fava. (Article) 'Fortuna at Palestrina' World History Encyclopaedia (2020)

TREVES, Piero. 'Brennus, Gallic Chieftain' Oxford Research Encyclopedia of Classics (2015)

TURCAN, Robert. 'The Cult of the Roman Empire' Wiley Blackwell (1996)

ULANSEY, David. 'Origins of the Mithraic Mysteries' Oxford University Press (1991)

VAGNETTI, L. 'Il deposito Votivo di Competti a Veio' Rome (1971)

WADKIN, David. 'The Roman Forum' Profile (2009)

WAGENVOORT, Hendrik. (Article) 'Diva Angerona' in Selected Studies in Roman Religion, Brill (1980)

WALSH, David. 'The Cult of Mithras in Late Antiquity – Development, Decline and Demise' Brill (2019)

WALSH, P. G. (Article) 'Making a Drama out of a Crisis – Livy on the Bacchanalia' in Greece and Rome 43 (1996)

WARRIOR Valerie M. 'Roman Religion' Cambridge University Press (2018)

WIEDERMANN, Thomas. (Article) 'The Festiales – a Reconsideration' Classical Quarterly Volume 36 (1986)

WILDFANG, Robin Lorsch 'Rome's Vestal Virgins' Routledge (2006)

WISEMAN, T. P. 'The Myths of Rome' Liverpool University Press (2004)

WISEMAN, T. P. 'Unwritten Rome' Liverpool University Press (2008)

WISEMAN, T. P. 'The House of Augustus – a Historical Detective Story' Princeton University Press (2019)

WITT, R. E. 'Isis in the Graeco-Roman World' Johns Hopkins University Press (1997)

ZAMMIT, Sir Themistocles 'The Prehistoric Temples of Malta and Gozo – a Description' Masterson (1997)

ZINK, David D. 'The Ancient Stones Speak – a Journey to the World's most Mysterious Megalithic sites' Penguin (1979)

Index

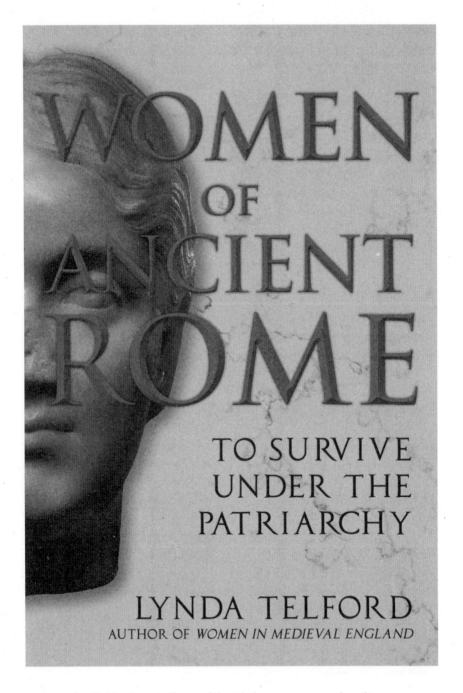